ESSAYS ON JACKSONIAN AMERICA

HRW Essays in American History Series
Paul Goodman, Editor

ESSAYS ON JACKSONIAN AMERICA

EDITED BY

FRANK OTTO GATELL

University of California, Los Angeles

HOLT, RINEHART AND WINSTON, INC.

New York · Chicago · San Francisco · Atlanta
Dallas · Montreal · Toronto · London · Sydney

Cover: George Caleb Bingham, "The County Election."
Courtesy of the City Art Museum of St. Louis.

Copyright © 1970 by Holt, Rinehart and Winston, Inc.
All rights reserved
Library of Congress Catalog Card Number: 70–102772
SBN: 03–077605–8
Printed in the United States of America
1 2 3 4 5 6 7 8 9

Preface

Traditionally, the Jacksonian period has been considered one of the most significant epochs in American history. While the nature of its importance has always been a subject for dispute, there is little doubt that fundamental changes occurred in nearly every aspect of American life during the years roughly embracing the second quarter of the nineteenth century. These changes extended from those of a most specific material nature to those of psychological import and symbolic value. Previous generations of historians, whether approvingly or disapprovingly, tended to concentrate on the political changes of the era, usually ascribing what was "liberal" or egalitarian to Andrew Jackson and the Democratic Party. It was the age of the "common man," and this new ruler, the humble citizen, was supposedly a consistent and loyal Jacksonian. He fought against the aristocratic Whig, the man who wore a shirt of broadcloth and ruffles, instead of homespun, and who tried to prevent the rise of democracy.

Such was the bare outline of the simple tale. Inevitably, in view of the complexity of the historical process, historians began to question it. The previously accepted certainties began to dissolve, and some historians would maintain that they entirely disappeared. In place of simplicity, the findings of the Jacksonian era revisionists offered diversity, a diagram of politics and society as complicated as that of any period in history. But in the opinion of the editor of this volume, the older overview, although severely revised, has not been completely eradicated. It was indeed an egalitarian age, and if the Jacksonians did not *monopolize* the instruments and institutions of egalitarianism, they nevertheless were more nearly the "popular" party than their opposition. This last statement is presented as a historical observation, not as a value judgment.

The revisionists have also contributed greatly in demonstrating the richness of that period, particularly in those nonpolitical areas that had been relatively neglected. For example, economic growth from 1815 to 1850 conditioned, and was itself conditioned by, the nature of political organization at that time. The effective penetration of the interior by a few surfaced roads at first, then canals, and finally railroads, gave Americans a physical mobility and a commercial latitude that were startlingly novel, a breakthrough unparalleled in history. The American was no longer a man tied to the soil, nor was his vision restricted to his immediate surroundings. By the mid-nineteenth century, the United States had changed profoundly as compared to what it had been in 1800. The Jacksonian period provided the watershed for this modernization.

The articles published in this volume offer the student closer views of important aspects of life during the Jacksonian period than can be drawn from text materials. An attempt has been made to obtain a chronological and topical spread. More advanced students and graduate students may refer to the journals in which the essays originally appeared, if they wish to consult the documentation and amplification of the footnotes that have been eliminated. From the data and interpretations of these monographs and others, a new comprehensive picture of the Jacksonian period is likely to emerge.

Frank Otto Gatell

Los Angeles
February 1970

Contents

Part IV SOCIAL TENSIONS 239

ESSAYS ON JACKSONIAN AMERICA

Part I

POLITICS
IN TRANSITION

1 / James Monroe and the Era of Good Feelings

Harry Ammon

In the years immediately following the end of the War of 1812, the United States enjoyed a period of apparent political calm known as the Era of Good Feelings. Of course, politicians fought as fiercely as ever, but with the almost total decline of the Federalist Party, only contending factions of the dominant Republican Party competed for power. In this essay Harry Ammon examines the maneuvers that took place behind the façade of party solidarity and the attempts made by the New England Federalists to salvage what they could from a critical situation. James Monroe emerges from these pages as a man with a great deal more political shrewdness than he is generally given credit for. But, more important, the essay illustrates that in a democratic society factionalism will inevitably grow into party opposition, this instance representing the transition between the first and second American party systems. In the 1790's, Washington and his associates had vainly tried to stem the growth of parties, attacking them as "factions," and in the decade from 1815 to 1824, the same antiparty campaign of reigning Republican presidents failed to accomplish its end. It was probably only the extreme vulnerability of Federalism that allowed the Republican one-party period to last as long as it did.

For further reading: George Dangerfield, *The Era of Good Feelings* (1951); Lynn W. Turner, "The Electoral Vote Against Monroe in 1820—An American Legend," *Mississippi Valley Historical Review*, XLII (September 1955), 250–273; Charles S. Sydnor, "The One-Party Period of American History," *American Historical Review*, LI (April 1946), 439–451; Shaw Livermore, *The Twilight of Federalism* (1962).

Virginia Magazine of History and Biography, LXVI, No. 4 (October 1958), 387–398. Reprinted by permission. Footnotes have been omitted.

3

The phrase, "Era of Good Feelings," so inextricably associated with the administration of James Monroe, was originally and most appropriately coined by a Federalist newspaper in Boston at the time of Monroe's visit to that city in 1817. In view of the many intense and bitter political animosities which developed during his presidency, the ironical implications of this term have always been stressed, and much has been written to show that it was anything but an era of good feelings—at least as far as the inner history of the Republican Party was concerned. It is not the purpose of this paper to attempt a reassessment of the interpretation of the phrase which designates this era, but rather to analyze and illuminate the policies formulated by President Monroe in regard to the party trends of this period.

It may seem rather startling to some that Monroe should be presented as having had clear-cut policies on the major problems of his own day, for he has been portrayed as a somewhat indecisive figure. This impression has arisen both from a lack of understanding of the man and of his methods in arriving at policy formulations. Not only was Monroe somewhat slow in reaching conclusions, but his approach to statecraft was vastly different from that of his two more famous colleagues in the Virginia Dynasty—Madison and Jefferson. Unlike his two fellow Virginians, Monroe was neither a philosopher nor a scholar. He viewed governmental problems from the standpoint of a practical politician. Because he possessed an unusual sensitivity to public opinion, Monroe's policies tended to be rather flexible. They were never formulated in such a dogmatic form as to preclude compromise, although they manifested at all times a consistent direction. Fully aware, as he was, of the conflicting personal rivalries within his party, Monroe often found it essential to delay final decisions until he had won the support of various factional leaders. His supposed tendency to drift with the current was in fact a skilled adjustment of his program to the constantly shifting complexities of the political scene during his administration. John Quincy Adams, Monroe's Secretary of State, who was inclined to judge men harshly for what he deemed to be weaknesses of character, did not attribute this slowness to indecisiveness, but to the complexities of the political situation which confronted him.

This approach to policy was fully apparent in the handling of one of the major party problems which confronted Monroe during his presidency, namely, the relationship between the parties. To this issue he gave much careful thought both before and after his inauguration. The idea of a reconciliation between the Federalists and the Republicans was not a concept which was original with Monroe, but one which was a widely discussed topic at this time. He had, after all, inherited a party which had advanced rather far on the road to Federalization, having incorporated both the bank and the protective tariff into the Republican program. The possibility of a closer rapprochement between the two parties was contemplated without any misgivings by Federalists and Republicans alike. The Federalists not only realized that their party had been ruined by their opposition to the War of 1812 and by the unpleasant odor which surrounded the Hartford Convention, but the less irreconcilable members of that party, such as Harrison Gray Otis of Massachusetts, understood that there was really no longer any basis for an opposition, since the Republicans had taken over all (as they saw it) that was of permanent value in the Federalist program. Otis had even anticipated the process of fusion with the Republicans by urging his friends to vote for Monroe in 1816 instead of wasting their ballots on Rufus King. Only by a reconciliation with the opposition could the Federalists be relieved of the stigma of disloyalty which still hovered about them as a result of the recent conduct of the more rabid members of the party. Most Republicans like former President Madison readily acknowledged the shift that had taken place within the Republican party towards Federalist principles, and viewed the process without qualms. As he expressed it, the Republicans during the course of time had "been reconciled to certain measures and arrangements which may be as proper now as they were premature and suspicious when urged by the champions of Federalism". Republicans of the younger generation, who did not have the problem of reconciling the past and the present, were apt to describe this process somewhat less tenderly. As Nicholas Biddle bluntly and sarcastically observed, the Republicans had finally "outgrown many of the childish notions with which they began their career twenty years since." The nation, he felt, was weary of the endless party squabbles.

This train of thinking on the part of the Republicans together with the atmosphere of the election of 1816 and the conduct of the Federalists after the war, when they had abandoned all organized opposition in Congress, led to the general anticipation that Monroe, who above all was looked upon as a man of moderation, would close the gap between the two parties. Monroe was well aware of this expectation, having received much advice as to how it should be accomplished both before and after his inauguration. Perhaps no bit of advice was more often given him than the suggestion that he include in his cabinet at least one Federalist as a sign that the party feuds had now ended and that the Republicans acknowledged the fundamental loyalty of the Federalists to the government. The most important figure to submit this kind of proposal was General Andrew Jackson, who on November 12, 1816, wrote to the president-elect to recommend the appointment of Colonel William Drayton, a South Carolina Federalist, as Secretary of War. The General, who here appears in the rather surprising role of a political peacemaker, urged Monroe to forget party feelings in forming his administration by drawing on the ablest men of both parties. Federalists such as Drayton, Jackson pointed out, had amply proven their loyalty during the war and deserved to be rewarded. Shortly after he received this letter Monroe sat down and wrote a lengthy and carefully worded reply, which revealed the extensive consideration he had given to this very question.

In this very important letter there are three significant elements. The first was Monroe's recapitulation of what might be called the Republican myth, that is, the belief, which was shared by all Republicans of his generation, that the ultimate goal of the Federalists had been the establishment of a monarchy by means of secret plots and cabals, which had verged on treason. The Federalists had never succeeded in this project, Monroe informed Jackson, because they had never found the right opportunity to act, and because Washington had opposed their aims during the formative period in the history of the republic. Of this desire to overthrow republican institutions, Monroe deemed the Hartford convention to be the most recent manifestation. In view of the past history of this party, he asked Jackson, how could these men be trusted? How could he risk appointing them to high posts, if to do so might mean the revival of this expiring but not entirely defunct party?

Secondly, in his letter Monroe stated his apprehension that a too rapid elevation of the Federalists would arouse opposition in his own party. After all should he not trust those who had stood by the government in its time of trial and who had valiantly supported the cause of republican government? Monroe (though he did not state this in his letter) was most anxious to avoid the party schisms which had plagued Madison and Jefferson and had arisen to a great extent on this very issue of Federalization of the Republican Party. Thirdly, and this is by far the most striking part of his statement of policy, was the over-all goal which he formulated for his own presidency, namely, not merely the absorption of the Federalists into the Republican Party but the elimination of all parties. Monroe told Jackson he was convinced that parties of any kind were contrary to the nature of republican institutions. That such parties had always existed in other republican governments, he admitted, but this did not strike him as meaningful, for he argued that we had removed in our constitution those defects which had inevitably given rise to these parties in ancient republics. He summed up his concept of the role which he intended to follow in the phrase that the president should be the head of the nation, not the chief of a party. If the experiment should fail, he concluded, it would be due only to an incorrect knowledge of all the factors to be considered and a want of judgment in the measures adopted.

In this line of thinking about the undesirability of political parties Monroe was revealing his deep affinity for eighteenth-century Republican theory, which had regarded parties as an evil arising only in societies with privileged orders and defective institutions. Washington had given this point of view a firm, if highly partisan statement, in his farewell address.

Monroe's motives in writing such a detailed exposition of his approach to the party problems of his day are quite clear. He wanted to be on record early in his administration as having taken a definite stand on this subject and thus be able to refute any charges that he was seeking to Federalize the Republican Party or that he was neglecting to appoint honest Republicans to office. This letter served its purpose, for during the next few years Monroe kept it (and Jackson's letter to him as well) conveniently at hand in his desk and read it to a number of congressmen who came to voice complaints from their constituents that Monroe was favoring the Federalists. Jackson also found his letter to the President useful in winning support from Tennessee Federalists in his presidential campaign. As the result of this private display the existence of these letters was widely known and Monroe's retained copy was removed by some person whom Monroe did not identify and published early in 1824 to Monroe's embarrassment and the General's irritation. The President was distressed not only because of what he had said about the Federalists, but also because the publication made him a party to the electioneering at a time when he was observing a precise neutrality. Rufus King, for one, was bitterly offended by the remarks about the Federalists in this letter, and abruptly ended the friendship that had sprung up between King and Monroe since 1817, refusing to call on the President again.

Although Monroe in this letter to Jackson declared that he was willing to embark on a "generous policy" towards the Federalists he made it quite clear that a period of de-Federalization would be necessary during which no offices would be available to members of this party. This attitude was not based upon any desire to further persecute the Federalists, but upon the practical necessity of getting the Federalists out of office in New England, where they still controlled all the state governments. To have advanced them by appointments to office would have indicated official approval of the party and would have entrenched them in power. Monroe's policy in effecting the desired reconciliation took two directions—first, he avoided in his public statements all references to the opposition which could be interpreted as a political attack upon that group. In his first inaugural, for example, he made no direct reference to the existence of another party. He merely confined himself to the general comment that the "increased harmony of opinion which pervades our Union" was most pleasing, for "discord does not belong to our system." Indeed his references to the Federalists in this address were so oblique that one contemporary observed that Monroe, rather than offering conciliation, was seeking to bury them in oblivion.

The second and more positive manifestation of his reconciliatory measures was in the form of gestures of personal friendship towards the Federalists. Federalist congressmen were freely received by the President, who willingly and openly discussed his policies with them. They were made to feel—and for creating this kind of atmosphere Monroe had a real talent—that no barrier existed between them and the President as a result of past party battles. Certainly his most effective action was the celebrated tour undertaken in two installments—to the East and Northwest in 1817 and to the South and Southwest two years later. Of these journeys the first was far more significant, for it took the President into the heart of Federalist dominated territory. As important as this tour was in restoring friendly relations with the Federalists, it is difficult to say when Monroe developed the plan or to what extent he was influenced by outside sources. Monroe said nothing about his tour until April 1817 and then merely announced his intention without any discussion. The analogy to Washington's tour is obvious, and since Monroe modeled other aspects of his conduct upon the example of the first president this is a not unlikely source. One possible source from which the proposal may have been derived was a suggestion made by Harrison Gray Otis six months before Monroe was elected (but after he had been nominated by the caucus). In the Monroe Papers in the Library of Congress there is a letter to Monroe written by Christopher Hughes from Boston on April 13, 1816. Hughes, a talented young diplomat, had stopped off in Boston on his way to a new assignment, and there he had been received in a most friendly fashion by Otis. Otis told Hughes that the Federalists were now divided into two factions, one of which would never approve of any measure of the Republicans, but the other (of which Otis was a member) would not obstruct any sound measure simply because the Federalists were not in power. Otis concluded this conversation by expressing "a strong wish that the leading men at Washington would travel during the recess more through the country and particularly to these states," where, Otis pointedly said, "the popular and general reception would be very pleasing, and . . . useful in its effect." Hughes, who was an intelligent and shrewd observer, recommended this idea to Monroe's attention. It is rather ironical to think that just as the name for his presidency was coined by a Federalist paper, so was the idea of the great good-will tour conceived in a Federalist mind.

Ostensibly Monroe's tour (which lasted three and a half months and took him as far west as Detroit) was for the purpose of inspecting military and naval installations. The very strong position that he had taken in his first inaugural in behalf of a larger military establishment and stronger fortifications made this seem a highly reasonable project. Although throughout his tour he diligently examined all installations, there was no doubt from the outset that it had larger intentions, and that it was designed to permit the Federalists by solemn public demonstrations to reaffirm their loyalty to the government and their acceptance of Republican control. Monroe was the ideal person for this task, for, unlike many of his contemporaries, he aroused no strong feelings of antipathy. After forty years in public office he had made almost no enemies apart from a few Federalist irreconcilables, who would have nothing to do with any Republican, and within his own party General John Armstrong was perhaps his only active enemy. Moreover, Monroe's personality was an attractive one. Most men immediately liked him, though it is true he rarely aroused the same kind of passionate devotion which Jefferson could among his associates. In manner Monroe was rather formal, having an innate sense of dignity, which allowed no one to take liberties. Yet in spite of his formality, he had the unusual ability to put men at their ease by his courtesy, his lack of condescension, his frankness, and what his contemporaries looked upon as the essential goodness and kindness of heart which he always radiated. These traits indeed seem not only to be vague but also rather unexciting ones—yet they are the ones most commonly noted by those who knew him. Abigail Adams, who was rarely taken in by anyone, summed up the attraction of the President when she wrote that all who met him were captivated by his "agreeable affability . . . unassuming manners . . . [and] his polite attentions to all orders and ranks." However difficult it is to describe Monroe's charm there can be no doubt that it was real. Of course the Federalists could have resisted the blandishments of the most dazzling personality had they not wanted to be charmed. But Monroe made it easy for them, leaving always the impression that the Federalists were honoring only the head of state, and avoiding any remarks that might humiliate them.

The President's tour turned into a love feast of fantastic proportions with Federalists and Republicans everywhere—except in Boston—uniting in feasting, parades, receptions, and an endless spate of addresses. In Boston, where the Federalists were still all powerful in political as well as social life, the Republican minority refused to join their opponents in receiving the President, and as a result a kind of race ensued as to which group could outdo the other in demonstrating its loyalty and affection. Without any question the Federalists easily won the day, displaying greater agility than the Republicans by rushing to Providence to welcome the President three days before he was due in Boston. The slower-footed Republicans did not catch up until the next day. In Boston it was not the Federalists who had to be reconciled by Monroe's tact, but the Republicans. Once in the city the President was feted royally by Otis, went to Braintree to dine with former President John Adams, and even found time in the course of a busy schedule to go to Waltham and eat a "strawberry" with the ailing Christopher Gore. Wherever he went the Federalists displayed so much eagerness to pay their respects that Abigail Adams wittily likened their endeavors to an "expiation."

As a capable politician well might do, Monroe sought to obtain a maximum result from this symbolic reaffirmation of loyalty with a minimum of commitment on his part. While some Federalists hoped that the President would eventually offer them offices, the shrewder among them, notably Rufus King and Jeremiah Mason of New Hampshire, were less sanguine. When the President was in Portsmouth, Mason found him quite willing to discuss all subjects in general terms, but, as he reported to King, Monroe "did not in any degree, designate the means by which he intended" to terminate the party conflict. Mason rightly concluded that Monroe was undoubtedly unwilling to conciliate the Federalists at the cost of alienating his old adherents. King concurred with this opinion, but both felt that the President had created a most favorable impression wherever he went.

Monroe was himself highly pleased with the results of the trip, and did not make the error of attributing the enthusiastic reception he had received to his personal popularity. After he left New England he summed up his reactions in a letter to Madison from Plattsburg:

> I have encounter'd more difficulties in my tour than I had formed any idea of. The pressure on me . . . by a crowded population, surpassed anything, that I ever witnessed. It was manifest to me, that a desire, in a body of the people to show their attachment to our union, and to republican govt., of which they seemed to be aware, there was just cause to certain doubts, from the events of the late war, was their ruling motive. The most distinguished in the opposition . . . seemed to seize the opportunity which my journey afforded them, to remove by the most explicit and solemn declarations, impressions of that kind, which they know existed, and to get back into the great family of the union.

In the years following his tour the President had good reason to consider his policy of conciliation successful. Every sign indicated that the era of party warfare was now at an end—by 1819 every New England state except Massachusetts was controlled by the Republicans, and in Congress there was not the slightest trace of an organized party opposing the administration on the old basis. The election of 1820 with its lone dissident elector seemed to be final proof, as Monroe observed in his second inaugural, that powerful causes had drawn the people together in a lasting unity of sentiment, of which he felt himself to be only the instrument and not the cause. He hoped that this new unity would now be equally apparent in all questions touching the interests of the nation.

With the process of de-Federalization this far advanced the next logical step would have been the appointment of former members of the opposition party to high office. However, during his second term, Monroe made the unhappy discovery that he, like his two Republican predecessors, was subject to criticism for having shown too much favor to Federalists. By and large the charge of a pro-Federalist orientation on the part of the administration was not really taken seriously by any one—it was part and parcel of the electioneering over the succession. However, Monroe dared not risk the creation of an organized opposition to the administration on this basis. Alarmed by the danger to which his domestic and foreign programs were already exposed, as a result of the ever mounting rivalry between the various presidential aspirants, Monroe had no choice but to discontinue making any further advances to the Federalists. That such appointments were not forthcoming was of little consequence as far as the objective of eliminating the opposition was concerned; the Federalists had gone too far on the road of reconciliation to be able to turn back now. However, to have given high office to a few Federalists would have been a splendid gesture with which to fully symbolize the Era of Good Feelings.

The complexities of this factional Republican rivalry lie beyond the scope of this paper, but several aspects deserve some comment, since they are so closely related to Monroe's policy of seeking to eliminate all parties. One of the most curious manifestations of this struggle was the extent to which it involved opposition to the policies of the administration. This state of affairs had been noted as early as 1818 by a number of observers, among them John Quincy Adams, who attributed it to what he called "a sort of instinctive impression that Mr. Monroe's administration will terminate by bringing in an *adverse* party to it." Even Monroe at the end of his first year in office had complained of the "querulous spirit" manifested by Congress, which had harassed the executive with unnecessary demands for information.

That the President's policies should have been involved is understandable, for of the five leading candidates, three—John Quincy Adams, William H. Crawford and John C. Calhoun—held cabinet posts, and a fourth, Andrew Jackson, held a number of important military appointments, and thus, like the others, was closely identified with policies Monroe was seeking to carry out. Henry Clay was the only presidential aspirant who occupied an independent position outside the official circle. The real object of the various attacks was to disgrace rival candidates, and, consequently, insofar as Monroe was concerned they were usually of an indirect or concealed nature, which made them difficult to cope with. A typical episode was the maneuvering which went on in Congress in connection with Jackson's conduct in the Seminole War, when the Crawfordites, in particular, wanted to damage the General's reputation as much as possible, and in so doing inevitably had to question the policy of the administration. Monroe, of course, found this kind of party warfare most taxing to deal with, and in complaining of it to Madison in 1822, sadly observed that one advantage of open party warfare was that it was grounded on principles which provided a basis to cheer and animate one to action.

Although these rivalries were a matter of much concern to Monroe, for they threatened to frustrate his program of eliminating all parties, their emergence was not a complete surprise to him. He had visualized this possibility before he entered the presidency, and sought to solve the difficulty by including in his cabinet the major contenders for the succession, who at the time of his election were Clay and Crawford. The latter was already in the cabinet, as Secretary of the Treasury, for Monroe had taken over those of Madison's cabinet willing to stay. Clay, however, declined the proffered secretaryship of war. Had Clay accepted then, Monroe would have begun his first term with two of the most potent political figures of the day committed to him. Much of the time consumed by Monroe's frequent cabinet meetings was not for the purpose of advice, but for the very practical objective of getting the members committed to a policy. Once committed in the cabinet, the President had a larger chance of getting his measures through Congress. In this task he was surprisingly successful until his last two years in office.

Vexatious as the complications of this intraparty struggle were, they did not shake Monroe's conviction in the correctness of his interpretation of the trend of public opinion. In 1822 in a letter to Madison in which he complained bitterly of the "embarrassment and mortification" which the party contest was causing him, he re-affirmed his belief that the nation had reached a "new epoch" in its political career—the Federalists had vanished and soon all party designations would disappear. He admitted to Madison that the course of this development had not been smooth, but he thought that this was only a temporary aberration and that public opinion would soon induce a more tranquil atmosphere. Madison, who had had his share of factional difficulties, sympathized with Monroe, but expressed a less hopeful opinion about the outcome. Madison felt that in all free governments there was a natural propensity for parties to form.

Even after his retirement from office and the advent of the bitter animosities of the Adams administration, Monroe continued to cherish the notion that parties would be eradicated, although he perhaps began to realize that this process was not going to be accomplished by sheer force of public opinion. In 1829 he began work upon an extended political essay, entitled "The People The Sovereigns," of which he completed only a small portion before his death. In this essay he intended to demonstrate by a comparative study of ancient and modern governments that the Constitution of the United States had eliminated the defects of ancient republics which had given rise to political parties. Since we had no class system and no privileged orders, there was no need for parties to act as the spokesmen of special interests, since all the people were sovereign. His notes for this work, it is true, do reveal much uneasiness over the continuing personal rivalries on the American political scene, but he still adhered to his optimistic faith that the virtue of the people would select men of talent and integrity, who would stand above personal ambition.

Although the eventual outcome of the political struggles of his administration was not what Monroe had envisaged, it cannot be said that he completely misunderstood his age. There were signs and indications which, when bolstered by Republican theories of an earlier age, could be interpreted as Monroe did. But if we were to take Monroe's statement to Jackson in 1816 that the failure to eliminate parties would result from a want of knowledge of all factors and a lack of judgment as to the measures to be adopted and ask what factors he ignored, I think the answer would be—the sectional ones. He was quite aware of their existence, but he did not fathom their divisiveness. To Monroe most of the problems presented by sectionalism were of a practical kind which should be solved by compromise. That many of his contemporaries did not feel this way he failed to perceive. If we were to ask what measures he failed to adopt, we pose an unanswerable question. It is difficult to say what more he could have done. One can only feel some amazement that he held together such inharmonious elements as long as he did. Monroe failed in his ultimate object of eliminating parties, but he created to a degree at least an appearance of unity in the nation, and to many of his contemporaries John Quincy Adams' conclusion in 1823 that the administration of James Monroe would be looked upon as a "golden age" in the history of the Republic may not have sounded as exaggerated as it does to us.

SOUTHERN CONFIDENCE IN NATIONAL POLICY

2 / Southern Support of the Tariff of 1816: A Reappraisal

Norris W. Preyer

In 1816 Congress passed several important pieces of legislation, including a new tariff that greatly strengthened American protectionism because it significantly raised import duties. Equally important, this tariff altered a great deal of the argument presented by the protectionists. Previously, they had supported higher duties by citing the national government's need for revenue. After 1816, the protariff advocates admitted more openly that protection of industry was their principal aim. The considerable Southern support for the tariff of 1816 has usually been explained by claiming that the South expected to industrialize as rapidly as the North and thus wanted tariff protection for a sectional interest then in the making. Norris W. Preyer submits evidence that Southern support did not originate in such expectations but rather derived from special circumstances in the two years after the Treaty of Ghent, circumstances that induced some Southerners to accept the higher tariff as a temporary measure. If held to be valid, this explanation clarifies a great deal of Southern politics after 1819, and the section's "rejection" of a national economic program that Preyer argues the South had never accepted. Preyer's article also illuminates some of the specific "bad feelings" that existed during the Era of Good Feelings, showing how the tariff became a major issue in the following decades and how competitive party politics continued to have issues on which to thrive.

For further reading: Charles M. Wiltse, *John C. Calhoun, Nationalist* (1944); Frank W. Taussig, *The Tariff History of the United States* (8th ed., 1931); Charles S. Sydnor, *The Development of Southern Sectionalism, 1819–1848* (1948).

Journal of Southern History, XXV (August 1959), 306–322. Copyright © 1959 by the Southern Historical Association. Reprinted by permission of the Managing Editor. Footnotes have been omitted except where they are necessary for an understanding of the text.

In 1816 the United States passed its first protective tariff, the principal aim of which was to place high duties on cotton and wool textiles. Historians, in examining this act, have been impressed by the strong support given it by the South. Especially was this support noticeable in South Carolina, where two of the South's strongest political leaders, William Lowndes and John C. Calhoun, voted for the measure.

The thesis invariably advanced to explain Southern support of the tariff of 1816 is that Southerners hoped and expected that textile manufacturing would develop in their section as it had in New England. This theory, to a great extent, hinges upon Lowndes and Calhoun. They are credited with having been the leaders of the drive to bring textile mills to the South, and it has been assumed that it was their influence which persuaded other congressmen below Mason and Dixon's line to vote for protection in 1816. Charles M. Wiltse believes that as a reward for their help on the tariff bill, Lowndes and Calhoun were considered for the office of Secretary of the Treasury. But was a desire to have manufacturing in the South the real consideration behind the voting of Lowndes, Calhoun, and other Southerners?

William Lowndes revealed definite hostility toward manufacturing in his voting. The only recorded votes during the debates of 1816 that deal specifically with protecting cotton and woolen manufacturers were those of April 2, 3, and 6. As such they constitute a better test of the willingness of Southerners to aid manufacturing than the final vote of April 8, in which a large number of extraneous factors (such as the need for revenue, fear of war, and Southern prosperity) played a part in the voting. The first two votes were on motions to reduce the duties levied on imported cotton goods. The third vote was on a motion to lower the duty on imported woolens. On all three motions Lowndes voted to lower the high protective duties that had been set.

Lowndes further demonstrated his hostility to high duties in his role as chairman of the powerful Ways and Means committee. It was to this committee that Secretary of the Treasury Alexander J. Dallas sent his report suggesting the rates that should be laid on manufactured articles to protect American entrepreneurs. When this message reached the committee it is reported that:

> Under the leadership of Lowndes the Committee of Ways and Means reduced the rates on several important articles—notably on textiles—below those recommended by Dallas when they presented their bill.

Lowndes' attempts to reduce textile rates were continued in speeches he made on the floor of Congress. On March 25 he spoke in favor of a motion which would lower the duties on imported cottons even below those which the Committee on Ways and Means had recommended. The following day he offered an amendment which would shorten the time that the high duties on manufactured woolen goods would be imposed. It is clear from these actions that Lowndes had no strong desire to protect cotton and woolen manufacturers.

John C. Calhoun, like Lowndes, is supposed to have supported the tariff of 1816 because of a desire to see manufacturing develop in South Carolina.[1] It should be

---

[1] The growth of this idea was probably due in large measure to Victor S. Clark who states in his *History of Manufactures in the United States* (3 vols., Washington, 1929), I, 368, that Calhoun founded a cotton factory on his plantation. Clark's statement is based on a letter that Calhoun wrote in January 1834, saying that "Mr. Davis has ceased to work on my mill and Gin. . . ." J. Franklin Jameson (ed.), *Correspondence of John C. Calhoun*, American Historical Association, *Annual Report, 1899* (2 vols., Washington, 1900), II, 331. This statement refers almost certainly to a grist mill which was to be found on nearly every plantation and not to a textile factory.

noted, however, that not once did Calhoun ever state that he expected industry to develop in South Carolina, or, for that matter, anywhere in the South. In his famous speech in support of the tariff of 1816, Calhoun referred specifically to the fact that his support was not based on any local manufacturing interests and that he was interested solely in agriculture as a means of livelihood for the South. On still another occasion Calhoun made the assertion that no mechanical enterprise would succeed in the Palmetto State.

That the actions of Lowndes and Calhoun reflected the sentiments of others in their home state is shown by the remarks of Langdon Cheves, one of the most prominent South Carolinians, who said that "manufacturing should be the last resort of industry in every country, for once forced as with us, they serve no interests but those of the capitalists who set them in motion and their immediate localities."

Like Calhoun and Lowndes, most of the other fourteen Southern congressmen who voted for the tariff of 1816 appear to have had something else in mind than a wish to bring manufacturing to their section. Eight of them voted the same as Lowndes (in favor of lowering the high duties that had been set) in the three earlier votes of April 2, 3, and 6. Three others—Samuel Smith of Maryland, Aylett Hawes and William McCoy of Virginia—were for reducing the rates set on cotton goods, but favored keeping the duties placed on manufactured woolen articles. Henry St. George Tucker of Virginia was also for keeping the duties on woolen goods but was absent during the voting of April 2 and 3 on cotton duties. Only two of the fourteen, William Mayrant of South Carolina and Thomas Newton of Virgina, voted on each of these earlier roll calls in favor of high duties. Mayrant had built a small cotton mill during the War of 1812, and in 1816 he was suffering as a result of British competition. Almost certainly he was motivated by these considerations in voting as he did. Newton had no textile mills in the district he represented, and his attitude toward manufacturing appears to have been similar to that of Calhoun. He favored the development of manufacturing in the Northeast and West, but seemed unaware that any textile plants were operating in the South and foresaw the role of the South only as a supplier of raw materials and food products to the rest of the nation. Protection, he felt, would "give to agriculture new life and expansion."

Another method of examining the thesis that Southerners supported the tariff of 1816 because they hoped that textile mills would develop there is to view the voting on this bill by states. If the thesis is valid one should expect to find that the states profiting most by it would give it the strongest support. In the South, Maryland was the state having the most cotton and woolen mills. Yet every Southern state, except North Carolina, cast a greater percentage of its congressional votes for the tariff than did Maryland.

It might be argued that one should not look at the voting of a whole state but just at that of the individual congressman having textile mills in his district. Seven representatives are known definitely to have had cotton or woolen mills in their districts in 1816, and four more probably had them. Of these eleven only three—Smith of Maryland, Tucker of Virginia, and Mayrant of South Carolina—cast final votes for the tariff.[2] On the other hand, thirteen representatives, including Lowndes and Calhoun, who had no textile factories in their districts in 1816, voted in favor of

---

[2] Georgia is omitted from this examination because her representatives were elected on a general ticket and so failed to represent any specific district.

protection. If any conclusion is to be drawn from these votes, it must be that Southern congressmen voted contrary to the manufacturing interests of their districts.

If most Southerners did not support the tariff of 1816 through a desire to have manufacturing, why then did they vote fot it? The true reasons may very well have been those given in the actual tariff debates. They were (1) the need to raise additional revenue and (2) the fear of a new war, making it essential that America protect what limited industry had been established.

Both protectionists and freetraders were in agreement that the country needed more revenue. This need became evident when, in December of 1815, Secretary of the Treasury Dallas presented his budget for the forthcoming year. It revealed that by the end of 1816 there would be a deficit of about three and one half million dollars. Dallas said that the only way that this deficit could be overcome and the budget balanced was by having a tariff with high duties. The accuracy of Dallas' budget figures or the fact that the country needed more revenue was never questioned by opponents of protection. The only point argued was whether a high tariff was the best way to bring in the necessary additional revenue. It was the contention of some Southerners that a high tariff would hurt the nation's revenue receipts because it would either stop people from importing goods entirely or else would lead them to smuggle in the wanted goods duty free.

Probably the greatest weakness in the position of those who said that high duties would not bring in more revenue was that they suggested no alternative means to increase the revenue.[3] Since no other solution for achieving this result, besides a high tariff, was ever advanced, most congressmen must have felt that they had at least to give the one method open to them a trial. Taking some action on the revenue problem, they reasoned, was preferable to doing nothing at all. Lowndes is an example of a Southerner who felt this way. Though he had opposed most of the high duties written into the tariff bill, he rose to his feet on the final day of debate to declare that he would still vote for the bill because it would help the revenue and general interests of the United States.

Possibly an even stronger consideration with Southerners, because their emotions played a stronger part in it, was the patriotic desire to build up America's defenses and to stop British goods from flooding the American market. It was clear from the speeches made in Parliament by Lord Brougham that this dumping of goods was done with malice aforethought. In connection with British exports to America, he was quoted by *Niles' Weekly Register* as saying that it was

> well worthwhile to incur a loss upon the first exportation, in order, by the glut, TO STIFLE IN THE CRADLE THOSE RISING MANUFACTURERS IN THE UNITED STATES, which the war had forced into existence, *contrary to the natural course of things.*

Only a year had elapsed since America had been at war with Great Britain. During

---

[3] The two alternatives that might have been tried were an excise and a direct tax. Both of these taxes were levied during the War of 1812 and were still in effect. The excise taxes were so unpopular that most were abolished or reduced when the war came to an end. Among Southerners the direct tax was equally unpopular, for it was levied on houses, land, and slaves. In March 1816, the South succeeded in having this tax reduced by one half. It is possible that there was a bargain made in which Southerners promised to support a protective tariff as a lesser evil in return for Northern aid in reducing the direct tax. These reductions, Dallas estimated, would increase the deficit in 1816 from $3,484,269 to $6,484,269.

the War of 1812 the South had been one of the strongest supporters of the administration. This support was based, in part, upon a deep hatred of Britain stemming from the many slights and injustices America had suffered at her hands. The South had entered the war determined to show Great Britain that America would take no more insults. Southern feeling against England was still strong in 1816, and few Southerners remained unmoved by the appeal that they now save from British flooding those industries which had helped America to survive during the war. There was, moreover, a strong feeling that occasion for using these industries might be close at hand.

One of the strongest speeches in favor of a protective tariff was made by John C. Calhoun. The entire speech was based on the fear that America might shortly be involved in another war with her ancient antagonist, Great Britain. After warning that war might break out at any time, Calhoun declared that America must not again be so poorly prepared to defend herself as she had been in 1812. This time she must be ready. The surest way to be ready was to aid, by means of a tariff, those industries which would make America self-sufficient. A letter written at about this same time reveals that, in addition to Calhoun, Henry St. George Tucker of Virginia, Alexander C. Hanson of Maryland, and Henry Clay of Kentucky were "in support of the grand system of preparation, in time of peace for war when it may come."

Fear of another war was justified. One of the British aims during the War of 1812 was to detach Louisiana from the United States. At the peace conference England carefully avoided any mention of the American boundary title to Louisiana. Americans consequently were apprehensive that Great Britain might again enter into war to acquire this large territorial region. The proposal made by the British commissioners during the negotiations at Ghent for the creation of an Indian buffer state in the Northwest must also have made Americans fearful that England would continue her aggressive frontier policy and her attempts to stir up the Indians. Certainly there was little in the Treaty of Ghent to relieve America's suspicions of Great Britain.

John Quincy Adams, who as Minister to Great Britain was in the best position to judge her intentions, shared entirely the views of Calhoun. In August 1816 he wrote his father that all the governments of Europe were deeply hostile to the United States and that Britain was using its influence to hurt America in every possible way. "How long it will be possible for us to preserve peace with all Europe," he wrote, "it is impossible to forsee. Of this I am sure, that we cannot be too well or too quickly prepared for a new conflict to support our rights and our interests,"

The argument that war was liable to break out again (an eventuality which would force reliance once again on the industries which had helped save America in the last war) made a strong appeal to the national patriotism of the South. This and the knowledge that the country needed more revenue combined to persuade Southerners to back the tariff of 1816. The attitude of the South at that time is probably best recalled in a speech made by Representative Eldred Simkins of South Carolina:

> To give some protection to those establishments which had greatly helped to save us in time of war, and without which no nation on earth can ever be truly independent or safe, as well as to raise a revenue, the Congress of 1816 passed a law, imposing a tariff, or system of duties, on the most of those foreign articles which could be made among ourselves, and the extravagant importations of which were about to bring ruin on our manufacturers! This was wise, it was patriotic, it was in fact the duty of the Representatives of the nation.

Offsetting, to some extent, the arguments advanced in favor of a high tariff was the consciousness on the part of Southerners that the burden of the tariff would be borne almost entirely by their section of the country while most of its benefits would accrue to other sections. It was because of this that most Southerners on April 2, 3, and 6 had tried to keep the tariff as low as possible by supporting amendments advanced toward that end. Yet on the final vote, when the question was no longer one of how high or low to have the duties but whether or not to have a tariff at all, Southerners voted for the tariff. Their common sense realization that the country must have more revenue and their patriotic feeling that America must be strong and resist Great Britain won out over their hatred of the high duties. For those wavering between which choice to make, three factors must have played a part in persuading them to cast their votes for the tariff. One was the belief that the high duties were to be a temporary expedient which would last only until June 1819. By that time, it was felt, the need for additional revenue and the danger to industry from British goods flooding the American market would be ended. A second factor was the promise by Representative Thomas R. Gold of New York that high protective duties would be laid only on cotton and woolen manufactures and would not be extended to other products. These promises together limited the tariff both as to time and extent. A final factor was that the South in 1816 was enjoying a period of great prosperity and so was in a position to make concessions.

Further evidence in support of the present interpretation of why the South advocated the tariff of 1816 can be found in Southern reaction to the tariff bill of 1820. The South was almost unanimously opposed to this new measure. The reason for this remarkable reversal may be found by considering the validity in 1820 of the arguments and promises which had influenced Southerners to vote for protection in 1816.

One of the most effective arguments protectionists used in 1816 was that which stressed the necessity of protecting America's war industries. In 1820 supporters of protection tried to make this the sole issue upon which the tariff issue would be discussed. Representative Henry Baldwin of Pennsylvania, making the principal speech in support of the tariff, declared that the increased duties were not based on whether manufacturers were prosperous or losing, but on national principles—the need of making America capable of defending herself in time of war. This argument had been very effective when John C. Calhoun voiced it in 1816, because at that time there was reason to believe that another war with Great Britain was imminent. Starting in 1817, however, with the Rush-Bagot agreement, a series of important events had taken place which served to dispel the fear of another war.

The Rush-Bagot agreement, demilitarizing the British-American frontier west to the Lake of the Woods, was an indication that Great Britain had decided not to contest American territory along that frontier. The old fear that England was trying to stir up the Indians and create a buffer state in the Northwest was now gone. The following year the Convention of 1818 was signed. Under its terms a boundary line was drawn between the United States and British North America along the forty-ninth parallel from the Lake of the Woods to the Rocky Mountains. This marked the first time that Britain recognized the northern boundary of the Louisiana Purchase and America's title to it. The Convention was significant in that it put an end to apprehensions, prevalent in 1816, that England planned to detach Louisiana from the United States.

The sincerity of Britain's new policy of friendship was put to the test when Andrew Jackson marched into Florida in 1818. While in Spanish territory he captured and executed two British subjects, Arbuthnot and Ambrister. British public opinion was incensed and Secretary of State Adams sent a defense of Jackson to Lord Castlereagh. But Castlereagh in January 1819, even before he received this defense, had already written his Minister in Washington that Britain would take no action in regard to Arbuthnot and Ambrister.

Another potential source of conflict between Britain and the United States came to an end on February 22, 1819, with the signing of the Adams-Onís Treaty between Spain and the United States. By the terms of this treaty Spain renounced all claims to West Florida and ceded East Florida to the United States. Spain had been loath to lose Florida and had dreamed of recovering Louisiana from America. She did not have the strength by herself to achieve these ends, but had hoped for English aid. As long as the Florida question remained unsettled there was always the danger that England, had she any aggressive intentions toward the United States, might use this as a pretext for conflict. William Lowndes, who was traveling in Great Britain at this time, worriedly wrote that "the reports now are that the Spanish government has refused to ratify our treaty [the Adams-Onís Treaty] and some people here are very gloomy upon the subject from the apprehension that a Spanish and ultimately an English war may ensue." England, however, would give Spain neither diplomatic nor military support, and it was largely because of lack of English backing that Spain settled the Florida Question with America.

By January 1820 even the usually pessimistic Secretary of State, John Quincy Adams, could inform the President that "in our foreign relations, we stood upon terms with England as favorable as can ever be expected. . . ."

As a result of these peaceful actions on the part of Great Britain, Southerners no longer saw any critical need to continue strengthening the national defense.

A second argument which had influenced Southerners to vote for protection in 1816 was that it might halt the flooding of the American market by cheap British goods. In 1816 this was a very real threat because Britain at that time was selling her goods at a loss in order to destroy American manufacturers, but by 1820 this threat, too, had vanished.

A third argument which had great effect upon Southerners in 1816 was that a high tariff was needed for revenue. In 1820 there again appeared a need for additional revenue. In December 1819, the Secretary of the Treasury had reported that the current year would end with a deficit estimated at one million dollars and a deficit of five million dollars was foreseen for 1820. Yet the proponents of protection did not raise the revenue argument even though it had served them so well in 1816. According to the late Charles Sydnor they did not raise the argument because everyone was in agreement on this point. But surely, in as closely fought a battle as that which took place over the bill of 1820, supporters of protection would not throw away one of their strongest weapons.

To understand why protectionists did not advance the revenue issue in 1820, it must be emphasized that the existing tariff had, up to 1819, been bringing in sufficient revenue. It had been estimated that the tariff of 1816 would bring in about seventeen million dollars in customs duties annually, but by the end of 1816 the new duties had brought in approximately twenty-seven and one half million dollars. The year 1816 was probably exceptional because the War of 1812 had ended only recently. Yet in 1817 the revenue from customs brought in approximately seventeen and one half million dollars. By January 1, 1818, the Treasury had turned its earlier deficit into a comfortable surplus of $6,179,883.38. The last complete figures available to the debaters on the bill of 1820 were those for the year of 1818 which showed a revenue from customs of nearly twenty-two million dollars.

The tariff was, therefore, bringing in sufficient revenue for any normal year. The deficit which was reported for 1819 and was expected to continue in 1820 was brought about by the Panic of 1819. The South, the leading buyer of imported goods in the United States, was hurt by the Panic and did not have the money to buy as before. Raising the tariff could only aggravate this situation. The Secretary of the Treasury, earlier in the session, had declared that an increase in the duties on woolens, cottons, and iron would impair the revenue and tend to introduce smuggling. This statement cut the ground from under the feet of the protectionists. Lowndes made use of it when he asked the rhetorical question: "Could it be necessary that we should interfere by law to diminish importations, at the moment when we see that an unparalleled reduction is effecting without our interference?" Thrown on the defensive, protectionists found themselves forced to argue that revenue should not come from the tariff but from other sources, such as excise taxes. This played right into the hands of the anti-tariff men. One of them, Mark Alexander of Virginia, was quick to point out that the country had always expected its revenue to come from customs. Thus, the revenue issue had become, by 1820, a potent weapon in the hands of the anti-protectionists.

The final argument used by supporters of the bill of 1820 was that manufacturers were in distress. Southerners tried in vain to determine if the hardships of manufacturers in 1820 were due to the Panic of 1819. If so, the manufacturers would need temporary help only, not a system of permanent duties such as the bill of 1820 envisioned. John Tyler of Virginia expressed what the South was thinking when, in the debates, he said:

> Are the present manufacturers in the United States really entitled to your aid? Where is the proof of it? We have asked for the proof, and the chairman of the committee [Henry Baldwin] frankly acknowledged that he did not possess it . . . . I wanted to be informed whether that interest only suffered in the same ratio with the others, and whether its sufferings were produced by similar causes.

The suspicion of the South that the troubles of the manufacturer were due solely to the Panic was never dispelled. Attempts by Baldwin to steer clear of that issue only heightened Southern suspicion. Baldwin, it must be remembered, had tried to make the need of a tariff for defense purposes the issue upon which the bill was to be debated. He strove to brush aside Southern questions as to the distress in which manufacturers found themselves by blandly saying "whether their establishments are productive or losing" is not the issue. This bill was supported on national principles.

Actually the Panic of 1819 aided manufacturing. The fall of prices which it brought about made the cost of raw materials cheaper and proved to be advantageous to manufacturers. The fact that prices dropped was no sign the Northern factory owners were suffering. Congressman Philip Barbour of Virginia pointed out that in 1816 cotton had sold at thirty cents a pound. Now it sold at not more than fifteen cents a pound. Therefore, "if, in 1816, cotton cloth sold at thirty cents per yard, and now it sells at twenty cents, it is substantially just as good a sale . . . ."

It must not be forgotten that it was the South and West which had been hurt most by the Panic of 1819. Manufacturing areas were hit only lightly while the rural areas suffered greatly. Although Northern manufacturers could profit from the low prices, there was no way by which Southern planters could do the same. In 1816, when Britain was dumping her goods on the American market, the South had gone along with the North in its time of need. At that time the South was enjoying great prosperity and could afford to be generous. Tobacco was selling at fifteen dollars per hundredweight, cotton at thirty cents per pound, and rice at $3.80 per hundredweight. But 1820 found a different situation. Tobacco now sold at only $5.25 per hundredweight, while the price of cotton had dropped to sixteen cents a pound (and in November fell to fifteen cents) and that of rice to $2.28 per hundredweight.

Another factor influencing the votes of Southerners was the memory of the promises which had been made to them in 1816. They had been led to believe that high tariff duties were to be a temporary expedient which would last just long enough to protect the American market from being flooded by British goods. But with the introduction of the tariff bill of 1820 all pretense that high duties would be temporary was brushed aside. The duties listed by the bill of 1820 were to be permanent. No longer was it stated or implied that when industry became strong, duties would be lowered or abandoned. A speech by Lowndes on April 28, 1820, shows that he was keenly aware of this.

> What he regretted, Mr. L[owndes] said, most, in the course pursued by the Committee of Manufactures, was, that they suggested no standard by which the sufficiency of the encouragement which they proposed could be tested, and promised, therefore, no limitation to the burden which might be imposed upon the country.

The other promise given in 1816 was that high duties would not be extended from cotton and woolen goods to other products.[4] The bill of 1820, however, proposed an extension of high duties to a long list of new items.

By 1820 the South realized that the earlier arguments and appeals of protectionists were no longer valid. In 1816 it was not a desire for manufacturing, but a combination of prosperity, patriotism, and promises that had swayed Southerners. None of these factors now existed to influence them. One consideration, however, which had always had a strong influence on the thinking of Southerners still remained—the need to defend their economic interests. Now, with no other views to challenge or obscure this desire, the South turned almost unanimously against the tariff bill of 1820. The brief Southern experiment in supporting protection had come to an end, and from then on that section would consistently oppose all protective tariffs.

[4] In 1818 a bill was passed which granted higher iron duties. Congressmen justified it, however, on the ground that iron duties should have been raised in 1816, since iron was a defense necessity which had been overlooked at the time.

3 / The Missouri Crisis, Slavery, and the Politics of Jacksonianism

Richard H. Brown

Another occasion for Southern apprehension came during and after the Congressional debates over the admission of Missouri into the Union that took place during 1819 to 1821. Although the formula for resolving this specific crisis now seems beautifully simple (the admission of Missouri as a slave state and Maine as a free state), the exchanges in Congress went beyond the immediate issues to broach the subject that the South always considered nonnegotiable: the then status and future of slavery. Almost every polemical point raised during the prolonged sectional crisis of the 1850's can be found 30 years earlier in the Missouri debates.

Richard H. Brown argues that the Missouri crisis fundamentally affected Southern politics for decades to come, and that in the 1820's the rise of Andrew Jackson can be understood in large measure as the success of a movement of Southerners upholding their sectional interests. They were joined by Northerners who agreed that their own advancement would be served by preserving the stability of Southern institutions. Martin Van Buren was the key man in reforging the Jeffersonian alliance between New York and Virginia. He sought to revive the Republican (soon to become the Democratic) Party by putting Andrew Jackson in the White House. Brown contends for the crucial role of Southern politics and interests in bringing this about. In support of this view, one might note that the Missouri debates added the term "doughface" (a Northerner with Southern principles) to the vocabulary of American political invective.

For further reading: Glover Moore, *The Missouri Controversy, 1819–1821* (1953); Philip F. Detweiler, "Congressional Debate on Slavery and the Declaration of Independence, 1819-1821," *American Historical Review,* LXIII (April 1958), 598–616.

South Atlantic Quarterly, LXV (Winter 1966), 55–72. Reprinted by permission.

From the inauguration of Washington until the Civil War the South was in the saddle of national politics. This is the central fact in American political history to 1860. To it there are no exceptions, not even in that period when the "common man" stormed the ramparts of government under the banner of Andrew Jackson. In Jackson's day the chief agent of Southern power was a Northern man with Southern principles, Martin Van Buren of New York. It was he who put together the party coalition which Andrew Jackson led to power. That coalition had its wellsprings in the dramatic crisis over slavery in Missouri, the first great public airing of the slavery question in ante-bellum America.

I

More than anything else, what made Southern dominance in national politics possible was a basic homogeneity in the Southern electorate. In the early nineteenth century, to be sure, the South was far from monolithic. In terms of economic interest and social classes it was scarcely more homogeneous than the North. But under the diversity of interests which characterized Southern life in most respects there ran one single compelling idea which virtually united all Southerners, and which governed their participation in national affairs. This was that the institution of slavery should not be dealt with from outside the South. Whatever the merits of the institution—and Southerners violently disagreed about this, never more than in the 1820's—the presence of the slave was a fact too critical, too sensitive, too perilous for all of Southern society to be dealt with by those not directly affected. Slavery must remain a Southern question. In the ante-bellum period a Southern politician of whatever party forgot this at his peril. A Northern politician might perceive it to his profit. There had been, Martin Van Buren noted with satisfaction late in life, a "remarkable consistency in the political positions" of Southern public men. With characteristic insouciance the Little Magician attributed this consistency to the natural superiority of republican principles which led them to win out in a region relatively untainted by the monied interest. But his partisan friend Rufus King, Van Buren admitted, ascribed it to the "black strap" of Southern slavery.

The insistence that slavery was uniquely a Southern concern, not to be touched by outsiders, had been from the outset a *sine qua non* for Southern participation in national politics. It underlay the Constitution and its creation of a government of limited powers, without which Southern participation would have been unthinkable. And when in the 1790's Jefferson and Madison perceived that a constitution was only the first step in guaranteeing Southern security, because a constitution meant what those who governed under it said it meant, it led to the creation of the first national political party to protect that constitution against change by interpretation. The party which they constructed converted a Southern minority into a national majority through alliance with congenial interests outside the South. Organically, it represented an alliance between New York and Virginia, pulling between them Pennsylvania, and after them North Carolina, Georgia, and (at first) Kentucky and Tennessee, all states strongly subject to Virginia's influence. At bottom it rested on the support of people who lived on that rich belt of fertile farmland which stretched from the Great Lakes across upstate New York and Pennsylvania, southward through the Southern piedmont into Georgia, entirely oblivious of the Mason-Dixon line. North as well as South it was an area of prosperous, well-settled small farms. More farmers than capitalists, its residents wanted little from government but to be let alone. Resting his party on them, Jefferson had found a formula for national politics which at the same time was a formula for Southern pre-eminence. It would hold good to the Civil War.

So long as the Federalists remained an effective opposition, Jefferson's party worked as a party should. It maintained its identity in relation to the opposition by a moderate and pragmatic advocacy of strict construction of the Constitution. Because it had competition, it could maintain discipline. It responded to its constituent elements because it depended on them for support. But eventually its very success was its undoing. After 1815, stirred by the nationalism of the postwar era, and with the Federalists in decline, the Republicans took up Federalist positions on a number of the great public issues of the day, sweeping all before them as they did. The Federalists gave up the ghost. In the Era of Good Feelings which followed, everybody began to call himself a Republican, and a new theory of party amalgamation preached the doctrine that party division was bad and that a one-party system best served the national interest. Only gradually did it become apparent that in victory the Republican party had lost its identity—and its usefulness. As the party of the whole nation it ceased to be responsive to any particular elements in its constituency. It ceased to be responsive to the South.

When it did, and because it did, it invited the Missouri crisis of 1819–1820, and that crisis in turn revealed the basis for a possible configuration of national parties which eventually would divide the nation free against slave. As John Quincy Adams put it, the crisis had revealed "the basis for a new organization of parties . . . here was a new party ready formed, . . . terrible to the whole Union, but portentously terrible to the South—threatening in its progress the emancipation of all their slaves, threatening in its immediate effect that Southern domination which has swayed the Union for the last twenty years." Because it did so, Jefferson, in equally famous phrase, "considered it at once as the knell of the Union."

Adams and Jefferson were not alone in perceiving the significance of what had happened. Scarcely a contemporary missed the point. Historians quote them by the dozens as prophets—but usually *only* as prophets. In fact the Missouri crisis gave rise not to prophecy alone, but to action. It led to an urgent and finally successful attempt to revive the old Jeffersonian party and with it the Jeffersonian formula for Southern pre-eminence. The resuscitation of that party would be the most important story in American politics in the decades which followed.

II

In Jefferson's day the tie between slavery, strict construction of the Constitution, and the Republican party was implicit, not explicit. After Missouri it was explicit, and commented upon time and again in both public and private discussion. Perceptive Southerners saw (1) that unless effective means were taken to quiet discussion of the question, slavery might be used at any time in the future to force the South into a permanent minority in the Union, endangering all its interests; and (2) that if the loose constitutional construction of the day were allowed to prevail, the time might come when the government would be held to have the power to deal with slavery. Vital to preventing both of these—to keeping the slavery question quiet and to gaining a reassertion of strict construction principles—was the re-establishment of conditions which would make the party in power responsive once again to the South.

Not only did the Missouri crisis make these matters clear, but it shaped the conditions which would govern what followed. In the South it gave marked impetus to a reaction against the nationalism and amalgamationism of postwar Republicanism and handed the offensive to a hardy band of Old Republican politicians who had been crying in the wilderness since 1816. In the early 1820's the struggle between Old Republicans and New would be the stuff of Southern politics, and on the strength of the new imperatives to which the Missouri conflict gave rise the Old Republicans would carry off the victory in state after Southern state, providing thereby a base of power on which a new strict construction party could be reared.

For precisely the same reason that it gave the offensive to the Old Republicans of the South—because it portrayed the tie between slavery and party in starkest form— the Missouri crisis put Northern Old Republicans on the defense. Doing so, it handed the keys to national party success thereafter to whatever Northern leader could surmount charges of being pro-Southern and command the necessary Northern votes to bring the party to power. For that reason Thomas Jefferson's formula for national politics would become, when resurrected, Martin Van Buren's formula for national politics. What has long been recognized as happening to the Democratic party in the forties and fifties happened in fact in 1820. After Missouri and down to the Civil War the revised formula for Southern pre-eminence would involve the elevation to the presidency of Southerners who were predominantly Westerners in the public eye, or of Northern men with Southern principles.

Because they shaped the context of what was to come, the reactions to the Missouri crisis in the two citadels of Old Republican power, Richmond and Albany, were significant. Each cast its light ahead. As the donnybrook mounted in Congress in the winter of 1820, the Virginia capital was reported to be as "agitated as if affected by all the Volcanic Eruptions of Vesuvius." At the heart of the clamor were the Old Republicans of the Richmond Junto, particularly Thomas Ritchie's famous *Enquirer,* which spoke for the Junto and had been for years the most influential newspaper in the South. Associates of Jefferson, architects of Southern power, the Old Republicans were not long in perceiving the political implications of the crisis. Conviction grew in their minds that the point of Northern agitation was not Missouri at all but to use slavery as an anvil on which to forge a new party which would carry either Rufus King or DeWitt Clinton of New York to the presidency and force the South from power forever. But what excited them even more was the enormity of the price of peace which alone seemed likely to avert the disaster. This was the so-called Thomas Proviso, amending the Missouri bill to draw the ill-fated 36°30′ line across the Louisiana Purchase, prohibiting slavery in the territory to the north, giving up the lion's share to freedom.

No sooner had the proviso been introduced in Congress than the temper of the Old Republicans boiled over, and with prescient glances to the future they leapt to the attack. Ritchie challenged the constitutionality of the Proviso at once in the

Enquirer, a quarter century before Calhoun would work out the subtle dialectic of a Southern legal position. Nathaniel Macon agreed. "To compromise is to acknowledge the right of Congress to interfere and to legislate on the subject," he wrote; "this would be acknowledging too much." Equally important was the fact that, by prohibiting slavery in most of the West, the Proviso forecast a course of national development ultimately intolerable to the South because, as Spencer Roane put it to Monroe, Southerners could not consent to be "dammed up in a land of Slaves." As the debates thundered to their climax, Ritchie in two separate editorials predicted that if the Proviso passed, the South must in due time have Texas. "If we are cooped up on the north," he wrote with grim prophecy, "we must have elbow room to the west."

When finally the Southern Old Republicans tacitly consented to the Missouri Compromise, it was therefore not so much a measure of illusion about what the South had given up, as of how desperately necessary they felt peace to be. They had yielded not so much in the spirit of a bargain as in the spirit of a man caught in a holdup, who yields his fortune rather than risk his life in the hope that he may live to see a better day and perhaps even to get his fortune back. As Ritchie summed it up when news of the settlement reached Richmond, "Instead of joy, we scarcely ever recollect to have tasted of a bitterer cup." That they tasted it at all was because of the manipulative genius of Henry Clay, who managed to bring up the separate parts of the compromise separately in the House, enabling the Old Republicans to provide him his margin of victory on the closely contested Missouri bill while they saved their pride by voting to the end against the Thomas Proviso. They had not bound themselves by their votes to the Proviso, as Ritchie warned they should not. If it was cold comfort for the moment, it was potent with significance for the future.

In fact, the vote on the Proviso illuminated an important division in Southern sentiment. Thirty-seven slave state congressmen opposed it, while thirty-nine voted for it. On the surface the line of division ran along the Appalachian crest and the Potomac, pointing out seemingly a distinction in interest between the South Atlantic states on the one hand and those in the Southwest and mid-Atlantic regions on the other—between those states most characteristically Southern and those which in 1820 were essentially more Western or Northern in outlook. More fundamental, within each section it divided Southerners between those who were more sensitive to the relationship of slavery to politics and those who were less so; between those who thought the party formula for Southern pre-eminence and defense important and those who thought parties outmoded; between particularists and postwar Republican nationalists; between the proponents of an old Republican polity and the proponents of a new one as defined in the years of postwar exuberance; between those closest to Jefferson, such as the Richmond Junto and Macon, and those closest to Monroe, such as Calhoun. It was a division which prefigured Southern political struggles of the twenties. When two years later 70 per cent of those congressmen from the South Atlantic states who had opposed the Thomas Proviso returned to the next Congress, compared to 39 per cent of those who had supported it, it was a measure of the resurgence of Old Republicanism. Two years after that, in the chaotic presidential election of 1824, the Southerners who had opposed the Proviso were the Southerners who sought to sustain the party caucus as a method of nominating in a vain attempt to restore old party discipline. Four years after that they marched back to power at last under the banner of Andrew Jackson, restoring to effectiveness in so doing a political system intended to make future Missouri crises impossible, and committed in due time to rectify the Thomas Proviso.

Equally important to the reaction in Richmond was what went on in Albany. There command of the state's Old Republicans was in the hands of the Bucktails, a group of which State Senator Martin Van Buren, at thirty-eight, was already master spirit. Opposed to the Bucktails was Governor DeWitt Clinton, an erstwhile Republican who drew a good deal of his support from former Federalists. With the Bucktails committed to the old Virginia-New York alliance, the Missouri question offered Clinton a heaven-sent opportunity; indeed there were those who suspected the ambitious governor of playing God himself and helping to precipitate the crisis. Whether or not this was true, Clinton tried desperately while the storm was raging in Washington to get a commitment from the Bucktails which would stamp them as proslavery, but the Bucktails acted cautiously. When a large meeting was called in Albany to indorse the prohibition of slavery in Missouri, Van Buren found it convenient to be off on circuit. When the Clintonians whipped a resolution indorsing the restriction through the legislature, not a Bucktail raised a voice in dissent. But for all their caution against public commitment it was generally understood both in Washington and New York that the Bucktails were anxious for peace, and that they supported the corporal's guard of Northern Republicans in congress who, retreating finally from the Missouri prohibition, made peace possible. Several of the Bucktail newspapers said as much, and despite the lack of public commitment on the part of party leaders, more than one Clintonian newspaper would brand them the "Slave Ticket" in the legislative elections which followed.

In private, Van Buren left no doubt where he stood, or where he meant to go once the storm had passed. No sooner had the compromise been adopted in Washington than the Little Magician got off a letter to his friendly rival Rufus King, promising at "some future day" to give that veteran Federalist his own views on the expediency of making slavery a party question, and remarking meanwhile that notwithstanding the strong public interest in the Missouri question, "the excitement which exists in regard to it, or which is likely to arise from it, is not so great as you suppose." It was a singularly important assessment of Northern public opinion for a politician who had fallen heir to a tattered Southern alliance, and in it King apprehensively saw the panorama of forty years of national politics stretching before him:

> The inveteracy of party feelings in the Eastern States [he wrote a friend], the hopes of influence and distinction by taking part in favor of the slave States, which call themselves, and are spoken of by others as the truly republican States and the peculiar friends of liberty, will keep alive & sustain a body considerably numerous, and who will have sufficient influence, to preserve to the slave States their disproportionate, I might say exclusive, dominance over the Union.

Twenty months after that, in the late fall of 1821, Van Buren set off for Washington as a newly elected United States senator. With his party having taken the measure of Clinton in the meantime, he carried with him into the lion's den of presidential politics effective command of the thirty-six uncommitted electoral votes of New York. If he would be the most disinterested statesman in all the land, he could not avoid for long the responsibility that went with that power. It was an opportunity to be used for large purposes or small, as a man might choose, and the Little Magician lost no time in indicating his intended course. Within weeks of his arrival he was pulling the strings of the New York delegation in the House to bring about return of the speakership to the slave states, from whom it had been wrested by a straight sectional vote upon Clay's retirement the year before. The new speaker was P. P. Barbour of Virginia, a leader of the Old Republican reaction in the South. Three months after that Van Buren was on his way to Richmond to plan the resurrection of the Old Republican Party.

That he should do so was partly for reasons of personal ambition, partly because the Bucktails after years of frustrating struggle with Clinton had their own clear reasons for wanting to redraw party lines. Beyond this there would appear to be the simple fact that Van Buren believed implicitly in the whole system of republican polity as Thomas Jefferson had staked it out. Committed to the principle of the least possible government, the Republican party was the defender of that republican liberty which was the sole political concern of the disinterested agrarian constituency for which, through life, Van Buren saw himself as a spokesman, and which constituted the majority of Americans. That majority was strongest where it was purest, least subject to the corrupting power of money. That was in the South. Slavery was a lesser issue than republicanism. Nor was it by any means clear in 1820 that agitation was the best way to deal with it. For while some who were nominally Old Republicans, such as Senator William Smith of South Carolina, were beginning to argue that slavery was a positive good, it was generally true that no men in America were more honestly committed to the notion that the institution was wrong than those men of Jeffersonian conscience who were the Old Republicans of the South. Eleven years later, in 1831, some of them would mount in the Virginia legislature the last great effort south of the Mason-Dixon line to abolish slavery. It required no very extended rationalization to argue in 1820 that the whole perplexing question would be best left in their hands, even if in fact the North had the right to take it up. Particularly was this true when, as Van Buren put it, the motives of those in the North who sought to take it up were "rather [more] political than philanthropical." Because he believed as he did, Van Buren's efforts to revive party distinctions and restore the Old Republican Party were to be more than a mere matter of machinations with politicians, looking toward the making of the Democratic party. He looked to Southern power, and he would quiet the slavery question if he could. He was dealing with the root principle of the whole structure of ante-bellum politics.

III

In the long history of the American presidency no election appears quite so formless as that of 1824. With no competing party to force unity on the Republicans, candidates who could not command the party nomination were free to defy it. They did so, charging that "King Caucus" was undemocratic. Eventually no fewer than four candidates competed down to the wire, each a Republican, every man for himself. Because they divided the electoral votes between them, none came close to a majority, and the election went to the House of Representatives. There, with the help of Henry Clay, John Quincy Adams outpolled the popular Andrew Jackson and the caucus nominee, William H. Crawford of Georgia, and carried off the prize.

Historians, viewing that election, look at King Caucus too much through the eyes of its opponents, who stated that the caucus represented an in-group of political officeholders attached to Crawford and anxious to preserve their own political power. In fact it was the Old Republicans who organized the caucus, not so much to sustain Crawford and preserve power as to revive the Virginia–New York party and regain power. They took up Crawford unenthusiastically because he came closest to the Old Republican pattern, and because he alone of all the candidates could hope to carry Virginia. They took up the caucus at the behest of Van Buren after two years of searching for a method of nominating which would command the support of all, because four years after Missouri the only hope of winning New York for a Southern candidate was to present him, however unpopularly, as the official party nominee.

Hidden in the currents and crosscurrents of that campaign was the reiterated issue of party versus amalgamation. Behind it, in turn, were repeated pleas by Old Republican presses, North and South alike, that unless genuine Republicans agreed on a method of choosing a candidate the division must be along sectional lines, in which case a Federalist or proto-Federalist might sneak into the White House. Behind it too was the repeated warning that party organization alone would make democracy work. Without it, the Old Republicans correctly prophesied, the election would end up in the House of Representatives, subject to the worst kind of political intrigue, and with the votes of the smallest states the equals of those of populous Virginia and New York.

When the caucus failed, it was because amalgamation had destroyed the levers which made party discipline possible. Exhortation could not restore them. Meantime the issue of democracy had been turned against the advocates of party, because in key states like New York and North Carolina they tried to use the power of the party organizations for Crawford, bucking more popular candidates such as Jackson and Adams. It was a bogus issue. The real issue was whether a party was necessary to make democracy work, and because they were more nearly right than their opponents about this, and the election in the House shortly proved it, the Old Republicans would recover quickly after 1824, after Crawford and the caucus issue were politically dead. Let circumstances limit the number of candidates, and tie up party and democracy on the same side, and the results would be different another time.

In the campaign of 1824 and the years immediately following, the slavery issue was never far below the surface. The Denmark Vesey conspiracy for an insurrection in Charleston (now a subject of controversy among historians) was to contemporaries a grim reminder of the Missouri debates, and it was attributed publicly to Rufus King's speeches on the Missouri question. In 1823–1824 some Southerners suspected that an attempt by Secretary of State Adams to conclude a slave trade convention with Great Britain was an attempt to reap the benefit of Northern anti-slavery sentiment; and some, notably Representative John Floyd of Virginia, sought to turn the tables on Adams by attacking him for allegedly ceding Texas to Spain in the Florida treaty, thus ceding what Floyd called "two slaveholding states" and costing "the Southern interest" four Senators.

Old Republicans made no bones about their concern over the issue, or their fear that it might be turned against them. In the summer of 1823 an illuminating editorial debate broke out between the New York *American,* which spoke the thoughts of the old Federalists in New York, and the Richmond *Enquirer*. So vehemently had the *American* picked up a report of a plan to revise the Illinois constitution to admit slavery that Ritchie charged its editors with reviving the slave question to put New York into the lap of the "Universal Yankee Nation" and to put the South under the "ban of the Empire." "Call it the Missouri question, the Illinois question, what you please; it was the *Slave question,*" Ritchie shrilled, which the *American* was seeking to get up for political purposes. Shortly, the Albany *Argus* got into the argument. The *Argus,* which got its signals from Van Buren and spoke the thoughts of New York's Old Republicans, charged the *American* with trying to revive the slave question to "abrogate the old party distinctions" and "organize new ones, founded in the territorial prejudices of the people." "The more general question of the North and South," the *Argus* warned, "will be urged to the uttermost, by those who can never triumph when they meet the democracy of the country, openly, and with the hostility they bear towards it." Over and over the debate rang out the argument that the attempt to revive party distinctions was an attempt to allay sectional prejudices, and by the time the debate was over only the most obtuse citizen could have missed the point.

Nor was the election of Adams destined to calm Southern fears on issues having to do with slavery. A series of incidents early in 1825 suggested that the New Englander's election had made anti-slavery advocates more bold, and Southern tempers grew shorter in the summer of 1825 than they had been at any time since Missouri. One of the incidents was a reported argument before the Supreme Court in the case of the South Carolina Negro Seaman's Act by Attorney General William Wirt, stating that slavery was "inconsistent with the laws of God and nature." A second was a resolution offered in the Senate a scant nine days after Adams' election by Rufus King, proposing to turn the proceeds from the sale of western lands to the emancipation and export of slaves, through the agency of the American Colonization Society. In the same week the New Jersey legislature proposed a system of foreign colonization which "would, in due time, effect the entire emancipation of the slaves in our country." John Floyd enclosed a copy of the New Jersey resolution to Claiborne Gooch, Ritchie's silent partner on the *Enquirer*, with salient warning:

> Long before this manifestation I have believed, connected with the Missouri question, would come up the general question of slavery, upon the principles avowed by Rufus King in the Senate. . . .
> If this indication is well received, who can tell, after the elevation of Mr. A. to the presidency—that he, of Missouri effort, or DeWitt C. or some such aspirant, may not, for the sake of that office, fan this flame—to array the non-slaveholding States against the Slaveholding states, and finally quiet our clamor or opposition, by the application of the slaves knife to our throats. Think of this much, and often.

Meantime, the New York *Commercial Advertiser* expressed publicly the hope that Adams' administration would introduce "a new era, when the northern, eastern, and non-slaveholding states, will assume an attitude in the Union, proportionate to their moral and physical power." Ritchie responded hotly in an editorial asking what the designs of such a combination would be against the "southern and *slave-holding* states." Soon in Georgia the Old Republican Governor George M. Troup, at the instigation of Senator John M. Berrien, put before the legislature a request for resolutions stating slavery to be exclusively within the control of the states and asking that the federal government "abstain from intermeddling." In May there was another violent editorial exchange between the New York *American* and the *Enquirer,* growing out of an *American* editorial which attacked the "slave press" and taunted the South with the comment that "the sceptre has departed from Judah, and those who have long ruled must be content to obey." Ritchie picked up the taunt as a challenge to the South, admitting that slavery was evil but insisting pointedly that the South had "too much at stake" to allow decisions on the matter by men ignorant of Southern "habits, manners, and forms of society." Ultimately, the Virginian concluded belligerently, Southern defense would be found in the traditional mechanisms of national politics: "Mr. John Adams the 2d is now upon his trial, [and] his friends consult as little his own interest as the public good, by conjuring up these prejudices against the *Slave people.* Should they persevere in their misguided policy, it will require no prophet to foretell that the son will share the fate of his father."

With the slavery issue thus drawn taut, the Old Republicans recovered quickly from the setback of 1824. Calhoun's inveterate foe William Smith was returned to the Senate from South Carolina, completing for the moment an Old Republican sweep of the South Atlantic states begun in 1821, a sweep which put Calhoun's political career in jeopardy and forced the Carolinian, now vice president, to break with Adams. For the Old Republicans, moreover, Adams made an infinitely better target than Monroe. The high-toned nationalism of the New Englander, combined with popular revulsion to the alleged bargain which secured his election, put the kiss of death on amalgamation as a political theory. The stage was set, under more favorable circumstances, for the Old Republicans to try again.

IV

For all the illuminating insights into Jacksonianism to which Americans have been treated in recent years, Jacksonian politics are still interpreted in Victorian terms, along classic lines descended from an early biographer of Jackson, James Parton, who recorded them one hundred years ago. To the Victorians, it is perhaps not too much to say, most of history could be ultimately attributed either to whores or to the unbridled pursuit of ambition. It was a simple view of history, and the Jacksonians got both barrels, one through the beguiling story of Peggy Eaton, the other through the notion of a sterile and essentially meaningless struggle for the succession between Van Buren and Calhoun. As Parton quaintly put it, "the political history of the United States, for the last thirty years, dates from the moment when the soft hand of Mr. Van Buren touched Mrs. Eaton's knocker."

When finally it rode to power, the Jacksonian party was made up of two clearly discernible and distinct wings. One comprised the original Jacksonians, those who had supported him in 1824 when he ran on his own, bereft, like all the rest, of party, and nearly of allies. As measured in that election this strength was predominantly in the West. It spilled over into a few states east of the mountains, most notably Pennsylvania, where the chaos of the existing political structure enabled Jackson as military hero to ride roughshod over all the rest. But this was all. The Western vote, especially when shared with Clay, amounted in electoral terms to little. Even with the votes of the Carolinas, thrown to him gratuitously by Calhoun and counting one-quarter of his total, he was far short of an electoral majority. To get even this much he had been formally before the public for two years, and all his considerable natural appeal as a Westerner and a hero had gone into the bargain.

After 1824 Jackson found himself the candidate of a combined opposition. The concrete measure of difference between defeat in 1824 and victory in 1828 was the Old Republican strength of the South Atlantic states and New York, brought to the Jackson camp carefully tended and carefully drilled by Van Buren. Nearly equal in size to the original Jackson following, they constituted a political faction far older, far more permanent, far more purposeful, far better led, and in the long run far more important. Their purposes were set forth by Van Buren in a notable letter to Ritchie in January, 1827, proposing support of the old hero. Such support, as the New Yorker put it, would be "the best and probably the only practicable mode of concentrating the entire vote of the opposition & of effecting what is of still greater importance, the substantial reorganization of the Old Republican Party." It would "restore a better state of things, by combining General Jackson's personal popularity with the portion of old party feeling yet remaining." It would aid Republicans of the North and middle states "by substituting *party principle* for *personal preference* as one of the leading points in the contest. . . . Instead of the question being between a Northern and Southern man, it would be whether or not the ties, which have hitherto bound together a great political party should be severed." Most important, its effects would be highly salutary for the South:

> We must always have party distinctions and the old ones are the best of which the nature of the case admits. Political combinations between the inhabitants of the different states are unavoidable & most natural & beneficial to the country is that between the planters of the South and the plain Republicans of the north. The country has once flourished under a party thus constituted & may again. It would take longer than our lives (even if it were practicable) to create new party feelings to keep those masses together. If the old ones are suppressed, geographical divisions founded on local interests or, what is worse, prejudices between free and slave holding states will inevitably take their place. Party attachment in former times furnished a complete antidote for sectional prejudices by producing counteracting feelings. It was not until that defence had broken down that the clamor agt. Southern Influence and African Slavery could be made effectual in the North. . . . Formerly, attacks upon Southern Republicans were regarded by those of the north as assaults upon their political brethren & resented accordingly. This all powerful sympathy has been much weakened, if not destroyed, by the amalgamating policy. . . . it can & ought to be revived.

Lastly, Van Buren noted, a Jackson administration brought to power by the "concerted effort of a political party, holding in the main, to certain tenets & opposed to certain prevailing principles" would be a far different thing from one brought to power by the popularity of a military hero alone. An administration brought to power by Old Republican votes would be governed by Old Republican principles. Van Buren would make himself the guarantor of that.

Because the Jacksonian party was what it was, Jacksonian policy was what it was, and Jacksonian politics as well. Because the administration rested on an Old Republican alliance which bridged the Mason-Dixon line and linked New York with the Old South, the two most important steps in the development of Jacksonian policy were the veto of the Maysville Road bill and the veto of the bill to recharter the Bank of the United States. Whatever the social and economic consequences of each, they were in their origins political measures, designed to solidify and hold together the Old Republican party; and they were predicated, each of them, on a strict construction of the Constitution. And, too, because its political base was what it was, the one great question of public policy which nearly brought the administration to disaster, one with which it could not deal and never did, was the tariff.

No less important, it was the structure of the Jackson party which gave meaning to—and dictated the course of—that struggle between Van Buren and Calhoun which bulks so large in the politics of the Jackson years. It was far more than an empty struggle for the succession. Its essence was competition between two conflicting ideas as to how best to protect Southern security in the Union, and thus, inferentially, how to preserve the Union itself. One of those ideas was the old Jeffersonian idea, resuscitated by Van Buren, sustained by the Jackson party and by the Democratic party until the Civil War. It was that Southern security rested ultimately on the maintenance in national office of a political party which would be responsive to the South because dependent on it for election. A political answer, not a doctrinaire one, it was product of the practical, pragmatic, and thoroughly political minds of Thomas Jefferson and Martin Van Buren. It depended for its success on the winning of national elections by a party which would maintain its identity in relation to the opposition as a states' rights—strict construction party, but which would at the same time be moderate, flexible, pragmatic in tone, able to win support in the North as well as the South if it would serve its purpose.

Counter to this was the proposition developed by John C. Calhoun. Last of the Southern nationalists, Calhoun had held to his position through 1824, long after the Old Republicans had routed Southern nationalism in every state but his own. In the mid-twenties, with his own political strength at rock bottom, his hold slipping even in South Carolina, Calhoun made his portentous switch from Nationalist to Sectionalist, squaring the two in his own mind with the development of a counter theory to that of the Jeffersonians. This was that Southern security was dependent in the last analysis on the maintenance of an effective Southern power to veto anything it didn't like—thus nullification—and that failing, on the right to secede. In contrast to the political and moderate remedy of the Old Republicans, this was a constitutional remedy, product of the brilliant legal, doctrinaire, and essentially nonpolitical mind of the great Carolinian.

That Van Buren won out over Calhoun in the Jackson years had nothing to do fundamentally with Mrs. Eaton or with a long chronicle of personal intrigue. It had everything to do with the fact that the Old Republican moderates controlled the South, all but South Carolina, almost that, in the twenties. While Calhoun brought only South Carolina and some personal support in Congress to the Jackson fold, Van Buren brought all the rest of the South, and New York as well. The fact was not lost on Jackson or his Tennessee friends, either before his election or after. Van Buren's triumph over Calhoun was won not on Washington backstairs after 1829 but on the Southern hustings in the early twenties. Two years before it came to power the Jackson party was already, in fact, a Jackson-Van Buren party.

V

There were postscripts, too, which harked back to the structure of the Jackson party, to the Missouri question, and to the political prophecies of Thomas Ritchie, woven into the very fabric of the party by the skilled political weaver from New York. First of these was that the Jackson party, the issue once raised, was committed to Texas. When in 1844 a new drumfire of antislavery sentiment in the North made it impossible for Van Buren to honor that commitment, Ritchie and Van Buren, after nearly a quarter century of fruitful political teamwork, would part company, and Van Buren would give up leadership of the party he had created. After 1844 the party of the Jeffersonian formula sustained itself in the face of the rising slavery issue by giving vent to its expansionist tendencies; and the Northern man with Southern principles who replaced Van Buren was in fact a Northwestern man with Southern principles, Stephen A. Douglas of Illinois. It was to be Douglas, governed by the irresistible logic of the party structure, who carried through Congress finally, in 1854, the repeal of the Missouri Compromise. And when three years after that the Supreme Court in the Dred Scott decision held the Thomas Proviso of the Missouri Compromise unconstitutional, as Ritchie and Nathaniel Macon had said it was thirty-seven years before, who were the judges who comprised the majority? Of six, one had been appointed in 1846 by "Young Hickory" James K. Polk, a second in 1853 by the next successful Democrat, Franklin Pierce. The four others were James M. Wayne of Georgia, coadjutor of Van Buren's Georgia lieutenant John Forsyth, appointed to the court by Jackson in 1835; Roger B. Taney of Maryland, appointed by Jackson in 1836; John Catron, Van Buren campaign manager in Tennessee, appointed by Jackson in 1837; and Peter V. Daniel of Virginia, long-time member of the Richmond Junto, confidante of Thomas Ritchie, appointed in 1841 by Van Buren.

Part II

GEOGRAPHIC EXPANSION AND ECONOMIC DEVELOPMENT

4 / The Frontier West as Image of American Society

Rush Welter

The attraction of the frontier West, as fact and symbol, has been a recurrent feature of American history. Even today when the United States is an industrialized and urban nation, this attraction continues to persist to some extent. During the Jacksonian era the western image exerted a formidable influence, as Americans spilled over the Appalachian Mountains to populate the great Mississippi Valley. In the following selection, Rush Welter attempts to view the phenomenon of the West from a new perspective, that of the eastern conservative, and simultaneously to demonstrate the irresistible power of the western experience on the American mind. The eastern conservatives moved slowly from outright deprecation to mixed reactions (always accepting the obvious economic benefits the West offered the nation, however) and finally toward a restrained but undeniably optimistic appraisal of western influence on American growth and national character. The changes in American society during the first third of the nineteenth century demanded such a revision of attitudes if American conservatism was to relate meaningfully to the realities of American life. In a frontier nation, one expanding across a continent, politicians and publicists who clung to the seaboard would soon find themselves without an audience.

For further reading: Frederick Jackson Turner, *The Frontier in American History* (1920); Henry Nash Smith, *Virgin Land: The American West as Symbol and Myth* (1950); Ray Allen Billington, *America's Frontier Heritage* (1966).

Mississippi Valley Historical Review (March 1960), 593–614. Reprinted by permission. Footnotes have been omitted except where they are necessary for an understanding of the text.

"In Europe," Alexis de Tocqueville wrote in the second volume of *Democracy in America,* "people talk a great deal of the wilds of America, but the Americans themselves never think about them; they are insensible to the wonders of inanimate nature and they may be said not to perceive the mighty forests that surround them till they fall beneath the hatchet. Their eyes are fixed upon another sight: the American people views its own march across these wilds, draining swamps, turning the course of rivers, peopling solitudes, and subduing nature. This magnificent image of themselves does not meet the gaze of the Americans at intervals only; it may be said to haunt every one of them in his least as well as in his most important actions and to be always flitting before his mind."

The French observer's description of American attitudes, antedating the homestead agitation and independent of the imagery of the yeoman farmer that supported it, admonishes us that we have not yet fully understood the image of the frontier West as a primary element of American social thought.* Indeed Tocqueville's statement is doubly significant, because it represents the opinions of ordinary men of affairs rather than literary figures, and because it is heavily influenced by the perspectives of conservative eastern spokesmen for American institutions, whom he mainly interviewed. On the one hand, the very emphasis it places on the difference between European images of a wild continent and American preoccupation with material conquest warns us that the predominantly literary antithesis between Nature and Civilization in the West that Henry Nash Smith has traced in *Virgin Land* may not have influenced the American people as much as their novels and some of their congressional rhetoric may suggest. On the other hand the statement also indicates that even during the early 1830's avowed conservatives in the East identified themselves with their emigrant countrymen's achievements in the West. If so, their sympathy with trans-Appalachian exploits reversed a tendency exemplified in several

---

* In the light of such pioneering studies as Albert K. Weinberg, *Manifest Destiny: A Study of National Expansion in American History* (Baltimore, 1935); Carter Goodrich and Sol Davison, "The Wage Earner in the Westward Movement," *Political Science Quarterly* (New York), L (June, 1935), 161–185, and LI (March, 1936), 61–116; Henry Nash Smith, *Virgin Land: The American West as Symbol and Myth* (Cambridge, 1950); John W. Ward, *Andrew Jackson: Symbol for an Age* (New York, 1955); and Arthur K. Moore, *The Frontier Mind: A Cultural Analysis of the Kentucky Frontiersman* (Lexington, Ky., 1957), this may well seem an ungracious if not an inaccurate statement. Yet while this essay owes much of its conceptual framework and many of its citations to their inquiries, its main focus is the development of a characteristic eastern perspective on the territorial possessions of the United States, which in one fashion or another each tends to neglect. Weinberg's focus is on attitudes toward territories outside our national boundaries. Goodrich and Davison are concerned with the "safety-valve" concept of our western lands to the exclusion of other matters. Ward concentrates on Andrew Jackson as popular hero reflecting fundamental American values, and Moore is concerned with the transfer of ancient stereotypes of Nature to the American experience of Kentucky. Even Smith, whose *Virgin Land* constitutes the main work in the field, and who has dealt with a wide range of literary and political ramifications of the American West, tends rather to pursue the development of a western literature and politics than to establish the perspective in which eastern spokesmen visualized the West.

Needless to say, my point in making these comments is not to deprecate the achievements of these scholars, but to identify my own somewhat different purposes more clearly. I should add that two other essays bear with particular relevance upon the problem I am dealing with here. One is Arthur E. Bestor, "Patent-Office Models of the Good Society: Some Relationships between Social Reform and Westward Expansion," *American Historical Review* (New York), LVIII (April, 1953), 505–526; the other, Barry Marks, "The Concept of Myth in *Virgin Land,*" *American Quarterly* (Philadelphia), V (Spring, 1953), 71–76.

decades of eastern thought—echoed, as Smith points out, by many of the literary figures of the Middle Period—to fear and hence to deprecate the influence and prospects of the West in the growth of the American nation. Within two generations after the founding of the republic, that is, eastern conservatives were apparently ready to embrace a West they had begun by rejecting.

It is the purpose of this essay to explore in some detail this shift in conservative perspective, which had large consequences for American social thought. It was probably to be expected that spokesmen for the democracy of the Middle Period should have adopted the frontier West (and the frontier westerner) as an image of their hopes. It was less to be expected, and for that reason more significant, that self-conscious eastern conservatives should also have done so. By adopting new perspectives on western settlement, indeed, conservatives helped to define the terms in which the whole nation was to see itself.

The most obvious and at the same time the most useful starting point for an analysis of shifting conservative opinion of the West is the disapproval of western religious mores that eastern commentators, and especially spokesmen for New England orthodoxy, expressed near the turn of the century. Indeed Timothy Dwight, Congregational clergyman and for twenty-one years president of Yale College, has become famous for the harshness of his criticism of the early settlers of Vermont, whom he took to be typical of a wider class of frontiersmen. On the one hand he believed that they were "too idle; too talkative; too passionate; too prodigal; and too shiftless; to acquire either property or character," and he complained that they were "impatient of the restraints of law, religion, and morality," not to mention likely to grumble at taxes, "by which Rulers, Ministers, and School-masters, are supported." On the other hand he also believed that the New England virtues might yet flourish among the departed children of Connecticut and Massachusetts. But the very fact that he expressed hope for Vermont amounted by implication to a perpetual condemnation of other regions that were to be settled by immigrants alien to New England ways; and (for that matter) his experience even of Vermont offered slight encouragement. "Intelligence and piety flourished under the fostering care of those, who founded Connecticut [he wrote]. They are growing up in Vermont, in spite of their founders."

A generation or so later three equally orthodox commentators were hardly more enthusiastic over the prospects of religion in the West. In 1828 an anonymous writer observed in the *Quarterly Journal of the American Education Society* that more schools and colleges and a better educated ministry were needed in the West "to dispel ignorance, check vice, and create a pure public opinion, favorable to sound morals and true religion." In December, 1834, a western missionary addressed himself, in the columns of the *Quarterly Christian Spectator,* to the same problem. The West is not hopelessly lost, he explained, but it is susceptible to ignorant doctrinal innovations as well as outright heresy, and it requires the intervention of a trained ministry, which the East must in the first instance supply. Eighteen months later the *Biblical Repertory and Theological Review,* discussing the qualifications for such a western ministry, made clear that in addition to heresy the West was troubled with dangerous forms of heterodoxy, which thanks to the influx of immigrants from many different lands threatened ultimately to destroy the republic. "It is evident [this essayist wrote] that we cannot be a mixed people and prosper. The permanency of our civil and religious institutions, and the happiness of all, demands that this mass of heterogeneous and discordant materials, be formed into one consistent and harmonious whole." Neither the sense of urgency nor the apprehensions that gave rise to it were restricted to New England.

Yet despite the eastern prejudices that obviously colored such evaluations of the West, the content of the attitudes expressed by eastern critics had begun to shift. Nor was the shift merely a reflection of the obvious wish to do something about the West while there was still time. It was, for example, neither missionary zeal nor infectious fear alone, but apprehension partly lost in admiration, that led the missionary author to say in the *Quarterly Christian Spectator* that "The immense extent, the unequalled fertility, and the future overwhelming influence of the west, are trite subjects. Every school-boy is by this time familiar with topics which have formed so large a part, not only of the epistolary eloquence and anniversary declamation of those who live there, and who may be viewed as interested; but of the more sober statements of judicious and unprejudiced observers." Even eastern critics were compelled to admit (in the words of the *Quarterly Journal of the American Education Society*) that "Before the present generation shall have passed off the stage, the 'star of empire' will have taken 'its way westward,' and the consequences will be either a blessing or a curse, just in the degree that virtuous or vicious principles prevail among the people"; or to concede, with the *Biblical Repertory,* that "every thing is springing up and growing into maturity with a rapidity unparalleled in the history of the world." If the hectic pace of western development stimulated orthodox fears, it also introduced something closely akin to pride into eastern contemplation of the frontier challenge.

The extent to which fear might turn into wonder was even more dramatically revealed in Lyman Beecher's *Plea for the West* in 1835. Like so many missionaries before him, Beecher had gone West to perpetuate orthodox New England belief, and the substance of his book was an appeal for funds in support of Lane Theological Seminary in Cincinnati, while its chief mode of argument was an appeal to anti-Catholic prejudice. Nevertheless the volume opened with a tribute to the power and future prospects of the West that matched anything its most ardent sons had yet delivered. It is plain, Beecher wrote, "that the religious and political destiny of our nation is to be decided in the West. There is the territory, and there soon will be the population, the wealth, and the political power. The Atlantic commerce and manufactures may confer always some peculiar advantage on the East. But the West is destined to be the great central power of the nation, and under heaven, must affect powerfully the cause of free institutions and the liberty of the world." Moreover, Beecher was at least half convinced of the approach of the Christian millennium, which he thought the prosperity of American institutions would insure if Protestantism kept pace with the westward expansion of the country. Hence he came, almost inevitably, to associate the millennium itself with the American West. "The West," his apostrophe continued, "is a young empire of mind, and power, and wealth, and free institutions, rushing up to a giant manhood, with a rapidity and a power never before witnessed below the sun. And if she carries with her the elements of her preservation, the experiment will be glorious—the joy of the nation—the joy of the whole earth, as she rises in the majesty of her intelligence and benevolence, and enterprise, for the emancipation of the world." *A Plea for the West* was striking evidence of the power of the West to move an essentially conservative imagination.

Nor was this exaggerated image of the West the property only of those who believed with Beecher in the advent of the millennium. The *Christian Review* acknowledged the appearance of a second edition of the book by disavowing Beecher's millennial expectations, pointing to evils abroad in the land that must prevent it from regenerating mankind. Yet the Baptist quarterly's objection hardly diminished the luster of its own vision of the West, for it quoted the whole of Beecher's millennial exhortation (including the paragraphs above) with evident appreciation. Moreover, in 1836 even a Boston Unitarian critical of western mores was moved despite the rationality of his faith to adopt a view of the West very much like Beecher's evangelical vision. Reviewing Mann Butler's *History of the Commonwealth of Kentucky* and James Hall's *Sketches of History, Life, and Manners in the West* for the *North American Review,* the Reverend James Freeman Clarke praised the western character but objected to its excesses and its laxity. As Henry Nash Smith points out, here was evidence that even a young and relatively radical minister could not escape prejudices inherited from early New England leaders. But there was also evidence of something else, for although Clarke observed that "Religious restraint is needed, moral principle is needed, wise guidance is needed" to discipline western character, he concluded his paragraph and his review by invoking an image of western perfectionism. "A deep reverence for truth [he said], a profound respect for law, a ready submission to right, a loyal allegiance to duty, these will make the western character as perfect as humanity can ever hope to become."

Clarke's reflections, like those of other religious commentators, indicated that even under the best of circumstances the new West would continue to seem a burden upon eastern virtues; neither New England nor the East as a whole would surrender its traditional religious authority easily or gracefully, and any aberration in the West would produce renewed concern over its safety and its morals. Yet his views also document the process of conversion that had undermined traditional eastern fears of the West. On the one hand, conservative apprehension over the heterodox West had stimulated ministers and other spokesmen for eastern orthodoxy to adopt the West as a special field for missionary endeavor. On the other hand, and although the missionaries went to impart the true faith, the magnitude of their responsibilities came to be matched in the eyes of eastern commentators by the magnitude of their opportunities. In spite of eastern prejudice, and to some extent because of it, the West conquered the imaginations of many of its most likely detractors.

More significantly still, the very terms in which religious commentators were wont to criticize western mores gradually became points of approbation of the region. That is, whereas it had once seemed a reproach to the pioneers that they fled the settled East, abandoning its traditions and careless of its institutions, their migration came in time to seem a measure of their achievement, and beyond that a mark of their country's future greatness. This process of redefinition is already apparent in Clarke's tribute to the potential western character as well as in Beecher's exaggerated hopes; it reached a climax some twenty years later when in the *North American Review* for January, 1855, the Reverend Charles W. Upham described the whole peopling of the American continent as an act of social and political "regeneration" of which no man knew the outcome. Dealing primarily with the future of the West in the struggle between proslavery and antislavery forces, Upham went on to associate the fate of liberty in the world with its fate in the western territories. "It is obvious [he said] that no issue can possibly arise, more important in its bearings upon the future of America or of mankind, than that which determines the character of the people who are to occupy the region just described and the institutions of government and society to be established there. It cannot but decide the destinies of the continent, and the last great experiment of humanity." If fear over the influence of the West motivated the eastern commentator, it took form nevertheless in a remarkable expression of belief in the West as embodying the mission of America.

Upham spoke for more than the ministry, however, for he had given up his pulpit in 1844 for reasons of ill health only to enter politics in 1848, and he was now a Whig congressman from Massachusetts. In other words, while his views marked a reversal of traditional religious prejudices against the West, they also reflected a reorientation of eastern political perspective. The shift of eastern attitudes toward the West as a force in American politics is as striking as the shift in religious perspective.

The political grounds of apprehension were already clear at the time of the Constitutional Convention. In his famous pronouncement, made during debate on provision for the admission of new states into the Union, Gouverneur Morris observed that "The Busy haunts of men not the remote wilderness, was the proper school of political Talents. If the Western people get the power into their hands they will ruin the Atlantic interests. The Back members are always most averse to the best measures." Subsequently Elbridge Gerry made much the same point, and even George Mason, speaking in behalf of the equal rights of states not yet founded, conceded that "If it were possible by just means to prevent emigrations to the Western Country, it might be good policy," only to explain, "But go the people will as they find it for their interest, and the best policy is to treat them with that equality which will make them friends not enemies." In political terms the West seemed a problem even when it did not present an overt threat to the East.

As Mason's argument suggests, one cause of eastern apprehension in 1787 was a feeling that Spain might either detach the trans-Appalachian settlements from the United States or cause them to involve the new nation in hazardous diplomatic controversies over the navigation of the Mississippi. In 1803, therefore, the acquisition of Louisiana should have seemed a sound political and diplomatic measure; but it elicited instead an opposition reminiscent of Morris and Gerry. During the debate that followed President Jefferson's message recommending the Louisiana Purchase to Congress, for instance, both Representative Roger Griswold of Connecticut and Representative Thomas Griffin of Virginia were struck with the political imbalance that the new territory would ultimately create. By the same token, Senator Samuel White of Delaware would not be reconciled to the purchase even if an attempt were made to contain the frontier population by establishing a permanent Indian reserve on the west bank of the Mississippi, for any prohibition on settlement would be useless, while the inevitable dispersion of population would be ruinous to national interests. Indeed Fisher Ames, commenting privately at the time, expressed a prevalent conservative view in his celebrated epitaph for the republic: "Our country is too big for union, too sordid for patriotism, too democratic for liberty."

During the course of his travels, meanwhile, Timothy Dwight had found no more reason to suppose that western politics would prove acceptable than to trust western morals. In a new society, he pointed out, political influence "is chiefly gained by those, who directly seek it: and these in almost all instances are the ardent and bustling. Such men make bold pretensions to qualities, which they do not possess; clamour every where about liberty, and rights; are patriots of course, and jealous of the encroachments of those in power; thrum over, incessantly, the importance of public economy; stigmatize every just and honourable public expenditure, arraign the integrity of those, whose wisdom is undisputed, and the wisdom of those, whose integrity cannot be questioned; and profess, universally, the very principles, and feelings, of him, with whom they are conversing." Yet in an equally invidious characterization of the "class of men" who "have already straggled onward from New-England, as well as from other parts of the Union, to Louisiana," Dwight strikingly reversed the political argument against emigration. Restless idlers constantly threaten the stability of free institutions, he said, and even New England's institutions have not been able to prevent their "noxious disposition" to be unruly. "In mercy, therefore, to the sober, industrious, and well-disposed, inhabitants," he concluded his harangue, "Providence has opened in the vast Western wilderness a retreat, sufficiently alluring to draw them away from the land of their nativity. We have many troubles even now: but we should have many more, if this body of foresters had remained at home."

The full significance of Dwight's political reflections lay in the future, when his bitterly critical characterization of the western democrat would give way to a positive national identification with precisely the traits Dwight had condemned. Yet his conception of a western safety-valve for eastern political institutions already served to present the new West in a perspective that threatened to undermine conservative fears. Dwight did not temper his prejudices, which operated indiscriminately to cloud his political as well as his religious judgment of the West, but in restating the role of the West he also restated its significance for the East. Already, under impeccable auspices, a process of conservative redefinition was in progress.

One of the ways in which that redefinition went on during succeeding decades was a practice that eastern commentators adopted of speaking about the West as a testing-ground for, rather than simply as a threat to, established republican institutions. Reviewing Timothy Flint's *Recollections of the Last Ten Years, Passed in Occasional Residences and Journeyings in the Valley of the Mississippi* for the *North American Review* in 1826, for example, James Flint observed that the new West "presents a fruitful theme of anxious contemplation and prophetic conjecture to the statesman and philanthropist," both as the "destined theatre" of events to come and as the scene of the "future trial" of the principles of free government and religious toleration adopted by the federal constitution. In conceding that a political experiment was in progress, of course, Flint acknowledged the possibility of a good as well as an evil outcome. By 1829, indeed, the *American Quarterly Review* was ready to say, in a review of the same author's *Condensed Geography and History of the Western States,* that the extension of republican institutions to the West had been an unqualified success. "The friends of civil liberty [it remarked] cannot but rejoice at the successful results of these experiments, tried as they have been in the wilderness, and under the most disadvantageous circumstances; for, if the elements of discord exist in our country at all, we should naturally look for them in new settlements, where people of opposing politics and various opinions, assemble from every quarter, and enjoy an equal voice in public affairs."

This was, perhaps, too optimistic and too urbane a view of western political institutions to be wholly acceptable to eastern conservatives during the 1830's, and the text suggests that the anonymous reviewer may have been both a westerner and a democrat. Nevertheless the sense that the United States was successfully engaged in a great republican experiment also affected unmistakably conservative writers, and it opened the way to a significant restatement of Timothy Dwight's safety-valve theory. For Dwight, the only political virtue the West possessed was that it drew off trouble-makers from the East. But for Edward Everett, reviewing Flint's *Condensed Geography and History* for the *North American Review,* it was something else. While what he wrote was intended to say no more than that the westward movement of population demonstrated the liberality of American political institutions, he also implied that a continuing reciprocal relationship existed between western expansion and eastern freedom. "The young men [he said], who have emigrated from the Atlantic coast to the West, did not, like the emigrants from Ireland and the Palatinate, leave potato-fare and six pence a day behind them. On the contrary, they left a country of high wages and hearty diet. If emigration be the safety-valve of states, ours is calculated to open at a very low pressure; in others, the governments have loaded it with additional weights, threatening the most disastrous explosions."

We shall consider the social and economic implications of Everett's statement in another place. What is important here is that the West has in its own right begun to take on positive political qualities that neither Dwight nor James Flint visualized; nor was Everett's doctrine the ultimate judgment of western influence. For within a dozen years at least one conservative easterner found himself acknowledging the republican habits of the West in terms that insisted upon westerners' shortcomings yet credited them at the same time with unique political virtues. In 1842, in reviewing Caroline Kirkland's *Forest Life* for the *North American Review,* Cornelius C. Felton of Harvard College observed that a "bold but not over-educated population" was growing up in the West, "with none of the restraints which fetter the characters of the working classes in other countries."

> No feudal feeling [he continued] tempers the natural overflowings of passion, and restrains the growth of individual humors. The sentiment of loyalty to any thing except a political party, does not exist to bind them in respectful obedience to a head and representative of the sovereignty of the nation. Each man is himself a sovereign by indefeasible right, and has no idea that another is his better in any one respect. Manners are, therefore, of the most unrestrained sort, and one accustomed to the conventions, and deferences, and distinctions, that have grown up even in our republican cities, is apt to find himself annoyed and embarrassed, when he gets into a circle of these tree-destroying sovereigns. But there are compensations for these things. There is more activity and stir in one of these new communities than in the ancient towns. Public affairs more engross the minds of men, and are more discussed, within doors and without. Poetry and art,—music, sculpture and painting,—the last new novel, to-morrow evening's concert, last evening's "Lowell Lecture," are things unheard of; but political disquisitions, not always of the wisest, stump speeches, the affairs of the town, county, or state, and the pretensions of rival candidates, are vehemently argued. *I* After a visit to the West, one cannot but be struck with the comparative apathy of the New England people. We look with wonder on communities of men who attend to their own business, and seem to care but little who is made President of the United States, or even County Commissioner.

Henry Nash Smith paraphrases this passage, inadequately I believe, as an instance of the "covert class bias" of easterners trained to the theocratic prejudices of New England. It has this quality, indeed; but what has happened is that the emotional context has shifted, until traditional fears have metamorphosed into a tacit recognition (however reluctant) that the West embodies American political institutions in their most characteristic form. Neither the principles nor the aberrations of Jacksonian Democracy have prevented the development of an image of western politics as peculiarly American.

Indeed in cataloguing the qualities of the Old Northwest for the readers of *Hunt's Merchants' Magazine* in 1840, James H. Lanman had already remarked that "A widely-diffused, deeply-stamped spirit of equality and republicanism extends throughout the whole social frame of the northwest"; and in subsequent essays on western topics he invoked the independent yeoman of the West as the surest guardian of republican institutions. Lanman was obviously a western booster, and not everyone was ready as yet to adopt the region with the enthusiasm he displayed, but in political terms his view of the West amounted to a complete inversion of early fears in which conservatives as well as innovators, easterners as well as westerners, might join. Far from threatening eastern political institutions, the West promised to guarantee their continuing prosperity.

Obviously Lanman's statement drew heavily upon the pastoral tradition of the self-sufficient farmer that is identified in American thought with the agrarian theory embraced by Thomas Jefferson. (For that matter, even Felton's review of *Forest Life* owed something to this tradition.) By the same token, it represented a significant modification of the social and economic as well as the political judgments of an earlier generation of conservative spokesmen. Although some aspects of this shift in attitudes have already become apparent during our discussion of religious and political estimates of the West, the change in social perspective is worthy of separate treatment here.

When traditional religious and political values were at stake, eastern commentators like Timothy Dwight saw little that was good in the westward movement. In their reflections on the character of the people who took up land in the West and on the social situation in which they found themselves, however, such conservatives betrayed a grudging admiration for men and social institutions they would not otherwise have respected. Their relative tolerance in this respect helped to prepare the way for an idealization of the man of the West as the American hero and of western society as the model of our social aspirations.

Dwight's ambivalence toward the westward movement as a social phenomenon is apparent in his identification of early emigrants from New England as those who "have met with difficulties at home" or who, "having large families, and small farms, are induced, for the sake of settling their children comfortably, to seek for new and cheaper lands," together with a number of "the discontented, the enterprizing, the ambitious, and the covetous." Even the adjectives are mixed, while the image of a society attractive to those who have met with difficulties at home is far less invidious than his comparable political image of restless idlers and potential trouble-makers straggling westward. Moreover, although he described the West as a means for drawing off socially undesirable individuals, Dwight also suggested that the acquisition of property makes the second type of settler, the "planter," actually civilized. In such pronouncements he was far from abandoning his fears of the religious and political hazards implicit in frontier expansion, but he imputed to the West a degree of economic opportunity, and a formative influence on human character, that made it seem in spite of its handicaps a promising vehicle for the social institutions of the East.

Other contemporaries who were no more enthusiastic than Dwight over the political prospects of the West also betrayed odd social sympathies when they sought to elaborate upon their hostility to further expansion. During debate over the Louisiana Purchase, for example, Senator White argued heatedly that a perpetual Indian reserve on the right bank of the Mississippi was impossible because of the "adventurous, roving, and enterprising temper of our people." For that matter even the most dogmatic social critic of the West was hard put to state the case against western expansion in unambiguous terms. During the same debate, Representative Griffin announced that he feared all of the consequences of the acquisition of Louisiana, without exception: "he feared the effects of the vast extent of our empire; he feared the effects of the increased value of labor, the decrease in the value of lands, and the influence of climate upon our citizens who should migrate thither." Griffin did not mean to praise western prospects, but the social and economic premises on which he based his condemnation threatened the very core of his argument.

This mixed perspective on western society continued to affect a later generation of conservative spokesmen for eastern interests. During his discussion of the obstacles that geographical dispersion placed in the way of intellectual and moral progress, for example, James Flint pointed out that the West "is an interesting country, as it will long continue to offer a wide field for the emigrating and enterprising population of the older states, and as the great receptacle of the shoals of foreigners, good and bad, that yearly cross the seas to seek, under the tutelary genius of American liberty, an asylum from the oppression, the poverty, or the justice of their native country." Even the *Biblical Repertory* described the problems that a mixed population would cause the United States in terms that glorified as well as criticized the westerners' challenge to the East. "The people of the west [it said], viewed as individuals, resemble the inhabitants of almost every clime; but taken as a whole, they are unlike every people under heaven. They have come hither from the four quarters of the globe, with manners and habits and genius and temperment, as different as the nations from which they severally sprung. Every thing is new, just coming into existence." In such phrases eastern critics of western character succeeded both in reiterating a whole complex of conservative fears and in paying reluctant tribute to the country and its people.

Such judgments as these, however, reflected a clear sense of the differences between West and East, which necessitated missionary efforts. Nevertheless other spokesmen for the East had already begun to depict the settlement of the West as an extension or an illustration of national character and institutions. This sense of identification was implicit in Edward Everett's portrait of the West as a republican safety-valve, and it became explicit in the *American Quarterly Review*, which expressed high praise in 1829 for traits that men like Dwight had criticized. A generation later, moreover, during the course of a critique of western educational institutions written for the *Biblical Repository and Classical Review*, the missionary president of Wabash College asserted that "All who have become acquainted with American society, have observed that its most marked feature, is restless activity. Enterprise is more characteristic of us than a high civilization; a passion for the glitter and parade of wealth, more than a tendency to substantial, unostentatious investments ad solid comforts. It has now become a universal statement and opinion, that a spirit of adventure and advancement, as also an actual forward and ascending movement, are no where in the country more apparent than in the Valley of the Mississippi. This ardor and progress, as is always the fact in new countries, respect the physical more than the intellectual; fortunes and honors more than facilities of knowledge and achievements of mind. All education is in a depressed condition." If there were still flaws visible in the western character, they now seemed to reflect national rather than merely regional traits—and (the article hastened to add) they did not interfere significantly with the progress of civilization in the West.

The aspect of western life that appealed most unambiguously to eastern commentators during this period, however, was the great material advantage that western society and western resources offered easterners who wished to migrate, which elicited in turn the most vigorous statements of national identification with the region. Moreover, this was no mere safety-valve doctrine such as Timothy Dwight and Edward Everett had expressed, for it made the West the focus of the American enterprise rather than simply a refuge from eastern poverty or a security against eastern political disturbances. During congressional debate on western land policy in 1830, for example, Representative Tristam Burges of Rhode Island clearly aligned himself against western interests in supporting distribution of the proceeds from land sales and in opposing a graduation proposal, yet he also appealed to an image of the West as the very definition of our social system. "In what other country," he asked, ". . . is freehold and inheritance so acquired as it is in the United States? Young men in the old States, who 'work out' from sixteen to twenty-one, and whose fathers receive one-half their wages for their clothing, their home, and subsistence while not employed, can then go to the West, purchase a farm, and, with labor and economy, they are, in a few years, independent and prosperous. Many, many have followed that course—they now find themselves well off in the world and members in the first rank of flourishing and highly cultivated communities. What would fathers, in any part of Europe, not willingly lay down in exchange, could they purchase such establishments for their sons?"

In 1844, furthermore, William H. Seward identified both our economic and our social institutions with the influence of the frontier West, when he told the Phi Beta Kappa Society of Union College that "A rapid increase of population in newly explored districts maintains labor at higher prices, the interest of money at higher rates, and science and skill in higher estimation, here than elsewhere. From these causes, as well as from the reverence of weary, down-trodden men, to our free institutions, we derive a perpetual influx of emigrants from Europe, with talent and capital in just proportion." Indeed Seward's words not only attributed American advantages to the West but also praised the immigrants whom it attracted, and thus inverted the judgments that both James Flint and the *Biblical Repertory* had applied to western settlement.

Obviously the major point of social and economic identification between East and West was the economic and social opportunity that western lands seemed to offer to every worthy citizen—a calculation of western advantages that led in time to the Homestead Act. The role that western spokesmen played, and the images they employed, in securing passage of a homestead law are familiar to us. It is equally significant, if less apparent, that with the growth of a favorable image of the West, eastern critics of homestead legislation were as likely to defend their views in essentially pro-western terms as to reiterate traditional fears of the region. The alternative perspectives were clearly demonstrated during the first major congressional debate on the homestead bill in 1852. Representative Josiah Sutherland of New York, a die-hard critic of liberal land legislation, undertook a bitter attack on the effect of free lands in raising the wages of eastern labor and hence the costs of manufacturing. In effect, the major vice he saw in the West was the social and economic promises it held out to eastern democrats. By contrast Representative Thomas J. D. Fuller of Maine, also an opponent of homestead legislation, defended the status quo as a great engine of progress. "Our present land system," he declared,

> operates like a great balance-wheel upon our political institutions. It regulates the value of real property; it controls the wages of labor; and so long as one day's work will purchase an acre of productive land, and secure a certain and sure title, directly from the Government—eastern manufactures can never control the wages of labor. . . . As our population increases and becomes more dense, they will emigate to this broad domain, occupy and cultivate the soil, establish schools and churches, and form settlements, and thereby avoid those evils incident to a more dense and thickly-settled country. . . . I trust, sir, that our public domain may be long so held, and that our children, and our children's children, may always have the privilege of resorting to it for settlement and support, and at an unvarying price, with a certainty of title, until the almost countless acres of our unoccupied domain shall be covered with a virtuous, industrious, and happy people.

Here, indeed, was a compelling image of the nation's future, which attracted those who might with good reason have continued to oppose the further extension of western settlement. Their anguish and their perspective were both well expressed by Senator John P. Hale of New Hampshire during debate over a proposal to cede additional lands to the state of Wisconsin in order to compensate for those in the original cession she had been prevented from exploiting. The senator observed that his state had never benefited from the public lands but he supported the measure anyway, remarking that "I know the lands will go West, and, what is worse, you will take our children, too; our young men and young women. You will take those who till the soil; those who give character to the State will go West, and carry our means with them. When we grant to the West, we grant to our own kindred, our own sons and brothers, who will leave the sterile and hard soil of the East to people the fertile valleys of the West; and so far as I am concerned my blessing shall go with them. . . . That is an inevitable destiny and a fixed fact *per se,* and I am not disposed to oppose it or cavil at the result." If Hale's statement echoed the attitudes toward the West that eastern spokesmen had expressed half a century earlier, the terms had been reversed. He not only conceded economic advantages to the region but also saw in it, in spite of eastern consequences, the greater fullfillment of his own people.

By such paths were conservative eastern prejudices against the West and its inhabitants converted into approbation and even identification with the region—in religion, in politics, in economic and social affairs. The process of conversion was twofold. On the one hand conservative attitudes simply shifted, until traditional apprehensions virtually disappeared, to be supplanted by recognition of the obvious achievements and prospects of the region. On the other hand, the very grounds of apprehension often metamorphosed into grounds of approbation: later generations of conservative commentators saw positive virtues in western institutional developments and traits of character that had once antagonized fearful easterners. Significantly, the *New Englander* suggested in 1846 that western expansion would encourage the spread of Puritan ideals because, in a new settlement, men are "thrown upon their own resources, and compelled to think and act; and hence, by the same law of necessity . . . forced to read, observe, and resort to all available sources for information."

We may account for these developments in several ways. Obviously, one's perspective on the West was more than likely to be shaped by sectional political interests. Hence a shift of sectional interests would tend to alter prejudices once expressed toward the West by eastern spokesmen. Indeed the political history of the Middle Period has very generally been written in terms of shifting sectional relationships to the West and shifting alliances for the exploitation of western resources and the disposition of the public lands. Yet the evolution of a characteristically optimistic evaluation of the frontier West was by no means a product wholly of such realignments. For one thing, many of the crucial sectional issues in American politics were not resolved in eastern minds until the 1850's, yet the image of the West as a special property of American civilization was already well on the way to being established by then, and it affected opponents as well as advocates of measures sponsored by western interests. Furthermore, even when easterners sympathized with western aspirations, their political situation gave them little reason to accept the West in the exaggerated terms that its own spokesmen were wont to use. Not all of them did, of course; but a sufficient number of representatives of what may be characterized as traditionally reluctant eastern interests had long since adopted a view of the region that owed more to the imagination than to sober conjecture.

In part, of course, the shift reflected the triumphs of Jacksonian Democracy, for however Andrew Jackson happened to win election he made the whole nation conscious of the West, and he attracted votes in New England. On the one hand, he undoubtedly appealed to eastern partisans who had little or no interest in the West or in its future, yet who were brought via their commitments to the man or to his party to value western qualities and attitudes that they had originally been taught to condemn. On the other hand, to the extent that Jackson stood for new ways to political success, eastern conservatives could hardly avoid catering to a self-consciously "western" population—as William Henry Harrison's log-cabin candidacy in 1840 clearly indicates. But though these circumstances may help to explain the evolution of a favorable image of the West in eastern democratic eyes, they are inadequate so far as many eastern conservatives are concerned: if they illuminate Democratic ideology they do not explain why, even before 1830, Whigs should also have begun to adopt a new perspective on the region.

Finally, the actual experience of two generations of western expansion and western travel undoubtedly influenced a number of eastern observers to feel more charitable toward western institutions and western innovations than had their immediate ancestors. But like other explanations this does not account for the enthusiasm with which sober eastern commentators came to portray the history and prospects of the land across the mountains. Experience may have taught them to be charitable (although it does not seem to have had the same effect on foreign travelers), but of itself it could not have persuaded them to be so optimistic. Somehow the West—the area of close settlement as well as the pioneer fringe, the urban future as well as the agricultural beginnings—enlisted powerful ideological commitments that were more lasting than political advantage, more powerful than the data of experience.

In other words the revision of conservative opinion of the West was more than a simple response to contemporary realities. It seems plausible to suggest, in fact, that far from being a mere datum in religion or politics or economics, the West served as a means of dramatizing fundamental conservative convictions. During the early years of the republic, when most institutions were unsettled and the future seemed clouded, apprehension predominated in conservative evaluations of the region, which already seemed likely to determine the course of our history. During later years, when the future of the republic appeared more promising, conservatives looked forward with greater confidence to the West's role in American life. The effect was to defind the West in the light of eastern needs; to shape its image according to eastern concerns.

If we accept this interpretation of eastern attitudes we recognize that what conservatives imagined was as significant as the act of imagining itself. Originally conservative spokesmen were apprehensive lest westward migration undermine the orthodox, republican, middle-class customs of the eastern seaboard. As time passed they came more and more to hope for the triumph of just these institutions on the frontier. Beyond this, however, they also tended to impute to the West a unique power and an extraordinary responsibility for such a triumph, until in some instances they portrayed the region as a virtual utopia. At their hands, that is, the West ultimately became more than a vehicle for eastern institutions; it embodied the lasting hopes of the American nation.

Above all it amounted to an economic and social utopia within the reach of every man. Significantly, even commentators who were thoroughly skeptical of the religious and political prospects of the West, for example Timothy Dwight, represented the region as an unmixed economic blessing to the American people. Even more significantly, the original safety-valve doctrine—the belief that western emigration might protect the East against heterodoxy or radicalism or poverty—metamorphosed into a positive identification of American hopes with unexploited land and resources in the West. Conservative writers ended by describing a perfected liberal society in which economic vice and economic virtue would receive their appropriate rewards; and even Timothy Dwight had been confident that in such a society economic opportunity would lead men toward moral and political stability.

In these terms the West was an invention of the conservative imagination that may well have served important partisan purposes. For it is plausible to argue that by appealing to the economic promise implicit in western settlement conservative spokesmen helped to divert democratic discontent in the East into harmless channels. Yet there is little reason to suppose that the conservative image of the West as middle-class utopia was deliberately adopted in order to achieve this effect. The chronology is wrong (conservative elaborations of the safety-valve doctrine antedated the social unrest of the 1830's), and conservative enthusiasm over the political and religious prospects of the West, which should have accompanied any deliberate remaking of the western image for partisan purposes, lagged behind the economic estimate. Rather, the conservatives' West would seem to have been an invention that reflected their deepest beliefs. It was not a product of experience alone, not simply a reflection of contemporary politics, but above all a vivid statement of commitment to the status quo in an era marked by drastic social change.

Yet it also corresponded in some degree to the reality, which almost everyone in the United States shared vicariously if not in practice. If there had been no West, that is, it would have been necessary for conservatives to invent it. Invent it they did, but with a sufficient degree of concreteness to make plausible their maturing hopes. As a result their social theory, far from being discarded as irrelevant, helped to shape the popular definition of American institutions according to their model of a western utopia. Their fears were not convincing, in a society of optimists. Their hopes were.

5 / The National Planning of Internal Improvements

Carter Goodrich

During the first half of the nineteenth century the United States changed profoundly. From a colonial nation, hugging its coastline, America transformed itself into an expanding nation that would eventually populate a large part of the most fertile portions of a continent. The transportation revolution made this possible, allowing for qualitative differences in economic growth that ultimately produced such startling quantitative results. These were the means of communication and trade that people in those days called "internal improvements." Without them the fertile lands could not have produced at the peak of their capacity for faraway and foreign markets. Large urban centers could not have developed while depending for their food upon farmers living far from the cities. The internal improvements provided the basis for a functioning national economic system—something that came into being long before the adjustment of American political institutions—to conform to economic realities.

Carter Goodrich, an economic historian who has studied the politics and economics of internal improvements, depicts the difficulties that beset attempts to rationalize these transportation needs on a national basis. Many such projects eventually came into being, but the neat plans of visionaries had remarkably little to do with actual accomplishments. National planning usually fell victim to states'-rights localism, strict constitutional construction, and sectional jealousies. However, economic expansion continued.

For further reading: George Rogers Taylor, *The Transportation Revolution, 1815–1860* (1951); Carter Goodrich (ed.), *Canals and American Economic Development* (1961); Albert Fishlow, *American Railroads and the Transformation of the Ante-Bellum Economy* (1965); Douglass C. North, *The Economic Growth of the United States 1790–1860* (1961).

Political Science Quarterly, LXIII (March 1948), 16–44. Reprinted by permission. Footnotes have been omitted.

Economic planning, it is now recognized, is by no means a new thing in American history. To be sure the term came into general currency only with the first Soviet five year plan and with the activities of the New Deal, and there is of course no American precedent for total planning of a national economy in the Russian sense. But, by the more inclusive definition under which the term has been used to refer to certain of the New Deal measures, the advocacy and practice of economic planning have long been significant parts of the American tradition. For the present purpose the term may be taken to mean the adoption by government or community of deliberate and concerted policies which are designed to promote economic expansion or prosperity and in which positive action to provide favorable conditions for economic activity is emphasized more strongly than negative regulation or the correction of abuses. In this broad sense our record shows many cases of economic planning.

From the time of the Puritans of Massachusetts Bay to that of the Mormons of Utah, the processes of colonization and settlement have often involved the concerted management of economic affairs for a common purpose by agencies wider than the individual household or the business enterprise. The early New England village divided its land resources according to an ordered plan and continued to make common decisions concerning their use. In the new nation, the famous reports of Alexander Hamilton, which should not be remembered merely for their advocacy of a protective tariff, have been described as constituting "a theoretical plan which is just now beginning to be appreciated." In the disposition of the public lands, in the organization of the banking system, and on many other issues, the government of the United States has throughout its history dealt with questions calling for positive action which could not be taken without some degree of conscious attention to the most general economic considerations.

In spite of changed circumstances, the study of cases like these may throw light upon the problem of planning in its present-day setting. Some of the earliest, to be sure, represent practices standing over from pre-industrial days and ideas that were soon to be swept aside in the rise of the doctrines of economic individualism. Yet the spirit of business enterprise was strong even in the early days of American settlement, and throughout our history it is possible to trace the shifting lines between the spheres of public and private enterprise. Sometimes the relations between the two have been those of competition and sometimes of cooperation. Government has on occasion acted to restrain or to supplant private business; on occasion also it has acted to stimulate or to subsidize or even to rescue it. The examination of this record may therefore be of interest today in relation to the continuing problem of how best to use government action and how best to use private enterprise in the promotion of the general good.

Among cases of planning one of the most interesting is that of the movement for internal improvements in the first half of the nineteenth century. The proposals to construct canals and turnpikes and other improvements, and later the railroads, at the public expense, were among the most important policy questions of the time. In certain respects, to be sure, the planning involved was of limited scope even as compared with other American cases. It implied, for example, no such surveillance of the economic system as a whole as is now asked of the President's Council of Economic Advisers. The work of the Tennessee Valley Authority offers a closer comparison, but the nineteenth-century planners of canals and turnpikes made no attempt to go beyond their engineering projects to the explicit social planning that is a notable and controversial feature of the T. V. A. The closest modern analogy, indeed, is to be found in the current projects of so-called underdeveloped countries such as those that are discussed by the Subcommission on Economic Development of the United Nations. In any case the internal improvements movement represented planning on no mean scale. It demonstrated boldness in conception and produced at least one national plan of remarkable scope. So much, indeed, was done by public initiative that the distinguished economic historian, G. S. Callender, declared that this country was at the time an early and a leading example of "the modern tendency to extend the activity of the state into industry."

Though internal improvements have been treated extensively by general and constitutional historians, and though the number of monographs devoted to particular undertakings continues to increase, there appears to be room for a review of the question in terms of the modern debate over the rôle of planning in the economy. The present article begins such a reëxamination. It will consider the movement for national rather than for state action from the administration of Jefferson to that of Jackson, and it will begin with the issues as they are raised in the document which was the movement's most comprehensive blueprint.

A NATIONAL PLAN

On April 4, 1808, Albert Gallatin, Secretary of the Treasury in the administration of Thomas Jefferson, sent to the Senate his report on roads and canals. It begins with the assertion that "the general utility of artificial roads and canals . . . is universally admitted." The question is, who should build them. In some countries, "these improvements may often, in ordinary cases, be left to individual exertion, without any direct aid from Government." In the American case, two major circumstances, "whilst they render the facility of communications throughout the United States an object of primary importance, naturally check the application of private capital and enterprise to improvements on a large scale." The first of these is the relative scarcity of capital. It is much more difficult than in Europe to attract investment by "prospects of remote and moderate profit." The second is "the extent of the territory compared to the population." With a sparse population, local traffic cannot be counted on to make profitable a local improvement. In general, a canal will be unproductive unless it opens "a communication with a natural extensive navigation which will flow through that new channel." For this reason, "some works already executed are unprofitable; many more remain unattempted, because their ultimate productiveness depends on other improvements, too extensive or too distant to be embraced by the same individuals."

"The General Government," declares the *Report,* "can alone remove these obstacles." Its resources are "amply sufficient for the completion of every practicable improvement." "With these resources, and embracing the whole Union, it will complete on any given line all the improvements, however distant, which may be necessary to render the whole productive, and eminently beneficial."

The argument continues:

> The early and efficient aid of the *Federal* Government is recommended by still more important considerations. The inconveniences, complaints, and perhaps

dangers, which may result from a vast extent of territory, can not otherwise be radically removed or prevented than by opening speedy and easy communications through all its parts. Good roads and canals will shorten distances, facilitate commercial and personal intercourse, and unite, by a still more intimate community of interests, the most remote quarters of the United States. No other single operation, within the power of Government, can more effectually tend to strengthen and perpetuate that Union which secures external independence, domestic peace, and internal liberty.

What, then, are the specific objects that on this argument require and justify action by the national government? Gallatin derives his answers from a broad view of the geography of the country. The main problems are to improve communications between the northern and southern states and to bring the settlers beyond the mountains into easy communication with the East. With respect to the former, he points out that the United States possesses "a tide water inland navigation . . . which, from Massachusetts to the southern extremity of Georgia, is principally, if not solely, interrupted by four necks of land." The four are Cape Cod, New Jersey between the Raritan and the Delaware, the peninsula between the Delaware and the Chesapeake, and the "marshy tract which divides the Chesapeake from Albemarle Sound." These should be cut by canals, which would total less than one hundred miles and would be useful "in peace or war" as protection against "storms and enemies." To this should be added "a great turnpike extending from Maine to Georgia . . . passing through all the principal seaports."

The problem of communication with the West presents a greater difficulty. From New York to southern Georgia, the way is blocked by the two great ranges of the Appalachians. "In the present state of science," it is useless to think of crossing them by canals. There are, however, places at which the upper waters of the western and Atlantic rivers are near enough together to make communication practicable. For each of four pairs of rivers, therefore—the Allegheny and the Susquehanna or the Juniata, the Monongahela and the Potomac, the Kanawha and the James, and the Tennessee and the Santee or the Savannah—the *Report* recommends improvements in navigation of the eastern river and a road connecting it with the western stream.

To the North geography opens a different possibility. The Hudson is the only river which "breaks through or turns all the mountains." "The tide in no other . . . comes within thirty miles of the Blue Ridge, or Eastern chain of mountains. In the North river it breaks through the Blue Ridge at West Point, and ascends above the Eastern termination of the Catskill, or great Western chain." Advantage should be taken of this obvious gateway to open communication with the inland navigation of the Great Lakes. . . .

These proposals are based on the "great geographical features of the country." Their benefits should "diffuse and increase the national wealth in a very general way." Yet the states through which these routes pass will receive more direct benefit than the others. Therefore, says Gallatin, "justice, and, perhaps, policy no less than justice," seem to require national aid to more local projects in other areas. For this purposed he adds $3,400,000 to bring his total to the round figure of $20,000,000.

How is this money to be raised and spent? "An annual appropriation of two millions of dollars would accomplish all these great objects in ten years." "In times of peace and under properous circumstances," this sum could be paid from the surplus revenues without new taxation. Indeed, an even larger total was being paid off on the national debt, now mainly discharged, from surplus revenue between 1801 and 1809. Or, as an alternative, the proceeds of the sale of public lands might be applied to this purpose. The improvements themselves would be of immediate and direct benefit to the purchasers of land, and "the United States, considered merely as owners of the soil . . . would be amply repaid" in the rise of value of the lands remaining unsold. If it were desired, also, the fund might be a revolving one. Projects once brought to profitable operation might be sold "to individuals or companies, and the proceeds applied to a new improvement."

Here then was a notable ten-year plan of national action. It was based on and buttressed by painstaking investigation. Its hundred-and-eighty folio pages of appendix, derived from answers to extensively circulated questionnaires, would do credit to a modern planning board with many times Gallatin's staff. They contain information, often including maps, charts, financial statements, and charter provisions, on some twenty-five canal enterprises, undertaken or projected, and deal, though more briefly, with several hundred turnpike companies. One of the *Report's* recommendations, moreover, is the next essential step in planning. "As an important basis of the general system," it asks Congress to authorize taking "the surveys and levels" of the routes proposed.

Certain problems which were to trouble the movement for internal improvements, however, received relatively little attention in the *Report*. In it the constitutional issue appears not at all formidable. The federal government can now make improvements only with the consent of the states concerned. For this reason the President has recommended an amendment "to remove every impediment to a national plan of internal improvements." Yet in these cases, since the improvements are of such obvious advantage, the problem of state consent should not be a difficult one. Again, the question of method is presented, perhaps for strategic reasons, rather as one of detail. The United States may have the work done "at their sole expense," or may subsidize private companies, preferably by subscription to their stock. The former method, Gallatin ventures, might, "by effectually controlling local interests," have the advantage of the "most proper general direction." The latter method might be more "economical" in the execution of details. Perhaps the two might somehow be "blended" to obtain the advantages of each.

Finally, the great problem of local and sectional conflicts in the choice of projects, to which the Secretary had already paid tribute in the item of $3,400,000 for local undertakings, is referred to in the closing paragraph in a sentence notable for its choice of conjunction:

> The National Legislature alone, embracing every local interest, and superior to every local consideration, is competent to the selection of such national objects.

When this *Report* was presented, there was much in the national situation to suggest the probability of favorable action. Geography itself appeared to point the way. The English observer, Harriet Martineau, began her chapter on "Transport and Markets" by exclaiming how much Nature had done for the United States "in this article of their economy" and how clearly it had "indicated . . . what remained for human hands to do." The economic need was manifest, particularly for the opening of trade connections for the western settlers. Out of a total population in 1810 of less than 7,250,000, more than a million were in the western states and territories, and many others living in western New York and Pennsylvania and in what is now

West Virginia were also beyond effective reach of the seaboard markets. In a speech supporting Gallatin's program, Congressman Peter B. Porter of western New York described the situation of these settlers in the following terms:

> The great evil, and it is a serious one indeed, under which the inhabitants of the western country labor, arises from the want of a market. There is no place where the great staple articles for the use of civilized life can be produced in greater abundance or with greater ease, and yet as respects most of the luxuries and many of the conveniences of life the people are poor. They have no vent for their produce at home, and, being all agriculturists, they produce alike the same article with the same facility; and such is the present difficulty and expense of transporting their produce to an Atlantic port that little benefit is realized from that quarter. . . . Such is the fertility of their land that one-half of their time spent in labor is sufficient to produce every article which their farms are capable of yielding, in sufficient quantities for their own consumption, and there is nothing to incite them to produce more.

Callender's study cited the Congressman's speech and confirmed his economics. A small quantity of livestock that could be driven long distances to market and a few commodities like furs were the only western produce that could reach the eastern cities. The main route to market was by way of the Mississippi, but even the river shipments amounted in 1816 only to about $2.70 per head of the western population. Here was a great untapped potential of trade. If it could be released by the provision of cheap transport, both East and West would profit.

The difficulty was to attract sufficient capital to get the work done. Of this contemporary accounts give abundant evidence. In Gallatin's summary of the experience of particular canal undertakings, the words, "suspended for want of funds," are a recurrent refrain. In the case of one project, his comment is: "The capital, which was inadequate, was not paid." Several small canals had been completed, one company had paid dividends, and two or three others were cited as having good prospects. The company which had started work in the Mohawk Valley had made "considerable progress" with substantial state aid; but even on this route—which was to provide the greatest triumph of the movement for internal improvement—navigation would not be profitable until works were constructed "at the two extremities"; and these "the funds of the company did not enable them to undertake." A number of observers described the difficulty at greater length and suggested explanations for it. The frontier regions, which would often benefit most directly, were particularly short of capital. The Dismal Swamp Canal Company had failed to receive "spirited patronage," partly because "the inhabitants of the circumjacent country" possessed "but little spare money" and were unwilling "to risk that little" in ventures of which the profits were doubtful or distant. Other accounts suggested the presence of more attractive alternatives. The Chesapeake and Delaware project began with "sanguine expectations," but "it soon became evident that a work of this kind, which required the toil and attention of several years to repay those who engaged in it, bore an unfavorable comparison with the banks, moneyed institutions, and private commerce of the United States, which gave immediate and large returns to the capital employed in them. Hence the ardor of the subscribers was soon perceived to cool." In a memorial to Congress, dated November 19, 1811, the sponsors of the Union Canal Company of Pennsylvania named "the allurements of external commerce" as the reason for their inability to raise the necessary funds.

More than thirty years before, Madison had written to Jefferson commenting on the "exuberant harvest" offered to investors in the prospectus of the James River Canal Company but adding that even these terms were judged "inadequate bait for subscription." Though there had been considerable capital accumulation in the intervening period, the prospect of "exuberant" profits was still required to draw out private funds or to lure them from the alternatives of commerce or land speculation. Except in a few fields, the American corporation, as Callender emphasizes, had not yet proved itself able to collect large sums of capital. There appeared, moreover, to be little prospect that canal and turnpike companies could raise the necessary funds from abroad. Up to this time there had been little foreign investment in American securities, and even on the domestic exchanges the only issues traded were those of federal and state governments and of banks and insurance companies.

The United States was still a "capital-scarcity" country. Private means unsupported by government appeared unequal to the task of opening the great lines of transportation. A number of private companies had already asked for aid from the national and state governments. The alternatives to failure appeared to be either government assistance of this sort or direct construction by government.

For national action to accomplish these purposes there was precedent as well as considerable political preparation. George Washington was not only an advocate of internal improvements but also the active promoter and president of the company formed to improve the navigation of the Potomac as a route to the West. His Farewell Address contains an eloquent statement of the importance for national unity of "the progressive improvement of interior communication by land and water." Though the internal improvements policy was to appear to some later observers more Federalist than Republican, it was under Jefferson that the first definite national step was taken. The act of 1802 providing for the admission of Ohio to statehood contained a clause setting apart a portion of the public lands for the construction of a road from the Atlantic waters "to the said state, and through the same." This was to be laid out "under the authority of Congress, with the consent of the several states" through which it was to pass. The first appropriation to carry out this policy was made in 1806, and by the end of that year the commissioners who were appointed to lay out the project had made their first report recommending a line from the Potomac, at Cumberland, to the Monongahela and the Ohio.

The immediate legislative background suggested strong support for the Gallatin plan. Jefferson's message to Congress in 1806 pointed out that, if peace continued, there would soon be surpluses in the Treasury. "Patriotism," he declared, recommended "their application to the great purposes of the public education, roads, rivers, canals, and such other objects of public improvement as it may be thought proper to add to the constitutional enumeration of Federal powers." The issue aroused lively discussion, particularly in the Senate, and the proposals put forward included several of the specific projects that were to be included in Gallatin's plan. As in the preceding session, there was active support for a government subscription to the stock of the Chesapeake and Delaware Canal Company. Henry Clay and others attempted to secure funds for a canal around the Falls of the Ohio at Louisville. Another proposal was that of a turnpike to connect "the Northeastern and Southwestern extremities of the Union." Moreover, the idea of a general concerted plan was beginning to emerge. Both senators from Delaware argued for the proposed canal across their own state as a "link" in a great chain. The report of a Senate committee had carried the point even further. The importance of the proposed canal, it declared, "though great in itself, is not justly appreciated by considering it as a separate work; it must be viewed as the basis of a vast scheme of interior navigation connecting the waters of the lakes with those of the most southern States; and if beyond the present means, unquestionably within the growing resources of the country."

John Quincy Adams, then in the Senate, gave part of the impetus toward a general plan. He was an effective opponent of separate action on the Chesapeake and Delaware project, and, on February 23, 1807, asked attention for the following resolution:

> That the Secretary of the Treasury be directed to prepare and report to the Senate, at their next session, a plan for the application of such means as are constitutionally within the power of Congress, to the purpose of making roads, for removing obstructions in rivers, and making canals; together with a statement of the undertakings of that nature now existing within the United States which, as objects of public improvement, may require and deserve the aid of government.

For the moment the proposal was unsuccessful. A few days later, however, Senator Thomas Worthington introduced a resolution similar to that of Adams, and on March 2, the Senate adopted by a vote of 22 to 3 the motion to which the Gallatin *Report* was the direct response.

Gallatin's plan, therefore, was by no means an isolated or merely quixotic effort. Its innovation lay not in the basic direction but in orderliness of thought and comprehensiveness of view. What it did was to give coherence and intellectual organization to the proposals of a movement that was already vigorous. For these proposals there was a strong economic argument, and for the movement there was apparently widespread political and popular support. Yet the great unified plan was never adopted, much less carried out, and only isolated fragments of an internal improvements program were undertaken by the federal government.

THE DEFEAT OF NATIONAL PLANNING

Thirty years later, John Quincy Adams, who described himself on the strength of the resolution quoted as "the first mover" of internal improvement "as a system"— that is as national planning—wrote bitterly of the defeat of the system:

> The great effort of my administration was to mature into a permanent and regular system the application of all the superfluous revenues of the Union to internal improvement. . . . I fell and with me fell, I fear never to rise again, certainly never to rise again in my day, the system of internal improvement by means of national energies.

Why, then, had this type of national planning been defeated? Adams' own answer was clear and simple. It was the work of "the Maysville road veto policy" and what seemed to him the related abominations of the administration of Andrew Jackson. Jackson was equally convinced of the decisiveness of his action. His Farewell Address expressed confidence that he had "finally overthrown . . . this plan of unconstitutional expenditure for the purpose of corrupt influence." The contrast between the policies of the two administrations was real and significant. In his first annual message, Adams expressed the hope that "the swelling tide of wealth" from the sale of public lands would be "made to reflow in unfailing streams of improvement from the Atlantic to the Pacific Ocean." Adams' first annual message asked the Congress to consider "the general principle" of internal improvement "in a more enlarged extent." This document may indeed be taken as the most "enlarged" expression of the philosophy of the movement. Substantial appropriations for internal improvements were made during Adams' administration. When, on the Fourth of July 1828, he turned the first earth for the Chesapeake and Ohio Canal, he declared that he considered this "the most fortunate incident" of his life.

Under Jackson, on the other hand, this "Great National Project" was, as one author puts it, "deserted by the Federal Government" and "left stranded on the southern shore of Maryland." Moreover, the Maysville Road veto and Jackson's second annual message stand as the historic replies to the Adams program. They denounced the mingling of government funds with those of private corporations and argued forcefully that the state rather than the federal government was the appropriate agency for internal improvement. Though they did not wholly rule out every possibility of national action, their practical effect was to administer the decisive check to the existing program of internal improvement "by means of national energies."

Yet an interpretation of the defeat of national planning must account for much more than the famous Jackson veto. What, after all, was the Maysville Road? It was a projected turnpike of some sixty miles, initiated by a private company. Though it was to continue the line of Zane's Trace, a pioneer route across Ohio, the road itself lay wholly within the state of Kentucky. It was therefore easy for the President to describe it as "a measure of purely local character . . . conferring partial instead of general advantages" and bearing "no relation to any general system of improvement." The organization of the project, moreover, made it vulnerable to Jackson's suggestion that it represented an artful expedient for saddling upon the government "the losses of unsuccessful private speculation." In these passages, it may be said that Jackson was in effect condemning the Maysville project precisely on the ground that it did not meet the specifications laid down by Gallatin. Certainly the Road made no part of the great geographic routes so carefully and so boldly outlined.

The same point does not apply to the four canal companies to which Congress had authorized stock subscriptions. The Louisville and Portland Canal around the Falls of the Ohio, the Chesapeake and Delaware and the Dismal Swamp canals in the proposed coastal navigation, and the Chesapeake and Ohio attempting one of the great connections between eastern and western rivers were all part of the Gallatin blueprints. But all of these, even the last, represented small beginnings. If over two decades the Gallatin plan had in practice come down to these and the Maysville Road, the defeat of the system cannot be laid entirely to the hands of Andrew Jackson. Why had not the proposals already resulted in the construction of a set of related major projects? Why, indeed, was the plan not adopted as a whole when it was first laid before Congress in 1808?

To this last question, the answer appears obvious. The great immediate obstacle was the danger of war. The Embargo Act was passed while Gallatin was at work on the *Report*. The document itself, as already noted, predicated its argument on the maintenance of peace. It added the further warning that if the nation should decide to maintain a large military establishment, even without war, "the objects of the report must probably be abandoned." When Porter rose early in 1810 to make his principal speech in favor of internal improvements, he felt it necessary to begin by pleading that important domestic questions should not be entirely crowded out of consideration by foreign affairs. Together with Senator John Pope of Kentucky, he introduced in the same session a measure including substantially the Gallatin list of projects. Their choice of method—in part no doubt influenced by the threat of war—was for subscription to the stock of state-chartered corporations rather than construction by the government, and for government borrowing on the security of the public lands as against direct appropriations. Gallatin himself was forced to modify his position and finally to lay aside the advocacy of internal improvement in order to protect the strength of the Treasury. In January 1812, he told a House committee that his opinion still remained the same "with respect to the general principles of the plan" and to the importance of the "system of improvement." The circumstances required only a change in the "manner" of proceeding. But Gallatin answered with an emphatic negative the committee's first question as to whether the present "state of the finances" allowed direct appropriation. The committee itself, to which had been referred memorials on behalf of the Chesapeake and Delaware and Union canals and the state of New York's proposed canal to the Great Lakes, came to the conclusion that "the inauspicious state of the United States, in regard to our foreign relations, renders it . . . improper, at the present time, to grant that effectual aid to the undertakings to which they are so well entitled." The committee's policy prevailed, and its conclusions were reinforced by the outbreak of actual war.

The return of peace removed these obstacles and revived the agitation for internal improvement. The war experience itself furnished a cogent argument. "How much did we suffer," exclaimed Calhoun, for lack of roads and canals. What the navy lost "for want of inland navigation along the seacoast," and the army by lack of proper transport to the Great Lakes, were points made again and again in the debates. The chartering of the Second Bank of the United States seemed to provide a special opportunity for action. During the session of 1816–17, Calhoun proposed a measure to set aside the government's bonus from the charter and its future income from the Bank for improvements. As the *Annals of Congress* reported, "Let us then, said Mr. C., bind the Republic together with a perfect system of roads and canals." The state of the nation was most favorable—"at peace with all the world, abounding in pecuniary means." To these two circumstances, Calhoun added a third which he described as of the most importance—"party and sectional feelings immerged in a liberal and enlightened regard to the general concerns of the nation."

The third point proved to be the crucial one. The conflict of state versus more general interests appeared at once in the Bonus Bill discussions. As introduced, the measure provided for a permanent national fund to be spent under the direction of Congress for improvements of national importance. As passed, it represented hardly more than a distribution of gifts to the states in proportion to their population. The fund was first to be carved into portions for the several states and then within each state applied to improvements under the concurrent direction of Congress and the state legislature. Clay and Calhoun and a number of others pointed out that this would make it very difficult to secure the construction of projects of national importance, citing as a favorite example the canal around the Falls of the Ohio which would be of more benefit to states up and down the river than to Kentucky. Yet they could secure only the proviso that a state might, if it wished, ask Congress to spend its portion of the fund within the borders of another state. Thus the bill which Madison vetoed as going beyond the powers of the federal government would, in any case, have given too little authority for the type of national planning called for by the Gallatin *Report*.

By this time most of the lines of the subsequent debate were well defined. President Monroe in his first annual message recommended a constitutional amendment to give the federal government specific authority to construct internal improvements. The suggestion was not welcomed by the strongest advocates of improvements, and most of the attempts to follow it were made by men willing to keep federal authority within the limits of the Bonus Bill provisions for the distribution of expenditures in proportion to population. In 1822 Monroe vetoed a bill providing for the collection of tolls on the Cumberland Road. If Congress did not possess the power to control and operate the Road effectively, there seemed no point in retaining responsibility. Title therefore was ultimately transferred to the several states within which it lay. The federal government's contribution had been to build "a highway seven hundred miles in length, at a cost of seven millions of treasure."

Agitation for other improvements continued, and some progress was made in the development of orderly methods for their consideration. Individual projects, and sometimes plans for more comprehensive action, were typically referred to the Senate and House Committees on Roads and Canals. An act of 1824 directed the government to institute a series of surveys of proposed routes, and reports by the United States Corps of Engineers and its Board of Internal Improvement began to play an important part in the discussions. A set of resolutions put forward in 1826 by Chairman Mercer of the House Committee, but not adopted, proposed a systematic plan, not unlike Gallatin's, which would make still further use of the Engineers and which would call on the Census to record the progress of internal improvements. Yet aside from appropriations for surveys, for improvements to the navigation of rivers and harbors, and for military and territorial roads, further actual appropriations for the construction of internal improvements were not made until after the election of 1824. Of the projects on the Gallatin list, the first to receive an appropriation was the Chesapeake and Delaware Canal. On his last day of office in 1825, Monroe approved a stock subscription for $150,000. Similar appropriations for the Falls of the Ohio and the Dismal Swamp projects followed the next year. In addition a new form of national encouragement for state undertakings had been worked out, and in 1827 and 1828 substantial grants of land were made to Illinois for the canal from Lake Michigan to the Illinois River, and to Indiana and Ohio for both roads and canals. Finally, in May 1828, the Congress authorized an appropriation of $1,000,000 for the greatest of the proposed projects, the Chesapeake and Ohio Canal which was the heir of Washington's Potomac Company. As with the other three monetary appropriations, the method chosen was that of subscription to the stock of a company; but in this case, the position of the federal government was to be the dominant one, and state and municipal contributions were to outweigh those of private subscribers. On the eve of Andrew Jackson's inauguration the record of appropriations for the four companies whose undertakings fell directly within the original Gallatin plan stood as follows:

Company	Appropriation	Date of Approval
Chesapeake and Delaware Canal	$300,000	March 3, 1825
Company	150,000	March 2, 1829
Louisville and Portland Canal	100,000	May 13, 1826
Company	up to 135,000	March 2, 1829
Dismal Swamp Canal Company	150,000	May 18, 1826
	50,000	March 2, 1829
Chesapeake and Ohio Canal Company	$1,000,000	May 24, 1828

Twenty years after Gallatin's *Report* and more than a decade after the close of the War of 1812, this was the point to which the movement for national internal improvements had come. One great segment of Gallatin's plan, the joining of the Hudson with the Lakes, had been carried through by a state instead of by the nation. For the rest, aside from the Cumberland Road, there were only beginnings. Yet the appropriations within four years of nearly two million dollars for the projects listed represented a substantial commitment, and it is clear that during Adams' administration the movement that was to be checked by Jackson's veto had begun to develop a mounting force.

THE ALTERNATIVES TO NATIONAL PLANNING

Adams spoke of the program of national improvements as giving way to the alternatives of state action and private enterprise. Since both of these methods seemed to him feebler than national action, he was not greatly concerned to distinguish between them. To the modern student, however, it is of particular interest to inquire which of these alternatives played the greater part in the opposition to national planning.

The constitutional obstacles clearly belong on the state side of the question. It is unnecessary to review the constitutional arguments so often repeated in these debates and so thoroughly discussed by later writers, or to attempt to reinterpret the relationship between the conflicting philosophies of government and the position of groups or sections whose interests would be furthered by a maximum or a minimum of federal action. For the purpose of the present discussion the essential point is a simple one. The constitutional issue turned solely on the respective rights of federal and state governments and not at all on the rights of private individuals or corporations.

Whatever the rôle of states' rights in the abstract, it is abundantly clear that conflicts of state and sectional interests were of major importance. Adams himself had no doubt as to the source of the defeat of national planning. It came from "the Sable Genius of the South" that had seen "the signs of his own inevitable downfall in the unparalleled progress" of the North and had therefore fallen "to cursing the tariff and internal improvements." Sable or not, the opposition was understandable. The protective tariff was clearly inimical to the interests of the South, and it was linked with internal improvements both in the politics of Clay's American System and as a principal source of the funds with which improvements might be constructed. But the North-South cleavage, however important, was not maintained consistently throughout the discussions nor was it by any means the only line of division.

When Miss Martineau singled out South Carolina for the fierceness of its opposition in the later stages of the internal improvements debate and for the unbounded character of its "sectional jealousy," she remarked that it had at one time been on the opposite side of the question. Its leaders, however, had found "how much larger a share of the benefit would be appropriated by the active and prosperous northern states." This was partly because the greatest of the specific improvements would serve to strengthen trade connections between the East and West, while without such intervention rivers carried western produce to the South and southern cotton to the sea.

In the earlier days of the controversy, the conflict appeared more often to be that of West against East. The advocates of improvements urged them as due recognition to the interests of western farmers, either as a just counterbalance to the favors being shown to manufacturers or as a partial offset to measures for the protection of the commercial interests of the seaboard. Congressman Porter even warned of the danger of revolt if the people of the West should come to believe that Congress "can constitutionally create banks for the accommodation of the merchant but cannot construct canals for the benefit of the farmer." Still another alignment divided states which had already spent substantial funds on improvements from those which had not done so. It was observed, for example, that representatives from New York, who had favored improvement legislation while they hoped for federal funds for the Erie Canal, discovered objections to national action after their state had completed the project by its own resources. A final comment on sectional jealousy relates to still another line of division. Robert Wright of Maryland complained that among the representatives "to the southward and westward of the Potomac" there had been scarcely a vote cast in favor of the Chesapeake and Delaware Canal. "And, sir," he exclaimed, "I regret that our legislative and proceedings do not wear a better aspect, but rather a more Southern and Western ascension, and a more Northern and Eastern decision." If such conflicts could not be resolved, the obvious recourse was to leave the matter to the several states.

The case for state action, moreover, rested on positive as well as negative grounds. Congressional orators frequently declared that the states were better equipped than the federal government to select projects wisely and to manage them efficiently. The same points were made by the enthusiasts for internal improvements who contributed to the influential *North American Review*. Jared Sparks declared that "the most direct and powerful means of improvement rest in the states individually." In supporting the statement he put first the argument that "The compass of each state is sufficiently narrow, and its legislative power sufficiently diffused, to render knowledge of its internal condition, wants, and resources easily attained," and only second the fact that each state "enjoys full authority, under the constitutional compact." The great example was New York State with its Erie Canal, "an undertaking of which the most powerful governments on earth might be proud." Similarly John L. Sullivan, though against parsimony on the part of the federal government, nevertheless found great satisfaction, "in a country as prodigious as ours," in the fact that the state could serve as the principal agency:

> . . . we are divided into independent communities so rich and powerful, that scarce any object of public utility is beyond the grasp of the resources of the single states; so that, after all, the care of individual objects of public improvement is

put into the hands of those most sure to be benefited by them, and most concerned by interest and most enabled by local situation to accomplish them with
zeal and economy.

States' rights, state and sectional interests, and a belief in the capacities of the
several states seem to have played the decisive rôle in the downfall of national planning. By contrast business enterprise offered less formidable competition. The possibility of conflict, to be sure, was lessened by the fact that proposals for federal
action so often took the form of partnership with private enterprise. Of the alternative
methods which Gallatin had set forth, direct government construction or subscription to the stock of private companies, the second was more often favored. For this
there were at least two reasons. In the first place, this method appeared to offer
a way around the constitutional difficulty. If the company's authority to construct
the improvement and to exercise the right of eminent domain derived from the
charter issued by a state, awkward questions of the state's assent to federal action
need not arise, and the national government could base its action on the appropriation power alone. This interpretation was suggested by Clay during the Bonus
Bill debates, was accepted by the House after long discussion, and was used again
and again by both supporters and opponents of internal improvements.

In addition, the opinion was widely held that stock subscription was in any case
the wisest method of government action. Sometimes the argument was simply that
the addition of private money would make that of the government go farther. In
1817, a House committee argued that individual and local enterprise should bear
half the cost and that Gallatin's twenty million dollar program could therefore be
accomplished with a government outlay of only ten millions. More often the argument ran that the work would be done more economically if the zeal of the private
enterpriser was also involved. James Buchanan of Pennsylvania declared that the
money of the government would be safest when invested jointly with private capital.
Though there seems never to have been a full-dress debate on the practical merits
of the two methods, the prevailing view was well summed up by a Senate committee
in 1817:

> Of the different modes which might be devised of applying public moneys to
> objects of internal improvements, that of authorizing subscriptions for a limited
> number of shares of the stock of companies incorporated for the purpose, appears,
> on every consideration, to be the most eligible. By limiting the number of shares
> to be subscribed to a third, or less than one-half, of the whole stock, there is
> more security that the Government shall not become engaged in impracticable
> projects for improvements, and also for the economical expenditure of the funds,
> than would be, on the plan of a direct application, by Government, of the public
> moneys.

In the closing years of the debate, objections to the practice began to develop.
Senator Thomas Benton of Missouri questioned the propriety of such "associations
between this Government and the people of the United States." A number of similar
references to "stockjobbing" and "executive patronage" and "pernicious copartner-
ships" illustrated the tendency that was to lead to Jackson's biting denunciation of
the mingling of private and public money and to the conviction of the Jacksonians
that the democratic solution of the improvements problem was to remove it from the
field of federal action. The great majority of the advocates of improvement, however,

remained convinced that the public interest would be furthered by the partnership with the "vigilance" and "sagacity" of private enterprise.

In his penetrating article, published in 1902, Callender remarked that the movement for public improvements in this period was not "due to any modern socialistic or populistic idea that the business of supplying transportation . . . to the community was not a safe and legitimate one, to be left to the management of private enterprise." It was almost universally assumed in the congressional debates that it was desirable to leave to individual business as much of the job as it could perform, and the view was rarely challenged outside. To a generation familiar with the controversies over public power and the Tennessee Valley Authority, it is equally interesting and perhaps more surprising to note how little of the *opposition* to national internal improvements seems to have been based on an *anti*-socialist philosophy, or on the desire of private business to take over the job for itself. Opponents occasionally included in their battery of arguments the proposition that the country was not ripe for improvements until they would yield a profit to those who undertook them. "The proper time is known," said Senator Nathaniel Macon of North Carolina, "by the industrious and careful people being ready to vest their money in them, for a reasonable profit." Striking by its isolation is a single case in which a congressman argued that the vested rights of existing corporations would be impaired by such powerful competition as that of the United States Congress. The conventional plea for internal improvements, as for example in Clay's much-quoted speeches, began with a recognition of the validity of laissez faire as a fundamental principle, but found no difficulty in establishing grounds for favoring public works. That stalwart defender of economic orthodoxy, Harriet Martineau, saw in this no inconsistency and had no doubts of the economic expediency of the improvements. Reporting to the Senate in 1817, Jeremiah Morrow of Ohio incorporated the policy in what was surely intended as a definition of laissez faire:

> To insure the pursuits of useful industry in a nation, a state of the greatest prosperity, it is only necessary to protect their interests from foreign aggression, to leave them unrestrained by artificial provisions, and to remove, or ameliorate, the natural obstacles to their erection, by public works, rendering conveyance practicable and cheap.

In these discussions the lines between public spirit and private interest were often indistinct. Specific projects for improvement were typically initiated by groups of leading citizens in local communities. In them a lively expectation of profit was combined with the desire to promote the progress of the area and the nation. When the project ran short of funds and its promoters "claimed the public patronage," their memorials to Congress or to the state legislature emphasized their civic purposes. Supporters of the Chesapeake and Delaware Canal were proud to point out that their project stemmed from a study made in 1769 by a committee of the American Philosophical Society composed of "Dr. Franklin" and other men "whose views, extending beyond themselves, [were] employed upon objects of general benefit and utility." Enthusiastic advocates of improvements addressed their exhortations impartially to the leaders of private and public undertakings. "Where there are public spirit, enlightened zeal, and honourable ambition," said Jared Sparks, "it is idle to talk about obstacles. . . . This remark will apply equally to individuals, corporate bodies, and state legislatures." A successful improvement would bring gains to those who owned land along the route and to those who would use it in their trade. In terms of their interests, as distinct from those of stockholders in the companies, the important thing was to get the improvement constructed. Whether it should be done by business or by government or by partnership between the two was a secondary consideration. Since various private interests were thus often on the side of public expenditure, and since corporations had not yet developed the financial strength to accomplish the major projects unaided, the issue of business versus government enterprise was posed much less sharply than in many modern controversies.

In his lament over the defeat of the national program of improvements, Adams discussed the prospects of the two alternative methods:

> With this system in ten years from this day the surface of the whole Union would have been checkered over with railroads and canals. It may still be done half a century later and with the limping gate of State legislature and private adventure.

This was better polemics than prophecy. Within the year in which he was writing, the outbreak of the panic of 1837 suggested that a number of the states had been too exuberant rather than too modest in their programs of improvement, and many of the canals constructed failed to survive the competition of the new means of transportation. The expansion of the railroads, after somewhat hesitant beginnings, was soon to proceed at much more than a "limping gate" under the control of great business corporations, some of which received extensive government aid. Yet in the period covered by the present articles these were not the agencies on which opponents of the national planning of internal improvements placed their chief reliance. For major undertakings such as those called for by the Gallatin plan, "private adventure" had not yet attained the stature of the principal alternative to national action.

6 / New York Port
and Its Disappointed Rivals

Robert G. Albion

Although much of the transportation revolution lacked coordination, and although many projects could be defended only on grounds of local interests, national economic expansion continued. In the decades following the War of 1812, the American economy grew enormously. This economic explosion was a prelude to the take-off period for American economic growth, the years immediately preceding the Civil War. The entire period between 1815 and 1860 provided the basis for American transformation from an affluent agricultural society into an even more affluent industrial society.

Some states and areas gained more from these changes than others. New York, after first requesting aid from the national government, built its great internal improvement project, the Erie Canal, on its own. The success of this venture effectively ended the negative economic significance of the Appalachian barrier. The port of New York City, already important in transatlantic and seaboard trade, then became the depot for much of the agricultural richness of the upper Mississippi Valley as well. This meant that the northeastern states could specialize economically, expanding their manufactures while obtaining food from western areas. Rival ports, as we see in the following article by Robert G. Albion, tried to compete, but New York City's primacy could not be prevented. The South, in particular, became almost a colony of the eastern merchants and bankers, most of whom were New Yorkers. A century later, President Calvin Coolidge would remark that "the business of America is business." If so, New York became the "capital" of the United States during the period 1815 to 1860.

Journal of Economic and Business History, III (August 1931), 602–629. Reprinted by permission. Footnotes have been omitted except where they are necessary for an understanding of the text.

For further reading: Edward C. Kirkland, *Men, Cities and Transportation: A Study of New England History, 1820–1900* (1948); Robert G. Albion, *The Rise of New York Port, 1815–1860* (1939); Ronald E. Shaw, *Erie Water West: A History of the Erie Canal, 1792–1864* (1966).

The very names of Salem and Liverpool suggest the sea, but in New York the docks of the East and North Rivers are overshadowed in the popular mind by Wall Street, Broadway, and Fifth Avenue. Yet it is highly doubtful whether those thoroughfares would be what they are today had it not been for the activity at the New York docks a hundred years ago.

The second quarter of the nineteenth century saw a lively and sometimes bitter contest among the American Atlantic seaports. New York had forged into first place and threatened to gain the lion's share of the nation's foreign trade. Thereupon the rival ports engaged in a desperate stern chase, doing all they could against New York and each other with canals, railroads, and liners. It was, however, a case of "To him who hath shall be given," and New York emerged from the contest secure in its primacy in population and finance as well as in commerce.

New York, Boston, and Philadelphia had long been America's "Big Three"; but Baltimore rose so rapidly during this period that it deserves to be classed with them. New Orleans, on the other hand, while it eventually attained second place in volume of trade, specialized to such an extent in cotton exportation that it was in a different category. Prominent in the second rank were Portland, Salem, Norfolk, Charleston, Savannah, and Mobile, to say nothing of Montreal and Quebec.

In estimating the relative advantages of these ports, we must take into account the combination of five distinct factors. The first three, which pertain to adaptability to transatlantic, to coastwise, and to inland trade, are geographical. The remaining factors are enterprise and the development of the hinterland.

There was a certain amount of predestination in the rise of New York. Nature had been more generous to her than to her rivals. New York has one of the finest harbors in the world, with the open sea right at hand. Long Island Sound offers an easy and sheltered approach to New England, while vessels coasting to the southward can get away with a quick start. The Hudson, navigable for some 150 miles, taps a rich back country. Combined with the Mohawk Valley, it forms a gap in the mountain wall that separates the coast from the West, providing what the New York Central still capitalizes as the "water level route." Other American ports surpass New York in particular geographical features, but no other one combines so well the advantages for foreign, coastal, and internal commerce.

The New England ports lie nearer Europe than does New York, but that is their sole advantage. They are rather far north for the coasting trade, and their back country cannot compare with New York's. Philadelphia and Baltimore are nearer the West than is New York, but the mountains lie across their path, nearly half a mile above sea level at the most advantageous points. Both are handicapped, especially in the coasting trade, by their distance from the sea. Norfolk has potential geographical advantages almost equal to those of New York, while Charleston, too, has a favorable position. New Orleans has unsurpassed natural connections with the interior, but the long trip around Florida is a decided drawback in transatlantic and coastwise commerce. Montreal and Quebec also have an excellent natural approach to the West and are nearer Europe than the ports of the United States, but the fogs at the mouth of the St. Lawrence are an impediment to navigation and the freezing of the river limits its seaborne trade to about half the year.

The influence of these geographical factors, however, was not absolute. Otherwise, Boston would never have surpassed Norfolk and Charleston in commerce. The element of enterprise can considerably modify the threefold geographical considerations. Ports might be classified as "active" and "passive." The active ports attract an import as well as an export trade, and engage in navigation as well as commerce. The passive ports are simply outlets for the products of the interior. The degree of activity increased progressively from south to north along the coast. The extreme contrast would be seen in the cases of Mobile and Salem. The former, close to the rich cotton region, exported a huge amount of that product, but its shipping was almost entirely in the hands of others and its imports were negligible. Salem, on the other hand, with a barren back country and not even much of a harbor, built up a lucrative and spectacular trade with the far corners of the earth.

New York was probably no more active on the whole than were its northern neighbors, but its activity was well timed. During the colonial period it had failed to capitalize its natural advantages to the limit. A concentration of energy and farseeing shrewdness at the critical time, however, gave New York a permanent position as "the great commercial emporium of America." Even though the New Yorkers then rested on their oars, that position was so secure that all the energy of their rivals could not shake it. New York differed from the active New England ports in that its own residents were not essentially a seagoing group. It was a city of merchants rather than mariners. Many of its leaders never trod a quarterdeck, but they were able to exert a widespread control over affairs afloat as well as ashore. It was characteristic that New York should use Maine ships and sailors to move southern cotton and should make the principal profits in such a transaction.

The success of New York, moreover, was not the work of a homogeneous group of men as was the case in the New England ports. New York, once its rise was under way, attracted outsiders who saw there the best career open to their talents. These new-comers fully held their own with the native New Yorkers. Many were foreigners but still more numerous were the Yankees from southern New England, who swarmed to New York like Scots to London. "It is a singular fact," wrote the garrulous historian of the old New York merchants, "that a foreign boy, or one from the New England states, will succeed in this city and become a partner in our largest firms, much oftener than a born New York boy. The great secret of this success is the perfect willingness to be useful and do what they are required to do, and cheerfully." Considering the fact that much of New York's commerce was carried on with ships and sailors from the eastward and that many even of her master minds, such as the Howlands, the Grinnells, and the Griswolds, also came from there, we might, in this study of maritime rivalry, almost regard New York port as a commercial outpost of New England.

The development of the hinterland is the final factor to be taken into account. During the colonial period, each port had served a relatively small portion of the adjacent back country. By the close of the Revolution, there was a rapidly increasing population beyond the mountains, ready to produce grain and other commodities, provided a suitable market could be found. Washington was tireless in urging the improvement of communication between the seaboard and the West. In 1784 he wrote: "The western settlers . . . stand as it were upon a pivot. The touch of a feather would turn them anyway. . . . smooth the road, and make easy the way for them, and then see what an influx of articles will be poured upon us; how amazingly our exports will be increased by them, and how amply we shall be compensated for any trouble and expense we may encounter to effect it." The various ports, with such a prize in prospect, were eventually to engage in a spirited contest for control of this "western front." The Mississippi and St. Lawrence were natural outlets for the region, but there was the possibility that any one of the larger ports from New York to Charleston might tap it by means of an overland route. Boston, more than any other major port, was handicapped in the race for this prize. It had hitherto held its own despite the lack of a rich agricultural hinterland, but it seemed too far away from the center to share in the new western trade. Its progress was slowed until railroads and factories finally gave it a more extensive sphere of influence than seemed possible at first.

To summarize the progress of the rivalry and to get statistics out of the way as soon as possible, we might resort to the naval conference type of ratio for the "Big Three" in combined imports and exports. Around 1700, Boston had enjoyed an easy first place. Philadelphia passed it before the Revolution and still maintained its leadership in 1791 when the ratio was Philadelphia, 9; New York, 8; and Boston, 6. In 1797, New York passed into first place in both imports and exports, and has held that position ever since except for an occasional year. The following ratios will give roughly the relative standing of New York, Boston, and Philadelphia respectively. By 1815, they stood 2–1–1. Ten years later, the ratio was 3–1–1. In 1841, they stood 7–2–1; in 1851, 10–2–1; and in 1860, 20–3–1. By 1860, Baltimore was on a par with Philadelphia, while New Orleans was ahead of Boston and Philadelphia combined. . . .

The narrative of the rivalry itself may be more clearly understood if the period between the War of 1812 and the Civil War is divided into four phases. The first, from 1815 to 1825, was New York's great decade. That port stole a march on its rivals by a series of brilliant innovations. The second phase, from the late 'twenties to the late 'thirties, saw the unsuccessful efforts of Philadelphia and Baltimore to divert the western trade by pushing communications over the mountains to the Ohio. The third phase, in the 'forties, found New York actually worried by Boston's success with railroads by land and Cunarders by sea. The fourth and final phase, overlapping the third and extending to the Civil War, saw the bitter resentment of the southerners at New York's profitable participation in their trade.

The first phase opened at New York immediately after the conclusion of peace in 1815. The time was propitious for development. For nearly a quarter of a century, the Anglo-French wars had produced hectic and abnormal conditions in American commerce. Unusually brisk and lucrative at first, it had finally ended in almost complete stagnation with embargo, nonintercourse, and war. With peace, there came an opportunity for a fresh start. New York, Boston, Philadelphia, and Baltimore were more evenly matched than they were ever to be again. The port which could adjust itself first to normal, peacetime trade would reap a rich harvest. England's factories had accumulated a huge surplus of cottons and woolens which called for a market even at sacrifice prices. The West was ready to pour its grain into the lap of the lucky port which would first open adequate communication. New York struck while the iron was hot. Its initiative at this juncture attracted to its magnificent port both the textiles and the grain. It drew the British manufactures with an attractive auction system and regular transatlantic packet service, while it extended its sphere of commercial influence in America by a net of coastwise lines and the Erie Canal. Commerce soon settled into regular channels leading to New York, and by the time the rival ports were aware of what was happening, they were faced with an accomplished fact. Historians have too often dismissed the rise of New York Port with the remark that upon the opening of the Erie Canal, New York became the leading seaport and largest city of the country. The canal has completely overshadowed New York's contemporary measures to develop its imports and its coastwise trade.

The British gave New York a lead over its rivals by selecting it as the dumping point for their surplus goods in 1815. Scarcely was peace declared when textile cargoes began to arrive in such quantities that the regular market was glutted. Goods were sold at auction for "whatever they would bring." Buyers flocked from all parts of the country to make the most of the opportunity. By the end of 1816, however, it seemed likely that the British would swing the bulk of their trade to fresher fields. New York was worried. Its auctioneers commissioned one of their number, Abraham Thompson, to propose to the governor a special form of auction legislation which, in Thompson's words, would "cause all the Atlantic cities to become tributary to New York." This was enacted in 1817, lowering the State auction duty to 1½ per cent on European goods. There was nothing novel in the idea of auctions themselves. There had been plenty of them in New York and the other ports for many years. Thompson explained the distinctive features of this New York system:

> Every piece of goods offered at auction should be positively sold, and to en-
> sure a sale, the duty should always be paid upon every article offered at auction.
> . . . The truth was, that both in Boston and Philadelphia, the free and absolute
> sale of goods by auction was not encouraged. (It did not appear to be understood.)
> In Philadelphia, goods were allowed to be offered, and withdrawn, free from
> state duty, and the purchaser went to the auction rooms of that city with no
> certainty of making his purchases. He was not certain that the goods would be
> sold to the highest bidder.

This device was successful in holding at New York the flood of British manufactures which had come there as a temporary measure in 1815. Dealers from far and wide continued to replenish their stocks in the New York auction rooms, lured by the hope of bargains. The auctions were anathema to the American manufacturers and importers, who could not hope to compete with the fluctuations of the auction rooms. The general methods of textile importations, in fact, underwent a radical change. Formerly, American importing merchants at various ports had purchased from the British exporting merchants and sold to the dealers in their vicinity. Now, the regular importers were largely crowded out of the trade in British goods. The British manufacturers, through agents in Liverpool and New York, sold their wares at auction direct to the American jobbers or storekeepers. Time and again, the regular importers at New York and other ports joined the manufacturers in petitioning Congress to modify or abolish the system, claiming that it led to numerous abuses. There were some changes in 1838, but New York retained its commanding position in the importation of British goods. A large part of the material for the nation's wearing apparel entered the country through the port of New York, forming the largest single item in the nation's imports. This particular trade in British manufactures gave New York its longest lead over its rivals. The tremendous volume offset the rather small commissions collected on such items. The British consuls, realizing New York's importance as a dumping ground for England's Industrial Revolution, referred to it time and again as "the greatest foreign emporium of British commerce."

Closely linked with the auction system was New York's development of the first line of American packets in 1817. The British Post Office at this time operated armed packet brigs between Falmouth and New York on a monthly service. These official packets carried mail and passengers but no freight, and their passages were lengthy and indirect. The bulk of the trade between European and American ports was carried at this time by "regular traders," which usually made two complete voyages each year—the so-called "spring" and "fall" sailings. Such "regular traders" carried passengers, mail, and freight not only for their owners but also for other merchants who chose to ship by them. The ships of the packet line (which was later called the Black Ball Line) rendered the same service as the regular traders, and in addition the most valuable service of a regular monthly sailing, rigorously maintained, on a specified day of each month. Three of the founders of this pioneer transatlantic line had come to New York about 1800 from the West Riding of Yorkshire as representatives of textile firms and received large shipments on their own packet ships, sending back cotton and other American staples in return. This packet service met with such success that by the end of 1822 there were four regular sailings a month between New York and Liverpool. A line of packets to Le Havre was also established in 1822, with a second line in 1823 and a line to London a year later. These sailing packets were for many years the crack ships of the Atlantic and their regularity gave New York the cream of the transatlantic passenger and freight business.

During the 'twenties, powerful shipping interests in New York also discovered the value of attracting the immigrant trade. This contributed to New York's greatness in at least a quantitative way. Such passenger service enabled the British to dump at New York not only their surplus textiles but also their surplus humanity. An ever-increasing proportion of the immigrants entering the country landed at New York. Many of them, particularly the Irish, tended to remain where they landed, thus increasing New York's primacy in population. By 1850, nearly half of New York's population was foreign born, more than half of the foreign born being Irish.

New York's third important step in its great decade was the development of the coastwise trade, in which its natural advantages have already been observed. "The coasting trade of the United States is great and New York ingrosses a very large proportion of it," wrote the British consul at Philadelphia in 1817. The New Yorkers, remarked Niles five years later, "will open a line anywhere it will pay," adding that they were determined that New York "shall become the place of arrival and departure of all who travel by land or water, inland, coastwise or from or to foreign countries." Long Island Sound and the Connecticut River were exploited so successfully that Boston claimed that it had even lost the trade of western Massachusetts to the New Yorkers. Lines were run down the New Jersey shore to New Brunswick, facilitating communication to the southward. There was a regular packet service to Charleston, and by 1816 a line was planned for New Orleans. Savannah and Mobile were also soon connected with New York by packets. Fulton's steamboat was of more use to New York than Fitch's had been to Philadelphia. By 1825, it was said that New York had 43 steamers, including 11 on the Sound and 4 running to the southward. The number of arrivals of coasting vessels was 3 or 4 times as great as the number arriving from foreign ports, and the volume of the trade may be judged from the fact that at one time New York's flour shipments to Boston alone were more than to all foreign ports. New York's sphere of commercial activity, originally limited to the Hudson Valley and to adjacent parts of Connecticut and New Jersey, was thus greatly increased.

It was enlarged even more widely by New York's fourth and most spectacular feat of the decade—the Erie Canal. This celebrated "ditch" has been so well advertised that it scarcely needs an introduction here. The idea of a canal from Albany to Lake Erie had been suggested even before the Revolution. In 1808 the New York legislature undertook the surveying of the route. De Witt Clinton led the fight to overcome the widespread skepticism and conservatism. On April 15, 1817, the very day on which the auction law was passed, the legislature undertook the 363-mile canal as a State project. It was finally completed on October 26, 1825. The great value of the Erie Canal lay, of course, in providing an easy outlet for the products of the West and a means for supplying that region with outside needs. Its influence was especially noticeable in the matter of flour. By 1822, when the middle section of the Canal was open for about 100 miles, New York passed Philadelphia as a flour market; by 1827 it had gained first place from Baltimore. It is worth noting, in view of the fact that the Erie Canal is often given sole credit for New York's rise, that the port's pre-eminence in imports has almost always been more marked than in exports, and that the combination of the auction system and packets had given New York commerce a decided boom several years before the Canal was opened.

At the end of its decade of activity it was quite evident that New York had achieved unusual success. It was becoming "the granary of the world, the emporium of commerce, the seat of manufactures, the focus of great monied operations, and the concentrating point of vast accumulating and disposable capital." Since commerce was the chief source of liquid capital in America at that time, it was natural that New York developed as the financial center of the country, with surplus capital for the promoting of further activity. It was estimated that the rest of the country probably constantly owed New York $50,000,000. The New York Custom House collected enough money in 1828 to pay all the running expenses of the national government, the remainder of the revenue going to pay off the debt. The prosperity of the city seemed to be general. It was reported in 1824 that "every vessel which is seaworthy is employed at New York, and that in the debtors' prison only four persons are confined." New York's commercial success was reflected in other fields. The British consul at Philadelphia twice remarked that at New York there was a greater opportunity "to obtain correct intelligence of passing events than at any other station in the United States—Washington not excepted." If we were making a study of the social history of New York we might find that the city's leadership in amusements arose from the demands of the tired business men from the provinces who flocked to the auctions. The New York merchants, having so successfully developed their foreign, coastal, and inland trade, were looking further afield. By 1825 they were even planning to furnish steamboat service on the Mediterranean and to dig a canal through Nicaragua!

It was evident during this same decade that New York's rivals had been caught napping. The comments of the British consuls stationed at the various ports furnish a more objective view of this situation than do those of the inhabitants of the rival cities. The consul at New York City reported in 1822 that "while the commerce of Boston, Philadelphia, Baltimore and the other principal ports has fallen off, that of New York has increased." The widespread slump in 1819 was reflected by the Baltimore consul who declared "the trade of this city was never more depressed, pecuniary embarrassment beyond anything ever before known, many failures, more expected, and no one knows who to trust." One year later Charleston began to show some signs of activity but, said the consul there, "these do not promise much." "There is a spirit of enterprize in the State of New York for improvements which has not been followed up by its neighbors," reported the Philadelphia consul, who went on to say that "at the same time there is in Philadelphia a manifest superiority as regards manufactures." As late as 1824, he remarked that the commerce of Philadelphia was "on the decline in all its branches. . . . Commercial men here seem to have lost all their accustomed enterprise."

The completion of the Erie Canal aroused the rivals from their lethargy. The middle twenties produced a prolific crop of editorials, speeches, prospectuses, and commission reports discussing ways and means of sharing in New York's surprising success. In some cases there was optimistic confidence that commerce could be diverted from New York; elsewhere there was a clamor for defensive measures to save the local trade that still remained. Not all were as generous in spirit as Hezekiah Niles of Baltimore who wrote: "The New Yorkers *deserve* success for their enterprise. There is a good spirit among the citizens to advance the business of New York. Let it be imitated—not envied." Whether the motive was emulation, envy, or fear, there was widespread conviction that something must be done and done quickly. Boston and Philadelphia had already started packet lines, but the opening of the Canal centered attention on the western front. The rivalry of the seaports thus became closely linked up with the development of the nation's transportation systems. [See table below.] Legislatures, cities, and individuals were ready to spend millions to divert the

PRINCIPAL EFFORTS TO LINK NORTHERN SEABOARD WITH THE WEST

Name	From	To	Length (miles)	Begun (year)	Finished (year)	Cost (millions)
Erie Canal	Albany	Buffalo	363	1817	1825	7
Pa. "Main Line" (canal & rail)	Philadelphia	Pittsburgh	395	1827	1835	14
Chesapeake & Ohio Canal	Georgetown	Cumberland	184	1828	1850	10
Baltimore & Ohio R.R.	Baltimore	Wheeling	379	1828	1852	20
7 roads (later N.Y. Central)	Albany	Buffalo	298	1830	1842	6
Western—Boston & Worcester R.R.	Boston	Albany	200	1832	1841	11
Erie R.R.	Piermont, N.Y.	Dunkirk, N.Y.	446	1836	1851	24
Hudson River R.R.	New York City	Albany	144	1847	1851	10
Pennsylvania R.R.	Philadelphia	Pittsburgh	331	1847	1852	25

golden stream from New York and to engage in any methods, fair or foul, to check the efforts of rival ports. The situation was complicated by the fact that just one month before the Erie Canal was finished, George Stephenson had run his pioneer locomotive over the Stockton & Darlington. The result was, as one consul reported, that the "rage for canals" became mixed up with the "Rail Road mania." Boston wisely rejected the idea of a canal to the West and bided its time for its successful railroad venture. What we might call the "second act" of the port rivalry centered in the efforts of Philadelphia and Baltimore to cross the Alleghenies to the Ohio River.

Philadelphia was alarmed by the situation. Its prestige, if not its prosperity, seemed to be at stake. In thirty years it had dropped from first to fourth place in volume of trade and it had lost to New York its old primacy in population. The fears were officially expressed that unless Pennsylvania "awakes to a true sense of her situation . . . she will be deprived of the sources of public prosperity . . . and instead of regaining the high commercial rank she once held, she will be driven even from her present station in the system of the Confederacy." Philadelphia scored a point against Baltimore in 1829 with the opening of the Chesapeake & Delaware Canal. This gave Philadelphia access to the southern coasting trade and to the Susquehanna, which empties halfway between the two cities. Philadelphia bungled its principal effort to rival the Erie Canal, however, by failing to appreciate the relative merits of canal and railroad. New York had been able to take the Alleghenies in flank, so a canal had served her purposes, but Philadelphia's route to Pittsburgh had to cross the mountains at 2,200 feet above sea level. Pennsylvania built a mongrel "main line" of alternate railroads and canals. This was opened in 1835, but the cost and difficulties of transportation over this mixed system did not make it a formidable rival of the Erie Canal, which had received a further stimulus from the opening of the Ohio Canal in 1832. For the same expenditure, Philadelphia might have built an all-rail route which could have done wonders. By the time Pennsylvania completed such a route in 1852, it was too late. Philadelphia not only failed to compete successfully for the trade of the West but it actually found its own territory invaded by its rivals. Baltimore pushed the Baltimore & Susquehanna to York, Pennsylvania, tapping one of the richest agricultural regions in the country, while New York ran the Delaware & Hudson Canal across to the Lackawanna mines to get its anthracite direct and to have an added market for its imports. Philadelphia gradually abandoned hope of more than moderate success in foreign commerce, contenting itself with manufactures and local trade.

Baltimore was more successful during the "second act." While Philadelphia was declining in relative commercial importance, Baltimore was "on the make." Its growth was surprisingly rapid. Little more than a hamlet in the colonial period, it ranked third in population by 1800. [See table below.] After the Revolution, it had begun to con-

POPULATION CHANGE (IN THOUSANDS) OF PRINCIPAL CITIES

	1790	1800	1810	1820	1830	1840	1850	1860
New York	33	60	96	123	202	312	515	1,174
Philadelphia	42	69	91	112	161	220	340	565
Baltimore	13	26	35	62	80	102	169	212
Boston	18	24	33	43	61	93	136	177
New Orleans	..	..	17	27	46	102	116	168

centrate the rich grain and tobacco trade of the Chesapeake region, up to that time widely scattered. An added boom came with the building of the Cumberland

Road, which for a time gave Baltimore the best position for trade with the West. Its fast little pre-clippers were active in commerce with the South and the West Indies, where Baltimore "Howard Street" flour had a high reputation. Baltimore was active for a while in developing the trade of the Susquehanna, but the opening of the Erie Canal shifted its main interest to the route up the Potomac and past Cumberland to the Ohio River at Wheeling. This is relatively level except for one short stretch where the Alleghenies rise even higher than on the Pennsylvania route. George Washington had been keenly interested in developing it as a natural pathway to the West but had sounded the warning that, if New York or Philadelphia should get into contact with the West first, there would be "the difficulty of diverting trade after connections are once formed." Baltimore was slower than Philadelphia in getting into action, but it acted more wisely. It realized that a railroad over its short route to the Ohio would be the best chance of beating the Erie Canal. On July 4, 1828, just a year after Pennsylvania had begun to dig the canals of its "main line," the Baltimore & Ohio Railroad was started. That same day, however, saw the beginning of the Chesapeake & Ohio Canal near Washington. Both were designed for that same route up the Potomac to Cumberland and over the mountains, so from the very outset the Baltimore & Ohio ran into the rivalry which was to hamper the whole course of its construction. Maryland supported both ventures, but Baltimore was more interested in its railroad. There were many fights among lawyers and laborers before the B & O secured the right to parallel the canal route up the Potomac. By 1835, it had reached Harper's Ferry and tapped the rich wheat fields of the Shenandoah. The railroad reached Cumberland, with its coal and iron deposits, by 1843. Then its progress over the mountains was delayed by Virginia, where Baltimore had been referred to as a "foreign port," and by Pennsylvania which fought the road, in the interest of its own, even to the extent of carrying the interesting "Wheeling Bridge Case" to the Supreme Court. It was not until the last days of 1852, just after three rival railroad lines had tapped the West, that the B & O finally reached Wheeling. In the meantime Baltimore had shown great energy in seaborne commerce, particularly to the southward where geographical conditions formed less of a handicap. From 1832 onward, Baltimore and Philadelphia ran neck and neck in exports, and by 1860 Baltimore's exports were so heavy that the two ports were practically equal in volume of trade. New York, however, had long ceased to be worried about them as rivals.

Its source of anxiety in the 'forties lay to the eastward. In the third phase of the rivalry, seagoing Boston enjoyed a monopoly of through railroad connection with the West. It had wisely abandoned the canal idea at the outset and by 1841 had opened its Western Railroad over the Berkshires to Albany. There it connected not only with the Erie Canal but also with a new series of seven railroads, roughly paralleling the Canal, leading to Buffalo. This new system, it was hoped, would accomplish two things for Boston. It might lure the Erie Canal traffic away from New York. It would in any case give Boston and the surrounding manufacturing region a cheaper supply of western products and an outlet for their products. Traffic on this future Boston & Albany increased all through the forties and the road paid good dividends.

For almost the only time in the whole period of the port rivalry, New York was definitely worried. Long overconfident in its Canal, it had neglected railroads. The enterprise which had characterized New York in its great decade seemed to have passed to its rivals. It had no direct connection with the West during the three or four months each year when the Hudson was frozen. It had, it is true, tried to obstruct Boston's new route to Buffalo. Its investors might take stock in Boston's railroads to Lowell and to Providence, but they would seldom subscribe to the Western line, which might hurt New York. The New York legislature tried to hamper the carrying of freight over the railroads parallel to the Erie Canal. But in constructive work, New York was deficient. The Erie Railroad, projected in 1835, was even then a matter of "delays and disappointments" and had progressed barely fifty miles ten years later. The Hudson River Railroad to Albany existed only on paper in 1845. Freeman Hunt sounded a warning to New York that year:

> The rapid increase of the city in population, weath, trade and commerce during the last fifteen or twenty years is attributable, for the most part, to the opening of the Erie Canal and other internal improvements. At the present moment, the tide of prosperity threatens to be checked by the superior enterprise of other cities on the seaboard, which are beginning to share in the advantages of those improvements, and thus to draw away much of the trade that flowed in this direction. Without great outlays of capital and enterprise, beyond what has already been made, New York must soon lose her proud pre-eminence among the cities of the Union, and add another example to the many the world has already seen, of the rapid decline of a commercial mart, by the operation of a decayed spirit of enterprise and successful competition in other places.

Boston was also threatening to steal the Canadian market from New York. The Canadians had watched the construction of New York's Erie and Champlain Canals with apprehension. A Quebec editor in 1821 had expressed indignation "that the bounty of nature, the finest navigable river in the world, should be rendered useless as an outlet to the sea, by works of art and artificial regulations." The completion of the Welland Canal in 1830, together with the improvements of St. Lawrence navigation, brought a large amount of trade to Quebec and to Montreal, which was created a separate port in 1832. Montreal gradually drew ahead of the older city, attracting most of the St. Lawrence imports, while Quebec still cleared more exports. The total volume of trade at the two ports was about equal to that of Philadelphia. By 1835 the British consul at New York was alarmed lest the United States ports should steal the cream of Canadian commerce during the winter months when the St. Lawrence was frozen. The designs of New York, Boston, and Portland were facilitated by the warehousing legislation passed by Congress in 1846. By 1850, Canada's import and export trade via the United States was nearly as great as the direct trade by sea. New York's canals had given it the original advantage in this field, but it was beaten by Boston and then by Portland. For once, geography favored New England. Boston in 1851 established direct rail communication with Montreal by way of Ogdensburg, New York.

Declining Boston's invitation to be present at the opening of this new road, Governor Hunt of New York wrote a letter, perhaps in a jesting spirit, which is interesting in connection with this port rivalry:

> We, the people of New York, claim to have some interest in the trade of the Great West, for which you are now reaching. Yet we have desired to act the part of friendly and generous neighbors toward you. We have seen you invading our soil, filling our valleys, boring our mountains at some points, levelling them at others, and turning your steam engines loose upon us to run up and down, roam-

ing at large throughout our borders. Indeed it has long been evident that you intended to ride over us in your efforts to entice away our western brethren. . . . I am somewhat curious to know at what point your next encroachments will begin. There are limits to human endurance and I must warn you to pause and take breath before making fresh tracks upon our territory. We have never desired to monopolize the Western trade. After yielding to you a share sufficient to satisfy any but an inordinate and grasping ambition, enough will remain for us.

But Boston did not limit its activities to the western front. It was natural that she should challenge New York also on the sea. Like Baltimore and Philadelphia, she had supported packet lines to Europe, but they had not accomplished much. The introduction of steam to transatlantic navigation, however, destroyed the pre-eminence of the old New York lines of sailing packets. In 1838 three rival English lines sent their steamships, the *Sirius, Great Western,* and *Royal William,* to New York. A year later Parliament subsidized with £60,000 a year the Cunard Line, which was to run from Liverpool via Halifax to Boston. While the new steamship lines to New York were meeting with reverses, the Cunarders, with their liberal government aid, were gaining first place on the transatlantic run. The Bostonians were so grateful that on the occasion of the freezing up of the harbor they sawed a seven-mile channel through the ice so that one of their first Cunard liners might sail on scheduled time.

If the New Yorkers were worried during the forties, the Bostonians were correspondingly confident. The British consul there referred in 1842 to the "superior situation of Boston in almost all matters of business, in comparison with New York, Philadelphia and other rival cities which are suffering under great commercial depression." The real cause for this, he continued, lay in "Boston's sound and wholesome currency, based on specie and steady principles of banking." The Bostonians pointed out that their commerce was really as profitable as New York's. The customs reports might show the latter's imports as three or four times those of Boston's, but it was necessary to look behind the figures. Three-quarters of New York's imports were on foreign account, simply yielding paltry commissions, while five-sixths of the Boston imports were on its own account, with much more lucrative profits. In New York the commission agents outnumbered the regular merchants two to one; in Boston it was just the reverse. Boston might send its cargoes from the Baltic, Mediterranean, and China to New York for sale but it, rather than New York, pocketed the principal profits. On top of all that, Massachusetts stood well ahead of New York in navigation and, as was remarked before, a large part of New York's ships and sailors came from the eastward.

The Massachusetts menace lasted throughout the forties. Then New York, roused from its lethargy, rallied with two railroads to the West and a virtual monopoly of the new government subsidizing of mail steamships. To compete with Parliament's support of Cunard, Congress determined in 1845 to back American competition in the field. New York received most of the subsidies, starting lines to Bremen, Le Havre, Havana, and Panama. Above all, it had the Collins Line to Liverpool. This line started in 1850 and, until the disasters to the *Arctic* and *Pacific,* temporarily put the Cunarders into the shade. The latter line had anticipated the Collins competition in 1848 by establishing direct service to New York, which gradually overshadowed its Boston run. By 1851 New York had its own Erie and Hudson River railroads completed, while three years later Portland, with its new Grand Trunk route, seduced the winter trade of Montreal away from Boston. That city had to abandon its hopes of equality with New York as a port, but it had made the most successful attempt of any of the rivals.

The fourth phase of the port rivalry, somewhat overlapping the third in time, saw the increasing discontent of the South with New York's domination of its commerce. New York was developing a new triangle, a figure as popular in our old commerce as in our modern fiction. It was carrying southern cotton to Europe, bringing the imports to New York, and finally shipping them to the South. It was also carrying cotton to the northern markets and shipping a considerable amount abroad from New York itself. In addition, it was advancing money to the planters and handling their business through the various stages. The steady accumulation of interest, commissions, freight charges, insurance premiums, and profits reached such a total, that, according to one estimate, New York was making forty cents profit on every dollar's worth of southern cotton it handled. "The South," declared one writer, "thus stands in the attitude of feeding from her own bosom a vast population of merchants, shipowners, capitalists, and others, who without the claims of her progeny, drink up the life-blood of her trade."

The southerners were particularly worried about the loss of their former direct import trade from Europe. Philadelphia's relative commercial decline was nothing compared with the slump in imports at the southern ports. In 1770, the colonies from Maryland south to Georgia had imported nearly half the goods brought into the country. In 1850, they imported only one-twentieth of the total. The actual value of their imports, moreover, had merely doubled in these eighty years, while New York's imports in that same period showed a fifty-fold increase. There had been occasional efforts to remedy the situation. Charleston had built its pioneer road to Hamburg at the very start of the railroad era. Early in 1837 it was planning a packet line to England and a railroad to Cincinnati. These, hopefully predicted the British consul there, promised to make Charleston's trade "second in importance to that of New York." In spite of these projects, the imports at Charleston fell off not only relatively but actually. In 1851, its exports amounted to 15 and its imports to only 2 millions. At New Orleans that year it was 54 millions against 12, while Mobile, the most extreme case, had exports of 18 millions with imports of less than half a million. The foreign commerce of the South was certainly passive, either because of the temperament of the people or because most of its capital was tied up in land and slaves.

The southerners endeavored to create a direct trade by means of conventions and resolutions. Feeling that the panic of 1837 would weaken New York, they held six commercial conventions within eighteen months. These culminated with a convention at Charleston in 1839, which drew up a lengthy report attacking New York's position in the southern trade. It was bad enough, the report said, to have a national tariff which discriminated against the South. In addition, "the direct trade, which was her own by every law of commerce and nature, and which should have grown and increased every year, grew less and less until it almost disappeared, being by this unpropitious policy transferred to the northern ports and people. . . . The importing merchants of the South became an almost extinct race, and her direct trade, once so great, flourishing and rich, dwindled down to insignificance." The report continued with a detailed analysis which attempted to prove that while the southern storekeeper might buy foreign goods more cheaply at the New York auctions than he could buy direct imports at Charleston, the latter would be much cheaper when one took into account the transportation from New York and other considerations. Though the European manufacturers and merchants showed an inclination to go halfway in developing a direct trade, nothing definite came from the movement. A second crop of commercial conventions, held annually during the fifties, was no more successful. Their tone was more belligerent than it had been in the late thirties. "So long as the Union lasts," wrote the editor of the *Charleston Mercury* in 1859, "Charleston and Savannah will be mere suburbs of New York and Boston. For our cities to be independent in trade, they must be independent politically of the North." The southern storekeepers, however, still made their annual pilgrimages to New York to replenish their stocks. One reason for failure of the direct trade movement seems to have been that the politicians dominated the conventions. "The leaders who were guides of the South," states one writer, "were parliamentarians rather than men of business. Their minds could conceive of the most wonderful enterprises, but they lacked the business acumen to carry them out. Even while their conventions were discussing ways and means, others reached for the prize and grasped it."

The matter of mail subsidies to steamship lines dragged the rivalry into Congress. Apparently there had been little opposition to the measure by the southerners when the original act was passed in 1845, but by 1852 the Senate committee on the Post Office favored the establishing of new lines from southern ports instead of more from New York. Five years later, Benjamin of Louisiana proposed in the Senate that any appropriations for New York lines should be matched dollar for dollar by grants for New Orleans. Some of the bitterest words in the rivalry of the ports were exchanged in the Senate debates of May 27 and June 9, 1858, over the renewal of the subsidy of the crippled Collins Line. "People get to thinking," declared one senator, "that there are no places in the world but New York and Liverpool. If you go to New York, they will tell you that it is the best place to buy at and to sell at, and they will make a sane man believe it." Cochrane of New York spoke in defense of his metropolis:

> I have listened with some degree of grief and surprise to opinions expressed in this House in deprecation of the favors claimed to be showered upon the locality which I in part represent. Sir, nothing which conduces to the advantage of the commerce of that great metropolis is or can be local in its nature; it is as important and general as commerce itself, universally absorbing . . . . Sir, it is nature and not art that constitutes the great emporium of trade. You might as well try to dip up and roll back Niagara with the hand as to turn aside the natural currents of commerce. New York enjoys her advantages, not by reason of the artificial influences of legislation, but because she sits enthroned, the queen of the seas. Into her lap flow the tides of commerce, because commerce follows the avenues and obeys the impulses of profit.

Jefferson Davis arose in rebuttal:

> He talks of New York as the queen of the seas. How does she happen to be queen of the seas? She has made the West tributary to her greatness. If she is, then, so much of a queen, how is it that she asks subsidies for her lines of steamers? . . . How are we to compete with New York lines of steamers when they get $300,000 for their lines and we do not get a dollar? . . . He says New York has natural advantages. Then let her look to her natural advantages, and not con-

tinually nauseate this House by the everlasting cry of give, give—demand of more, more. Let her be content with her natural advantages or grant unto others what she seeks for herself.

Davis probably realized even then that the deep purse and far-flung commerce of New York would be dangerous to the South in the impending crisis.

New York's prosperity on the eve of the Civil War was certainly enough to incite envy. Her lead over her rivals had increased steadily in spite of all they could do. By 1860 New York was handling two-thirds of all the nation's imports and one-third of its exports. The combined imports of Boston, Philadelphia, and Baltimore were less than New York's imports of textiles alone. Those 3 rivals together exported less grain and meat products than did New York, whose hold on the West had not been seriously affected by the Baltimore & Ohio, the Boston & Albany, and the Pennsylvania roads, all started with such high hopes. In fact, out of well over a thousand individual items distinguished in the customs reports, New York ranked first among the seaports in all except 7 articles of domestic export and 24 in importation.

Geographically, New York's influence was equally widespread. Boston still maintained its primacy in part of the Baltic and Mediterranean trade, but elsewhere around the world, New York stood first. Its well-traveled transatlantic track to Liverpool, Bremen, and Le Havre may seem prosaic compared with the path of the Massachusetts mariners past Java Head to Canton and the "Salem East Indies." But a ship from New York had blazed that route to the East, and the ships laden with Canton tea and Manila hemp set their course not for Boston Light but for Sandy Hook. So, too, did two-thirds of the clippers coming around the Horn from California. The ships on these various routes probably attracted the most attention as they came into New York, but the long procession through the Narrows included many lesser craft, some with coffee from Rio, some with hides from the Argentine and Africa, and others from still more remote corners of the world, wherever a cargo offered promise of a profit.

The various rivals on the Atlantic coast have since remained in about the same relative position that they held in 1860, but several new-comers on the Gulf and the Pacific coast have crowded in among them. Philadelphia has overtaken Boston, which, however, still ranks second in imports. Both have been passed by San Francisco, and are closely tied with Houston and Galveston. Baltimore stands still lower in the scale, for Seattle and Los Angeles have passed it, to say nothing of the Lake ports, Buffalo and Detroit. But far above them all, New York still stands as "the great commercial emporium of America." One has but to mention railroad differentials to hear from the rival cities the same disgruntled complaints that were made a century ago. That old competition of the American ports was, however, simply a semifinal round for New York. Not content with its national championship, it has finally overtaken London, Liverpool, and Hamburg and has gained first place among the seaports of the world.

Part III

POLITICS
IN JACKSONIAN
AMERICA

7 / Jacksonian Democracy and the Rise of the Nominating Convention

James Staton Chase

In the quarter century before Andrew Jackson came to power in 1829, American politics underwent important changes. The form and style of politics altered fundamentally. Whether or not Jackson originated or merely benefitted from these changes remains a point in dispute among historians. But all agree that by the late 1820's, egalitarianism became a permanent factor in American politics. Not only did more men exercise their right to vote, but the symbolic importance of the campaigns against property qualifications for the franchise and for officeholding contributed significantly to the demise of the old order. What has been aptly termed the age of "deference politics," in which the lower classes accepted the leadership of the rich and well-born as almost a matter of course, came to an end.

The new order demanded more modern forms of political organization and voter stimulation. Not only did strong national parties begin to appear, ending the Republican one-party reign, but such practices as outright electioneering by candidates (something previously frowned upon) and the frankly political use of government patronage occurred with increased frequency. The following article by James Staton Chase deals with the rise of one of the peculiarly effective organizational forms of the period, the nominating convention. Chase shows how this device could be used for the dual purpose of strengthening the party apparatus, while simultaneously providing the illusion of greater popular participation in the nominating process. The legislative and congressional nominating caucuses had acquired the stigma of aristocracy, and whatever their practical uses, they had to be abandoned because of the stigma. The convention proved an ideal substitute, one that party managers quickly utilized to strengthen their machines.

Mid-America, XLV (October 1963), 229–249. Reprinted by permission. Footnotes have been omitted.

For further reading: Chilton Williamson, *American Suffrage: From Property to Democracy, 1760–1860* (1960); William G. Morgan, "The Decline of the Congressional Nominating Caucus," *Tennessee Historical Quarterly,* XXIV (Fall 1965), 245–255; Michael Wallace, "Changing Concepts of Party in the United States: New York, 1815–1828," *American Historical Review,* LXXIV (December 1968), 453–491.

Through most of the ninteenth century and part of the twentieth the organizational structure of the major American political parties could be easily described by reference to the convention system. Delegates to county, district, state and national conventions, presumably chosen by the grass roots membership of the sponsoring party, met shortly before each election to nominate candidates for the offices under their particular jurisdiction. They also performed the important task of appointing the party's central committees, which in turn controlled the electioneering machinery, and passed resolutions defining the party's position on public questions. Thus, during much of our history, the party could be equated roughly, and absolutely from the standpoint of the law, with the convention. And even though today local and state conventions have given way to the party primary for nominating candidates, they still retain in many states their function of choosing the state and county central committees and enunciating the platform. Of course the greatest hold-over of the system is the national convention, which continues effectively to reduce the voters' choice for president to two names. In view of the past and present importance of the convention system, an investigation of the causes responsible for its initial adoption would, hopefully, shed considerable light on party development in the United States.

Although the nominating convention was by no means the creation of the age of Jackson, since the first one of record had been held by the Pennsylvania Antifederalists in 1788, it was during the ten years from 1822 to 1832 that the ascendency of the convention over other nominating methods was fully established. Significantly, the same period also witnessed the final break-up of the old Republican Party and the emergence of a revitalized two party system. Lacking an unquestioned favorite to succeed James Monroe or a viable opposition party, the superficial national solidarity of the Republicans shattered under the impact of personal and sectional rivalries prior to the election of 1824. The bitter factionalism of state politics in the Era of Good Feelings became the regimen for the nation as was indicated by the presence of four major contenders to replace Monroe, all carrying valid Republican credentials. John Quincy Adams' election by the House of Representatives in 1825 began the slow but steady polarization of politics around the standards of the new President and his principal opponent, Andrew Jackson. This dualism, re-enforced after 1828 by Henry Clay's taking over the defeated Adams party, was seemingly marred by the rise of the Antimasons, but they functioned in national politics more as an anti-Clay faction within the larger force opposed to Jackson than as an independent third party.

Revival of organized competition for the presidency and lesser offices greatly stimulated the spread of the convention because of its superior ability, as will be shown, to concentrate large numbers of voters behind a single candidate or slate of candi-

dates. No party can successfully vie for power unless it can prevent the fragmenta-
tion of its own supporters and this elementary fact was not lost on the rising class
of professional politicians faced with conducting campaigns among a numerous and
geographically diffused citizenry who were empowered to fill an incomprehensibly large
number of public offices. In the interval between the elections of 1824 and 1832
the parties and their factions used the convention with increasing frequency at the
state and local levels. When the Antimasons, National Republicans and Democrats
nominated their presidential and vice-presidential candidates in national conventions
before the 1832 election, it signaled the predominance of the system in a majority
of the states. The switch from self-announcement, mass meetings and legislative
caucuses took place gradually and unevenly. Different parties adopted the convention at different times for a variety of reasons, and its first use in a county, city,
district or state often depended on a number of unique circumstances.

But in spite of the complexities of such glacial change, the maze of electoral
divisions and the welter of competing groups which obscure the transition process,
two relatively comprehensive reasons for the convention's growing popularity stand
out. The convention prevailed over other nominating methods because it best satisfied
the ideological demands of the Jacksonian era that government should be responsive to the people's direction. It also solved the technical difficulties of conducting politics in a democracy. In the nominating convention, idea and experience
harmonized; a popular theory created an institution which passed the pragmatic test
imposed by politicians.

The convention's appeal to the democratic instincts of the age is rooted in the
historical significance of the word itself. The convention concept derived from the
English constitutional struggles of the seventeenth century when two irregularly appointed parliamentary bodies (in 1660 and 1689) settled the government of the
kingdom by pretending to express the will of the whole nation. During and immediately after the American Revolution this usage proved invaluable as both the
former colonies and the nation needed a means compatible with the natural rights
philosophy of government for writing and ratifying their new constitutions. Implicit
in the convention was the idea that its delegates incarnated the sovereignty of the
people; its sessions enacted the social compact. Private associations, such as the
great religious denominations, whose large and scattered memberships made primary meetings impracticable, also employed the convention after 1776 as the
supreme governing body of their organizations. These conventions possessed, on a
more modest scale, the same sovereign functions as the state constitutional conventions and the delegates proceeded on the assumption that their authority sprang
directly from the rank and file.

Another user of the convention, one particularly active in the age of Jackson,
was the pressure group engaged in securing the passage of a favored bill through
Congress or a state legislature. Often representing narrow special interests, the lob-
byists endeavored through the holding of conventions to give the appearance of
speaking for a majority of the voters. The *Richmond Compiler* observed in 1831
that "This seems to be the age of Conventions—not for forming Constitutions, but
for shaping the measures of the People." To marshal the support of "the People"
and impress legislators, public meetings appointed delegates to conventions where,
obedient to their instructions, they endorsed resolutions requesting the people's legal
representatives to build some internal improvement, raise the tariff (or lower it),

encourage observance of the Sabbath, promote temperance, stimulate trade or revise the militia laws. In 1827, well before the Antimasons held the first national nominating convention, friends of domestic manufactures met in a national convention and in 1831 both protectionists and free traders convoked similar assemblies. By the time party warfare was sufficiently developed to warrant its use, convention theory and practice were well known and the politicians had an instrument fashioned to their needs.

The convention satisfied the great political touchstone of Jacksonian democracy—popular sovereignty. Every public question was to be decided by the people acting through their chosen agents; elected officials were considered, even by themselves, mere agents reflecting the voters' desires. Any other course constituted a dangerous tendency toward aristocracy, or even monarchy, and many legislative careers were ruined by the exercise of independent judgment. The defeat of the Western congressmen who voted for Adams in 1825 was an object lesson to legislators who thought of flouting their constituents' instructions. "The cry of aristocracy takes with certain folks," wrote John C. Spencer to a fellow Antimason, Thurlow Weed, in 1831, "and there is no way to meet it but to clamor louder than our adversaries. . . ." Few remarks typify the demands of Jacksonian politics with greater precision, for in their efforts to prove their devotion to democracy politicians were forever clamoring louder than their adversaries. Belief in democracy was the price of being allowed to compete for office, and the convention, composed of delegates directly commissioned by the entire membership to make a nomination for a particular office, certified that the party met this requirement. In a day when polls of steamboat passengers, grand juries and militia musters were accepted as indices of public opinion the ability to stage conventions was the best available evidence that the party's nominee enjoyed wide approval.

Party conventions, in keeping with the intrinsic meaning of their underlying concept, usually affected to speak for all the voters, not just a segment of them. After 1816, when the Federalist party had all but vanished, the Republican nomination was ordinarily the equivalent of election and as long as this situation lasted party conventions could reasonably claim to speak for the whole community. If the Republicans split each faction declared its nominee the people's choice. After a regular Republican district convention in New York failed to renominate Representative John W. Taylor in 1824, the delegates supporting him withdrew and "proceeded to nominate and form a ticket to suit *themselves the sovereign people.*" In 1830 Clay's Kentucky friends, calling themselves National Republicans, decided to nominate him for president in a state convention called solely for that purpose. They solemnly announced that the proposed convention would speak for all the state's citizens:

> Issuing directly from the people, it will bear and proclaim their genuine sentiments. Essentially popular in its character and composition, it will command respect and secure confidence by its plain straightforward movement, without intrigue, without the corrupt agency of caucus management, without any other motive of origin but the spontaneous impulse of the people themselves.

Opponents' conventions, on the other hand, were notoriously unrepresentative, consisting of office holders, drunks, lawyers or, worst of all, Federalists. The Working Men's party of Boston broke with the Republican organization in that city because, it contended, the regular nominating conventions while "assuming to be the organs of public opinion" were notorious for the fact "that the mass of the people were neither consulted nor represented. . . ." But except when making odious comparisons convention participants seldom indulged in theorizing. The revival of the two party system after 1825, spurred by the rivalry between Adams and Jackson, caused the convention to be accepted more and more as the voice of the party only, although the casual nature of party membership meant that a careful distinction was not always observed. The convention was democracy applied to party government.

Homage to popular sovereignty made it necessary to determine the people's choice of candidates, but the consultation did more than implement a theory; it paid off in the mundane task of winning elections. The convention not only united large numbers of voters in support of a candidate but it created an organization capable of waging a successful campaign in his behalf. For this reason it had a special appeal to the new breed of managers generated by the rise of national parties in a period of increasing political participation by the masses. These were men vitally interested in ways of holding amorphous groups together within a single organization which they could wield to hoist themselves into power.

To nominate a candidate for Congress in the Middle Atlantic states, where the convention system was first and most fully developed, necessitated mass meetings in each township for the election of delegates to a county convention. The delegates from the townships met and appointed delegates to a district convention which nominated the candidate. All of the not inconsiderable number of persons who participated in these meetings and conventions, or who identified themselves with the sponsoring party, were expected to abide by the decision of the majority and support the nominee. The observation made by the politician-historian Jabez D. Hammond on the binding nature of the caucus applied with equal force to the convention:

> If you suspect [he wrote] that the determination will be so preposterous that you cannot in conscience support it, then you ought on no account to become one of its members. To try your chance in a caucus, and then because your wishes are not gratified, to attempt to defeat the result of the deliberations of your friends, strikes me as a palpable violation of honor and good faith.

The convention's democratic form reduced the chances of intraparty competition for the same office even more than the caucus since, unlike the caucus, every geographic and electoral division of government was directly consulted in the choice of nominees. Unless some clear infraction of the democratic process had transpired in the election of delegates there could be little justification (other than thwarted ambition) for a losing aspirant to declare himself an independent candidate.

Even if the disappointed candidate for the nomination were insensitive to the moral obligation of abiding by the majority's decision, the fact that the convention nominee wore the tag of the "regular" candidate discouraged revolt, because the party's label exerted a powerful influence over the voters. An independent candidate favorable to Jackson stood little chance of winning although he might siphon enough votes from the regular nominee to elect the Adams man. Certainly, the greatest threat to victory at the polls lay in the possibility that the party's vote would be split among several candidates while the opposing forces were solidly behind one man or ticket. By providing a device whereby the full weight of the party could be brought to bear in an election, yet one which allowed for a democratic selection and gave scope to individual ambition, the convention helped perpetuate the two party system.

The convention's efficacy in concentrating the support of a party was not lost on office seekers. One New York politician wrote in 1823:

> I am one of six candidates in this District to fill Mr. Rochesters [sic.] place in Congress, if I succeed in getting the nomination by the District convention (which will shortly take place) I will be elected, but should I fail in geting [sic.] the nomination, I shall in all probability be a member of our next [state] legislature. . . .

In the West, where the convention developed slowly, the lack of party cohesion was a severe handicap, particularly to the anti-Jackson forces. Henry Clay in 1829 wrote to a congressional candidate in Kentucky that he

> should be most happy to learn that any mode had been adopted to concentrate on yourself, or any other friend, the votes of those who concur in their political principles. Can no such mode be fallen upon? Is it not yet practicable to convene persons from all parts of the district?

A Clay newspaper, noting the disastrous results of plural nominations against an undivided enemy, denounced self-nomination as "anti-republican." An easterner in 1832 asked Clay plaintively if

> our Western brethren [could] be sufficiently innoculated with the caucus [i.e., convention] virus to enforce a wholesome political action among them at future elections. In New York the most jarring personal feelings are made to yield to the furtherance of a great publick purpose.

Another advantage enjoyed by the convention nominee over his independent rivals was the campaign organization incidental to the system. Every township meeting, held to elect county convention delegates, appointed a committee of correspondence which, in turn, provided for committees of vigilance for the school districts and polling places. Each county, district and state convention also appointed similar committees and on this network, reaching down to the smallest subdivision of government, rested the burden of winning the battle on election day. Whatever their official duties these committees operated as command posts, coordinating operations against the adversary. They distributed campaign literature, printed ballots, won over the undecided voter, conducted friends to the place of election and compiled lists of the voters within their jurisdiction, indicating how each would vote, and forwarded them on to the state committee. No maverick could possibly match this organization produced as a by-product of the convention and placed at the disposal of its nominee.

The propaganda value of the convention was immense. Meetings of county and district conventions were reported not only in the local papers but in friendly sheets throughout the state. A state convention for the nomination of governor and lieutenant governor provided copy for several months. The state central committee issued the call to arms, inviting the counties to send delegates to a state convention. Townships meetings then chose delegates to county conventions which appointed delegations to the state convention and, if state senators or congressmen were to be elected, also appointed delegates to a district convention. Invariably, each of these meetings adopted resolutions and sometimes an address expressing the delegates' opinions on local, state and national issues, all duly reported in the newspapers. Legislators were instructed how to vote, complimented or censured for past behavior, and the delegates might even recommend persons to the governor or president as fit for appointive office. Finally, after the preliminary conventions had run their course the state convention met. The importance of its task made it an object of great interest and even opposition newspapers took notice, if only to scorn and ridicule.

Almost without exception the proceedings and the address of state conventions were published as pamphlets for dissemination as campaign literature. Ten thousand was an average issue and in Pennsylvania many copies were printed in German while in Louisiana a large portion were ordered in French. Publication of the proceedings and the address, in addition to their duplication in newspaper columns, put them into the hands of voters who might never attend a partisan rally. Although these closely printed documents would not be considered effective propaganda today, campaign managers in the 1820's eagerly sought them for distribution.

Apart from the benefits of unity, organization and propaganda, the bringing together of like-minded men from scattered communities, many meeting one another for the first time, kindled enthusiasm and fortified party morale. A correspondent of the Rochester *Anti-Masonic Enquirer* exultingly reported his party's state convention:

> It is a *glorious* Convention. Lobbies, galleries, and all, are overflowing. I am proud of Anti-Masonry. What principles beyond all estimation brings honest plain farmers from the extreme bounds of the State, at the dead of winter. The masons and the Regency look pale, at the view, and in the anticipation, with which such a Convention must present to their minds.

A discouraged Adams supporter in New York looked forward to the state convention in hopes that "An exhibition such as might and I trust will be made at the convention will create a new feeling among us—and provide the happiest results in the River Counties." In the meetings of delegates, as Alexis de Tocqueville observed in 1831, "men have the opportunity of seeing one another; means of execution are combined; and opinions are maintained with a warmth and energy that written language can never attain." Every convention was a party rally whose enthusiasm was transmitted to the faithful back home.

The convention's advantages become quite clear when the meeting of the Adams state convention of Virginia in 1828 is examined closely. Called for the purpose of designating presidential electors, it was the first state convention held in the Old Dominion and its influence extended far beyond the Commonwealth's boundaries.

Despite Adams' efforts at reconciling Virginia to his election by appointing its citizens to important positions, a preponderant majority of the old Republican party, under the leadership of the so-called Richmond Junto, showed unmistakable Jackson proclivities. So hopeless did the President's prospects for carrying Virginia appear that for two and one-half years following his inauguration in 1825 his partisans made no serious effort to organize a state-wide party in his behalf. Somewhat tardily, in the summer of 1827, important administration leaders attempted to give the President at least a fighting chance to carry the state. The critical feature of their plan was a scheme for holding a state convention. The proposal was publicly unveiled in James H. Pleasants' *Richmond Whig* and through its columns popularized among the demoralized friends of the administration who enthusiastically endorsed it as a means of rallying their forces.

Virginians in 1827 bitterly debated the question of revising the state constitution. For years the large, western counties had been complaining about discrimination in favor of the slaveholding eastern counties in the apportionment of legislative seats. A nominating convention would identify the Adams party with the cause of constitutional reform by emphasizing the reliance of the Junto on a legislative caucus to nominate Jackson electors. Like the legislature, the caucus, the Junto's traditional method for nominating its candidates, was controlled by the planter class. A convention would proclaim the democracy of the Adams party while capitalizing on the general unpopularity of caucus nominations, particularly keen in the underrepresented counties. "The plan of a Convention of Anti-Jackson delegates at Richmond," wrote an Adams supporter, would be "a strong political weapon, which the opposite party will dread exceedingly. It will give confidence at home and abroad, and neutralize the influence of the small counties in the Legislature." Once the convention was proposed newspapers friendly to Adams began denouncing the caucus as "an absolute despotism," "an unclean thing" and "a self-constituted body . . . undertaking to dictate the choice of a President. . . ." Through a convention the people of Virginia "for the first time" would be "given an opportunity to form their *own* Ticket, and thus practically to vote for the President of their choice. . . ."

With Clay's blessing a public meeting in September at Fredericksburg, presided over by the Secretary of State's good friend, Francis T. Brooke, officially invited those opposed to Jackson to participate in a convention at Richmond in early January, 1828. The invitation stressed the contrast between a convention, emanating from the people, and the caucus, imposing its will upon the voters. Dozens of counties subsequently appointed delegates at special public meetings which also passed resolutions praising the administration (condemning Jackson and the caucus), and appointed committees of correspondence. For the first time Adams had a local organization in Virginia, created by the necessity of choosing delegates to a central convention "which like the throbbing of the heart" communicated "its pulsations to the distant extremities."

Foe, as well as friend, felt the effects of the scheduled meeting. Congressman William C. Rivers tried to minimize its impact by reassuring a New York colleague, Guilian C. Verplanck, that the Adamsites "may, no doubt, have a convention, (as indeed what party is so poor as not to have it's [sic.] convention, in these times), but Virginia will be Virginia no more, if she can ever be propitiated towards Adams & Clay. Fear not, then, for us." The *Richmond Enquirer,* joined by a chorus of other Jackson papers, attacked the convention by pointing out the small percentage of voters who attended the county meetings. Simultaneously, it defended caucus nominations as far more representative of the people's thinking since the Adams convention acted on dictation from Washington while the legislators mirrored the opinion of their constituents.

Nevertheless, it became clear that the Adams maneuver was operating effectively on the public mind. Several Jacksonian meetings, "aware that strong objections exist on the part of many persons" to caucus nominations, specifically authorized their legislators to nominate electors. One meeting even suggested the caucus be abandoned entirely in deference to popular prejudice. When the caucus met in December it delayed nominating electors so that special delegates could be chosen in those counties whose legislators were not members of the Jackson party. This call for a mixed caucus, a transitional step from the pure legislative caucus to the delegated convention, was the Junto's first cognizance of the inequities of caucus nominations. By allowing the counties represented in the legislature by Adams men to elect delegates the Jackson managers invested the caucus with the appearance of greater democracy, a reaction to the appeal of the Adams convention. In setting a date for a subsequent meeting the December caucus nervously avoided convening on the same day as their adversaries "lest it might by possibility be misinterpreted into the slightest alarm about the result of the Adams Convention." Instead, it would meet a week later, on January 14, "so that the antidote should be administered so soon after the poison as possible. . . . By assembling on the 14th, we shall meet at once this Mammouth convention, which is now agglomerating itself and threatening like an Avelanche, to fall upon our heads."

Beginning on January 8, the anti-Jackson delegates met for four days in the state capitol building. The *Enquirer* admitted that the list of delegates "embraced some of the ablest men in Virginia. . . ." An electoral ticket headed by James Madison and James Monroe was nominated which the *Whig* understandably called "the most powerful ever formed by any state of this union." A state central committee was appointed. The convention address, written by Chapman Johnson, received lavish praise and 30,000 copies were ordered printed; each member of a county committee was allotted a portion. Other copies of the address were apparently printed outside Virginia and found effective use throughout the nation. Congressman Henry Storrs of New York thought the convention had a decidedly good effect on the whole Adams campaign. The Jackson press, including the *Albany Argus,* conspired to ridicule the convention address, but William L. Marcy wrote with some concern to Azariah C. Flagg (both members of the Jackson-oriented Albany Regency) that Silas Wright's district was flooded with it. From faraway Missouri came news that "the ingenious, and persuasive ability of the address, of the Virginia administration convention, has done some good here."

The fact that Virginia, reputed to be overwhelmingly opposed to the nationalist administration, could muster such a formidable convention heartened the Adams party everywhere. Within Virginia it briefly revived the spirits of the flagging cause. Unquestionably, the convention gave Adams what he previously lacked in the Old Dominion—an organization capable of waging a campaign, one extending into almost every county, but responding to central direction. It also united the party behind a single slate of electors. The convention's effect was hardly less important for members of the Junto, since it compelled them to abandon the pure legislative caucus for the mixed variety and thus move one step closer to the adoption of the convention.

The caucus was best suited for nominating candidates to state offices .although occasionally used for local ones. The convention, however, was easily adaptable to the smallest unit of government, provided there were subordinate divisions which could elect delegates. State conventions were usually composed of representatives from the counties, but congressional districts were sometimes used. District conventions, for the nomination of congressmen or state senators, also relied upon the counties. Township public meetings elected delegates to county conventions in the Northern and Northwestern states while election districts (within each county) in Maryland and the hundreds in Delaware served the purpose in those two states. The South had no such convenient county subdivision, accounting at least in part for that section's slowness in developing a full-fledged convention system, and a county-wide public meeting substituted for a county convention in selecting the delegates to infrequent state conventions.

Where the system was well established procedural rules governing the entire convention process were developed to regulate personal and factional struggles for control of the organization thereby assuring the competitors of fair play. The most important consideration was the size of the delegations from each subordinate unit. A recognized standard of apportionment prevented the partisans of one candidate from packing the convention and negated the advantage a few towns or counties derived from their proximity to the meeting site. For state conventions the apportionment prescribed for representation in the lower house of the legislature was the general rule; for the county conventions each township ordinarily elected an equal number of delegates. However, these provisions were not always rigidly enforced and this lack of form reflected the convention's role as a party rally when observance of quotas seemed less important than a full house. Each party bragged about its "numerously attended" conventions, deriding the sparse numbers their opponents mustered, and turned nomination meetings into a numbers game. "I think if we can get a meeting to nominate our County Ticket of 400 or 500 Persons," one New York politician wrote, "it will have a good effect upon the election. It will do more to stimulate our Friends to activity than anything else. . . ." The advantages of sheer bulk over adherence to a quota were succinctly stated in a letter to Congressman Taylor in 1828:

> On reflection I think we have erred in confining the number of Delegates to our county convention to 3 from a town—1st Because we should endeavor to make our convention as numerous & respectable as possible 2nd Because we cannot by thus restricting the number gratify all who might be ambitious of acting in the convention. However numerous the meeting, order & a judicious selection of candidates may be secured by appointing a subcommittee—Would it not be well therefore to leave the towns free to choose as many on their Delegations as they please & for the central committee to request the attendance of as many (whether Delegates or not) as may find it convenient to be present.

Authority to call a convention could be vested in a number of agents. The most common was the central committee appointed by the last convention and explicitly authorized to call its successor. Sometimes a convention set the date for a future meeting and legislative caucuses might summon the state convention, but any instrumentality could serve—public meetings, newspapers, self-appointed individuals or anonymous circulars. Taverns and churches housed most county conventions although a private home might suffice. State conventions frequently convened in the state capital and sat in a legislative chamber, but if called for a town other than the capital a court house, town hall, church, or privately owned hall fulfilled the need. County or district conventions normally required one day to dispatch their business while state conventions, often involving considerable travel for the delegates, usually lasted longer and as many as five days might expire, but two or three days was general.

No matter what the type of convention, the organization and agenda were essentially the same; yet no two were exactly alike, for the parts of the convention mechanism were interchangeable. Its basic form was that of a public meeting: a group of citizens assembled to express their opinions on public questions by adopting resolutions. To this simple formula the convention added refinements in keeping with its representative character.

A temporary chairman, usually a member of the central committee, opened the convention. Permanent officers, at least a president and secretary and frequently plural vice-presidents and secretaries (up to four of each), were elected, followed by an invocation, after which the delegates submitted their certificates of election to a credentials committee for approval. Honorary members, including distinguished guests or visitors from other states, next gained admission. Occasionally, spectators were· absorbed as delegates, although this privilege might be restricted to persons from places not represented by regularly elected delegates. A delegate would then move that a committee to draft resolutions and an address "expressive of the sentiments of this convention" be appointed. Following a recess the resolutions committee reported, the nomination of candidates more than likely included among the resolutions. Possibly, the nominees were selected by a separate committee composed of one or more delegates from each unit represented. Naming a candidate by having the delegates ballot occurred only rarely. Sometimes the business and agenda were prescribed by a special committee appointed after the election of permanent officers. The work of the convention might be divided among half a dozen or more special committees on finance, local organization, publication of the proceedings, candidate notification and the like. Convention sessions were consumed in debating committee reports sandwiched between endless orations.

That important decisions, including the selection of the nominee, were made by committees rather than by all the delegates perhaps indicates the convention was not truly democratic in its operation. The large number of delegates made a deliberative assembly virtually impossible and any attempt to make it into one would have invited chaos and encouraged personal and geographic rivalries. Party leaders dreaded an eruption into violence and newspaper accounts of convention proceedings emphasized their "respectable" character. The delegates were only asked to approve a choice made by the inner circle of party leaders. This power elite, if they held any official position in the party at all, were members of the corresponding committee. Thurlow Weed, a member of the Antimasonic state central committee of New York, alleged that

> during the five or six years following the organization of a party opposed to Freemasonry, what was known as the Morgan Committee . . . enjoyed its full and uninterrupted confidence. Candidates for all important offices were indicated by our committee, neither of whom would accept office themselves.

The process of candidate selection could be, as Weed recalled, disarmingly simple. When the man he selected as the nominee of an Antimasonic congressional convention declined the honor a substitute was required on short notice:

> The difficulty of this task was not diminished by the circumstances that I was compelled to leave Buffalo in the stage at nine o'clock the next morning to attend a senatorial convention in Batavia. Rising at daylight, and on my way to another hotel to find the Chautauqua and Niagara delegates, I encountered Ebenezer F. Norton in the street, and inquired whether he would accept an Anti-Masonic nomination for Congress. His reply was, "I cannot afford to decline any nomination for Congress. . . ." I found Colonel Flemming and Mr. Boughton, of Niagara, and Messers. Mixer and Plumb of Chautauqua, and hastily arranged with them the nomination of Mr. Norton. . . .

The power of decisions was not always formalized in a committee; anyone possessing the confidence of the party might exercise it. In New York and Virginia where the Regency and Junto, the most notorious examples of centralized management, held sway control was not restricted to the central committee. The Albany Regency took a keen interest in local nominations, its members making trips over the state to effect the arrangements. Azariah C. Flagg earned the sobriquet of "the Traveling Regency" for his efforts. When the Regency decided to support Jackson for the presidency in 1828 it was able surreptitiously to arrange for the nomination of Jackson men to the legislature, much to the alarm of the Adams men within the Regency-dominated party. But this type of influence was not unique and its presence may be assumed even though the evidence for it seems slight. Elections were too important to leave to chance. "I have neither the time nor inclination at present," penned a disgusted observer, "to give you a detail of all the paltry intrigues & machinations, which were resorted to, to effect the nomination of some Gentlemen."

The belief that politicians are bent on personal gain at the public's expense persisted throughout the history of the early republic. Whether or not the convention system masked an undemocratic contrivance to carry office-seekers with greater ease to the public trough cannot be answered categorically. Some viewed the convention as a retreat rather than an advance toward greater democracy. A holder of this position unburdened himself to Congressman Taylor:

> I most heartily congratulate you on your triumph over the caucus [i.e., convention] candidate (Mr. Palmer). Not that I have anything personal against Mr. P. but I think it all important that *this taking out of the hands of the people* the choice of their rulers should have an end. At last fall's election in the State of Ohio several of the Congressional districts had 6 candidates some 5 and some 4, but few that had only 2. The choices were completely the people's without any forestalling or attempt at it. Many important reforms that we need can never take place until choices of our legislators shall come direct from the people.

An affirmative answer assumes that talk of programs and principals is humbug to win over guileless voters. The organization provided by the convention could be, and often was, used for narrow and selfish ends, but the system at least allowed for popular participation in the choice of candidates. The convention was effective only if it reflected public opinion, only if its nominee won elections. If "order & a judicious selection of candidates" were usually achieved by a few professionals, the delegates could, and occasionally did, reject the designated nominee. It cannot be assumed that the delegates or the rank and file disagreed with their leaders simply because the vast majority of conventions accepted decisions handed down from above. The price of party victory, desired by leader and led, was discipline.

It is not clear though that the convention was more democratic than the legislative caucus, public meeting, or self-announcement which it replaced, as none of them operated in an opinion vacuum. Congressmen and state legislators were elected directly by the people and were answerable to them if their nomination proved unpopular. Furthermore, caucus members were guided in making their nominations by all the devices for measuring public opinion available to convention delegates— letters, newspapers and public meetings. Conventions could be manipulated no less than caucuses. Legislators were presumed corruptible because they stood to gain patronage and influence if their candidate succeeded, but was this less true of convention delegates? Admittedly, most of them could not expect great rewards if only because they were so numerous, yet this did not necessarily prevent them from being bought. Only the price may have been cheaper. The greatest test for all nominating methods came on election day when the voters registered their approval or disapproval of the candidates preselected for their suffrage.

The triumph of the convention was achieved without a protracted struggle between its advocates and those of other techniques. Self-announcement continued as an acceptable way of running for office, albeit unsuccessfully, and the public meeting, incorporated into the convention system, lost none of its significance. Even the conflict between the convention and the caucus has been overdrawn. Whether anti-caucus rhetoric ever won many votes for convention-nominated candidates is doubtful. In no election does the legislative or congressional caucus appear to have been the deciding issue. The caucus did not disappear after it ceased making nominations, and it remained an important institution for formulating party policy. Ironically, the first National Republican and Democratic national conventions were both called by legislative caucuses. The convention owed its ascendancy to its superior ability to meet the theoretical and practical requirements of democratic politics: candidates nominated by conventions, wrapped in the mantle of popular sovereignty and backed by an organization no independent could equal, were likely to be elected.

8 / New Perspectives on Jacksonian Politics

Richard P. McCormick

Traditionally, historians have refrained from using statistics and the quantifying method partly because they have felt strongly the need to maintain the prominence of the literary aspect of their craft. However, in the past few years the lure of percentiles and computers has proved increasingly difficult to ignore, and some historians have accepted the new methodological challenges that the quantifying techniques impose and the opportunities they offer for broadening our knowledge of the past.

One of the most successful of these efforts is the following article by Richard P. McCormick. McCormick probed beneath the surface of the fact that in 1828 Jackson won the Presidency with a vote considerably larger than the vote of 4 years previously, and he showed that although Jackson's election had great significance, it was not the "popular revolution" at the polls that several generations of historians had described. McCormick tabulated the presidential vote in the Jacksonian period (up to 1844) in terms of percentages of eligible voters who participated, a much more meaningful figure than the raw vote alone. When it first appeared, this article upset many previously held notions about the Jacksonian "explosion at the polls." Yet the student should not lose sight of the fact, as clearly demonstrated by McCormick's data, that the Jacksonian campaign of 1828 did begin to "nationalize" voting —it brought the percentage of eligible voters participating in a presidential election up to the levels of previous percentage highs in many state elections.

For further reading: Richard P. McCormick, *The Second American Party System: Party Formation in the Jacksonian Period* (1966); Robert V. Remini, *The Election of Andrew Jackson* (1964); Arthur M. Schlesinger, Jr., *The Age of Jackson* (1946).

American Historical Review, LXV (January 1960), 288–301. Reprinted by permission. Footnotes have been omitted except where they are necessary for an understanding of the text.

The historical phenomenon that we have come to call Jacksonian democracy has long engaged the attention of American political historians, and never more insistently than in the past decade. From the time of Parton and Bancroft to the present day scholars have recognized that a profoundly significant change took place in the climate of politics simultaneously with the appearance of Andrew Jackson on the presidential scene. They have sensed that a full understanding of the nature of that change might enable them to dissolve some of the mysteries that envelop the operation of the American democratic process. With such a challenging goal before them, they have pursued their investigations with uncommon intensity and with a keen awareness of the contemporary relevance of their findings.

A cursory view of the vast body of historical writing on this subject suggests that scholars in the field have been largely preoccupied with attempts to define the content of Jacksonian democracy and identify the influences that shaped it. What did Jacksonian democracy represent, and what groups, classes, or sections gave it its distinctive character? The answers that have been given to these central questions have been—to put it succinctly—bewildering in their variety. The discriminating student, seeking the essential core of Jacksonianism, may make a choice among urban workingmen, southern planters, venturous conservatives, farm-bred *nouveaux riches*, western frontiersmen, frustrated entrepreneurs, or yeoman farmers. Various as are these interpretations of the motivating elements that constituted the true Jacksonians, the characterizations of the programmatic features of Jacksonian democracy are correspondingly diverse. Probably the reasonable observer will content himself with the conclusion that many influences were at work and that latitudinarianism prevailed among the Jacksonian faithful.

In contrast with the controversy that persists over these aspects of Jacksonian democracy, there has been little dissent from the judgment that "the 1830's saw the triumph in American politics of that democracy which has remained pre-eminently the distinguishing feature of our society." The consensus would seem to be that with the emergence of Jackson, the political pulse of the nation quickened. The electorate, long dormant or excluded from the polls by suffrage barriers, now became fired with unprecedented political excitement. The result was a bursting forth of democratic energies, evidenced by a marked upward surge in voting. Beard in his colorful fashion gave expression to the common viewpoint when he asserted that "the roaring flood of the new democracy was . . . by 1824 foaming perilously near the crest. . . ." Schlesinger, with his allusion to the "immense popular vote" received by Jackson in 1824, creates a similar image. The Old Hero's victory in 1828 has been hailed as the consequence of a "mighty democratic uprising."

That a "new democracy, ignorant, impulsive, irrational" entered the arena of politics in the Jackson era has become one of the few unchallenged "facts" in an otherwise controversial field. Differences of opinion occur only when attempts are made to account for the remarkable increase in the size of the active electorate. The commonest explanations have emphasized the assertion by the common man of his newly won political privileges, the democratic influences that arose out of the western frontier, or the magnetic attractiveness of Jackson as a candidate capable of appealing with singular effectiveness to the backwoods hunter, the plain farmer, the urban workingman, and the southern planter.

Probably because the image of "mighty democratic uprising" has been so universally agreed upon, there has been virtually no effort made to describe precisely the dimensions of the "uprising." Inquiry into this aspect of Jacksonian democracy has been discouraged by a common misconception regarding voter behavior before 1824. As the authors of one of our most recent and best textbooks put it: "In the years from the beginning of the government to 1824, a period for which we have no reliable election statistics, only small numbers of citizens seemed to have bothered to go to the polls." Actually, abundant data on pre-1824 elections is available, and it indicates a far higher rate of voting than has been realized. Only by taking this data into consideration can voting behavior after 1824 be placed in proper perspective.

The question of whether there was indeed a "mighty democratic uprising" during the Jackson era is certainly crucial in any analysis of the political character of Jacksonian democracy. More broadly, however, we need to know the degree to which potential voters participated in elections before, during, and after the period of Jackson's presidency as well as the conditions that apparently influenced the rate of voting. Only when such factors have been analyzed can we arrive at firm conclusions with respect to the dimensions of the political changes that we associate with Jacksonian democracy. Obviously in studying voter participation we are dealing with but one aspect of a large problem, and the limitations imposed by such a restrictive focus should be apparent.

In measuring the magnitude of the vote in the Jackson elections it is hardly significant to use the total popular vote cast throughout the nation. A comparison of the total vote cast in 1812, for example, when in eight of the seventeen states electors were chosen by the legislature, with the vote in 1832, when every state except South Carolina chose its electors by popular vote, has limited meaning. Neither is it revealing to compare the total vote in 1824 with that in 1832 without taking into consideration the population increase during the interval. The shift from the legislative choice of electors to their election by popular vote, together with the steady population growth, obviously swelled the presidential vote. But the problem to be investigated is whether the Jackson elections brought voters to the polls in such enlarged or unprecedented proportions as to indicate that a "new democracy" had burst upon the political scene.

The most practicable method for measuring the degree to which voters participated in elections over a period of time is to relate the number of votes cast to the number of potential voters. Although there is no way of calculating precisely how many eligible voters there were in any state at a given time, the evidence at hand demonstrates that with the exception of Rhode Island, Virginia, and Louisiana the potential electorate after 1824 was roughly equivalent to the adult white male population.[1] A meaningful way of expressing the rate of voter participation, then, is to state it in terms of the percentage of the adult white males actually voting. This index can be employed to measure the variations that occurred in voter participation over a period of time and in both national and state elections. Consequently a basis is provided for comparing the rate of voting in the Jackson elections with other presidential elections before and after his regime as well as with state elections.

[1] The only states in which property qualifications were a factor in restricting voting in presidential elections after 1824 were Virginia and Rhode Island. New York did not completely abolish property qualifications until 1826, but the reform of 1821 had resulted in virtually free suffrage. In Louisiana, where voters were required to be taxpayers, the nature of the system of taxation operated to confine the suffrage to perhaps half of the adult white males. . . . To be perfectly accurate, estimates of the size of the potential electorate would have to take into account such factors as citizenship and residence requirements and, in certain states, the eligibility of Negro voters.

Using this approach it is possible, first of all, to ascertain whether or not voter participation rose markedly in the three presidential elections in which Jackson was a candidate. Did voter participation in these elections so far exceed the peak participation in the pre-1824 elections as to suggest that a mighty democratic uprising was taking place? The accompanying data (Table I) provide an answer to this basic question.

In the 1824 election not a single one of the eighteen states in which the electors were chosen by popular vote attained the percentage of voter participation that had been reached before 1824. Prior to that critical election, fifteen of those eighteen

TABLE I

PERCENTAGES OF ADULT WHITE MALES VOTING IN ELECTIONS

State	Highest Known % AWM Voting before 1824		Presidential Elections					
	Year	% AWM	1824	1828	1832	1836	1840	1844
Maine	1812ᵍ	62.0	18.9	42.7	66.2*	37.4	82.2	67.5
New Hampshire	1814ᵍ	80.8	16.8	76.5	74.2	38.2	86.4*	65.6
Vermont	1812ᵍ	79.9	—	55.8	50.0	52.5	74.0	65.7
Massachusetts	1812ᵏ	67.4	29.1	25.7	39.3	45.1	66.4	59.3
Rhode Island	1812ᵍ	49.4	12.4	18.0	22.4	24.1	33.2	39.8
Connecticut	1819¹	54.4	14.9	27.1	45.9	52.3	75.7*	76.1
New York	1810ᵍ	41.5	—	70.4*	72.1	60.2	77.7	73.6
New Jersey	1808ᵖ	71.8	31.1	70.9	69.0	69.3	80.4*	81.6
Pennsylvania	1808ᵍ	71.5	19.6	56.6	52.7	53.1	77.4*	75.5
Delaware	1804ᵍ	81.9	—	—	67.0	69.4	82.8*	85.0
Maryland	1820¹	69.0	53.7	76.2*	55.6	67.5	84.6	80.3
Virginia	1800ᵖ	25.9	11.5	27.6*	30.8	35.1	54.6	54.5
North Carolina	1823ᶜ	70.0#	42.2	56.8	31.7	52.9	83.1*	79.1
Georgia	1812ᶜ	62.3	—	35.9	33.0	64.9*	88.9	94.0
Kentucky	1820ᵍ	74.4	25.3	70.7	73.9	61.1	74.3	80.3*
Tennessee	1817ᵏ	80.0	26.8	49.8	28.8	55.2	89.6*	89.6
Louisiana	1812ᵍ	34.2	—	36.3*	24.4	19.2	39.4	44.7
Alabama	1819ᵍ	96.7	52.1	53.6	33.3	65.0	89.8	82.7
Mississippi	1823ᵏ	79.8	41.6	56.6	32.8	62.8	88.2*	89.7
Ohio	1822ᵏ	46.5	34.8	75.8*	73.8	75.5	84.5	83.6
Indiana	1822ᵍ	52.4	37.5	68.3*	61.8	70.1	86.0	84.9
Illinois	1822ᵏ	55.8	24.2	51.9	45.6	43.7	85.9*	76.3
Missouri	1820ᵏ	71.9	20.1	54.3	40.8	35.6	74.0*	74.7
Arkansas	—	—	—	—	—	35.0	86.4	68.8
Michigan	—	—	—	—	—	35.7	84.9	79.3
National Average			26.5	56.3	54.9	55.2	78.0	74.9

* Exceeded pre-1824 high   # Estimate based on incomplete returns
ᵍ Gubernatorial election   ᶜ Congressional election
ᵖ Presidential election   ¹ Election of legislature

states had recorded votes in excess of 50 per cent of their adult white male population, but in 1824 only two states—Maryland and Alabama—exceeded this modest mark. The average rate of voter participation in the election was 26.5 per cent. This hardly fits the image of the "roaring flood of the new democracy . . . foaming perilously near the crest. . . ."

There would seem to be persuasive evidence that in 1828 the common man flocked to the polls in unprecedented numbers, for the proportion of adult white males voting soared to 56.3 per cent, more than double the 1824 figure. But this outpouring shrinks in magnitude when we observe that in only six of the twenty-two states involved were new highs in voter participation established. In three of these— Maryland, Virginia, and Louisiana—the recorded gain was inconsiderable, and in a fourth—New York—the bulk of the increase might be attributed to changes that had been made in suffrage qualifications as recently as 1821 and 1826. Six states went over the 70 per cent mark, whereas ten had bettered that performance before 1824. Instead of a "mighty democratic uprising" there was in 1828 a voter turnout that approached—but in only a few instances matched or exceeded—the maximum levels that had been attained before the Jackson era.

The advance that was registered in 1828 did not carry forward to 1832. Despite the fact that Jackson was probably at the peak of his personal popularity, that he was engaged in a campaign that was presumably to decide issues of great magnitude, and that in the opinion of some authorities a "well-developed two-party system on a national scale" had been established, there was a slight decline in voter participation. The average for the twenty-three states participating in the presidential contest was 54.9 per cent. In fifteen states a smaller percentage of the adult white males went to the polls in 1832 than in 1828. Only five states bettered their pre-1824 highs. Again the conclusion would be that it was essentially the pre-1824 electorate—diminished in most states and augmented in a few—that voted in 1832. Thus, after three Jackson elections, sixteen states had not achieved the proportions of voter participation that they had reached before 1824. The "new democracy" had not yet made its appearance.[2]

A comparison of the Jackson elections with earlier presidential contests is of some interest. Such comparisons have little validity before 1808 because few states chose electors by popular vote, and for certain of those states the complete returns are not available. In 1816 and 1820 there was so little opposition to Monroe that the voter interest was negligible. The most relevant elections, therefore, are those of 1808 and 1812. The accompanying table (Table II) gives the percentages of adult white males voting in 1808 and 1812 in those states for which full returns could be found, together with the comparable percentages for the elections of 1824 and 1828. In 1824 only one state—Ohio—surpassed the highs established in either 1808 or 1812. Four more joined this list in 1828—Virginia, Maryland, Pennsylvania, and New Hampshire—although the margin in the last case was so small as to be inconsequential. The most significant conclusion to be drawn from this admittedly limited and unrepresentative data is that in those states where there was a vigorous two-party contest in 1808 and 1812 the vote was relatively high. Conversely, where there was little or no contest in 1824 or 1828, the vote was low.

[2] It may be suggested that it is invalid to compare voter participation in each state in the presidential contests of 1824, 1828, and 1832 with the highs, rather than the average participation in each state prior to 1824. The object of the comparison is to ascertain whether the Jackson elections brought voters to the polls in unprecedented numbers, as has so often been asserted. Moreover, it is hardly feasible to compare average participation in elections before and after 1824 in many states because of the changes that were made in the methods of electing governors and presidential electors or—in certain instances—because the state had only recently entered the Union. . . .

TABLE II

PERCENTAGES OF ADULT WHITE MALES VOTING IN PRESIDENTIAL ELECTIONS

State	1808	1812	1824	1828
Maine	Legis.	50.0	18.9	42.7
New Hampshire	62.1	75.4	16.8	76.5
Massachusetts	Legis.	51.4	29.1	25.7
Rhode Island	37.4	37.7	12.4	18.0
New Jersey	71.8	Legis.	31.1	70.9
Pennsylvania	34.7	45.5	19.6	56.6
Maryland	48.4	56.5	53.7	76.2
Virginia	17.7	17.8	11.5	27.6
Ohio	12.8	20.0	34.8	75.8

When an examination is made of voting in other than presidential elections prior to 1824, the inaccuracy of the impression that "only small numbers of citizens" went to the polls becomes apparent. Because of the almost automatic succession of the members of the "Virginia dynasty" and the early deterioration of the national two-party system that had seemed to be developing around 1800, presidential elections did not arouse voter interest as much as did those for governor, state legislators, or even members of Congress. In such elections at the state level the "common man" was stimulated by local factors to cast his vote, and he frequently responded in higher proportions than he did to the later stimulus provided by Jackson.

The average voter participation for all the states in 1828 was 56.3 per cent. Before 1824 fifteen of the twenty-two states had surpassed that percentage. Among other things, this means that the 1828 election failed to bring to the polls the proportion of the electorate that had voted on occasion in previous elections. There was, in other words, a high potential vote that was frequently realized in state elections but which did not materialize in presidential elections. The unsupported assumption that the common man was either apathetic or debarred from voting by suffrage barriers before 1824 is untenable in the light of this evidence.

In state after state (see Table I) gubernatorial elections attracted 70 per cent or more of the adult white males to the polls. Among the notable highs recorded were Delaware with 81.9 per cent in 1804, New Hampshire with 80.8 per cent in 1814, Tennessee with 80.0 per cent in 1817, Vermont with 79.9 per cent in 1812, Mississippi with 79.8 per cent in 1823, and Alabama with a highly improbable 96.7 per cent in its first gubernatorial contest in 1819. There is reason to believe that in some states, at least, the voter participation in the election of state legislators was even higher than in gubernatorial elections. Because of the virtual impossibility of securing county-by-county or district-by-district returns for such elections, this hypothesis is difficult to verify.

Down to this point the voter turnout in the Jackson elections has been compared with that in elections held prior to 1824. Now it becomes appropriate to inquire whether during the period 1824 through 1832 voters turned out in greater proportions for the three presidential contests than they did for the contemporary state elections. If, indeed, this "new democracy" bore some special relationship to Andrew Jackson or to his policies, it might be anticipated that interest in the elections in which he was the central figure would stimulate greater voter participation than gubernatorial contests, in which he was at most a remote factor.

Actually, the election returns show fairly conclusively that throughout the eight-year period the electorate continued to participate more extensively in state elections than in those involving the presidency. Between 1824 and 1832 there were fifty regular gubernatorial elections in the states that chose their electors by popular vote. In only sixteen of these fifty instances did the vote for President surpass the corresponding vote for governor. In Rhode Island, Delaware, Tennessee, Kentucky, Illinois, Mississippi, Missouri, and Georgia the vote for governor consistently exceeded that for President. Only in Connecticut was the reverse true. Viewed from this perspective, too, the remarkable feature of the vote in the Jackson elections is not its immensity but rather its smallness.

Finally, the Jackson elections may be compared with subsequent presidential elections. Once Jackson had retired to the Hermitage, and figures of less dramatic proportions took up the contest for the presidency, did voter participation rise or fall? This question can be answered by observing the percentage of adult white males who voted in each state in the presidential elections of 1836 through 1844 (Table I). Voter participation in the 1836 election remained near the level that had been established in 1828 and 1832, with 55.2 per cent of the adult white males voting. Only five states registered percentages in excess of their pre-1824 highs. But in 1840 the "new democracy" made its appearance with explosive suddenness.

In a surge to the polls that has rarely, if ever, been exceeded in any presidential election, four out of five (78.0 per cent) of the adult white males cast their votes for Harrison or Van Buren. This new electorate was greater than that of the Jackson period by more than 40 per cent. In all but five states—Vermont, Massachusetts, Rhode Island, Kentucky, and Alabama—the peaks of voter participation reached before 1824 were passed. Fourteen of the twenty-five states involved set record highs for voting that were not to be broken throughout the remainder of the ante bellum period. Now, at last, the common man—or at least the man who previously had not been sufficiently aroused to vote in presidential elections—cast his weight into the political balance. This "Tippecanoe democracy," if such a label is permissible, was of a different order of magnitude from the Jacksonian democracy. The elections in which Jackson figured brought to the polls only those men who were accustomed to voting in state or national elections, except in a very few states. The Tippecanoe canvass witnessed an extraordinary expansion of the size of the presidential electorate far beyond previous dimensions. It was in 1840, then, that the "roaring flood of the new democracy" reached its crest. And it engulfed the Jacksonians.

The flood receded only slightly in 1844, when 74.9 per cent of the estimated potential electorate went to the polls. Indeed, nine states attained their record highs for the period. In 1848 and 1852 there was a general downward trend in voter participation, followed by a modest upswing in 1856 and 1860. But the level of voter activity remained well above that of the Jackson elections. The conclusion to be drawn is that the "mighty democratic uprising" came after the period of Jackson's presidency.

Now that the quantitative dimensions of Jacksonian democracy as a political phenomenon have been delineated and brought into some appropriate perspective, certain questions still remain to be answered. Granted that the Jacksonian electorate—as revealed by the comparisons that have been set forth—was not really very large, how account for the fact that voter participation doubled between the elections of 1824 and 1828? It is true that the total vote soared from around 359,000 to

1,155,400 and that the percentage of voter participation more than doubled. Traditionally, students of the Jackson period have been impressed by this steep increase in voting and by way of explanation have identified the causal factors as the reduction of suffrage qualifications, the democratic influence of the West, or the personal magnetism of Jackson. The validity of each of these hypotheses needs to be reexamined.

In no one of the states in which electors were chosen by popular vote was any significant change made in suffrage qualifications between 1824 and 1828. Subsequently, severe restrictions were maintained in Rhode Island until 1842, when some liberalization was effected, and in Virginia down to 1850. In Louisiana, where the payment of a tax was a requirement, the character of the state tax system apparently operated to restrict the suffrage at least as late as 1845. Thus with the three exceptions noted, the elimination of suffrage barriers was hardly a factor in producing an enlarged electorate during the Jackson and post-Jackson periods. Furthermore, all but a few states had extended the privilege of voting either to all male taxpayers or to all adult male citizens by 1810. After Connecticut eliminated its property qualification in 1818, Massachusetts in 1821, and New York in 1821 and 1826, only Rhode Island, Virginia, and Louisiana were left on the list of "restrictionist" states. Neither Jackson's victory nor the increased vote in 1828 can be attributed to the presence at the polls of a newly enfranchised mass of voters.

Similarly, it does not appear that the western states led the way in voter participation. Prior to 1824, for example, Ohio, Indiana, and Illinois had never brought to the polls as much as 60 per cent of their adult white males. Most of the eastern states had surpassed that level by considerable margins. In the election of 1828 six states registered votes in excess of 70 per cent of their adult white male populations. They were in order of rank: New Hampshire, Maryland, Ohio, New Jersey, Kentucky, and New York. The six leaders in 1832 were: New Hampshire, Kentucky, Ohio, New York, New Jersey, and Delaware. It will be obvious that the West, however that region may be defined, was not leading the "mighty democratic uprising." Western influences, then, do not explain the increased vote in 1828.

There remains to be considered the factor of Jackson's personal popularity. Did Jackson, the popular hero, attract voters to the polls in unprecedented proportions? The comparisons that have already been made between the Jackson elections and other elections—state and national—before, during, and after his presidency would suggest a negative answer to the question. Granted that a majority of the voters in 1828 favored Jackson, it is not evident that his partisans stormed the polls any more enthusiastically than did the Adams men. Of the six highest states in voter participation in 1828, three favored Adams and three were for Jackson, which could be interpreted to mean that the convinced Adams supporters turned out no less zealously for their man than did the ardent Jacksonians. When Van Buren replaced Jackson in 1836, the voting average increased slightly over 1832. And, as has been demonstrated, the real manifestation of the "new democracy" came not in 1828 but in 1840.

The most satisfactory explanation for the increase in voter participation between 1824 and 1828 is a simple and obvious one. During the long reign of the Virginia dynasty, interest in presidential elections dwindled. In 1816 and 1820 there had been no contest. The somewhat fortuitous termination of the Virginia succession in 1824 and the failure of the congressional caucus to solve the problem of leadership succession threw the choice of a President upon the electorate. But popular interest was dampened by the confusion of choice presented by the multiplicity of candidates, by the disintegration of the old national parties, by the fact that in most states one or another of the candidates was so overwhelmingly popular as to forestall any semblance of a contest, and possibly by the realization that the election would ultimately be decided by the House of Representatives. By 1828 the situation had altered. There were but two candidates in the field, each of whom had substantial sectional backing. A clear-cut contest impended, and the voters became sufficiently aroused to go to the polls in moderate numbers.

One final question remains. Why was the vote in the Jackson elections relatively low when compared with previous and contemporary state elections and with presidential votes after 1840? The answer, in brief, is that in most states either Jackson or his opponent had such a one-sided advantage that the result was a foregone conclusion. Consequently there was little incentive for the voters to go to the polls.

This factor can be evaluated in fairly specific quantitative terms. If the percentage of the total vote secured by each candidate in each state in the election of 1828 is calculated, the difference between the percentages can be used as an index of the closeness, or one-sidedness, of the contest. In Illinois, for example, Jackson received 67 per cent of the total vote and Adams, 33; the difference—thirty-four points—represents the margin between the candidates. The average difference between the candidates, taking all the states together, was thirty-six points. Expressed another way this would mean that in the average state the winning candidate received more than twice the vote of the loser. Actually, this was the case in thirteen of the twenty-two states (see Table III). Such a wide margin virtually placed these states in the "no contest" category.

A remarkably close correlation existed between the size of the voter turnout and the relative closeness of the contest. The six states previously listed as having the greatest voter participation in 1828 were among the seven states with the smallest margin of difference between the candidates. The exception was Louisiana, where restrictions on the suffrage curtailed the vote. Even in this instance, however, it is significant that voter participation in Louisiana reached a record high. In those states, then, where there was a close balance of political forces the vote was large, and conversely, where the contest was very one-sided, the vote was low.

Most of the states in 1828 were so strongly partial to one or another of the candidates that they can best be characterized as one-party states. Adams encountered little opposition in New England, except in New Hampshire, and Jackson met with hardly any resistance in the South. It was chiefly in the middle states and the older West that the real battle was waged. With the removal of Adams from the scene after 1828, New England became less of a one-party section, but the South remained extremely one-sided. Consequently it is not surprising that voter participation in 1832 failed even to match that of 1828.

Here, certainly, is a factor of crucial importance in explaining the dimensions of the voter turnout in the Jackson elections. National parties were still in a rudimentary condition and were highly unbalanced from state to state. Indeed, a two-party system scarcely could be said to exist in more than half of the states until after 1832. Where opposing parties had been formed to contest the election, the vote was large, but where no parties, or only one, took the field, the vote was low. By 1840, fairly well-balanced parties had been organized in virtually every state. In only three states did the margin between Harrison and Van Buren exceed

TABLE III

DIFFERENTIAL BETWEEN PERCENTAGES OF TOTAL VOTE OBTAINED BY
MAJOR PRESIDENTIAL CANDIDATES, 1828–1844

State	1828	1832	1836	1840	1844
Maine	20	10	20	1	13
New Hampshire	7	13	50	11	19
Vermont	50	10	20	29	18
Massachusetts	66	30	9	16	12
Rhode Island	50	14	6	23	20
Connecticut	50	20	1	11	5
New York	2	4	9	4	1
New Jersey	4	1	1	4	1
Pennsylvania	33	16	4	1	2
Delaware	—	2	6	10	3
Maryland	2	1	7	8	5
Virginia	38	50	13	1	6
North Carolina	47	70	6	15	5
Georgia	94	100	4	12	4
Kentucky	1	9	6	29	8
Tennessee	90	90	16	11	1
Louisiana	6	38	3	19	3
Alabama	80	100	11	9	18
Mississippi	60	77	2	7	13
Ohio	3	3	4	9	2
Indiana	13	34	12	12	2
Illinois	34	37	10	2	12
Missouri	41	32	21	14	17
Arkansas	—	—	28	13	26
Michigan	—	—	9	4	6
Average Differential	36	36	11	11	9

twenty points, and the average for all the states was only eleven points. The
result was generally high voter participation.[3]

When Jacksonian democracy is viewed from the perspectives employed in this analysis, its political dimensions in so far as they relate to the behavior of the electorate
can be described with some precision. None of the Jackson elections involved a
"mighty democratic uprising" in the sense that voters were drawn to the polls in
unprecedented proportions. When compared with the peak participation recorded
for each state before 1824, or with contemporaneous gubernatorial elections, or most
particularly with the vast outpouring of the electorate in 1840, voter participation
in the Jackson elections was unimpressive. The key to the relatively low presidential vote would seem to be the extreme political imbalance that existed in most
states as between the Jacksonians and their opponents. Associated with this imbalance was the immature development of national parties in connection with the
Jackson elections. As balanced, organized parties subsequently made their appearance

[3] Careful analysis of the data in Table III will suggest that there were three fairly distinct
stages in the emergence of a nationally balancd two-party system. Balanced parties appeared first
in the middle states between 1824 and 1828. New England remained essentially a one-party
section until after Adams had passed from the scene; then competing parties appeared. In the
South and the newer West, a one-party dominance continued until divisions arose over who
should succeed Jackson. Sectional loyalties to favorite sons obviously exerted a determining influence on presidential politics, and consequently on party formation, in the Jackson years.

from state to state, and voters were stimulated by the prospect of a genuine contest, a marked rise in voter participation occurred. Such conditions did not prevail generally across the nation until 1840, and then at last the "mighty democratic uprising" took place.

9 / The Presidential Election of 1832 in New Hampshire

Donald B. Cole

The second statistical article, by Donald B. Cole, is a microanalysis of a single state, New Hampshire, during one presidential election. Whereas McCormick concentrates upon voter participation and extends his analysis over a 20-year period, Cole does not compare the New Hampshire vote of 1832 with previous or subsequent elections. Instead he attempts to isolate socioeconomic factors existing in the state at that time, factors that may inferentially but logically be interpreted as determinants of voting behavior. This is admittedly treacherous ground for the political scientist as well as for the historian. Not only are usable socioeconomic factors difficult to isolate, but the "correlation game" requires much sophistication if it is not to become sophistry, or what Lee Benson calls establishing "spurious relationships."

Nevertheless, when strongly correlative patterns, such as Cole has found, can be matched against the votes of small units such as townships, the results allow for something more than guesswork about class and party within that constituency. However, they do not permit generalizations applied to the country as a whole.

For further reading: Lee Benson, *The Concept of Jacksonian Democracy: New York As a Test Case* (1961); Frank Otto Gatell, "Money and Party in Jacksonian America: A Quantitative Look at New York City's Men of Quality," *Political Science Quarterly*, LXXXII (June 1967), 235–252.

Historical New Hampshire, XXI (Winter 1966), 33–50. Reprinted through the courtesy of the New Hampshire Historical Society. Footnotes have been omitted.

Historians have long been concerned with identifying the eastern Jacksonian Democrats. Frederick Jackson Turner in *The United States 1830–1850* contended that they "found their rural following among the less prosperous towns"; while Arthur Schlesinger, Jr., in the *Age of Jackson,* called particular attention to the urban worker wing of the eastern Democratic Party. From Turner and Schlesinger developed the now traditional thesis that the eastern "Democracy found its strength among the poorer people," especially the farmers in the "hilly mountainous districts" and the factory workers in the cities.

Recently this traditional view of Jacksonian Democracy has been under attack. In *The Concept of Jacksonian Democracy: New York as a Test Case,* Lee Benson rejects the Turner-Schlesinger thesis. By studying the presidential vote in New York State in 1844, he demonstrates that the rank order of Democratic vote in the cities as well as towns did not coincide exactly with any ranking of economic status. The very poorest communities were not necessarily those with the strongest Democratic vote. Benson goes on to reject the entire concept of Jacksonian Democracy, preferring to call the period the "Age of Egalitarianism" instead of the "Age of Jackson."

The purpose of this article is not to debate the concept of Jacksonian democracy, nor to detract from Benson's excellent book, which has forced scholars to take a fresh look at the entire period. Instead the purpose is to test the Turner-Schlesinger thesis again—particularly for rural areas—by studying the presidential election returns for 1832 in New Hampshire. The election of 1832, coming at the height of Jacksonian Democracy when the bank war was hot, provides a better test of the traditional thesis than the election of 1844, which turned on expansion and slavery rather than on economic issues. Since historians have paid more attention to the urban vote than the rural vote during the Jackson years, the study of a farm state like New Hampshire seems appropriate.

New Hampshire in 1832 had been electing Democratic governors and Congressmen by wide margins since 1829. The Democratic machine, called the Concord Regency, was the envy of Democrats across the land. The leading Jacksonians were Isaac Hill, the small hunchbacked publisher of *The New Hampshire Patriot,* who served in the United States Senate and the kitchen cabinet, and urbane Levi Woodbury, Secretary of the Navy. In the election of 1832 Jackson received over 25,000 votes to barely 19,000 for Henry Clay. Since all males 21 and over were eligible to vote and since about 75% actually turned out, the statistics provided a reliable guide to voting patterns of the state. Sufficient economic, geographic, and religious data exist to correlate with the election returns.

The 44,000 votes in New Hampshire came from a population of 270,000, living in 209 towns. Three-quarters of the people depended on farming for their living. They farmed irregular fields spread over ridges and valleys; lived in rambling wooden farmhouses; shopped at cheerful general stores; attended town meetings once a year. They identified readily with their town, less easily with the state, and had difficulty comprehending the nation. The Jackson program with its emphasis on local authority appealed to them.

The state consisted of seven geographic regions: in the south reading from east to west were the seacoast, the southeast uplands, the Merrimack Valley, the southwest uplands, and the Connecticut Valley; in the north the lake region and the White

Mountains. Population was most dense along the seacoast and in the two river valleys. The statistics that follow divide the towns between those located in the low regions (the seacoast and the two river valleys) and those in the high regions (the upland, lake and mountain districts):

	Low Towns	High Towns	Total
Clay	39 (48%)	24 (19%)	63 (30%)*
Jackson	39 (48%)	103 (81%)	142 (68%)

* A tie vote in four towns (three in low regions, one in high) accounts for the fact that the percentages do not add up to 100%.

While the high regions were obviously for Jackson, giving him four towns out of five, the low regions were evenly divided. If the statistics are arranged by candidates, the results are similar:

	Clay	Jackson	Total
Low Towns	39 (62%)	39 (30%)	81 (39%)
High Towns	24 (39%)	103 (70%)	128 (61%)

The greater proportion of Jackson's strength came from the high towns (seven out of ten); but most of Clay's support came from low towns (six out of ten).

The details cited in the footnotes are also instructive. While over half of the communities in the high areas gave 2/3 or more of their vote to Jackson, only one-seventh of those in the low areas were that committed. Among the 79 towns that voted 2/3 or more for Jackson, 86% were in the high regions. Almost every town in the southeastern hills, the lake district, and the White Mountains voted for Jackson. The Connecticut Valley, on the other hand, was just as solidly National Republican, for only seven of the 23 communities supported Jackson and six of those were on higher land on the outer fringes of the valley. The statistics only support what Isaac Hill's *New Hampshire Patriot* kept saying, that the sturdy upland farmers were loyal Democrats and that the opposition lay in the Connecticut Valley, where Federalism and Congregationalism had been strongest. From colonial days the Connecticut had brought men, goods, and ideas from Massachusetts. In 1814 the valley sent unofficial delegates to the Hartford Convention. With a history of Federalism the valley voted National Republican; with a history of Republicanism the uplands voted Democratic.

The statistics also support the *Patriot's* claim that villages were Jacksonian and larger communities often National Republican.

	Population of Towns		
	Under 2,000	2,000 and Above	Total
Clay	50 (28%)	13 (46%)	63 (30%)
Jackson	127 (70%)	15 (54%)	142 (68%)

At the same time a much greater proportion of Clay towns than Jackson towns were large: 21% of those for Clay had more than 2,000 people compared to only 11% of those for Jackson.

Geological and agricultural surveys make it possible to distinguish between the good and bad farm land in the state and to generalize about the economic basis of Jacksonian Democracy. The figures that follow show that farmers in the poor areas (generally less prosperous farmers) were far more likely to vote for Jackson than for Clay.

	Good Agricultural Regions		Bad Agricultural Regions		Total*	
	Number of Towns	Percentage	Number of Towns	Percentage	Number	Percentage
Clay	43	40%	20	20%	63	30%
Jackson	62	58%	80	77%	142	68%

* Four towns with a tie vote are not listed.

Even the towns in the good areas supported Jackson but by a much smaller margin. Over half of the towns on poor farm land gave 2/3 or more of their votes to Jackson. When arranged by candidate rather than by region the results are even more startling:

	Clay Towns	Jackson Towns	Total
Good Agricultural Regions	43 (68%)	62 (44%)	107 (51%)
Bad Agricultural Regions	20 (32%)	80 (56%)	102 (49%)

Almost 70% of the Clay towns were in good regions, while almost 60% of the Jackson towns were in bad regions.

Once again the statistics support Hill's claim that the poor farmer working rocky upland soil was his most loyal supporter. The figures on arable land give Hill additional support. The statistics that follow divide the towns according to the number of acres of arable land per 100 eligible voters. Towns with more acres per voter would have larger, more prosperous farms and according to Hill should be for Henry Clay.

	Acres of Arable Land per 100 Eligible Voters		
	0-150 Acres	151 plus Acres	Total*
Clay Towns	38 (25%)	13 (52%)	63 (30%)
Jackson Towns	116 (74%)	10 (40%)	142 (68%)
Ties	4	0	4

* 3 towns with no acreage statistics and 25 manufacturing towns included in the Total column but not in the other two columns.

Hill was right. Though he lost the state by a wide margin, Clay actually did better than Jackson in the communities with large farms while Democrats took three-quarters of those with small farms. Furthermore, only one of the towns with small farms gave 2/3 of its vote to Clay, while ten gave 2/3 to Jackson. Hardly any of the towns for Jackson had large farms compared to a quarter of those for Clay.

	Clay Towns	Jackson Towns	Total*
0-150 Acres/100 Polls	38 (75%)	116 (92%)	154 (83%)
151 plus Acres/100 Polls	13 (25%)	10 (8%)	23 (17%)

* 4 tied towns, 3 towns with no acreage statistics, and 25 manufacturing towns omitted from all columns.

No matter how the figures are arranged the towns with small farms were Democratic.

The best way, however, to separate the prosperous towns from the poor towns is to study the tax figures. New Hampshire rated each community according to the number of dollars it had to contribute for every $1,000 to be raised in state taxes. Where the tax rate was high in proportion to the population, the community was presumably prosperous with well-to-do farmers. In the manufacturing towns, however, where the rate was high because of capital invested in factories, most of the inhabitants were poor mill hands.

The table below divides the towns according to their tax rate per $1,000 of state taxes and per 1,000 population. Hampton Falls, on rich farm land, paid the highest tax in the state—$3.26 for 582 people or $5.60 for 1,000 population. Nearby Newcastle, a poor fishing harbor, was next to the bottom with $1.41 for 850 people or $1.66/1,000. Dover, a manufacturing city, paid a rate of $4.67/1,000, one of the highest in the state.

TAX APPORTIONMENT FOR TOWNS PER $1,000 STATE TAXES
AND PER 1,000 POPULATION

	Below $3.00	$3.00-$3.49	$3.50-$3.99	$4.00-$4.49	$4.50 Plus	Total*
Clay	5(14%)	14(23%)	17(32%)	13(39%)	14(58%)	63(30%)
Jackson	29(83%)	44(77%)	35(66%)	20(61%)	9(35%)	142(68%)
Tie	1		1		2	4(2%)

* Five Jackson towns with no apportionment figures available are included in the Total but not in the other columns.

The percentage of poorer towns for Jackson was much higher than the percentage of more prosperous towns. As the tax apportionment climbs, the percentage for Jackson drops.

When the same figures are arranged according to party, they show that almost half of the Clay towns were well-off, compared to barely one out of five Jackson towns.

Apportionment	Clay Towns	Jackson Towns	Total
Below $4.00	35 (56%)	108 (72%)	143 (72%)
$4.00 Plus	28 (44%)	29 (21%)	57 (28%)

On the evidence to this point it appears that villages with small farms on poor upland soil were the Jacksonian strongholds. It appears also that Turner, Schlesinger, and Isaac Hill were right.

But one part of New Hampshire—the hill region in the southwest running from Sullivan east to Amherst—fails to fit into the pattern. These small, upland villages on poor soil with small farms should have voted for Jackson and yet 14 of the 16 were for Clay and 12 gave Clay at least 2/3 of their vote.

SIXTEEN TOWNS FROM SULLIVAN TO AMHERST
Number of Towns

On High Land	16
Population under 2,000	16
In Poor Farm Regions	13
With Less than 101 Acres of Arable Land/100 Eligible Voters	13
For Jackson	2
2/3 or More for Clay	12
51-66% for Clay	2

In tax apportionment, however, the Sullivan-Amherst towns do fit the established pattern, The fourteen Clay towns should have had a relatively high tax rate and indeed they did:

TAX APPORTIONMENT OF CLAY TOWNS IN THE SULLIVAN-AMHERST
REGION COMPARED TO ALL CLAY TOWNS IN THE STATE

	State	Sullivan-Amherst Region
Below $3.00	5 (8%)	0
$3.00-$3.49	13 (21%)	1 (7%)
$3.50-$3.99	17 (27%)	6 (43%)
$4.00 Plus	28 (14%)	7 (50%)

The consistency of these figures strongly suggests that tax apportionment is a more valid key to the nature of the Jackson movement than height of land or size of farms; it also suggests that the traditional view that Jacksonian Democrats were poor farmers is reasonably accurate.

Another part of the traditional view held that factory workers were Democratic. In New Hampshire, however, the manufacturing towns were evenly divided and the largest manufacturing towns were almost all for Clay.

	All Manufacturing Towns	Eight Leading Manufacturing Towns	Total Towns
Clay	12 (48%)	7 (88%)	63 (30%)
Jackson	13 (52%)	1 (12%)	142 (68%)

Since the population in the eight towns was made up mostly of workers, it follows that mill workers were probably National Republicans. Since the votes in those eight towns were not broken down by precinct, it is not possible to say definitively that the workers were the ones voting for Clay, but the strong probability is that they were. Hill, the *Patriot,* and the Democrats showed little interest in the workingman. 1832 is rather early to generalize about labor and Jacksonian Democracy. New Hampshire was not heavily industrialized and Jackson had not taken the hard money stand that would make him the favorite of workingmen's groups. Nevertheless, the evidence is against those who would equate labor and Jacksonian Democracy. Poor farmers were Democrats, but poor workers probably not.

In Protestant New Hampshire religious affiliation also had an important impact on voting. The *Patriot* linked Congregationalists with Federalists and later with National Republicans. The evidence in 1832 confirms the *Patriot's* view.

NUMBER OF CONGREGATIONAL CHURCHES IN TOWNS
SUPPORTING CLAY AND JACKSON

Towns Voting	Towns	Number of Congregational Churches
67% Plus for Clay	25	24 (9.6/10 towns)
51%-66% for Clay	38	34 (8.9)
51%-66% for Jackson	63	45 (7.1)
67% Plus for Jackson	79	37 (4.7)

In Coos County, furthermore, where 79% of the vote went to Jackson, only 36% of the churches were Congregational, while in Cheshire, 64% for Clay, almost 60% were Congregational. The Democratic way was not the Congregational way.

According to the statistics already presented the poorer non-Congregational towns in New Hampshire were likely to be Democratic. It remains to be seen whether the poorest towns according to tax apportionment were also the strongest Jackson towns, that is, whether an exact correlation existed between economic rank order and political voting order. When the top 25 Jackson towns were compared with the poorest 25 towns, some correlation did exist—ten were on both lists. The correlation of the top 25 Clay towns was less exact,—only five were on the list of the 25 most prosperous towns. The correlation was better, however, when deviations were studied. None of the leading Jackson communities ranked among the 25 leaders in apportionment; in fact the highest was Lee, which ranked 66th. Nor did any of the top Clay communities rank in the bottom group in apportionment. Furthermore, the median tax apportionment for the Jackson group was extremely low ($2.93); the Clay median very high ($3.92). The extent of the correlation may be summarized as follows:

	25 Leading Jackson Towns	25 Leading Clay Towns
Median Apportionment	$2.93	$3.92
Number among Bottom 25 in Apportionment	10	0
Number among Top 25 in Apportionment	0	5
Highest in Apportionment*	No. 66	No. 15
Lowest in Apportionment†	No. 3	No. 27

* From the top
† From the bottom

And the correlation is even more persuasive when the poorest and richest towns are studied:

	25 Poorest Towns	25 Richest Towns
Jackson 2/3 Plus	15	5
Jackson 51%–66%	7	3
Clay 51%–66%	3	10
Clay 2/3 Plus	0	5
Tie	0	2
Total Jackson Vote	68%	46%
Total Clay Vote	32%	54%

Though the correlation is not exact, it is certainly pronounced. The probability is that the very poorest towns were Jacksonian and the very richest National Republican. Turner is close to being right.

The religious correlation of the leading Jackson and Clay towns is even stronger than the economic:

	25 Leading Clay Towns	25 Leading Jackson Towns
No Church	1	8
3–4 Churches	5	1
Congregational Churches	23	5
Freewill Baptist or Methodist Churches	4	14
Total number of Churches	47	27

The Democratic Party flourished in towns that either had no churches at all or had the less aristocratic churches such as the Freewill Baptist. The National Republicans were strongest in communities with several churches including a Congregational Church. Congregational upper class towns went to Henry Clay.

The following statistics complete the profile of the leading Jackson and Clay towns:

COMPARISON OF THE 25 LEADING CLAY TOWNS AND
THE 25 LEADING JACKSON TOWNS

	Clay	Jackson
Among the 25 Poorest Towns	0	10
Number of Congregational Churches	23	5
Towns on High Land	13	22
Towns on Bad Farm Land	11	17
Towns with Population under 1,000	10	19
Towns with 0-50 Acres/100 Eligible Voters	1	5
Manufacturing Towns	5	0

As might have been expected from the patterns already established, the leading Clay communities were much more prosperous and had more Congregational Churches, more textile mills, and larger farms than the leading Jackson communities. And predictably those for Jackson were small ones on high land with poor soil. But it is surprising that so many of the ranking Clay towns were also small on high land and on poor soil. The reason is simple: twelve of them were among the sixteen towns in the southwest running from Sullivan to Amherst, which failed to fit into the earlier patterns. Even though they were small upland villages, they backed Henry Clay because they were prosperous and were close to the Connecticut Valley, which was first Federalist and then National Republican. The Democratic influence reached southwest from Concord but not as far as Sullivan and Keene, which had always opposed Isaac Hill. No Jacksonian newspaper was published in the Keene region, where the National Republican *New Hampshire Sentinel* dominated politics. Farmers on small farms in the southwest hills voted against Jackson because they were conditioned to oppose the Democratic machine in Concord.

Furthermore, this upland Clay area was close to the Massachusetts border and thus much more accessible than the rest of the hilly region, which generally went to Jackson. Accessibility rather than height distinguished Clay towns from Jackson towns. Almost all of those strongest for Clay were south of a line drawn from Exeter to Sullivan, barely twenty miles north of the Massachusetts border; while almost all of the ranking Jackson towns were north of the line. Furthermore, practically every leading Clay town was on a main road, but fifteen of the 25 Jackson towns were on back roads. Eleven of the Clay group were communication centers: Exeter, Chester, Keene, Milton, Jaffrey, Claremont, New Ipswich, Rindge, Winchester, Fitzwilliam and Marlborough; only Barnstead of the Jackson group was a center. Each of the six main highways entering New Hampshire from Massachusetts went though several of the Clay communities. The road to Exeter continued on to Brentwood on its way to Concord; the road to Derry passed through Windham and Chester; the road to Nashua went on to Milford, Temple, and Dublin; they were all leading Clay towns. And so it went: the Clay towns were in the swim of things; the Jackson towns were out of it.

A typical Jackson community was Jackson, New Hampshire, once called Adams, but renamed for the new president in 1829. With a population of 515, Jackson lay far to the north in the mountains tucked under the mass of Mount Washington. While a road of sorts ran from Lake Winnipesaukee north to Jackson, travel was light; and during the long winter months Jackson was isolated. Farms were small, averaging between fifty and 100 acres for every 100 eligible voters; the soil was rocky. With an apportionment of only $2.62 (only fifteen units were lower), it was poor. Few homes or buildings of distinction marked the center of Jackson; the sole church was Freewill Baptist. When the votes were counted in 1832 the record read: Jackson 85—Clay 0.

Exeter, typically National Republican, was another world from Jackson. Settled in 1638, it had always been one of the leading communities in New Hampshire. The hub of Revolutionary activity, it became the first state capital. The center of New Hampshire Federalism, it was the home of John Taylor Gilman, longtime Federalist governor. Its stately Congregational Church gave it a link with the past; the Exeter Manufacturing Company, which produced cloth, looked to the future. Elegant colonial homes and graceful elms lined Main, Water, Court and High Streets. In 1832 Phillips Exeter Academy, over fifty years old, had already educated Daniel Webster, John Parker Hale, and George Bancroft. Exeter had over 3,000 people, boasted two Congregational Churches, and paid a tax rate of $4.14. Busy roads led to Portsmouth, Concord, and Boston. Ships sailed for Great Bay, Portsmouth, and the Atlantic. The *Exeter News-Letter* kept people informed. Barely a dozen miles from the ocean, Exeter lay on low fertile meadows. The vote read Clay 307, Jackson 140.

The strongest Democratic towns in New Hampshire were Democratic principally because they were rural, poor, small, non-Congregational, and out of the mainstream of New Hampshire life. As Turner put it, the "Democracy found its strength among the poorer people," especially the farmers in the "hilly mountainous districts." The poor textile workers, however, were more likely National Republican than Democratic. The patterns are not exact. Newcastle, the next to poorest town in the state, voted for Henry Clay; Sharon, the next to richest town, voted 46–23 for Andrew Jackson. Benson is right to a degree; exact economic patterns do not exist. But there is enough evidence in New Hampshire to conclude that the traditional Turner interpretation of Jacksonian Democracy is still sound.

10 / Andrew Jackson and the Judiciary

Richard P. Longaker

Jackson was by far the strongest chief executive up to his time, and one of the most forceful in all American history. The office of the Presidency, after a strong beginning, declined in importance during the Era of Good Feelings. However, Jackson reversed that trend, and during his first administration offered several examples of powerful presidential leadership.

In retrospect it might appear that Jackson's reaction to the nationalistic opinions of Chief Justice John Marshall were wrongheaded if not simply petulant. Judicial supremacy in the interpretation of the Constitution has since become an accepted fact, but in the 1830's this was not yet the case. Jackson maintained that he, like other officers of the federal government, had sworn to uphold the Constitution, and he could see no reason why the Supreme Court should necessarily act as the final arbiter of all constitutional questions, particularly in those cases involving executive powers. Richard P. Longaker argues that Jackson, far from acting irresponsibly to destroy the Court's power and prestige, was seeking to protect the executive branch from *judicial* encroachment. It can be, and was, argued that such a growth of judicial power exceeded the intentions of the Constitution's framers. The fact that this specific Jacksonian crusade ultimately failed does not detract from the validity of the attempt nor its importance in the development of the Presidency.

For further reading: Leonard D. White, *The Jacksonians: A Study in Administrative History, 1829–1861* (1954); Carl B. Swisher, *Roger B. Taney* (1935); Robert V. Remini, *Andrew Jackson* (1966).

Political Science Quarterly, LXXI (September 1956), 341–364. Reprinted by permission. Footnotes have been omitted execpt where they are necessary for an understanding of the text.

In 1822, protesting a recent attack on the judiciary, a future President of the United States wrote to his nephew, "the constitution is worth nothing and a mere buble [sic] except guaranteed to them by an independent and virtuous judiciary." President Jackson is not remembered as a great defender of "an independent and virtuous judiciary" but instead has gained notoriety and fame for the legendary statement, "John Marshall has made his decision; now let him enforce it." Because this statement appears with bothersome regularity in studies of our constitutional past, it seems appropriate to reinvestigate Jackson's views on the place of the judiciary in our governmental system.

Reëxamination of Jackson's attitude toward the judiciary reveals more than the defiance historians have associated with Jackson's conflict with John Marshall during the famous Georgia controversy. Jackson's attitude was ambivalent and to some extent contradictory. He was defiant, but mixed with his defiance were two other significant elements: the belief that the executive was independent of judicial control in certain situations and an attitude of deep-rooted respect for the judicial function in others. The President did not try to resolve his ambivalence, although in retrospect all three components of his attitude—defiance, independence and respect—were based on the shifting constitutional sands of the separation of powers.

Respect for the Marshall court was not a part of the Jacksonian creed. The Jacksonians, as lineal descendants of the Jeffersonians, were vigorous critics of the federal judiciary, and Jackson's election in 1828 was in part a popular repudiation of the institutional aggrandizement of the judicial branch. All Americans revered the Constitution but worship of the document did not presuppose worship of the Supreme Court or the Chief Justice, whose nationalism, according to Jackson men, threatened the soverignty of the states. There is no evidence, however, that the President shared the extreme hostility of many of his lieutenants, and at no time did he cooperate with their proposals for drastic judicial reform.

Before discussing the President's attitude in specific instances it is necessary to mention the rôle which personal feelings played in contributing to an antagonistic environment. Jackson certainly objected to the institutional imbalance resulting from the Court's aggressiveness under John Marshall, but his displeasure was as much personal as institutional. It is a mistake to confuse Jackson's lack of esteem for John Marshall with presidential hostility toward the judiciary.

The famous statement reads, "John Marshall has made his decision . . . ," not "The Supreme Court has made its decision. . . ." As a republican, Jackson could be expected to frown upon the Chief Justice as a symbol of centralization, but his republican objections were far outdistanced by his attitude toward Marshall the man. Marshall had offended Jackson in the campaign of 1828 by siding with Clay and Adams. Jackson was personally affronted and believed Marshall had gone beyond the bounds of "non-partisanship." In 1828 Marshall allegedly declared, "should Jackson be elected, I shall look upon the government as virtually dissolved," and stated his intention to vote for the first time in twenty years to contribute to Jackson's defeat. His subsequent denial of this report did little to assuage the mercurial Jackson, for Marshall publicly admitted

> having said in private that though I had not voted since the establishment of the general ticket system and had believed that I should never vote during its continuance, I might probably depart from my resolution in this instance, from the strong sense I felt of the injustice of the charge of corruption against the President and the Secretary of State.

Such statements were not calculated to evoke presidential sympathy. Thus Jackson's personal resentment toward Marshall was compounded with a prejudice against the federal judiciary among some of his advisers to produce an environment that was, superficially at least, unfriendly to the courts. The personal factor, Marshall's nationalism, and the President's view of the separation of powers and the nature of the Union were mixed together in opposition and accord in the whirlpool of events in the 1830's. The result was not simple hostility but a more complex equation of defiance, independence and respect.

PRESIDENTIAL DEFIANCE: THE GEORGIA CONTROVERSY

One of the most explosive problems in John Quincy Adams' bequest to his successor was the Indian question in the South and Southwest. The storm center was in Georgia, where the Governor and legislature exhibited increasing resistance to Adams' efforts to enforce treaties with the Indians. Jackson was known to be sympathetic to the interests of the whites in this region and this was a major factor in his electoral success there in 1828. Emboldened by Jackson's election and offended by the efforts of the Cherokee tribe to establish its own government within the bounds of the state, Georgia passed stringent laws invalidating the Indian enactments and authorizing the division of Cherokee lands. Georgia's action was in apparent conflict with treaties negotiated by the Cherokees and the United States but especially an act of 1802 in which the state had ceded all the lands now comprising Alabama and Mississippi to the United States on the condition that the government extinguish the Indian titles by negotiation as soon as possible. Included in the Act of 1802 was a guarantee that intruders on Indian lands be ousted by the federal government until the land titles were extinguished.

In three instances the Cherokees or persons identified with them engaged the state of Georgia in litigation in the federal courts and in all three cases Georgia, with the tacit approval of the President, ignored the mandates of the Supreme Court. The first incident concerned an Indian, George Tassels, who was convicted of murder under the laws recently extended throughout the Cherokee territory. On appeal from the decision of the Georgia courts the Supreme Court issued a writ of error which was ignored by Governor Troup, and Tassels was executed. The failure of the President to enforce the Court's writ led John Quincy Adams to observe: "The Constitution, the laws and treaties of the United States are prostrate in the State of Georgia . . . because the Executive of the United States is in league with the State of Georgia. He will not take care that the laws be faithfully executed."

A second incident occurred two years later when one James Graves was tried and convicted of murder in Georgia. Again the state refused to obey an order issued by the Supreme Court to show cause why a writ of error should not issue.

Of greater importance was the trial of two white missionaries to the Cherokees who had violated state law. The incident culminated in the famous case of *Worcester v. Georgia*. In this instance the President not only defied the Supreme Court by refusing to enforce the mandate but coöperated with Georgia by removing Worcester from a postmastership as a reprimand. The Georgia law of December 1830 required licenses and an oath of all whites in Cherokee territory, and when Worcester refused to apply for the license he was convicted in the Georgia courts.

On appeal John Marshall held the Georgia statute unconstitutional because it was in conflict with the Act of 1802 and treaties with the Cherokees. Marshall asserted that "the treaties and laws of the United States contemplate the Indian territory as completely separate from that of the states." Directing a personal blow at Jackson, Marshall pointed out that Worcester had been sent to Georgia by the President with a commission granted under the laws of the United States to instruct the Indians. He called the decision of the Georgia courts a "violation of the acts which authorize the chief magistrate to exercise this authority." The President again refused to execute the mandate of the Supreme Court, an action which would have required the removal of all Georgia authority, forcibly no doubt, from the Cherokee lands.

On what constitutional grounds did the President base this doctrine of defiance and inaction? In reply to a Senate resolution inquiring why he had not enforced the Act of 1802, the President gave a partial answer. Jackson said that, though the purpose of the statute was to remove white intruders from Indian lands, "The authority of the President . . . is not imperative." The President believed it was lawful to use military force to remove intruders only in cases where military force was absolutely necessary. In this instance, he reasoned, it was unnecessary and would violate the rights of Georgia, for the statute was applied only so long as Georgia did not "extend her laws throughout her limits." In a rare and uncharacteristic case of broad statutory construction the President concluded that because Georgia had extended her laws throughout the state the statute was no longer applicable within Georgia's boundaries.

Secondly, Jackson did not accept the Court's holding that the Cherokees had rights independent of state authority. Under the Constitution Congress possessed the power "to regulate commerce with Indian tribes," but only dangerous construction, the President contended, could bestow on Congress the power to interfere with a state's jurisdiction over Indian lands within its limits; for the clause was designed to give "the General Government complete control over the trade and intercourse of those Indians only who were not within any state." To give the Chief Executive the power to interfere with the relations between a state and the Indians within the state would, from Jackson's point of view, "place in his hands a power to make war upon the rights of the States and the liberty of the country—a power which should be placed in the hands of no individual."

The President said that if he were to execute the writs of the Court or its mandate in favor of Worcester, he would be going beyond his own power and compounding the erroneous decision of the Supreme Court with his own unconstitutional action.

Finally, the President denied that he was empowered to enforce the law against a state. In a letter to the Secretary of War he wrote, "No feature in the Federal Constitution is more prominent, than that the general powers conferred on congress, can only be enforced, and executed upon the people of the Union." He closed his argument by saying he could not enforce a decision which violated the constitutional provision, "no new state shall be formed or erected within the jurisdiction of any other state . . . without the consent of the legislatures of the States as well as of the Congress."

These are Jackson's arguments, and when one recalls his opposition to the Nullifiers in South Carolina less than a year afterward, the constitutional reasoning falls far short of a full explanation for his defiance of the Supreme Court. Besides a vague urge to defend the rights of the states against an aggressive Court, it seems that the President, during the Georgia controversy, was singularly unclear about his obligations to the Constitution. Since Jackson's constitutional argument was largely feeble rationalization, it is necessary to turn elsewhere to discover the underlying reasons for his defiance and inaction.[1]

Jackson's resistance to the Court was certainly conditioned by a personal distaste for John Marshall, but this was not all. Among other reasons was Jackson's lack of sympathy for the Indians and his apprehension lest any concession damage the core of his Indian policy—removal across the Mississippi. Long experience in fighting and negotiating with the Indians convinced Jackson years earlier that removal was the only sound policy. He informed Congress in his First Annual Message that the Indians had already been told "that their attempt to establish an independent government would not be countenanced by the Executive . . . [and had been advised] to emigrate beyond the Mississippi or submit to the laws of the states." Also, as an Indian fighter turned president he could not easily forget "the prowling lion of the forest who has done us so much injury." In short, he had respect for Indian rights so long as they were exercised on the western bank of the Mississippi. But there were more urgent reasons for the avoidance of a clash with Georgia, particularly when, as Jackson knew, armed force would be necessary to carry out the mandate. Paradoxically, a President who is noted for his quick temper and rashness often attained his goal by being temperate and avoiding an open struggle. This factor has too often been overlooked in past commentary on the Georgia controversy. Jackson's forbearance was rooted partly in his aversion to the use of military force. Also, the President was in the midst of his fight with the Bank of the United States and was soon to stand for reëlection. Certainly he did not forget that Georgia, largely in reaction to Adams' inflexible Indian policy, had repudiated Adams and strongly supported Jackson in 1828. A proper Indian policy was important for holding Georgia, Tennessee, Alabama and Mississippi within the party during a crucial election year. Finally, Jackson needed Georgia's support against the South Carolina Nullifiers. If Jackson did not consider this the primary justification for his defiance of the Supreme Court, history should. While the President saw the Indian problem as a temporary one, the nullification issue presented a basic national crisis. He and his advisers were not unaware that the Nullifiers counted on him to chastise Georgia and thus draw that state into their ranks. As one Jacksonian wrote:

> They [South Carolinians] hope to see Georgia embroiled with the General Government, in which they may join and make a common cause . . . [a permanent injunction by the Court] will be disregarded by Georgia, and any attempt to enforce it will be promptly resisted. This is precisely the State of Things which our Nullifiers are anxious to see brought about. And should this happen, I can see

---

[1] Several authorities contend that Jackson was not empowered to enforce the *Worcester* decision since an effort to give the decision legislative sanction failed of passage in the House. Charles Warren contends it is "clearly untrue" that Jackson defied the court decree. The crucial fact is, of course, that Jackson did not want to enforce this particular decision and, had he wanted to, his ingenuity would have found a way. Commentators like Warren perhaps forget that the Act of 1802 was still good law despite Jackson's interpretation of it. He might just as well have read the statute in favor of the executive instead of the states. Also he was not beyond using his autonomous power to execute the laws faithfully during the Nullification crisis in South Carolina. No doubt if Jackson had believed it possible and desirable to enforce the law against Georgia he would have done so.

no other result but civil war and the dismemberment of the Union. . . . One thing is certain, General Jackson will not lend his official aid to enforce the injunction. This may avert disaster for awhile. . . .

Of utmost importance as a cause of Jackson's defiance of the Supreme Court was his awareness that enforcement—had he wanted to act—would be difficult and bloody. Here it seems is the significance of Jackson's refusal to enforce Marshall's decision. Whether or not the famous statement is apocryphal is a moot question, although it does not seem out of character and expressed the President's feelings.[2] But what does the sentence mean? It certainly suggests defiance of Marshall, but it means more. Drawing on a declaration that is similar and expands the cryptic pronouncement, one is led to believe Jackson meant not only that the Chief Justice and the Supreme Court were institutionally incapable of enforcing the mandate but that all of the national government would be unable to coerce Georgia:

> The decision of the supreme court has fell still born and they find it cannot coerce Georgia to yield to its mandate . . . if orders were issued tomorrow one regiment of militia could not be got to march to save them from destruction and this the opposition know, and if a colision was to take place between them and the Georgians, the arm of the government is not sufficiently strong to preserve them from destruction. . . .

Jackson might have expanded his original statement to read: "John Marshall has made his decision and he can try to enforce it. I cannot. Even if the Executive wished to enforce the mandate it is not powerful enough to oppose the tide of feeling in the South."

Added to the note of personal defiance of Marshall and the inference that the Court was powerless without the coöperation of the executive is the President's recognition of political reality. In sum, Jackson's defiance of the Court was compounded of constitutional argument, personal and political considerations, and an awareness of what was politically and militarily feasible. Considering the prospect of active resistance in Georgia and the explosive situation in South Carolina at the time, one is left to wonder whether Jackson should not be praised for prudence instead of being condemned for inaction.

PRESIDENTIAL INDEPENDENCE: THE BANK VETO

In 1832 President Jackson vetoed the bill rechartering the United States Bank despite a clear expression of Congressional will favoring the Bank and the Supreme Court's recognition of the Bank's constitutionality in *McCulloch v. Maryland* some years before. In the Veto Message the following statement appears:

> Each public officer who takes an oath to support the Constitution swears that he will support it as he understands it. . . . It is as much the duty of the House

[2] The statement can be traced to Horace Greeley's *American Conflict: A History of the Great Rebellion in the United States of America, 1860–65* (Hartford, 1864), I. 106. Greeley said, "I am indebted for this fact to the late Governor George N. Briggs, of Massachusetts, who was in Washington as a member of Congress when the decision was rendered." The quotation as Greeley transcribed it is as follows: "Well: John Marshall has made his decision: *now let him enforce it.*"

of Representatives, of the Senate, and of the President to decide upon the constitutionality of any bill or resolution which may be presented to them for passage or approval as it is of the supreme judges when it may be brought before them for judicial decision.

Two key ideas appeared in this passage and the later refinements of the veto by administration leaders in the ensuing Senate debate: (1) the President has an unqualified right to use the veto power to block "unconstitutional" legislation despite judicial precedents affirming the constitutionality of similar statutes; (2) the President is not required to enforce "unconstitutional" statutes.

Jackson clearly believed he possessed an independent right to judge the validity of legislation even if the judgment were contrary to judicial precedent. In reply to friends of the Bank who contended that *McCulloch v. Maryland* settled the question of the Bank's constitutionality, Jackson declared: "Mere precedent is a dangerous source of authority, and should not be regarded as deciding questions of constitutional power except where the acquiescence of the people and the states can be considered as well settled."

Drawing upon his power as representative of the whole people and his oath to support the Constitution, Jackson said in effect that if the President believed the statute in question was a "danger to our liberty," and the people and the states agreed with the President, then the Chief Executive's opinion was superior to mere judicial precedent in judging questions of constitutionality. He averred as well that the instant case dealt with new facts and a new situation which could not be governed by *McCulloch v. Maryland*, and therefore "ought not control the coordinate authorities of the Government." This assertion of independence was based on Jackson's belief that it was the autonomous duty of the executive to pass on constitutional questions in preparing his veto:

> Each public officer who takes an oath to support the Constitution swears that he will support it as he understands it, not as it is understood by others . . . the opinion of the judges has no more authority over Congress than the opinion of Congress has over the judges, and on that point the President is independent of both.

But was the President obligated to enforce statutes which he considered to be unconstitutional? The controversy and confusion over this question arose partly from the opening words of the passage cited above—"Each public officer who takes an oath to support the Constitution swears that he will support it as he understands it." The President's opponents seized on this as a flagrant extension of executive power and an effort to destroy the judiciary. The point at issue was serious enough to lead Taney to write the following passage in a letter twenty-six years later. He defended the President:

> He [Jackson] was speaking of his rights and his duty, when acting as part of the legislative power and not of his right or duty as an executive officer. For when a bill is presented to him and he is to decide whether, by his approval, it shall become law or not, his power or duty is as purely legislative as that of a member of Congress, when he is called on to vote for or against a bill. . . . But General Jackson never expressed a doubt as to the duty and the obligation upon him in his executive character to carry into execution any act of Congress regularly passed, whatever his opinion might be of the constitutional question.

Taney's interpretation after the fact seems acceptable. But Martin Van Buren inadvertently introduced conflicting evidence when he wrote years later that Jackson "contented himself with frequent and unreserved concurrence in the views which had been taken of the subject, on the floor of the Senate by Judge White."

An examination of White's interpretation of the veto, however, shows it to be in direct contradiction of Taney:

> If either of these coordinate departments is . . . called upon to perform an official act, and conscientiously believe that performance of that act would be in violation of the Constitution, they are not bound to perform it, but, on the contrary, are as much at liberty to decline acting, as if no such decision had been made. . . . They ought to examine the extent of their constitutional powers for themselves; and when they have had access to all sources of information within their reach, and given to everything its due weight, if they are satisfied that the constitution has not given a power to do the act required, I insist they ought to refrain from doing it.

It it impossible to reconcile these two conflicting statements, for there is no extant evidence of Jackson's view written in his own hand. Since Taney assisted in the preparation of the Bank veto perhaps his word should be given more weight than Judge White's. It seems safe to conclude, however, that Jackson, Taney, Van Buren and White were one and all confused about the matter. If Jackson agreed with White's speech in the Senate, it was agreement with an extreme claim of executive independence; but Taney, who was closer to the President, denied in later years that this was the proper interpretation. This enigma notwithstanding, there remains the generous extension of executive independence in Jackson's vigorous assertion that he, in judging constitutionality, while considering a veto, was not bound by the precedents of the Supreme Court.

PRESIDENTIAL INDEPENDENCE:
KENDALL V. UNITED STATES

Of equal importance in illustrating a broad doctrine of the executive independence were the arguments put forward by two of Jackson's advisers, Amos Kendall and Benjamin F. Butler, in *Kendall v. United States, United States v. Kendall,* and *Kendall v. Stokes.* Although *Kendall v. United States* was decided against Kendall, the Postmaster General, the doctrine expressed by representatives of the President before the Court typifies the Jacksonian view of presidential independence. There is no positive evidence of the President's opinion on the outcome of these famous cases, but it is believed his attitude can be established by inference.

The parties involved in *United States v. Kendall* were the Postmaster General and Stockton and Stokes, a mail-carrying firm. Kendall succeeded William Barry as Postmaster General in 1835 and upon reviewing the departmental accounts disallowed a claim awarded to Stockton and Stokes by his predecessor. Kendall considered the claim excessive, in some respects fraudulent, and refused to pay the firm. Stockton and Stokes turned to Congress and after a brief investigation Congress passed a resolution directing the Solicitor of the Treasury to review the claim, a review which ended in an order for payment. Once again Kendall refused to honor the claim and Stockton and Stokes appealed to the President. Jackson replied that since Congress was then in session, "and the best expounder of the intent and meaning of their own law, I think it right and proper, under existing circumstances, to refer it to that body for their decision."

The second appeal to Congress resulted in a Senate resolution affirming the carriers' claim for the full amount and Kendall countered once again by arguing that only the Senate had ordered payment, not both Houses of Congress. In desperation Stockton and Stokes turned to the Circuit Court for a writ of mandamus. In June 1837, three months after Jackson's departure from office, the Circuit Court held that a mandamus should issue to force Kendall to pay the award, a decision which the Supreme Court affirmed in January 1838. The Court declared that an act of Congress, empowering the Solicitor of the Treasury to pass on the claim and the subsequent resolution of the Senate, imposed a ministerial duty on the Postmaster General who had no choice but to pay the award.

Two documents express the administration viewpoint: a letter to Chief Justice Cranch written by Kendall explaining his refusal to obey the mandamus and an opinion written by Attorney General Benjamin F. Butler at Kendall's request. Both Kendall and Butler denied the right of the federal courts to issue a writ forcing an executive officer to perform any act, and both based their argument on a strict interpretation of the separation of powers.

Kendall's letter to Judge Cranch contained an unqualified denial of the power of any judicial officer to control the acts of the executive. Kendall reasoned that under the separation of powers the President alone has the power to execute the laws. If the mandamus issued by the Circuit Court was valid, Kendall argued, "the effective and controlling Executive of this great republic will not be the Chief Magistrate elected by the people, but three judges of the Circuit Court for the District of Columbia."

In sum, the proper function of the judiciary was to expound the law, the executive's to enforce it. Kendall assured the Court that he did not consider an executive officer above accountability, for each officer was responsible to the President and ultimately to Congress.

In his exegesis the Postmaster specifically denied to the judiciary the power to issue a writ for the execution of a ministerial duty:

> No such distinction is to be found in the Constitution. It is the duty of the President to "take care that the laws be faithfully executed"—*special* laws as well as *general;* but no such duty is enjoined upon the judiciary. . . . The officer whose particular province it is to execute the law is under the immediate eye of the President, holds office at his will, and may be removed if he refuses. . . . The Executive power is ONE—*one* in principle—*one* in object. Its object is *the execution of the laws.* It is not susceptible of subdivisions and nice distinctions as to its duties and responsibilities. To execute the laws, and *all the laws,* are its duties.

To yield to the writ, Kendall declared, would violate his oath to discharge the duties of his office faithfully and to support the Constitution.

At the Postmaster's request Attorney General Butler prepared an opinion supporting his fellow cabinet officer. He agreed with Kendall that the mandamus should not issue, for it involved a crucial surrender of executive independence. No law, Butler wrote, "can confer on any court in the United States the power to supervise and control the action of an executive officer of the United States in any official matter, properly appertaining to the Executive Department in which he is employed." Butler emphasized that the President could resist actively a writ of mandamus, a fact which exhibited "in the clearest light, the incapacity of any court to issue such a writ."

It is difficult to determine Jackson's attitude toward these extreme claims of executive independence. Butler and Kendall were the President's constitutional advisers and Jackson did declare at one time that he would, and his cabinet officers should, defer to the Attorney General in questions of this nature. The case arose at the end of the President's second term, however, and he either did not have a sustained interest in the problem or was busy with other affairs of state. The only written record touching on Kendall's difficulty with the courts was a comment Jackson made in defense of Kendall when Stockton's search for a settlement led to a private suit for damages against Kendall. Jackson was in retirement at the Hermitage and wrote to Kendall:

> I have just received your letter of the 19th instant, and it rends my heart with sorrow to read that you who so ably and faithfully watched over the interests of the government as Postmaster Genl. should be crushed and deprived of your personal liberty, by such a cruel and unjust judgement against you. . . . This precedent must lead to make the President and all the heads of Depts., subject to be harassed by suits, by every villain who wished to put his hand into the public crib, and is prevented by them. . . .

Unfortunately Jackson made no direct comment about the other decisions, *Kendall v. United States* or *United States v. Kendall*. Congress was the proper board of appeal as "the best expounder of the interests and meaning of [its] own law."

Although the President's attitude can be established only by inference,[3] three facts point to his tacit acknowledgement of an ample interpretation of presidential independence. Jackson was emphatically opposed to the private suit against Kendall and saw the dangers to the executive in such a suit; he stated a specific preference for a settlement in Congress, not the courts; and, despite a thorough search, there is no evidence of presidential disagreement with the reasoning of his constitutional advisers. Their mildest argument placed the President beyond the arm of the judiciary when Congress had not made its intentions crystal clear. In its most extreme form the interpretation empowered the executive to resist a writ even in the face of a clear statement of Congressional intent. Both arguments presumed an ample area of presidential freedom in determining how the laws were to be executed and a guarantee against judicial "legislation." Submission to a writ of mandamus, these advisers contended, would do injury to the separation of powers, confound the proper rôle of the judiciary, and place an irresponsible superior above the highest representative of the people. The theory fits the Jacksonian pattern, and the most cautious generalization is that the President's advisers, in their arguments before the courts, expressed a Jacksonian view of executive independence, and probably the view of the President himself.

[3] Jackson's successor believed the mandamus was a violation of the separation of powers and hinted that Jackson agreed with him when he advised Kendall to resist the writ and added that he "considered the disposition made by his predecessor as final."

THE PRESIDENT AND THE COURTS

Defiance and independence only partially characterize Jackson's attitude toward the judiciary. Hidden behind the traditional description of Jackson, the antagonist of the judiciary, is evidence of deep-rooted respect and support for the judicial function. It can be argued that the courts were stronger in 1837 than in 1828 partly because of Jackson's defense of the federal courts during the Nullification controversy and his apparent unwillingness to succumb to proposals for far-reaching judicial "reform."[4]

Before investigating these aspects of the President's relations with the judiciary mention should be made of an unusual theory of executive accountability which arose during Jackson's presidency. In three separate instances Jackson or his advisers claimed that the President was personally liable to private suits while in office—a doctrine that ceased to be good law (if ever it was) after *Mississippi v. Johnson*.

This argument was used on two different occasions by counsel for Kendall in *Kendall v. United States*. Benjamin Butler told the court:

> Where the President has controlled and directed the action of the inferior executive officer, they [counsel for Stokes, defendant in error] contend that the inferior is not responsible; and, as the President's liability to private action has been doubted, there will then, it is said, be no responsibility. The answer is, that whenever the President takes an active part in an illegal action, to the injury of an individual, though it be done by the hand of his subordinate, he will be responsible in a civil suit, along with that subordinate: and that the latter cannot be excused from doing an unlawful act, by pleading the command of his official superior.

There is no evidence in Jackson's correspondence that he subscribed to this principle of accountability but it is mentioned in one of his major messages to the Senate. Since Jackson reviewed and helped to write all of his important messages, he certainly knew that the following statement appeared, although he may not have realized its implications. Reviewing the ways in which the President could be held accountable Jackson said in his Protest to the Senate, "He is also liable to private action of any party who may have been injured by his illegal mandates or instructions in the same manner and to the same extent as the humblest functionary."

One can hardly believe, knowing Jackson's character and his views of executive independence, that he would have submitted to a private suit for any reason while in office. But there is a trace of respect for the judicial function and the need for executive accountability which deserves mention.

The President's attitude toward the federal judiciary during the Nullification con-

[4] It can be argued that Jackson's appointments to the Supreme Court strengthened the judiciary by replacing Marshall nationalists with Taney moderates. The President wanted to be assured that potential appointees reflected his interpretation of the Constitution and he was willing to consider a candidate only "if his principles on the Constitution are sound, and well fixed." He was aware of the importance of life tenure as a vehicle for transporting his beliefs beyond his years in the presidential office. . . . Jackson relieved some of the pressure on the judiciary by appointing men sensitive to contemporary social trends. None of Marshall's decisions were overturned but many were made more palatable to a new generation. . . .

troversy is more conclusive and enduring. One major tenet of the Nullifiers' creed was the freedom of state power from the judgments of the federal courts. The radical doctrine of the Nullifiers was not accepted by Jackson. Although the President did not hesitate to assert his own freedom from court precedent under the separation of powers and appeared to believe in a large degree of administrative independence, it did not follow in Jackson's reasoning that a state could ignore the federal judiciary and the supremacy of national law. If South Carolina objected to the tariff acts of 1828 and 1832, according to Jackson, her proper recourse was to the courts, not nullification. He condemned this heresy. South Carolina, the President wrote, "has not only not appealed in her own name to those tribunals under the Constitution and laws of the United States but has endeavored to frustrate their proper action on her citizens by drawing cognizance of cases under the revenue laws to her tribunals."

The President declared that there were two avenues of appeal from an unconstitutional law: a constitutional amendment or a suit in the federal courts. Unilateral action by one state to nullify a law—the right which South Carolina believed was hers—would destroy the supremacy of national law that the President, the Congress and the Supreme Court were duty bound to defend. It is of the utmost significance that Jackson, reputedly an opponent of the Judiciary Act of 1789, affirmed the usefulness and validity of this statute in his Special Message to Congress on Nullification and his Proclamation to the people of South Carolina:

> The Constitution declares that the judicial powers of the United States extend to cases arising under the laws of the United States and that such laws, the Constitution, and treaties shall be paramount to the State constitutions and laws. The judiciary act prescribes the mode by which the case may be brought before a court of the United States by appeal when a State tribunal shall decide against this provision.

By defending the federal courts against the destructive doctrine inherent in nullification Jackson put his stamp of approval on the usefulness of judicial review in a federal system and showed his respect for the judiciary. His enemies attacked him for his behavior during the Georgia controversy and their opinions have been passed down as the correct view of the President's attitude toward the judiciary. Nevertheless, his greatest antagonists, Story and Marshall, recognized the President's service to the judiciary. As Story wrote to his wife, "since the last proclamation [on nullification] and message, the Chief Justice and myself have become his warmest supporters." In the final analysis, Jackson's defense of the Judiciary Act of 1789—the cornerstone of the federal judicial power—was possibly more important than his record of defiance and independence. While affirming the rôle of the judiciary in maintaining the integrity of the Union, Jackson rose above narrow partisanship and dissolved some of the odium associated with his defiance of the Supreme Court in the Georgia controversy. As we have seen, in fact, the two events were closely related in Jackson's mind.

It should be recalled that many of Jackson's followers were children of the Jeffersonian era and consequently hostile to the judiciary. Jackson's alliance with the courts in his struggle with the Nullifiers is all the more impressive because of this. The decade preceding Jackson's first term burgeoned with court decisions—*McCulloch v.*

Maryland, Ogden v. Saunders, Cohens v. Virginia, and *Craig v. Missouri,* to name only a few—which aroused the fear of the South and the West and stored up resentment which threatened to explode in a burst of legislation designed to cripple the federal judiciary. In the early years of Jackson's presidency frequent attempts were made in Congress to weaken the judiciary, although they seemed to taper off after Marshall's death and the influx of Jackson appointees into the federal courts.

The attacks usually centered on the 25th Section of the Judiciary Act of 1789. In January 1831, for example, the Committee on the Judiciary reported favorably on a bill to repeal the 25th Section but it was defeated on the floor of the Senate soon afterward. As was to be expected, most of the attacks originated with the delegations from the South and West. They did not hesitate to propose repeal of the entire Judiciary Act of 1789, a constitutional amendment limiting the judges to seven years' tenure, unanimity in the Supreme Court on questions of constitutionality, and an outright prohibition against decisions touching on the rights of the states.

The President certainly felt the force of demands for "reform", for important members of his inner circle of advisers were among the most vigorous critics of the judiciary. The atmosphere of hostility was doubtless charged by the attitude of Martin Van Buren, Amos Kendall, Louis McLane and Andrew Stevenson, all close presidential advisers. Van Buren attacked the Supreme Court while a member of the Senate in 1826 and while John Marshall lived feared his control over the Court. Like many Jackson men he followed Jeffersonian doctrine; when Jefferson told him of his proposal to limit judicial tenure to four or six years, Van Buren recalled: "Fresh from the Bar, and to some extent at least under the influence of professional prejudices, I remember to have thought his views extremely radical, but have lived to subscribe to their general correctness."

Thomas Hart Benton in the Senate and Andrew Stevenson in the House, both legislative lieutenants of the President, deplored Marshall's invasion of state sovereignty. Stevenson was Judge Spencer Roane's protégé, Marshall's most celebrated opponent in the states, and carried his prejudice against the Court with him to Congress. Amos Kendall's hostility toward the judiciary dated from his experience as an editor in Kentucky and the rise of the New Court party there. At one time he proposed a special court to which each state was to appoint a judge to handle conflicts between the states and the federal government. Louis McLane, another presidential confidant, proposed to Van Buren that judicial tenure be limited and the President be given power to remove judges on petition of two thirds of the state legislatures. And a Tennessee politician, in one of many similar letters, asked Jackson to propose to Congress a change in the Judiciary Act which would restrict appeals from the state to the federal courts.

There is abundant evidence that Jackson was subjected to arguments against the judiciary by influential presidential advisers and political leaders in the states. Some men close to the President, such as Edward Livingston, Roger B. Taney and James Buchanan, did not take part in the attack. James Buchanan, in fact, wrote the minority report of the Judiciary Committee which had reported favorably on repeal of the Judiciary Act of 1789. But the unfavorable climate of opinion and the commitment of many of his advisers to judicial reform suggest that if the President had used his popularity and power to support anti-judicial legislation, "reform" would have carried the day. The fact is that Jackson did not recommend proposals to weaken the judiciary in his messages to Congress, nor is there evidence of hostility in his correspondence. On the crucial issue of repeal of the Judiciary Act of 1789 he was persistently silent.

Conclusion

What were the results of eight years of defiance, independence and respect? The President brought with him to office party leaders who were hostile to the federal judiciary and demanded reforms that included the recall of judges and repeal of the Judiciary Act of 1789. The President did not put his weight behind these efforts. For more significant and complex reasons than dislike of John Marshall and loyalty to states' rights, Jackson defied the Supreme Court during the Georgia controversy, argued for the President's independence of the Supreme Court on constitutional questions in his Bank veto and inferentially in his attitude toward the Kendall episode. On the other hand, defiance and independence are only the most obvious parts of an involved picture. The President also reaffirmed the value of judicial review during the Nullification controversy when the integrity of the Union was at stake and indirectly strengthened the federal judiciary by appointing men who were more in tune with their times than their aging predecessors. Jackson did claim a coördinate and independent standing for the President but it did not follow that the states were independent of the federal judiciary. These observations indicate that caution should be exercised when quoting that highly quotable remark, "John Marshall has made his decision; now let him enforce it." This statement has been accepted generally as the touchstone of Jackson's attitude toward the judiciary. One can argue, conversely, that this was the exception to a rule of guarded but genuine respect for the judiciary based on Jackson's constitutional sense and his own past. Closer scrutiny suggests that a happy but probably apocryphal statement should not be accepted as conclusive evidence of Jackson's disposition toward the judiciary.

11 / "Liberty and Union": An Analysis of Three Concepts Involved in the Nullification Controversy

Major L. Wilson

In the first half of the decade of the 1830's, leading American politicians engaged in a significant debate over the nature of the Union. A growing national economic system and the nationalization of political institutions made such a debate necessary and probably inevitable. It extended from the Webster-Hayne debates of 1830 (ostensibly over public land policy), to the struggles over Indian removal and the national bank, and culminated with the justifications and attacks on South Carolina's attempt to nullify the federal tariff law. The following article by Major L. Wilson seeks to categorize the major threads of argument over Liberty and Union and it analyzes the thoughts of three principal spokesmen—Daniel Webster, John Quincy Adams, and President Andrew Jackson—who sought to combat the nullification doctrines of John C. Calhoun.

Jackson's position as a unionist lay in the center of the spectrum. This in great part accounted for his strength as a national politician, and at the same time it helps account for the fact that viewed from one end of the unionist spectrum or the other, Jackson appeared to be a member of the opposing side. He may not have been well-versed in constitutional theory, but as the President he acted upon a firm belief in the divided sovereignty created by the Constitution. And only such a nonabsolutist approach ensured the preservation of the most vital absolute, the Union.

Journal of Southern History, XXXIII (August 1967), 331–355. Copyright 1967 by the Southern Historical Association. Reprinted by permission of the Managing Editor. Footnotes have been omitted.

For further reading: Paul C. Nagel, *One Nation Indivisible: The Union in American Thought, 1776–1861* (1964); Louis Hartz, "South Carolina vs. the United States," in Daniel Aaron (ed.), *America in Crisis* (1952); William W. Freehling, *Prelude to Civil War: The Nullification Controversy in South Carolina* (1966).

The period from 1828 to 1833 witnessed a great debate over the policies which freemen in the Union ought to pursue. The very nature of the Union and its destiny came in, as a consequence, for profound consideration. The ideas of nullification and secession served to precipitate the debate and to provide much of its form. But there was far more on the other side then just the matter of preserving the Union. Opposition to the Nullifiers, it was true, reflected widespread agreement that liberty and the Union were not to be so easily separated. Within this consensus among the defenders of the Union, however, real and significant differences did obtain. The idea of freedom could, with peculiar urgency, lend itself to many interpretations in a society still in the process of being built. The nullification controversy thus involved not alone the decision to save and to order the existing Union; it pointed as well to the kind of liberal society to be realized on the yet unsettled continent.

As many contemporaries saw it, the impending retirement of the national debt provided a unique occasion for the seminal debate. John G. Watmough of Pennslyvania told the House of Representatives in January 1833 that he had long feared "the gratifying period" for the Union "could not arrive without bringing with it evils and developing springs of political action which might shake her to her very foundation. . . ." A New York representative, Churchill C. Cambreleng, likewise remarked how the issue of the debt had "substituted for debates about woollens, cottons, iron, and sugar, questions involving not only constitutional powers, but the fundamental distinction between a confederate and a national Government." The end of the debt, he added significantly, had placed the nation "in a new latitude." In Jeffersonian terms it meant that the land at last belonged to the living. What the living generation did at such a crucial juncture would be of unusual importance. Any new policy to be adopted would necessarily involve the more fundamental question about the nature of the nation's venture in freedom. By legislating on a particular matter at this time Congress thus functioned in some degree as a constituent assembly.

In the dialectic of debate, John C. Calhoun had the first say. With the *Exposition and Protest* in December 1828, he supplied a systematic challenge to the consolidating tendencies of the protective tariff and its related policies. He conceived the Union to be a partnership of sovereign states and the government an agent for achieving ends narrowly defined in the constitutional compact. Later pronouncements merely refined these views and spelled out in greater detail the technique of nullification. The Union, as he formulated the matter in his toast at the Jefferson Day Dinner in 1830, was next to liberty most dear, a means for freemen and not an end in itself. When a new revision of the tariff in 1832 left the principle of protection unchallenged, Governor James Hamilton, Jr., of South Carolina pronounced the system "as fixed as fate." On November 24 a state convention in South Carolina thereupon put theory into practice by solemnly absolving the citizens from any obligation to pay tariff duties after February 1, 1833. "CONSTITUTIONAL LIBERTY is the only idol of our political devotion," it further proclaimed.

In opposition to these views swelled a chorus for the Union. "Liberty and Union," Daniel Webster affirmed in reply to Senator Robert Y. Hayne in 1830, were "one and inseparable." As an indispensable means for the pursuit of happiness, he said in effect, the Union was an end in itself. John Quincy Adams in like spirit closed a Fourth of July oration to his constituents in 1831 with the sentiment of *"independence and Union forever."* The Union was the sum of all possible good, President Andrew Jackson proclaimed to the people of South Carolina the following year, designed by Providence as "the only means of attaining the high destinies to which we may reasonably aspire." All pronounced the experiment of Union undertaken by the Founding Fathers a success, and the tremendous response of the people seemed to ratify the view.

It was one thing to decide that freemen still shared a common destiny, but it was quite another thing to determine what that destiny ought to be. The Union to be saved from the threat of the Nullifiers remained, in the minds of its different defenders, a particular kind of Union after all. Three fairly distinct conceptions of it, indeed, found expression during the nullification controversy. Webster thought of the Union as an absolute, as a grand corporation cutting across time to bind all generations together. His predilection for order and his legal cast of mind, however, disposed him to stress the prescriptive force of the past far more than any positive vision of its future. With no blueprint of policies to be initiated with the expiration of the debt, he wanted the guidelines of the past to direct the nation in a more organic way. Adams, by contrast, considered the Union in far more prospective and instrumental terms. He called for the government to serve as a positive agent in improving the nation's estate. The collective and cumulative nature of the pursuit of happiness meant, in this view, that the progressive development of the country as a whole would enable freemen in it to attain ever higher levels of self-realization. With the resources of the country about to be relieved from debt, he wanted his age to incorporate future generations more fully in the grand venture of Union. President Jackson, meanwhile, placed the Union on a far different basis. He supposed it to be indissoluble because it rested on the will of a growing majority of citizens who, like himself, looked to the Union as the giver of identity and the guarantor of the future. The Union held freemen together as they went their several ways, yet a glorious destiny for the nation was in the process of being fulfilled. Essential freedom from past prescriptions and from future controls at once comprised the nature and assured the greatness of the Union.

Order, improvement, freedom from control—these were the vital principles of Union held respectively by Webster, Adams, and Jackson. Of the three, Jackson's views actually supplied a creative basis for compromise in 1833. Jackson agreed with Webster and Adams that the Union must be preserved, yet he shared with Calhoun the belief that freemen should be allowed to pursue happiness without fundamental direction from the government. In transcending the older categories, Jackson spoke as a nationalist against the Nullifiers and as an advocate of state rights against the American System of policies. He could enlist Webster in support of the Force Bill while he approved the new tariff adjustments. By favoring with equal facility both parts of the compromise, he served as the enforcer of the peace. On the fateful issue of slavery, however, this synthesis was to prove unable to keep the peace by 1860.

Among the champions of Union, Webster spoke first. He gave in the Senate debate with Hayne in January 1830 a systematic answer to the "Carolina doctrines." By emotional appeal, economic argument, and constitutional affirmation he pleaded for the Union as an "absolute and vital necessity to our welfare." Later public addresses developed more fully the theme of its "transcendent value," while the speech against Calhoun on the Force Bill in February 1833 brought into fullest form his legal argument for the Union as an end in itself.

Throughout the nullification controversy Webster stressed order as the highest good of the Union. Nowhere else did he express this so effectively as in the reply to Hayne, for here he made the Union to appear as essentially religious in its highest function. The Union under the Constitution gave stable form to liberty, he had earlier observed, thus enabling each generation of freemen to relate itself meaningfully in "the great chain of being." Primal chaos, in such a view, was the only alternative to Union. By using a chain, a temple, or a constellation as a symbol, Webster dramatized the awful possibility that the snapping of any link, the collapse of a single column, or the bolting of any one star would involve the whole in ruin. Nullification led to secession, he warned, and secession from the "happy constellation" of Union could not stop until all had descended, "star after star, into obscurity and night." The practical import of Hayne's position, as he changed the figure, brought the nation to "the precipice of disunion" and threatened a fatal plunge to "the depth of the abyss below." Repelled by the very thought of disunion, he chose "not to penetrate the veil" to see what might lie hidden in "the dark recess behind."

Less emotional appeal marked Webster's later speeches, for popular approval assured him that the Union was safe. But the attribute of order remained central in his thought about its nature and destiny. With regard to economic policies, he spoke for the status quo. Many at the time hailed the end of the debt as a propitious opportunity for putting the country on a new course. Webster, alarmed rather by the "morbid sort of fervor" on the subject in some quarters, wanted to cling to the existing policies. "The duty of the Government, at the present moment," he said in reference to the tariff, "would seem to be to preserve, not to destroy; to maintain the position which it has assumed . . . ." As a spokesman for free-trade interests in New England, he had long opposed government aid to industry. With much capital in his section now converted to manufacturing, he argued for protection as the "settled course of public policy." Personal and sectional interests also helped to inspire his protest against Jackson's veto of the bill for rechartering the Second Bank of the United States. "This message," he declared ominously, "calls us to the contemplation of a future, which little resembles the past." Against the constitutional scruples of the President he pitted the authority of a nation's acquiescence in the Bank for forty years. He deplored as well the dislocation which the end of the Bank would cause in an economy adapted to its powerful and benign influences. He was alarmed, he confessed, by the "unaccountable disposition to destroy the most useful and most approved institutions of the Government."

As he looked to the future, then, Webster adduced no new system of policies to shape the destinies of the country. He wanted its course to unfold in a more organic fashion under the steady direction of past policies. Whatever changes there were to be made, he supposed, should reflect the new and imperious needs of the time. His votes for Western improvements and for special pre-emption laws provided a case in point and illustrated as well his ability to transcend narrow sectional interests. The government was less a planner of the future, in his way of thinking, than a positive broker to comprehend new interests and to harmonize them all. "The interests of all must be consulted, and reconciled, and provided for, as far as possible," he explained, "that all may perceive the benefits of a united government." His earlier reluctance to place the great interests of the country under the patronage of government had arisen from the professed belief that harmony could come only where all were left alone. Now Webster saw the statesman's task as a positive and creative one. His earlier fears that freedom for most people would be doomed in an industrial age likewise gave way to the hope that laborers under the protection of the government might also acquire "a stake in the welfare of that community."

A recent biographer, taking note of his conversion by 1828 from a negative to a positive concept of government, has concluded that Webster was essentially a player of roles. Webster sought, in any case, to conserve what he took to be the realities of developing national unity. While the tariff and related policies reflected already the facts of interdependence, he rejoiced that one effect of those policies would be to create even greater ties of mutual interest. Retrospectively, indeed, he imputed that same purpose to the Founding Fathers. Consolidation had been, he thus affirmed, "the very end of the constitution." As the bonds of Union grew stronger, he believed that a fuller "national character" would continue to emerge out of more disparate elements. Nor did this process rule out a moderate growth for the Union across territory already in its possession. He would "bring the interests of these new States into the Union," he told a New York audience in 1831, "and incorporate them closely in the family compact." But Webster did anticipate here his later opposition to new territorial acquisition, for he assumed that there were geographical limits to the development of a homogeneous nation. The destiny of the Union thus involved in large measure the realization of the existing elements of solidarity.

Freedom for each generation caught up in this process had about it a distinctly historical quality. The will of the numerical majority within its constitutional sphere, Webster protested to Calhoun in 1833, did express the true will of the nation. But it was to be limited by the prescriptions of the past, ultimately by the interpretation of the courts. Without the judiciary, Webster ever argued, the Union would cease to exist. In contrast to Jackson's predilection for "mere majorities," he thought the Union of freemen rested on the collected will of all generations. In larger perspective, he deemed freedom in America to be in the family line of English liberties gained and disciplined through the centuries. The American Revolution, in this light, represented a supremely conservative act. Freedom was not to be regarded as a universal impulse in man, but as a social product with a history and a pedigree. It was, he explained, "our established, dear-bought, peculiar American liberty."

In his formal thought about the Union, Webster managed quite well to conserve the new order. He remained, with some reservations, within the contract school of thought. On one of its tenets, namely, the notion of divisible sovereignty, he was quite explicit. He wrote off as totally "European" the contrary idea Calhoun was using as a bulwark for the state-rights position. In the peculiar system of America, he asserted, all power lay with the people and was capable of division. The people had, as a matter of fact, delegated some power to the central government and some to the states. Each level of government, he furthermore noted, was supreme in its sphere and the judge of its own powers. But the division of power could not be, in the very nature of the case, an exact and absolute thing. By considering the meaning of the Constitution as in part the kind of thing that grew from precedent to precedent, Webster rather provided for a gradual but real shift in power to the federal government. He supposed the shift necessary in order to accommodate the centralizing tendencies in American life. Calhoun's appeal to state sovereignty and his idea of the concurrent majority amounted to a call for a moratorium on change. By his dynamic view of the divided powers of sovereignty, Webster sought a basis for orderly change.

It was only with considerable qualification that Webster could hold a second principle of contract theory. He assumed, to be sure, that the Union was "artificial and founded on agreement." By the way he thought of the parties to the agreement and of the time when it was made, however, he apparently took new ground. Accepting as a literal fact the preamble phrase, "We the people," he insisted that the Constitution had been formed by the people as a whole and not by several peoples separately organized into state communities. This position involved the further notion that the people as a whole had been organized before 1787, that the Union was older than the Constitution. With the First Continental Congress in 1774, Webster thus affirmed, the people had constituted themselves "in some measure, and to some national purposes," a body politic. But the agreement in this case could not have been a very conscious one, for none could possibly have realized the full consequences of the act. To the degree that the contract in 1774 was unconscious, then, Webster flirted with organic theories which held the state to be the product of cultural needs. In effect, he read back into the period before 1787 that sense of nationality which developed subsequently. It was, in any event, good psychology, if not good history. An admirer praised Webster for teaching "the citizens in general what their relation to the Federal government is . . . ." The chief surprise, he concluded, was that someone had not thought of it sooner.

In the way he conceived the nature of the constitutional agreement, Webster diverged most of all from the contract school. He deemed the Constitution to be, not a continuing agreement among freemen, but an executed contract. In the same sense that a law "is not the agreement, but something created by the agreement," he noted, the Constitution ". . . . is itself not the compact, but its result." Ratification by the people terminated agreement and gave to the document the force of law. "The compact is executed," he went on, "and the end designed by it attained. Henceforth, the fruit of the agreement exists, but the agreement itself is merged in its own accomplishment . . . ." Webster had earlier argued before the Supreme Court that the Dartmouth College charter was of this nature. As an irreversible grant it had brought a private corporation into existence and stamped it with perpetuity. The Constitution in like fashion had created a corporation with "a will of its own" and the "powers and faculties to execute its own purposes." His view of the constitutional agreement as a self-liquidating one did provoke considerable criticism, yet it served his purpose well. It gave legal form to his view of the Union as a grand instrument of order comprehending all generations. Each generation retained the power of amendment, he admitted, and the right of revolution. But such a concept of Union tended more than ever to reduce revolution to the starkness of naked insurrection.

By taking certain liberties with an older way of thinking, Webster was thus able to provide a solid basis for the Union as an absolute. He did move in some ways toward the organic school which by mid-century was to regard the Union as a natural product of underlying realities rather than an artificial body created by consent. But he did not move all the way. He would have found unthinkable in 1833, for example, the proposition broached by Senator William H. Seward in 1850 that a new Union would rise phoenixlike from the ruins of the old. As a champion of order, Webster supported "the Constitution as it is and . . . the Union as it is." No matter how unlimited its future, he never forgot that the Union had been made by human hands and ever required the solicitude of the statesman. If the existing Union failed despite the nearly ideal conditions for freedom on a virgin continent, none other could ever succeed. Nor was Webster prepared for any substantial reform, even with regard to the unequal provision for the three-fifths representation of slaves. The Union was an absolute in the first instance, not because it was strong enough to stand any shock, but because the shock of its dissolution would reduce life to nothing. In language reminiscent of Edmund Burke, he gave a summary definition of the Union:

> The Union is not a temporary partnership of States. It is the association of the people, under a constitution of Government, uniting their power, joining together their highest interests, cementing their present enjoyments, and blending, in one indivisible mass, all their hopes for the future. Whatsoever is steadfast in just political principles, whatsoever is permanent in the structure of human society, whatsoever there is which can derive an enduring character from being founded on deep laid principles of constitutional liberty, and on the broad foundations of the public will—all these unite to entitle this instrument to be regarded as a permanent constitution of Government.

While Webster revered order, John Quincy Adams deemed improvement the highest good of the Union. "The constitution itself," he exulted in 1833, "is but one great organized engine of improvement—physical, moral, political." Assuming that freedom in America had already been tamed, he looked to the fruitful consequences of its full sway. Liberty meant power, the power of men freed from the trammels of the past to work out their own destinies. "It is the purpose," he exclaimed, "for which intellectual power was given to man by his Maker . . . ." Hopefully, the dominion of mind and the arts of peace were in process of replacing the reign of prejudice, exploitation, and war. By taking thought, he believed, men could truly advance toward a higher stage of civilization. While holding with the Law of Progress, he did not suppose it to be a self-fulfilling one. It rather prescribed the sustained effort of freemen. In this perspective, the Union was a positive means for progressive improvement.

Basic to Adams' thinking was the assumption that happiness for the individual necessarily required the improvement of the whole community. The pursuit of happiness was, in the nature of things, a collective and cumulative enterprise. Social progress created ever-widening opportunities for self-realization. In its social and economic aspects, the ideal community possessed a relatively stable and compacted population, a balance of rural and urban elements, and great variety in its occupations. Such a community gave scope to the diversity of talents and interests in men, thus conducing "to their own elevation in the scale of being." Against the agrarian rhetoric of the day Adams pleaded for a more collective mastery over the forces of

nature. The task would also require time and the co-operation of oncoming generations. Freemen in any one age would find fulfillment through their participation in
the long-range goal of building a better common life. Freedom here involved far
more than a brute absence of restraint. It was less a quantitative function of open
space and more a qualitative function of time. The Union, in this sense, could best
be seen as a teleological entity, as something yet to be fulfilled. It was in its grand
prospective dimensions "an union of all classes, conditions, and occupations of men;
an union coextensive with our territorial dominions; an union for successive ages,
without limitation of time."

Because the full measure of the Union's grandeur lay in the future, Adams professed to see the impending retirement of the national debt as a truly rare opportunity.
It was given to his age, he supposed, to become the greatest link of the Union.
In a very significant figure he compared the American people to the children of
Israel. After its own travail of forty years, the nation could at last "survey from the
top of Pisgah the happy and promised land reserved for" its reward and use. By
paying the debt his generation participated with the Founding Fathers in the glory
of gaining freedom. By diverting more of the unencumbered resources of the country
to the improvement of the nation's estate, his age could then incorporate future
generations more fully in the grand pursuit of happiness. Whereas Webster lamented
the end of the debt as another bond of Union set loose, Adams hailed the great
freedom it allowed. He wanted to do something with freedom.

The policies to be adopted at such a seminal moment were thus of unusual
importance. Adams appreciated no less than Webster the role of the government as a
positive broker for harmonizing the great interests. But he brought to the defense of
the American System of policies a much greater spirit of system. He wanted the
government to direct in an active and self-conscious way the course of the country.
He saw in the protective tariff a way to continue the diversification of pursuits and
in the Bank a salutary means to stimulate and regulate the development of the
country. Much of his opposition to the policy of Indian removal arose from the fear
that too rapid a settlement of the West would create imbalance in the community.
In part for the same reason he resisted the numerous proposals for the speedy
disposal of the public lands. With the continued revenues from these lands, moreover,
Adams wanted to finance the key feature in his system, namely, a vastly expanded
program of internal improvement. Such things as roads and canals would quicken
industry and intercourse among all parts of the country. They would also serve to
increase land values and, hence, the amount of revenue available to the government
for promoting education and the arts. Though favoring direct appropriations by the
central government, Adams also approved the plan of Henry Clay for distributing
land revenues among the states. Controlled development, in any case, remained the
goal of policy. A supporter of Adams in the House expressed quite clearly this vision
of the future. "Population, settlement, education, and improvement, will hold their
united march," Tristam Burges of Rhode Island observed in 1830, "until your whole
territory, cultivated and improved, is filled with a well educated, great, and prosperous people.

The spirit of the planner came out as well in the way Adams argued for the
constitutional power of the central government to direct the pursuits of the people.
While Webster invoked the authority of past policies, Adams boldly pointed to the
growing needs of "the common defence and general welfare." In a public letter,

which sought to answer the strictures of former President James Madison against consolidation, he set forth this position at length. He made no claim that the provision for the common defense and general welfare was in itself a substantive grant of power. It did, however, represent a statement of the larger purposes of Union for whose fulfillment the taxing power had been granted. To this argument Adams also brought the skill of a partisan debater. President Thomas Jefferson, he tellingly observed, had appealed to the common defense and general welfare in justifying the acquisition of Louisiana. He had, in effect, used "a broad and liberal construction" in order to shape the nation's destiny by external expansion. With equal right and greater justice, Adams triumphantly concluded, the government should direct the energies of the nation in the task of internal improvement.

Many of his formal pronouncements about the Union, it was true, appeared to belie this urge to centralization. Adams repudiated, for example, the idea of the executed contract which Webster found useful for that purpose. The Senator had "hung his cause upon a broken hinge," he declared, for "all constitutional government is a compact." Adams also subscribed to the notion of divisible powers of sovereignty. All powers "emanate from the people," he insisted, and the people had used the power to erect a complex system of state and federal government. His praise for the ability of the system to apply the republican principle successfully over an area "exceeding that of the Roman Empire" likewise showed his regard for the federative nature of the Union.

At the heart of his thought, however, remained the view of a nation already organized for great common tasks. By calling the Declaration of Independence a "social compact," Adams pushed back to 1776 the moment when the people gave conscious expression to the sense of their common destiny. The people, "speaking in the first person," thereafter adopted the Constitution and attained the more perfect form for securing the blessings of liberty—"the most exalted purposes of human action, upon this side [of] the grave." In private correspondence at the time Adams went much farther in arguing for the primacy of the Union. He maintained, as President Abraham Lincoln was to do, that "the sovereignty of each State was the child and creature of the Union." Webster was interested in the orderly change toward greater unity, but Adams assumed the existence of national order and looked to accelerated change.

The Union, for Adams, was thus a grand instrument for realizing the vast potential of freedom on a relatively undeveloped continent. This teleological emphasis came out most clearly in the way he conceived of the two enemies of the Union during the nullification controversy. One of them was the rising democratic spirit of the time. "Democracy has no forefathers, it looks to no posterity," he complained, "it is swallowed up in the present, and thinks of nothing but itself." If such a spirit should prevail, all hopes for a glorious future must perish. Democracy represented in the body politic the element of passion rather than reason. The sum of its philosophy, he contemptuously remarked, was "comprised in the maxim of leaving money in the pockets of the people." Against the charge that business corporations were monopolistic, Adams protested that, under wise management, they served rather to pool the energies of many and promote the larger good. He yearned in like fashion for leaders of "resolution, intelligence, and energy" to rise above the popular passions and give positive direction to the nation's course.

The slave power, in Adams' view, was the second enemy. The unequal representa-

tion given in the three-fifths clause, when added to the sectional solidarity created
by the slavery appeal, threatened to place the Union under the permanent control
of a declining minority. Though he deemed slavery to be alien to the principles of
freedom embraced by the nation in 1776, Adams was willing to tolerate it so long
as it remained a quiescent force. But he now warned that it was becoming an
aggressive force. The slaveholders' new concept of the Union as "a partnership of
corporate bodies" boded ill for any hopes of a corporate pursuit of happiness. Impending compromise in 1833, he furthermore professed to believe, came in part at the
dictation of the slave power and tended to the destruction of the American System.
That his own moral strictures may have been one cause for the new aggressiveness
of slaveholders, he did not see fit to discuss. He was ready, however, to declare
publicly by 1833 that an irreconcilable conflict of interests and ultimately of principles
obtained in the Union. "It cannot be denied," he observed,

> that in a community spreading over a large extent of territory, and politically
> founded upon the principles proclaimed in the declaration of independence, but
> differing so widely in the elements of their social condition, that the inhabitants
> of one-half the territory are wholly free, and those of the other half divided into
> masters and slaves, deep, if not irreconcilable collisions of interest must abound.
> The question whether such a community can exist under one common Govern-
> ment, is a subject of profound, philosophical speculation in theory. Whether it
> can continue long to exist, is a question to be solved only by the experiment
> now making by the people of this Union, under that national compact, the con-
> stitution of the United States.

Would the "experiment now making" lead to disunion? Or could the conflict
somehow be resolved within the Union? On these matters during the latter part of
the nullification controversy, Adams displayed that ambivalence about the Union
later to come out in the petition fight, the controversy over Texas, and the more
general issue of slavery expansion. He appeared, on the one hand, to believe that
disunion was possible. Because improvement was central in his thought about the
Union, he tended to feel that the destruction of the policies necessary for its improvement might destroy the Union itself. To "dash from the lips of our prosperity the
cup of joy" might be to make the Union not worth while. He professed to see
the compromise in 1833, in this light, as the work of Jackson and at one with the
President's successful war on all parts of the American System. Jackson's veto of the
bank bill and of internal improvement measures, the reduction of the tariff duties,
the removal of the Indians, and especially the call for a more liberal land policy
convinced Adams that the President was embracing "a complete system of future
Government for this Union directly tending to its dissolution . . . ." He had sold
out to the slave power and the democracy, Adams bitterly noted, "to the nullifiers of
the South and the land-robbers of the West." In pronouncing the "epitaph" of the
American System, Adams suggested that it might be the epitaph of the Union as
well.

But Adams thought of the Union at other times as an absolute in the present no
less than in the possible grandeur of its future. It was strong enough to resolve the
conflict of interests and then to resume its more constructive tasks. The resolution of
the conflict could come in two ways: slavery might be destroyed or the slave power
as an effective political force might be contained. For these purposes Adams here
regarded the Union less as the product of voluntary agreement and more as the

organic expression of physical, economic, and political necessities. The interdependence of economic interests, as Lincoln was also to argue, the geographical propinquity of the sections, and the imperious needs of the upper Mississippi Valley for an outlet to the sea all dictated the Union as an absolute. Adams warned would-be secessionists that the two parts of the country "would remain in the same relative geographical position to each other, each still employed in the same occupations, and with the same irreconcilable and opposite interests, without that link of union between them . . . ." War to reunite the sections would surely follow, he implied, with the abolition of slavery a most likely incident of the struggle. His vigorous use of these ideas in support of the Force Bill and in opposition to tariff compromise evoked the charge that he had "thrown a firebrand" into the House. Cries of "Robespierre" likewise greeted similar views expressed by Representative Samuel F. Vinton of Ohio.

Short of war and abolition, Adams proposed to resolve the conflict by making the slave power a declining voice in the councils of the nation. The political tactic he suggested for this purpose foreshadowed much of Free Soil and Republican politics in the 1850's. In order to unite freemen in the majority section of the North, it would be necessary to divide the two elements—the democracy and the slave power—which he had elsewhere considered as the common enemies of the Union. He must, in other words, show that the real foes of the people were not the Northern advocates of positive government, but rather the spokesmen of the slave power. The three-fifths provision for representation, he thus could note, made slaveholders the only element of aristocracy in the Union. By playing upon the divisions natural in the open society of the North, he furthermore argued, the aristocratic element was able to become the balancing power in the government. Under these conditions thus arose the spectacle of one-twentieth of the people shaping the destinies of an overwhelming majority. Nor was the voice of the slaveholders a negative one, for the effect of their control on the people was direct and malignant. Using the prolabor argument for positive government that became so commonplace later on, Adams charged that the slave power sought by opposing protection to "rob the free working man of the North of the wages of his labor; to take money from his pocket and put it into that of the Southern owner of machinery." By his absolute resolve to oppose the further admission of slave areas into the Union, Adams also helped to define the later issues of controversy.

The abolition of slavery or the containment of the slave power actually amounted to a program of internal reform. It involved on moral grounds the effort to make the essential principle of freedom—avowed in 1776—the ruling political force in the Union. Once the alien element of slavery had been checked, Adams then supposed that freemen could resume the business of improvement. His own activities after the compromise in 1833 were to suggest this priority of tasks. Whether he was an abolitionist or merely the "prince of fellow travelers" is not entirely clear. But he behaved, in either case, like a man with a job to do. The emphasis Webster placed on order tended to rule out any effort at substantial change. For Adams, by contrast, reform would remove the obstacle to the higher realization of the Union.

Jackson, the third champion of Union, conceived of it in a very different way. No basic reform was called for in his view; no teleological essence remained to be fulfilled. The Union existed in the fullness of its nature at that time. His quantitative concept of freedom, indeed, made this necessarily the case. As a political good, freedom was not the kind of thing pointing beyond itself to progressive development through time. It meant then and forever the freedom of the individual from any essential direction in his pursuit of happiness. It was a thing to be possessed and enjoyed in its entirety at the time. For a Union of freemen, the future would be one that reproduced the present; its destiny would simply be more of the same. Not until 1843 did Jackson hit upon the happy phrase, "extending the area of freedom," but the substance of the notion inhered in his thought during the nullification controversy. The true destiny of the Union, in these terms, could best be seen in its quantitative growth across space rather than in any qualitative change through time.

Jackson's view of the Union, from his Western vantage point, furthermore transcended the categories of nationalism and state rights. While holding with Webster and Adams that the Union must be preserved, he shared Calhoun's idea of it as a Union of severely limited powers. In two basic state papers during the nullification crisis—the fourth annual message on December 4, 1832, and the proclamation six days later—he gave rounded expression to this position. He would consolidate power to save the Union from the Nullifiers, yet he was prepared to dismantle the American System of policies and devolve power on the states and the people. Many contemporaries, it was true, saw nothing but inconsistency in the two messages. But the equal support he gave to the Force Bill and to new tariff adjustment showed in a practical way the underlying unity of his thought. The "preservation of the rights of the several States and the integrity of the Union," he declared on the very morrow of compromise, constituted two "necessarily connected" goals of his administration.

On the nationalist side of his thought, Jackson based the Union on the will of the majority. Whereas Webster invoked the will of all generations and Adams the prospects of a glorious future, Jackson found the Union as an absolute in the hearts of the people. The "united voice of the yeomenry of the country" in response to the Nullification Proclamation confirmed his belief that the Union was theirs. While opposing the "federalist" heresies in the proclamation, Representative Churchill C. Cambreleng of New York had to admit that the people passed over its theories because the sentiments "make them think and feel like men." Since order of the most solid sort already existed, Jackson could dismiss the call by Webster and others to forge by positive policies new material bonds of Union. "In thus attempting to make our General Government strong," he protested, "we make it weak." He would "rivet the attachment" of the people by simply leaving them alone.

The Union was deemed dear, not for anything specific which it did, but for the identity it gave to freemen as they went their several ways. At no time during the nullification crisis did Jackson express a regard for the "old thirteen" as the link with the past and the future. He could only judge as "madness" and "folly" the disposition of the plain people in South Carolina to follow the Nullifiers. They were becoming, he exclaimed in disbelief, "the destroyers of their own prosperity and liberty." The Union was, in the order of Providence, the "only means" for freemen. That great freedom which Jackson claimed for destroying the policies of the past stood in stark contrast to the reverence with which he bowed before the absolute Union. "Providence," to use the categories of John William Ward, here sharply defined the area in which "Will" could operate.

On the state-rights side of his thought, Jackson spoke for the new part of the Union. Because growth was for him the most dramatic evidence of its vitality, he took the "federal" nature of the Union to signify a proper division of power and not a compact theory of origins. Though it was made possible through the surrender of power by the old states, he called for the central government in turn to devolve power on the new areas of development. Freemen, as carriers of the nation, could hence go forth without essential direction from the center and yet remain in the Union, whose federative aspect was uniquely suited to comprehend what it did not control. It was very significant, in this light, that the "one absurdity out of thousands" in the Carolina doctrines which Jackson saw fit to refute was one pertaining to a new state. "We gave five millions for Louisiana," he explained to Martin Van Buren, "we admitted her into the Union, [and then] she too has the right to secede, close the commerce of six states, and levy contribution both upon exports and imports." Such a position, he protested, was "an insult to the understanding" of the Founding Fathers no less than a violation of the natural unity decreed by the Mississippi River. By his efforts at the time to acquire Texas, Jackson also displayed his direct relation to the ideas of "manifest destiny" in the following decade. Texas ought to be brought into the Union, he pleaded, because "the god of the universe had intended this great valley to belong to one nation".

The fusion of nationalist and state-rights elements also found expression in confusion of Jackson's more formal thought about the Union. The inconsistencies marking his statements suggest that he transcended the terms within which the issue had been previously debated. In his Nullification Proclamation, for example, three separate dates were mentioned for the origin of the Union. By calling the Constitution "our social compact," he appeared to favor 1787. Yet if the Union were "coeval with our political existence," as he also stated, then the year 1776 had a better claim. Elsewhere he declared that even "before the declaration of independence we were known in our aggregate character as *the United Colonies of America.*" A fourth date was given in his private correspondence, for here he supposed the "confederated perpetual union" to have been established by the Articles of Confederation. Contradiction also obtained in his thought about the parties who formed the Union. In the proclamation he leaned toward the view of Webster and Adams that the Union had been formed by the people as a whole. He elsewhere argued that it was the creature of the state governments or of the people as separately organized in state communities. Complete silence on all theoretical considerations, finally, characterized his special message to Congress on January 16, 1833, recommending the Force Bill. But consistent theories were not needed to convey his most fundamental sentiment: "the Constitution and the laws are supreme and the *Union indissoluble.*"

On one matter vital to the preservation of the Union, however, Jackson did remain consistent. He thought of the constitutional compact, whether made by the states or the people, as one of binding obligation. In this he stood once more between Webster and Calhoun. Against the notion of the executed contract, he contended for the Constitution as a continuing agreement. But he also opposed the claim by Calhoun that the parties to the compact had retained the independent power to judge its terms. "Because the Union was formed by a compact," Jackson observed, "it is said the parties to that compact may, when they feel themselves aggrieved, depart from it; but it is precisely because it is a compact that they can not." "The preservation of the Union," he likewise reminded the wavering Van Buren, "is the supreme law."

Along with this determination to consolidate power for saving the Union, Jackson also stood ready to devolve much of its power on the states and the people. The

Union's presence ought to be felt, he said in the Bank veto, "not in its power, but in its beneficence; not in its control, but in its protection; not in binding the States more closely to the center, but leaving each to move unobstructed in its proper orbit." Jackson assumed the right to destroy the Bank and to undo any other policies of the past which violated this principle. In opposition to the misgivings of conservatives, he affirmed that "Mere precedent is a dangerous source of authority . . . ." Nor could he accept the prospect of future controls which Adams called for. He wanted to free individuals from any basic control so that each could define and pursue happiness for himself. The true exercise of power by the government, in this way of thinking, was to remove the obstacles to larger liberty. Harmony and unimpeded growth for the country could then come, not by government patronage, but by leaving all interests alone.

By the end of 1832 Jackson gave a systematic formulation to the policies for the country. His fourth annual message amounted in substance to a call for destroying the American System. He repeated here his earlier condemnation of the national bank and internal improvements as examples of special legislation for monopolists. To this list he now added the protective tariff. Most significant of all, however, was his proposal for the public lands. With the burden of the national debt about to be lifted, he argued that "the speedy settlement of these lands constitutes the true interest of the Republic." He proposed a reduction in the price of land for actual settlers to a level barely sufficent to cover the costs of administration. Two important goals, he pointed out, could be achieved. The rapid disposal of the lands would, by hastening the removal of the federal administrative machinery from the states, help to redress the balance of power in the Union. It would, moreover, multiply freemen and thus extend the area of freedom. His plan suggested in dramatic form the way the government could devolve power and control. It was little wonder that Adams damned the President's proposal as a virtual "dissolution of the Union, an inextinguishable brand of civil war."

There was in Jackson's "system," to be sure, much of the spirit of a negative broker. He seemed disposed, in effect, to do away with any existing policy where appreciable discontent existed. The growing unrest of "a great sectional interest" in the West, for example, provided one good reason for changing the land policy. While agreeing that a protective tariff might, "in the abstract be beneficial to our country," Jackson likewise contended that the heartburnings in the South far outweighed any possible good. On the matter of internal improvements, indeed, he fashioned a precise formula for negative brokerage. If one more than one-fourth of the states rejected an amendment for that purpose, then the good of the whole called for no action at all.

But there was as well an affirmative mood in Jackson's thought about the proper policies for the future. The end of the debt made possible a truly new departure. "In regard to most of our great interests," he thus exulted, "we may consider ourselves as just starting in our career, and after a salutary experience about to fix upon a permanent basis the policy best calculated to promote the happiness of the people and facilitate their progress toward the most complete enjoyment of civil liberty." With the earth at last in the hands of the living, he wanted to secure an equal right to posterity. By destroying the established policies of the past and by overruling future controls, he would perpetuate the freedom of the eternal present.

Jackson's views enabled him to enforce the peace. His firm resolve to save the Union first of all served as an efficient means for pacification. On January 21, 1833, just five days after he had called on Congress to pass the Force Bill, an unauthorized group of leaders in Charleston put off beyond February 1 the time when nullification would go into effect. It was this action which paved the way for tariff adjustment, Clay then recognized, for it allowed Congress to make concessions without appearing to bow before a faction. Jackson did not, it was true, dictate the specific provisions of the compromise tariff. The Verplanck bill which had administration backing was replaced by the measure agreed on by Clay and Calhoun. By calling for an end to protection, however, Jackson did put pressure on Clay to come up with an alternative. On one substantive matter, at that, he did participate in the tariff part of the compromise. He gave a pocket veto to the bill for distributing land revenues to the states, which Clay pushed through Congress along with the tariff. The measure, passed with the help of Southern votes, was regarded by many Northern protectionists as "an equivalent for the Tariff bill." By his veto Jackson thus dictated a compromise settlement more in line with his policies.

In the name of the people Jackson thus saved the Union. By the people, as Marvin Meyers has well argued, the President meant "the great social residuum after alien elements have been removed." Ranged on one side against the Union were the Nullifiers and on the other side the seekers of special privilege. In his own postmortem on the compromise Jackson clearly defined these enemies of the people. "Nullification, the corrupting influence of the Bank,—the union of Calhoun and Clay, supported by the corrupt and wicked of all parties," he wrote to James Buchanan, "engaged all my attention." The destruction of nullification and the American System, in this light, comprised a single act. Liberty and Union were inseparable because the Union reposed on the will of freemen who wanted only to be left alone.

This Jacksonian synthesis would not be able, however, to keep the peace in the future. By absolutizing the majority, first of all, Jackson made it possible for the government to become a positive broker. The actual increase in appropriations for internal improvements during his administration was a token. While he opposed on principle any "system" of improvements, unsystematic log-rolling developed apace. Carolina spokesmen called for an absolute veto power in the states to check consolidation. Jackson placed all reliance on the veto power of the President and the virtue of the people. He wanted the government to leave the people alone, but he provided no way to make the people leave the government alone.

On the fateful issue of slavery, most of all, the synthesis would break down. The attitude of Adams at the time suggested that the compromise in 1833 could not be a permanent peace. Within Jacksonian ranks by the 1840's division would also appear. David Wilmot wanted the government to stop the spread of slavery. Such action, he reasoned, would remove an obstacle and let freemen pursue happiness without further direction. Lewis Cass and Stephen A. Douglas, by contrast, thought that popular sovereignty gave a better reading to the Jacksonian faith. With Webster and Clay, they were able to effect a new compromise in 1850. But in the crisis a decade later they could only fly to the defense of the Union. The people during the nullification crisis wanted their Union to be preserved, and Jackson's concept of liberty and Union provided a creative basis for saving it by peaceful means. But it was to be an uneasy peace.

12 / Jackson, Biddle, and the Bank of the United States

Bray Hammond

Jackson's war against the Second Bank of the United States was one of the most dramatic campaigns of his Presidency. In addition to the significant economic consequences of this struggle, it had important political results as well. Their effect on the office of the Presidency, the organization and realignment of political parties, and the problem of federal-state relations have all been argued by historians with a good deal of the heat that enlivened the contemporary debates.

The first stages of these arguments, those of open adulation or searing denunciation, have given way to studies that seek to probe motivations and evaluate the many interest groups influencing or influenced by the Bank War. Arthur Schlesinger's *Age of Jackson* (1945), the capstone of pro-Jackson accounts, praised the President's attack on Bank "aristocracy," and fixed the ideological center of radical Jacksonianism in the anti-Bank Democracy of the eastern cities. On the other hand, one of the most distinguished and widely read of those who view Jackson negatively is Bray Hammond. Hammond, a nonacademician, spent many years studying the Bank War from a particularly favorable observation post, as an officer in the Federal Reserve System. His sensitivity to the nuances of public finance make him one of the few historians writing on the Bank War to possess a practical and expert knowledge of banking, and his Federal Reserve post kept him acutely aware of those aspects of the operation of the Second National Bank that made it an early central bank.

The Bank War of this essay is thus not an account of "Andrew the Good" battling against the "Biddle Monster," and it runs counter to many of the versions the student may have previously encountered.

Journal of Economic History, VII (May 1947), 1–23. Reprinted by permission. Footnotes have been omitted except where they are necessary for an understanding of the text.

For further reading: Bray Hammond, *Banks and Politics in America from the Revolution to the Civil War* (1957); Fritz Redlich, *The Molding of American Banking, Part I* (1951); Thomas P. Govan, *Nicholas Biddle: Nationalist and Public Banker* (1959).

More than forty years have passed since Catterall's monograph on the second Bank of the United States was published, and, though that account has never been superseded, it antedates all recent literature on central banking and therefore presents inadequately the public purposes of the bank. Furthermore, it includes nothing about the bank's Pennsylvania successor, which failed, and thus omits the denouement of Biddle's conflict with Jackson. The inevitable effect of the failure, in the rough justice of history, was to make Jackson seem right and Biddle wrong; and this impression, especially in the absence of attention to the purpose and functions of the bank, seems in recent years to have been strengthened. I think it needs correction.

I

The Bank of the United States—the B.U.S. as Biddle and others often called it— was a national institution of complex bginnings, for its establishment in 1816 derived from the extreme fiscal needs of the federal government, the disorder of an unregulated currency, and the promotional ambitions of businessmen. The bank had an immense amount of private business—as all central banks then had and as many still have—yet it was even more definitely a government bank than was the Bank of England, the Bank of France, or any other similar institution at the time. The federal government owned one fifth of its capital and was its largest single stockholder, whereas the capital of other central banks was wholly private. Government ownership of central-bank stock has become common only in very recent years. Five of the bank's twenty-five directors, under the terms of its charter, were appointed by the President of the United States, and no one of these five might be a director of any other bank. Two of its three successive presidents—William Jones and Nicholas Biddle—were chosen from among these government directors. The charter made the bank depository of the government and accountable to Congress and the secretary of the Treasury.

On this depository relation hinged control over the extension of credit by banks in general, which is the essential function of a central bank. The government's receipts arose principally from taxes paid by importers to customs collectors; these tax payments were in bank notes, the use of checks not then being the rule; the bank notes were mostly those of private banks, which were numerous and provided the bulk of the money in circulation; the B.U.S. received these notes on deposit from the customs collectors and, becoming thereby creditor of the private banks that issued them, presented them to the latter for payment. Banks that extended credit properly and maintained adequate gold and silver reserves were able to pay their obligations promptly on demand. Those that overextended themselves were not. The pressure of the central bank upon the private banks was constant, and its effect was to restrict their lending and their issue of notes. In this fashion, it curbed the tendency of the banks to lend too much and so depreciate their circulation.[1] Its regulatory powers were dependent on the private banks' falling currently into debt to it. The regulatory powers now in effect under the Federal Reserve Act depend upon the opposite relation —that is, upon the private banks' maintaining balances with the Federal Reserve Banks. The private banks were then debtors to the central bank; they are now creditors. The regulatory powers of the United States Bank were simpler, more direct, and perhaps more effective than those of the Federal Reserve Banks, though they would not be so under present-day conditions.

It was notorious that large and influential numbers of the private banks and official state banks resented this regulation of their lending power. All but the more conservative found it intolerable to be let and hindered by the dunning of the B.U.S. and forced to reduce their debts instead of enlarging their loans. Many of them had the effrontery to insist as a matter of right that they be allowed to pay the central bank if and when they pleased. The effort of various states, especially Maryland and Ohio, to levy prohibitory taxes on the United States Bank's branches reflects this desire of the private banks to escape regulation quite as much as it reflects the states' jealousy of their "invaded" sovereignty; the efforts were economic as well as political.

In 1831, Gallatin commended the bank for its conduct during the twenties; it had "effectually checked excessive issues" by the state banks; "that very purpose" for which it had been established had been fulfilled. On the regulatory operation of the bank, "which requires particular attention and vigilance and must be carried on with great firmness and due forbearance, depends almost exclusively the stability of the currency . . ." The country's "reliance for a sound currency and, therefore, for a just performance of contracts rests on that institution." In 1833 he wrote to Horsley Palmer, of the Bank of England, that "the Bank of the United States must not be considered as affording a complete remedy," for the ills of overexpansion, "but as the best and most practicable which can be applied"; and its action "had been irreproachable" in maintaining a proper reserve position "as late as November 1830." Though Gallatin did not say so, this was in effect praise of Nicholas Biddle's administration of the bank.

The powerful expansion of the economy in the nineteenth century made it necessary for the regulatory action of the bank to be mostly one of restraint, but there was occasion also for it to afford ease as holder of the ultimate reserves and lender of last resort. One of the first things it did was to end the general suspension that the country had been enduring for more than two years; and a crucial factor in the willingness and ability of the private banks to resume payment of their obligations was the pledge of the United States Bank that it would support them. This, Vera Smith writes, was "a very early declaration of the view that it is the duty of the central bank to act as lender of last resort."

The regulatory functions of the bank were not always well performed. Its first president, William Jones, was a politician who extended credit recklessly, rendered

---

[1] I use the term "private banks" in preference to the common term "state banks" because it brings out the essential differences between the central bank and the units of the banking system regulated by it. I therefore include as private those "state banks" proper owned in whole or part by state governments; for functionally these "state banks" proper differed little if any from the private banks.

the bank impotent to keep the private banks in line, and nearly bankrupted it—all in a matter of three years. Langdon Cheves put the bank back in a sound condition by stern procedures that were unavoidably unpopular. When Nicholas Biddle succeeded Cheves in 1823, the bank was strong in every respect but good will. Biddle repressed the desires of the stockholders for larger dividends, keeping the rate down and accumulating reserves. The art of central banking was not so clearly recognized then as it has since become, but Biddle advanced it, and with better luck he might well be memorable for having developed means of mitigating the tendency to disastrous, periodic crises characteristic of the nineteenth century in the United States.

But Biddle, with all his superior talents, was not very discreet. He had an airy way of speaking that shocked his more credulous enemies and did him irreparable harm; and, when he described the functions of the bank, he contrived to give a livelier impression of its power than of its usefulness. Once when asked by a Senate committee if the B.U.S. ever oppressed the state banks, he said, "never": although nearly all of them might have been destroyed, many had been saved and still more had been relieved. This was ineffable in a man of Biddle's exceptional abilities. It put a normal situation in a sinister and uncouth light. A wanton abuse of regulatory powers is always possible, and abstention from it is not to be boasted of—any more than a decent man would boast of not choosing to be a burglar. By talking so, Biddle made his opponents feel sure he had let the cat out of the bag. For Thomas Hart Benton he had proved entirely too much—that he had a dangerous power "over the business and fortunes of nearly all the people." Jackson referred in his veto to Biddle's remark, and Roger Taney was still shuddering at the disclosure many years later. He believed then and he believed still, he wrote, that there was a scheme to close every state bank in the Union. He believed "that the matter had been thought of, and that the manner in which it could be done was well understood." That people believed such things, Biddle had his own jauntiness, naïveté, and political ineptitude to thank.

II

When Jackson became president in 1829, the B.U.S. had survived what then seemed its most crucial difficulties. The Supreme Court had affirmed and reaffirmed its constitutionality and ended the attempts of unfriendly states to interfere with it. The Treasury had long recognized its efficient services as official depository. The currency was in excellent condition. Yet in his first annual message, Jackson told Congress that "both the constitutionality and the expediency of the law creating the bank were well questioned by a large portion of our fellow-citizens, and it must be admitted by all that it has failed in the great end of establishing a uniform and sound currency."

There is nothing remarkable about Jackson's doubts of the bank's constitutionality, for he did not defer his own judgment to John Marshall's nor, in general, had the Supreme Court's opinions attained their later prestige. His statement that the bank had failed in establishing a good currency is more difficult to understand, for it was plainly untrue in the usual sense of the words. But he was evidently using the words in the special sense of locofoco hard-money doctrine, according to which the only good money was gold and silver; the Constitution authorized Congress to coin it and regulate its value; the states were forbidden to issue paper and the federal government was not empowered to do so. Jackson, wrote C. J. Ingersoll, "considers all the state banks unconstitutional and impolitic and thinks that there should be no currency but coin. . . ." There were practical considerations no less important than the legal. It was evident to the antibank people that banking was a means by which a relatively small number of persons enjoyed the privilege of creating money to be lent, for the money obtained by borrowers at banks was in the form of the bank's own notes. The fruits of the abuse were obvious: notes were overissued, their redemption was evaded, they lost their value, and the innocent husbandman and mechanic who were paid in them were cheated and pauperized. "It is absurd," wrote Taney, "to talk about a sound and stable paper currency." There was no such thing. So, in Jackson's opinion, if the United States Bank was not establishing a metallic currency, it was not establishing a constitutional or sound and uniform one. His words might seem wild to the contaminated, like Gallatin and Biddle, but they were plain gospel truth to his sturdy antibank, hard-money agrarians.

Hard money was a cardinal tenet of the left wing of the Democratic party. It belonged with an idealism in which America was still a land of refuge and freedom rather than a place to make money. Its aim was to clip the wings of commerce and finance by restricting the credit that paper money enabled them to obtain. There would then be no vast debt, no inflation, no demoralizing price changes; there would be no fluctuant or disappearing values, no swollen fortunes, and no grinding poverty. The precious metals would impose an automatic and uncompromising limit on the volatile tendencies of trade. "When there was a gold and silver circulation," said an agrarian in the Iowa constitutional convention of 1844, "there were no fluctuations; everything moved on smoothly and harmoniously." The Jacksonians were even more devoted to the discipline of gold than the monetary conservatives of the present century.

There was also a pro-bank, "paper-money wing," which harbored the Democratic party's less spiritual virtues. Its strength lay with free enterprise, that is, with the new generation of businessmen, promoters, and speculators, who found the old Hamiltonian order of the Federalists too stodgy and confining. These were "Democrats by trade," as distinguished from "Democrats in principle"; one of the latter wrote sarcastically in the Democratic Review in 1838, "Being a good Democrat, that is to say, a Democrat by trade (Heaven forefend that any son of mine should be a Democrat in principle)—being a good Democrat by trade, he got a snug slice of the public deposites." Fifty years before, business had fostered the erection of a strong federal government and inclined toward monopoly; in the early nineteenth century it began to appreciate the advantages offered by laissez faire and to feel that it had more to gain and less to fear from the states than from the federal government. This led it to take on the coloration and vocabulary of Jacksonian democracy and to exalt the rugged individualism of the entrepreneur and speculator along with that of the pioneer.

The private banks and their friends had helped to kill the first Bank of the United States twenty years before, but the strength they could muster against the second was much greater. Herein lies the principal difference between the situation of the old bank when Jefferson became president in 1801 and the situation of the second when Jackson became president in 1829. Both men disapproved of the national bank and yet were inhibited by its being accepted in their own party and performing well its evidently important functions. There were also the differences that Jefferson was more amenable to reason than Jackson, that he had in Gallatin a better adviser than any Jackson had, and the bank was under a more passive management in his day than in Jackson's. But of most importance was the greater pressure the private banks were able to exert in Jackson's time than in Jefferson's. Between 1801 and 1829 their number had greatly increased, as had the volume of their business and the demand for credit. The records indicate that in 1801 there were 31 banks, in 1829 there were 329, and in 1837 there were 788—an increase of 140 per cent during Jackson's administration alone. These banks were associated to a marked extent with the Democratic party, especially in New York. Their opposition to federal regulation was therefore far greater in 1829 than in 1801, and it did more for Jackson's victory over the national bank than did the zeal of his hard-money locofocos. De Tocqueville wrote that "the highest observation" enabled one to see the advantages of the B.U.S. to the country and mentioned as most striking the uniform value of the currency it furnished. But the private banks, he said, submitted with impatience to "this salutary control" exercised by the B.U.S. They bought over newspapers. "They roused the local passions and the blind democratic instinct of the country to aid their cause. . . ." Without them, it is doubtful if the Jacksonians could have destroyed the B.U.S.

The Jacksonian effort to realize the hard-money ideals was admirable, viewed as Quixotism. For however much good one may find in these ideals, nothing could have been more unsuited than they were to the American setting. In an austere land or among a contemplative and self-denying people they might have survived but not in one so amply endowed as the United States and so much dominated by an energetic and acquisitive European stock. Nowhere on earth was the spirit of enterprise to be more fierce, the urge for exploitation more restless, or the demand for credit more importunate. The rise of these reprobated forces spurred the agrarians, and as business itself grew they came to seek nothing less than complete prohibition of banking.[2] Yet they chose to destroy first the institution which was curbing the ills they disapproved, and to that end they leagued with the perpetrators of those ills. Jackson made himself, as de Tocqueville observed, the instrument of the private banks. He took the government's funds out of the central bank, where they were less liable to speculative use and put them in the private banks, where they were fuel to the fire. He pressed the retirement of the public debt, and he acquiesced in distribution of the federal surplus. These things fomented the very evils he deplored and made the Jacksonian inflation one of the worst in American history. They quite outweighed the Maysville veto, which checked federal expenditures on internal improvements, and the specie circular, which crudely and belatedly paralyzed bank credit.

As a result, Jackson's, presidency escaped by only two months from ending like Hoover's in 1933. Far from reaching the happy point where the private banks could be extirpated and the hands of the exploiters and speculators could be tied, Jackson succeeded only in leaving the house swept and garnished for them; and the

[2] In a number of western states and territories they achieved prohibition: in Arkansas, Illinois, Iowa, Wisconsin, California, and Oregon—though in the last two the impetus was more than agrarian.

last state of the economy was worse than the first. He professed to be the deliverer of his people from the oppressions of the mammoth—but instead he delivered the private banks from federal control and his people to speculation. No more striking example could be found of a leader fostering the very evil he was angrily wishing out of the way.

But this was the inevitable result of the agrarian effort to ride two horses bound in opposite directions: one being monetary policy and the other states' rights. Monetary policy must be national, as the Constitution doubly provides. The agrarians wanted the policy to be national, but they eschewed the practicable way of making it that and, instead of strengthening the national authority over the monetary system, they destroyed it. Where they were unencumbered by this fatal aversion to centralized power, they accomplished considerable. In Indiana they set up an official State Bank, with branches, which from 1834 to 1853 was the only source of bank credit permitted and yet was ample for all but the most aggressive money-makers, who finally ended its monopoly. In Missouri they established the Bank of Missouri, with branches, a state monopoly which lasted from 1837 to 1857, when it too succumbed to free enterprise. And in Iowa, another monopoly, the Bank of Iowa, with branches, was in operation from 1858 till 1865, when free banking penetrated the state under authority of the National Bank Act. These instances indicate that if the hard-money agrarians had had a conception of national government less incompatible with their social purposes, they might have tempered rather than worsened the rampant excesses of nineteenth-century expansion that so offended them.

But as it was, they helped an acquisitive democracy take over the conservative system of bank credit introduced by Hamilton and by the merchants of Philadelphia and New York and limber it up to suit the popular wish to get rich quick. Wringing their hands, they let bank credit become the convenient key to wealth—the means of making capital accessible in abundance to millions of go-getting Americans who otherwise could not have exploited their natural resources with such whirlwind energy. The excesses of that energy have forced the Jacksonian hard-money heroics to be slowly undone: the federal government's authority over money, the Treasury's close operating contact with the banking system, and the central-bank controls over credit have been haltingly restored. Credit itself, in the surviving American tradition, is not the virus the agrarians held it to be but the lifeblood of business and agriculture, and the Jacksonian hard-money philosophy has been completely forgotten, especially by Jackson's own political posterity.

III

Jackson had not committed himself against the bank during the early part of his first term but worried both those who wanted him to support recharter and those who wanted him to prevent it. In November 1829 he was friendly to Biddle and assured him that he had no more against the B.U.S. than against "all banks." The next month he slurred the bank in his message to Congress. In 1831 when the cabinet was changed, two important portfolios went to friends of Biddle: Livingston became Secretary of State and McLane Secretary of the Treasury. Both wanted the bank continued and hoped to influence Jackson. Biddle deferred to their hopes, but the tension was evidently too severe for him. The bank's enemies were growing more provocative, and in the summer of 1831 his brother, a director of the bank's St. Louis branch, was killed in a duel, more than usually shocking, which arose from the controversy over recharter. Whatever the reasons, he let impatience get the upper hand and decided that the bank, without further temporizing, should ask Congress that the charter be renewed.

Jackson was offended by this direct action, and notwithstanding improvements in the new charter and concessions to his views, he vetoed the bill of renewal. The economic reasoning of the veto message was, in Catterall's language, "beneath contempt," and the most appealing allegations in it were "demonstrably and grossly false." Biddle was deluded enough to have 30,000 copies printed and distributed in the bank's own interest. One may regard this as evidence of contempt for Jackson or of a faith in the democracy as sincere as Jackson's own; but it is also evidence of the limitations on Biddle's political sense. In the election that fall the bank was the leading issue, and hopes for recharter went to nothing with Jackson's over-whelming majority. Jackson's purpose was now to stop using the bank as government depository. How firmly accepted it was in Washington as the peculiar agency of the government is indicated by the resistance he encountered. He had to get rid of two Treasury heads successively before he found a third who would execute his wishes, the law giving only the Secretary of the Treasury the power to remove the government's deposits from the bank; and he had also to disregard a House resolution declaring that the government deposits were safe as they were.

With loss of the deposits, the bank lost the means of regulating the private banks' extension of credit. Biddle had made enough mistakes already, but he now made the fatal one of failing to resign and let the bank be liquidated; there is a limit beyond which the head of a central bank cannot decently go against the head of the government, even when he is right and the head of the government is wrong. Moreover, although a central bank is a very useful institution, it never possesses the kind of virtues that count in conflict against an intensely popular leader. By resigning, Biddle would have stultified Jackson and justified himself, as it turned out; for when the panic came in 1837, Jackson would have got the blame, with considerable justice. Furthermore, Biddle would have spared himself a tragic end. The bank was in a better condition than it came to be later, and conditions were much more favorable for liquidation, in spite of the recession of 1833–1834. Incidentally, this recession was produced, it was averred, by a vindictive curtailment of the bank's loans. There certainly was resentment mixed into the bank's policy, but on the other hand, the bank could not go out of existence, as its enemies desired, without cur-tailing its credit, and curtailment is always unpopular, scarcely less in a period of general expansion than in one of depression.

Instead of going out of existence the bank became a private corporation under Pennsylvania charter in February 1836, a fortnight before its federal charter ex-pired. A little more than a year later the panic of 1837 broke. It began May 10 and involved all the banks in the country, about 800 in number, with an aggregate circulation of $150,000,000 and deposits of $125,000,000. It precipitated three distinct monetary programs—one of hard money by the anti-bank administration in Washing-ton, one of easy money by Biddle in Philadelphia, and one of convertibility by the banks of Wall Street under the sage but incongruous leadership of the venerable Jeffersonian, Albert Gallatin.

The administration, with Van Buren now president, took the opportunity to urge an independent Treasury system, with complete "divorce of bank and state." Its course was that urged by Jackson, who wrote, July 9, 1837:

> Now is the time to separate the Government from all banks, receive and disburse the revenue in nothing but gold and silver coin, and the circulation of our coin through all public disbursements will regulate the currency forever hereafter. Keep the Government free from all embarrassments, whilst it leaves the commercial community to trade upon its own capital, and the banks to accommodate it with such exchange and credit as best suits their own interests—both being money making concerns, devoid of patriotism, looking alone to their own interests—regardless of all others. It has been, and ever will be a curse to the Government to have any entanglement or interest with either, more than a general superintending care of all.

Wall Street paid little attention to this program but set about preparations to resume specie payments as soon as possible, getting its own house in order and urging the banks elsewhere to send delegates to a convention "for the purpose," in Gallatin's words, "of agreeing on a uniform course of measures and on the time when the resumption should take place."

Nicholas Biddle took a course opposed to that of both Wall Street and the administration. He demanded that the Treasury scheme be abandoned and the specie circular repealed. He contended that Jackson's policies were responsible for the financial distress and that the basic condition of recovery was their repudiation by Congress. Till these things were done, the banks should not resume redemption of their notes. Wall Street's program he denounced as premature and sacrificial. He advocated instead an active and flexible policy that should be remedial for the prostrate economy—that should check the credit contraction and the fall of prices. His own objects during the past eighteen months, he wrote James Gordon Bennett, October 1838, had been "to sustain the national character abroad by paying our debts and at the same time to protect the securities and the staples of the country from the ruinous depreciation to which they were inevitably sinking." It was evident to him, he wrote John Quincy Adams in December, "that if resort was had to rigid curtailments, the ability to pay would be proportionally diminished; . . . the only true system was to keep the country as much at ease as consisted with its safety, so as to enable the debtors to collect their resources for the discharge of their debts." Lenity for the banks would mean lenity for their debtors, foreclosures and bankruptcies would be avoided, and values protected from collapse. Suspension, he had already said, was "wholly conventional between the banks and the community" and arose from "their mutual conviction that it is for their mutual benefit."

The situation was one in which the more conservative settled back to let deflation, as it came to be called a century later, run its bitter course; and the hard-money agrarians sardonically joined them in hoping for the worst. But both the agrarians and Wall Street testified to the popularity of Biddle's ideas. Governor Ford of Illinois observed, with the sarcasm of a hard-money Democrat, that although the banks owed more than they could pay and although the people owed each other and the banks more than they could pay, "yet if the whole people could be persuaded to believe the incredible falsehood that all were able to pay, this was 'confidence.'" In Wall Street it was said that suspension made lawbreakers of every one. "Instead of the permanent and uniform standard of value provided by the Constitution, and by which all contracts were intended to be regulated, we have at once fifty different and fluctuating standards, agreeing only in one respect, that of impairing the sanctity of contracts." The believers in Biddle were themselves eloquent in the new faith. Following the later debacle of the B.U.S., the Philadelphia *Gazette* said: "The immediate effect of the suspension will be an ease in the money market, a cessation of those cares and disquietudes with which the business men of our community have been annoyed. . . . The great error . . . to which all subsequent errors are in a measure to be traced was in the premature resumption in August 1838. . . . The banks are just as good, and better and more solid, under a season of suspension as under its opposite."

Meanwhile, the New York banks had succeeded in resuming payment of their obligations, May 10, 1838, the anniversary of the suspension. This was a real hard-money achievement, due largely to Gallatin and the Bank of England, in which the professedly hard-money administration had little if any part. Instead it had to violate with its eyes open the professions that Jackson had violated without knowing what he was doing. While still trying to distribute a federal "surplus" which had turned into a deficit, it had to resort to issues of Treasury notes, which its hard-money zealots believed unconstitutional. It had to go still further and tolerate what Biddle had demanded: the specie circular was repealed in May 1838, the subtreasury bill was defeated in June, and in July the Treasury had to accept—to its substantial relief—a credit of four million dollars on the books of the Bank of the United States in anticipated payment of amounts due the government in liquidation of its shares. This last transaction made the bank a depository of the government some five years after Jackson had ordered that its predecessor, a better institution, cease to be used as depository.

By the fall of 1838, banks everywhere were back on a specie basis, and, although this was mainly due to the efforts of Wall Street and Albert Gallatin, it was Biddle who had the prestige. He was riding on the crest. "All that it was designed to do has been done," he wrote John Quincy Adams in December 1838; and he was about to retire. Two months later, February 1839, he was Van Buren's guest of honor at the White House. "This dinner went off very well," according to James A. Hamilton, "Biddle evidently feeling as the conqueror. He was facetious and in intimate converse with the President." A month later Biddle retired from the bank, its affairs being, he said, in a state of great prosperity and in able hands. The same day the directors were unanimous in describing him as one who had "performed so much and so faithfully" and was leaving the bank "prosperous in all its relations . . . . and secure in the respect and esteem of all who are connected with it in foreign or domestic intercourse."

Six months later, in the fall of 1839, the bank suspended payment of its obligations. It resumed and then suspended again. In 1841, after two years of dismayed inquiry and recrimination, it was assigned to trustees for liquidation.

The stockholders were stunned, and then they turned on Biddle. In the summer of 1840 he was told that he owed the bank an "over-advance" of about $320,000 on an old account. This he denied. Nevertheless, "though he did not recognize the claim" and although "neither law or equity made it necessary to pay," he did so—mostly in Texas bonds which were accepted at more than market value. The stockholders next turned to litigation and thereafter seem to have kept Biddle continuously in the courts. In January 1842, he and former associates in the bank were arrested on charges of criminal conspiracy and put on $10,000 bail each. The charge was that they had conspired "to cheat and defraud the bank by obtaining therefrom large advances upon shipments of cotton to Europe," and "by the unlawful receipt and expenditure of large sums of money, the application of which is not specified upon the books." The court of General Sessions was occupied two weeks with habeas corpus hearings, twenty witnesses being examined and "all the books and papers of the bank brought into court, where they underwent a most searching investigation." Biddle's attorneys let his case stand on the evidence of the prosecutors. "As soon as the testimony for the prosecution was finished, the counsel for Mr. Biddle offered to leave the matter to the court without argument." The court found evidence lacking that the acts charged involved fraud; for they were known to the directors and approved by them. Of any fraudulent coalition it found nothing to justify even a reasonable suspicion. Two judges concurred in this decision; one dissented.

A few weeks later another suit was instituted. The stockholders filed a bill of equity in which they asked that Biddle and one of his former associates be required to account for $400,000 of the bank's funds. The bill was dismissed December 1844, the court holding that information which might incriminate the defendants could not be required of them. But Biddle was no longer living. He had died ten months before, February 27, 1844, aged fifty-eight.

IV

The failure of the B.U.S. leaves two questions one would like to have answered: What was the actual condition of the bank? How responsible was Biddle for it? The Jacksonians had easy answers, of course, and jeered triumphantly; matters had proved to be even worse than they had said, Biddle had known the bank was rotten, and having enriched himself he had striven to leap clear in time but had been caught. The Democratic press was hot with invective and ribald ridicule of the great Regulator, the old Nick, the prestidigitatorial wizard who had crowned a career of astounding performances by consummately destroying everything he had done, and himself with it.

To say with Biddle's political enemies that the bank was "rotten" is putting it both vigorously and vaguely. No one can be precise in such a matter, for in a long and complicated liquidation involving suits and technical decisions respecting the admissibility of claims, the completeness of the settlement must be subject to interpretation. But, according to a trustee quoted by Knox, the creditors were paid in full, principal and interest, though the bank's capital was entirely absorbed, and the stockholders got nothing. This would mean a shrinkage of about one fourth of the value of the bank's assets, roughly speaking. The 7,000 bank failures in the United States in the ten years, 1921–1930, entailed estimated losses of about one third of the total deposit liabilities. The comparison is crude, but I think it warrants the opinion that the condition of the B.U.S. was rotten only in a hyperbolical sense. Moreover, it is to be borne in mind that values usually diminish in liquidation, that the portfolio to be liquidated was the country's largest, and that the process, which ran to 1856, had to be undertaken in a period when buyers were not eager nor prices buoyant. The stockholders in 1841 insisted to the legislature that the bank could pay all its creditors and requested lenity so that losses might be minimized. These things make me think that the bank in 1839 may have been in a situation little if any worse than that which Jones had got its predeccesor into twenty years before and from which Cheves rescued it.

As for the second question—Biddle's responsibility—it seems to me clear that policies put into effect by him led to the bank's failure but that he had no realization or suspicion of what was developing. The policies included prodigal loans on stocks, especially to officers and directors of the bank, heavy investments in corporate stocks and speculative bonds, and purchases of cotton and other agricultural commodities for export. The cotton transactions were undertaken in the emergency of 1837 as a means of sustaining domestic commodity prices and providing European exchange. They succeeded initially, but once begun they were hard to stop, and they produced loss, litigation, and recrimination that was probably more damaging to Biddle himself than to the bank. The loan and investment policy was begun as early as 1835 when it looked as if the bank would have to liquidate: the active assets were converted into loans on stocks in preparation for a long period of liquidation. But when the Pennsylvania charter was obtained, the policy was not abandoned. Instead it was adapted to the vaster prospects of manifest destiny and empire building. Loans were made with a lax grandiosity. "It seems to have been sufficient," according to a stockholders' committee report later, "to obtain money on loan, to pledge the stock of 'an incorporated company,' however remote its operations or uncertain its prospects." Partly from choice and partly from the extortionate requirements of its charter— which Biddle should never have accepted—the bank also became the owner of such stocks outright; in 1840 it had shares in more than twenty other banks, some of which it wholly controlled, and great holdings in railways, toll bridges, turnpikes, and canals, besides speculative bonds issued to finance "public improvements." These investments immobilized the bank's funds so that it was without active means to repay the government for its stock, to honor its $20,000,000 of circulating notes, which soon began to be rapidly presented for redemption, and to meet its charter obligations, which in five years made it divert more than a third of its capital "to purposes of the state." To meet these requirements, the bank was driven into the market as borrower, both at home and abroad. These borrowings were begun by Biddle, and his successors turned to them more and more. Hence the bank came to be progressively incurring new obligations harder to meet than the old. The pressure mounted swiftly, so that a situation of apparent comfort in the spring of 1839 had passed into one of agony in the fall. These were the six months between Biddle's retirement and the bank's suspension. The bank had for years been growing more and more illiquid, but the condition had remained concealed by confidence. Once the illiquidity was suspected, however, the bank's creditors woke up with a start, and its obligations became instantly menacing. The suddenness of the change depended not on existence of the condition but on recognition of it.

According to one view, Biddle cannot be blamed for the bank's failure—it happened six months after he had retired. Well, granted that Biddle was gone, the bank was in the hands of successors who besides being heirs to his policies had been trained in his school. And this school, according to the evidence of stockholders' reports and court records, was one of extreme administrative inefficiency. The directors, dazzled by Biddle, knew nothing and approved everything. There were special procedures for special transactions, items being carried in the teller's drawer till it was expedient to post them. Accounts of the old bank were continued on the books of the new as if the corporate continuity was unbroken; and the notes of the old were kept in circulation by the new—a practice which particularly outraged Gallatin. It was in this atmosphere that Biddle's successors learned to manage the bank, and if they came to grief if cannot be said that it was merely because they had not his ability. He would have come to grief himself.

That Biddle must bear responsibility for the bank's condition is one thing; but that he had a guilty consciousness of its condition is quite another. Although the tradition of his dishonesty is held both by the Jacksonian partisans and by some scholars, I think it rests on a trite and stiffly moralistic view of the facts. If he realized how seriously wrong things were, it was an instance of objective analysis and cold self-appraisal unique in his career. I cannot believe him capable of it. He was eminently of a sanguine disposition, as is emphasized in the characterization of him by Catterall, who had given him more attention than any other historian. Caution and modesty were probably never among his more conspicuous virtues, and Jackson's attack did not enhance them. In the years 1836 to 1839, when he was laying down a new course for the bank, he was at the height of his career, it then seemed, and flushed with victory. He had blundered when he forced the issue of recharter in 1832, and Jackson had whipped him in the elections that year, in the veto, and in the removal of the deposits in 1833. But by 1838 he seemed to have retrieved his blunder and defeat. He had found sanctuary for the bank in the Pennsylvania jurisdiction, where Jackson could only gnash his teeth at it. He could point scornfully at the situation compounded of the panic of 1837, the specie circular, and distribution of the federal surplus. By 1839 he was the honored guest of Van Buren in the White House, and he could boast that the bank was again a government depository, that the independent Treasury scheme was rejected, and that the specie circular was repealed. He had triumphed over the Jacksonians on the points he cared most about. He even claimed credit for resumption, patronized Wall Street, and acted as the impresario of national monetary policy. It was in the fatuous mood of wishful thinking and expansive imagination stimulated by these illusive developments that he administered the bank after the failure of Jackson's attempt to annihilate him. If Biddle, at the height of his success in the winter of 1838–1839, examined his achievements objectively and concluded that all he had done mounted up to either a colossal fraud or a colossal mistake, he must have been a very remarkable character indeed. Yet that is what the tradition of his moral guilt requires one to believe. I find more credible the less dramatic possibility that, being a man of very sanguine susceptibilities, he was simply carried away by success and self-confidence, by the grand scale of his activities, and by the daily exercise of more power, as he put it, than the President of the United States possessed. I believe he had lost the faculty of recognizing his own mistakes. The series of letters he wrote in 1841— prolix, specious, declamatory compositions in which he unconvincingly insisted that the bank had been in sound condition when he left it—seem to me the pathetic efforts of a man confounded by other things than guilt: by surprise, incredulousness, grief, anxiety, and shock. His friends were at no less a loss; the most they could say in his favor was to protest at those who had been his sycophants while hoping to prosper but who turned against him with a "malicious prosecution" when their common fortunes collapsed.

The hostility of Jackson to the Bank of the United States was in the first instance a matter of principle, the bank belonging to a monetary system and to a theory of federal powers which he disapproved; but later he and his followers could allege also that the bank was rotten and Biddle dishonest. That allegation was, in fact, emphasized more than the original principle. But if the bank was not rotten and Biddle was not dishonest, then what may be called the moral grounds for Jackson's action disappear leaving no defense except in charity to his good intentions. All he did was destroy a wisely developed monetary system. The administration of that system by the B.U.S. was admirable but might have been strengthened and improved had not Jackson's views been so radical and his temper so intransigent. In particular, had his demoralizing attack never been made Biddle would not have been stimulated to undertake his later grandiose and tragic course. But the blame must be shared by Biddle. The fury and the folly of these two ruined an excellent monetary system—as good as any the country has ever possessed—and left a reckless, booming anarchy.

When the career of Nicholas Biddle is given the study its importance deserves, it may appear that the earlier part of it, when he was a central banker, was something less than brilliant and that the later part, when he was an empire builder, was something worse than overweening. But, as it is, the evidence indicates an inventive, facile, dynamic person—vain and not too painfully honest under pressure—who encountered a bigoted interference with his extremely able management of an institution purposing to restrain the inflationary abuse of bank credit; who naïvely trusted the rightness of his position, contemned his adversary, defied him, and, after a smart defeat which he refused to acknowledge, achieved an illusory victory; who then, with overblown confidence in his own judgment, in the economic future of the country, and in the alchemic powers of bank credit, committed himself to empire building; who did things the ingenious if not the right way; and who reckoned on a faster and less fluctuant growth than the country actually had. In all this he went with the times. When an opposition that was locofoco on one side and laissez faire on the other overcame him, he joined the latter and likelier of the two. Having been stripped of the Hamiltonian garments of central control, he gladly put on the gayer ones of free enterprise. Yet Biddle was attracted more by the statesmanship of enterprise than by enterprise itself. As a central banker, his policy had been governed properly by public interest rather than profit. As empire builder also he led the bank into affairs of national scope and purpose. He upheld the nation's foreign financial obligations. He intervened with both parties on behalf of Texas, whose government he had financed. He resisted Jackson's monetary measures with a determination more patriotic than discreet. His retirement from the bank at the age of fifty-three must have been greatly influenced, and very reasonably, by political ambitions. Only a few weeks before announcing that he would retire, he had been advised by Thomas Cooper that his candidacy for president of the United States was not immediately practicable because of the "prevailing ignorance and prejudice about banks"—the general suspension being still a recent matter—and that "some years hence" prospects might be better. The bank's difficulties from 1839 on blanked out these prospects wholly. They did more. Biddle had rebounded from the earlier frustration that ended his career as central banker; from the disaster to his later career he had no power to turn. John Quincy Adams had dinner with him *en famille*, November 22, 1840, and talked long with him. "Biddle," he wrote, "broods with smiling face and stifled groans over the wreck of splendid blasted expectations and ruined hopes. A fair mind, a brilliant genius, a generous temper, an honest heart, waylaid and led astray by prosperity, suffering the penalty of scarcely voluntary error—'tis piteous to behold." He died a little more than three years later, in reduced circumstances if not insolvent.

Besides the Jacksonian view of Biddle and the view that I have opposed to it, there is another I have already mentioned. Its distinction is its calm silence about the unhappy events, whether discreditable or tragic, of Biddle's last years. In R. C. McGrane's *Panic of 1837*, the bank's failure is alluded to, and Biddle's connection with it is dismissed in a footnote: "It should be noted that Biddle was now out of office, and can not be held responsible for what the bank did at this period." In the published correspondence of Nicholas Biddle, edited by Mr. McGrane, there is nothing that deals with the things that made Biddle's last years so miserably unlike those of his prime—the bank's failure, the loss of money and esteem, the prosecution of suits against him. And similarly in the article on Biddle in the *Dictionary of American Biography*, no mention is made of his last years' being clouded by any trouble whatsoever. Such reticence and piety contrast genteelly with the bitterness he actually suffered and with the judgment that he belonged in jail.

Two things combined to give Biddle's fall a supererogatory blackness. One was the sheer drama of the event. The largest corporation in the country—one of the largest in the world—had fallen suddenly from its splendid success into sprawling collapse at the very feet of the genius who had only recently with grand gestures relinquished its management. It was a denouement that stimulated the imagination to make worse what was already bad enough. The other aggravation of the story came from political motives. Biddle and the bank had never been warmed to by the Whigs, and Biddle's own ties were less with them than with the Democrats, but the latter naturally sought to make the bank seem Whig.[3] They had great success; the debacle helped to disintegrate the Whigs and strengthened the Jacksonians immeasurably. As a result, partisan views have dominated subsequent judgments and given Biddle the incidental and thankless role of darkened background to the glories of Andrew Jackson; and his achievements in credit policy, especially in the earlier and more admirable phase when he was a pioneer central banker, have been forgotten. Nowhere has he been studied adequately in his own right as a man of significant accomplishments, shortcomings, and misfortunes. Yet, in intellectual capacity, force of character, public spirit, and lasting influence, he was comparable with any of the contemporaries of his prime.

The withering that overtook Biddle's fame did not extend to his philosophy and example, which turned out to be triumphant, though with no acknowledgment to him. The monetary views of Gallatin and of Jackson are both obsolete, but Biddle's have a sort of pragmatic orthodoxy. He sought to make monetary policy flexible and compensatory rather than rigid. His easy-money doctrine had its source in a vision of national development to which abundant credit was essential. The majority of his countrymen have agreed with him. They have dismissed the man, but they have followed his ideas, especially his worse ones. They have shared his bullishness and

---

[3] It is not clear which party Biddle supposed might make him president. The Second Bank of the United States was both nurtured and destroyed within the Democratic party. Its creators and friends included Madison, Monroe, Gallatin, and Crawford; its three presidents, Jones, Cheves, and Biddle, were party members. Its greatest enemies were likewise pillars of the party—Jackson himself, Benton, and Taney. Jackson's cabinet was divided. The Whigs championed the bank less for its own sake than because Jackson's course left them no choice, and they abandoned it with relief as soon as they could. They were not interested in having bank credit restricted.

his energy. They have not liked Jackson's primitive ideals of a simple, agrarian society, except in their nostalgic moods. They have not understood Gallatin's noble aversion for the fierce spirit of enterprise. They have exploited the country's resources with abandon, they have plunged into all the debt they could, they have realized a fantastic growth, and they have slighted its cost. Gallatin personified the country's intelligence and Jackson its folklore, but Biddle personified its behavior. They closed their careers in high honor—he closed his in opprobrium and bewilderment.

13 / Sober Second Thoughts on Van Buren, the Albany Regency, and the Wall Street Conspiracy

Frank Otto Gatell

The Hammond interpretation of the Bank War, which emerged as part of an anti-Jacksonian historiographical school of the 1950's, has already been challenged several times. In the following essay the editor of this volume first offers a direct challenge to one of Hammond's principal theories about the political origins of the Bank struggle. Hammond contended that Martin Van Buren, chieftain of the Albany Regency, New York State's Democratic machine, actively fomented the Bank War, acting in the interest of New York City's Wall Street. Gatell then goes on to comment upon the lines of political power existing in the nation's largest state (the geopolitics of New York), and their relation to the Jackson administration in Washington. Some of the anti-Jackson accounts almost read the President out of the Bank War, contending that he was the foolish and innocent dupe of wily manipulators who were trying to "make a fast dollar" by destroying the Bank. This essay reasserts the primacy of Jackson himself in consideration of the origins of the Bank War.

For further reading: Charles Sellers, "Banking and Politics in Jackson's Tennessee, 1817–1827," *Mississippi Valley Historical Review,* XLI (June 1954), 61–84; Robert V. Remini, *Andrew Jackson and the Bank War* (1967); Frank Otto Gatell (ed.), *The Jacksonians and the Money Power, 1829–1840* (1967).

Journal of American History, LIII (June 1966), 19–40. Reprinted by permission. Footnotes have been omitted.

The assault on traditional pro-Jacksonian historiography during the past decade and a half has extended into nearly every aspect of the Jacksonian era. Nowhere has it achieved more apparent success than in the field of banking and politics—the Bank war of the 1830s. During the early decades of the twentieth century American historians described a Bank war of elemental splendor, a struggle between democracy and privilege, between Andrew Jackson and Nicholas Biddle. It was as though Francis P. Blair lived on, and from his Silver Spring mansion sent out the word to middle period historians in terms little changed from his *Globe* editorials of the 1830s. Not everyone concurred, but until recently the dissenters and the banking historians remained barely tolerated.

The recent swing of the pendulum more than made up for previous slights to Biddle. Jackson's ignorance of finance and Biddle's grasp of central banking became the battle cries of the new Bank war army. And as the President's stature diminished (for not even his best friends could make a financier out of the "Old Hero"), accounts appeared which all but left Jackson out of the Bank war, some *sotto voce*, others *voce piena*. In the former category, Lee Benson, in *The Concept of Jacksonian Democracy*, asserts that Jackson was not primarily responsible for the Bank war, that "he served primarily as an instrument of other men. At present, however," Benson concludes, "that belief is only impressionistic." Bray Hammond's work, *Banks and Politics*, is less tentative. This massive and brilliant tour de force argues on two levels: first, on the economics of banking, particularly the advantages of coordinated central banking; and second, on the fundamentals of Bank war politics, that is, who got what and why? New York gained most. With the Bank of the United States crippled and dying the financial center of the country shifted from Phila-delphia to New York City. Wall Street defeated Chestnut Street, and, argues Hammond, the general who directed hostilities was not the President from Tennessee, but Martin Van Buren, urbane commander of the Albany Regency, America's finest political legion.

Hammond treats Van Buren with respectful distaste. He ascribes almost super-human managerial abilities to the "Red Fox," a man of profound discretion and limitless deception. He calls him the Bank's least conspicuous but most important enemy, and goes whole hog in claiming that in October 1829, at a conference in Richmond, Van Buren launched the Bank war after selling the idea to Jackson and the Kitchen Cabinet. Van Buren toyed with Jackson, citing national political and constitutional considerations for opposing Biddle, all the while masking his and the Albany Regency's real aim, to shift financial primacy to New York.

At first glance the Hammond view (not original with him, of course, but his is the best and most sustained development), seems refreshingly tenable in its sim-plicity. That New Yorkers would do all they could to increase the power of their state seems axiomatic, and a powerful New York politician, head of a superbly drilled state machine and high in national councils, would naturally further New York interests to the fullest extent possible. A second, closer look at banking in New York state buttresses the New York Albany Regency conspiracy thesis. Demo-cratic power in Albany banking is too well known to require repetition, and study of the New York City banking community of the 1830s reveals heavy Democratic influence there as well. With Democratic bankers at Albany and in New York City wielding extensive power, Hammond's case appears closed. But were Democrats in both cities united? Were the Regency men of Albany and the Tammany Bank

Democrats of New York City one and the same, and did they agree on economic objectives? Did Van Buren and the Albany Regency connive in bringing about the primacy of Wall Street and New York City?

The only specific evidence which Hammond offers concerning the Van Buren conspiracy is the "Richmond cabal" of October 1829, which, allegedly acting under the New Yorker's promptings, decided the Bank's fate. In the summer of 1830 Henry Clay learned from "one of the most intelligent citizens of Virginia" that the dirty business had been started the previous autumn—a warning he immediately relayed to Biddle. Also, notes Hammond, Senator Felix Grundy was present at Richmond, a party to it all, at the very moment he was hawking a plan for a new national bank.

Close examination of these sources weakens the conspiracy case considerably. For one thing, Clay's Virginia correspondent was Judge Francis Brooke, who may well have been "one of the most intelligent citizens" in the commonwealth, but as a reliable source of political information, this garrulous, over-sanguine leader of the tiny pro-Clay corps in the Old Dominion, left much to be desired—as any reader of his ever-prescient, seldom-accurate prognostications in the Henry Clay Papers can attest. Brooke's account of the meeting rested on no special knowledge beyond the then-current rumors—and let it not be forgotten that Van Buren left a trail of rumors behind him wherever he traveled. Grundy had indeed informed Jackson on October 22 that he would soon depart Nashville for Richmond, and he enclosed a sketch for a new national bank. But, as Grundy noted, every politician who could make it was then heading for Richmond to hear the debates in the state constitutional convention. It is also noteworthy that Grundy's confidential bank suggestions did not include a change of venue for the mother bank. He proposed that the national bank, however modified, remain in Philadelphia.

Compromised as these sources became from internal criticism, the Nicholas Biddle Papers provide additional counterarguments to the conspiracy thesis. Particularly significant are two letters received by Biddle, again from Richmond, but this time from the cashier of the Richmond branch of the BUS, James Robertson.

A year after the alleged anti-Bank conclave, Robertson informed his chief:

> With regard to the story of a combination between certain politicians and the Secretary of State [Van Buren], against the Bank of the U. S., I never did, and do not now believe that there was the slightest foundation for it. . . . It was absurd on the face of it, as it must have been plain to every one acquainted with matters here, that a part of the paragraph in the President's Message which gave rise to the story, could not be otherwise than obnoxious, in every point of view, to the political sentiments and personal concerns of the parties alluded to. . . . The most prominent of these men, have several times in the course of conversation, voluntarily declared to me, unsought in any way, in the most solemn manner, that during the Secretary's visit to Richmond, they never heard the name of the Bank, nor an allusion to it, escape their lips.

Robertson closed by promising to send more details later, and within a few days he complied:

> The dinner given by the Editor of the Enquirer [Thomas Ritchie] to Mr. V[an Buren] was got up with a few hours' notice, was a small one, and mixed as to politics—in fact there were hardly any politicians there—the prominent men in that way in the city, were all engaged to dine with another gentleman. I have

conversed with several gentlemen who were present, one of whom in particular, who is a thoroughgoing Anti-administration man, assured me that during dinner and afterwards he was seldom out of the reach of Mr. V[an Buren]'s voice; and there was no discussion on politics, and he is confident that the B.U.S. was never once mentioned or alluded to. . . . I do not mean to say that Mr. V[an Buren] may not have had private interviews with his political friends; and that there may not have been some discussion about men and measures, and parties in relation to the general government.—But I do not believe there was much of it; and if we reflect, that at that time the most absorbing questions, in regard to the constitution of Va. engaged daily and I may say hourly, the most serious consideration of all the statesmen and politicians then in Richmond, it is very unlikely that much of their time, or attention, would be given to any matters that might or might not be introduced into the President's message.

These statements do not demand automatic acceptance. As Robertson admitted, Van Buren may have talked pertinently about "Bank and Biddle" during the visit, and however much the first Jackson message surprised Biddle, key administration men, including Van Buren, surely knew by October 1829 that it would mention the Bank hostilely. Robertson was a man close to the scene, who had no reason to whitewash Van Buren and the Richmond *Enquirer* clique or to deceive Biddle, and his opinions merit consideration. They must rank at least as high as the rumors which Biddle received from Brooke, via Clay. The Robertson letters (and several other similar statements) reopen the case—a case which Hammond's selective display of evidence had apparently closed.

Central to the conspiracy thesis is its typecasting of Jacksonians as entrepreneurial and get-rich-quick Democrats, prattling about agrarianism and strict construction, but actually cramming their pockets in a Jacksonian prelude to the Gilded Age. It is extremely difficult, however, to fit many of the Regency leaders into this mold.

Under the rubric "The Jacksonians," Hammond provides sketches of sixteen prominent Democrats who helped Jackson destroy the Bank. In doing so, Hammond stresses the acquisitiveness of the men. Included are five New Yorkers: Van Buren, Churchill C. Cambreleng, Benjamin F. Butler, Jacob Barker, and James A. Hamilton. He omits such important Regency leaders as Silas Wright, William L. Marcy, John A. Dix, and Azariah C. Flagg, and even the principal Regency businessmen, Benjamin Knower, Thomas W. Olcott, Charles E. Dudley, Edwin Croswell, and Erastus Corning.

Of the five men Hammond mentions, one may dismiss Barker, the controversial figure of the Exchange Bank lawsuits of 1826. He had no political power during the Bank war. Hammond cites Van Buren's autobiography to the effect that Barker was "always my personal friend," but he leaves out the rest of the sentence: "altho' never my co-adjutor." Although Hamilton helped draft the message of 1829, his friendship with Jackson and Van Buren cannot be equated with power in the Regency, nor was he a power in New York City financial circles. Cambreleng, a New York City merchant before entering Congress, obviously had business interests in the city, as well as interests—particularly in railroad promotion—which extended beyond the city. Although he did not hold any bank directorship during the 1830s, he was the leading anti-BUS Democrat in the city following declaration of the Bank war.

When moving upstate and examining the Regency itself, the entrepreneurial thesis collapses—especially if one tries to equate Regency leadership with Wall Street power. It was not that Van Buren and his friends disliked money, but many of them were more interested in political success than in making a million dollars, and even the Regency businessmen looked westward for their gains rather than southward to the metropolis.

The first category, the politicos, starts with the leader, Van Buren. Hammond quotes a New York City Whig who in 1837 called Van Buren "a very rich man" although he did not specify the level of opulence. If so, the accumulation of wealth came about with none of the stock-jobbing frenzy of the supposedly typical entrepreneurial Jacksonian. He acquired his competence, "fairly earned," through the law, and kept it by prudent management. With regard to both politics and material delights, Van Buren could distinguish between first and second quality goods. That he enjoyed so many of the former is attributable not to the prodigality of the *nouveau riche* but to the calculating parsimony (political as well as financial) of the top-level county seat lawyer. Van Buren resembles John Quincy Adams, another political squire, much more than he resembles John Jacob Astor. Butler was a lawyer who was Van Buren's professional alter ego. No amount of innuendoes based on the fact that some of the suits he handled involved "very large sums of money" can make a Wall Street plunger out of him. Marcy's kingdom was also of the political world, and Comptroller Flagg minded the political store at Albany, while Adjutant General Dix reviewed the state militia. No one, not even in the wildest flights of entrepreneur excess, has tried to make a William Zeckendorf out of the St. Lawrence County potato farmer, Silas Wright.

The most important Regency businessman of the early 1820s was Marcy's father-in-law, Knower. His overly strong tariff stand, and declining financial condition, had by 1830 weakened his influence markedly. Olcott, cashier and then president of the Mechanics and Farmers Bank, the "Regency Bank" at Albany, played an important part in state business affairs, but he had no controlling influence on the New York City money market. The same applies to such men as Senator Dudley, also influential at the Mechanics and Farmers Bank; Croswell, editor of the Albany *Argus* and a director of Albany's Canal Bank; and Corning, iron merchant, mayor, banker, and railroader. The Regency's economic power, considerable though it was, extended primarily west from Albany, along the Erie Canal to Buffalo and into the western states. This is an admitted oversimplification, but there was nothing in New York City itself akin to the Regency overlordship of many of the state banks along the Canal. In New York City two financial centers existed, Wall Street and Pearl Street, and while the incidence of Democratic control ran high—especially on Pearl Street and in the newly-chartered banks—this represented Tammany strength which was not subject to the direct orders of the Regency.

Regency conservatism in economic affairs was deep-rooted, and the field of banking proved no exception. When Jackson became President in March 1829 the Regency had just fashioned its major contribution to banking legislation, the Safety Fund System. During his three-month governorship, Van Buren obtained passage of this law which provided for collective responsibility for bank indebtedness through the imposition of a tax on bank capital, and the establishment of the first permanent state banking commission. Significantly, the Regency did not repeal the restraining laws which made banking illegal for private citizens, nor the constitutional provision which required a two-thirds vote of the legislature to obtain bank charters or pass amendments.

If the Regency men had been the speculative type described by the entrepreneurial school, they would hardly have supported these restrictive, conservative measures. Important minority segments of the New York Democracy favored repeal of the restraining laws and as much freedom for banking as for any other business, but this was not Regency policy. Instead, Van Buren provided a reasonable curb on the banking business, intended to provide protection to the noteholder, who would have been told by the laissez-faire advocate that regulation was no concern of the government. Also, the retention of the restraining laws meant that bank incorporations would proceed at a restricted pace. Banking capital increased after the passage of the Safety Fund Act, but there was only a trickle, not the flood of new incorporations which would have occurred in an unregulated situation. Even after the fall of the BUS and the subsequent reduction in the state's banking capital, the number of banks did not multiply uncontrollably. Not until 1838, with the passage of the Free Banking Act, could New York capitalists enter the banking business at will.

Hammond deals with the Safety Fund System in detail, but it does not conform to his overview, and ultimately proves unmalleable. The example of responsible regulation runs counter to his general proposition, and thus must be dubbed a Van Buren political engine, intended to cement state political power through the power of the purse (the anti-Masons consumed reams of paper on that theme), or it can be tied in with the BUS—that is, Van Buren produced the Safety Fund System as a model state substitute for the national bank already marked for destruction. To substantiate the latter charge, Hammond cites only the 1837 opinion of James Gordon Bennett. Perhaps it happened that way; anything is possible until disproved. But to see conspiracy in *every* Regency move is to write a cabalistic history of the state of New York. If one examines the state of the banking issue in New York politics by 1829—especially its need for some system to operate upon the increase of banking capital sure to come—the more plausible view emerges that the Safety Fund System represented a constructive though imperfect piece of legislation, meant to give the state of New York system and security in that branch of business which not only meant profit or loss to investors, but which also provided the medium of exchange.

It is a severe commentary on the application of the entrepreneurial thesis in New York politics to note that the Regency consistently opposed repeal of the restraining laws during the 1830s; that only massive discontent with Regency conservatism over its denial of many new bank charters and the suppression of small notes forced Governor Marcy's belated support of free banking in 1838; and that free banking came about through the votes of a Whig-controlled legislature. Van Buren's financial legacy was the Safety Fund System, not free banking. He bequeathed conservative restriction, not economic liberty.

Too much has been written about the opposition of New York City banks to the BUS and not enough about the prolonged peaceful coexistence between the national bank and most Democratic leaders in the city. According to the accepted view, financial hostility between New York City and Philadelphia was a constant factor in the Bank war equation. A standard account notes that "relations between the Bank of the United States controlled in Philadelphia, and the state-chartered banks which had been established in New York [City], were not always of the friendliest." This charming understatement refers to the first national bank. The Second Bank, still located at Philadelphia, supposedly did nothing to change that feeling of distrust and jealousy, particularly after New York City outstripped Philadelphia in both domestic and foreign commerce. In restating this theme, Hammond treats Wall Street's interests and state interests as if they were identical. And an earlier Hammond, Jabez D., charged over a century ago that the machinations of greedy, anti-BUS, New York City banks carried the city for Jackson in 1832.

The reverse side of the coin deserves inspection. Many Jackson party leaders in New York City had no trouble living with Biddle's monster during the 1820s, and some of them served that monster effectively and enthusiastically. Their subsequent political hostility to the BUS resulted from the call for party discipline following declaration of the Bank war. Jackson had cracked the whip, and most Jacksonians responded. Some Democrats did not comply, thus providing one faction which comprised the Whig coalition. Such important Jacksonians as Gulian C. Verplanck and Dudley Selden, both New York City congressmen, refused to swallow the administration bank line (the former balked at the veto, and the latter bolted over removal of deposits). Since defection to Whiggery may make these two men suspect as examples of pro-BUS Jacksonism, the following pages will discuss several others—a trio of New York City Democrats, Walter Bowne, Campbell P. White, and Cambreleng. All three were loyal Jacksonians before and after the Bank war.

In the course of a decade—from 1823 to 1833—Bowne went full circle with regard to the BUS. A prominent Tammany sachem and mayor of the city, he joined the board of the New York City BUS branch in 1822. Bowne played an important role in BUS affairs, and during 1825 he helped thwart an attempt to wrest management away from Biddle and his New York City lieutenants, Robert Lenox and Morris Robinson. Biddle weathered that storm, and he reassured Bowne: "I am desirous that an old and large stockholder like yourself should know that the institution is prospering." Bowne remained at his post and did his best to ensure the continuation of BUS prosperity. But the demands of Bank war politics changed that. He joined the war against the monster, and fought it from a new position: president of New York City's most Democratic bank, the Seventh Ward Bank, which was chartered in April 1833, a few months before the removal of deposits, and which later became a pet bank. To label Bowne a pet-bank president and Tammany leader is accurate but insufficient, and to draw inferences from these two facts alone is risky. Bowne's previous harmonious relationship with the BUS requires equal emphasis.

Another Tammanyite of importance in the New York City money market who worked easily with Biddle was Campbell P. White. The Whites were a remarkable Irish family. The immigrant father prospered in Baltimore, distilling gin, and of his many sons, one, John C., became Biddle's cashier in that city. Two others, Robert and Campbell, went to New York City and shortly took over the Bank of the Manhattan Company. Robert became the bank manager; Campbell became the politician who sat in Congress for almost a decade, where he combined his Democratic politicking with a growing interest in public finance and banking. The BUS approached Campbell White warily, fearful he might not keep secrets from brother Robert and the Manhattan Bank; but once sealed, the bond between Campbell White and Biddle remained strong—for several years, at any rate. White joined Bowne in protecting the BUS's New York City flank, a job he performed even after

Jackson's muted but unmistakable declaration of war in December 1829. A year before that, White had congratulated Biddle on the sound condition of the BUS, observing that "it is eminently entitled to the confidence of the public." But Campbell White's higher chief, Jackson, thought otherwise. The President's anti-BUS message surprised and disappointed White, who had believed that Jackson favored the Bank. White did not withdraw his support of Biddle at that time, and Biddle continued to rely upon him, with waning confidence, until early in 1832, when he decided to drop as BUS board members all who were members of Congress. White thereupon adjusted to the new situation dictated by events, and his brother Robert's Manhattan Company soon became the beneficiary of attentions formerly lavished by Campbell White upon the BUS. Another BUS man had been transformed into a pet banker. White did not agonize over Biddle's misfortunes, but he had been a hard worker for the BUS (for a longer period than most Democrats) despite his political creed and his intimate connection with one of the city's principal state-chartered banks.

Cambreleng was Van Buren's man in New York City. More than any other city politician, he enjoyed Regency confidence. His BUS stand, therefore, acquires additional significance. Like Bowne and Campbell White, Cambreleng found that he could live very well with the monster. In 1827 Philip P. Barbour of Virginia introduced a resolution in the House of Representatives calling on the federal government to sell its BUS stock. Cambreleng rushed to calm Biddle: "I hope you will not let Mr. Barbour's resolution disturb you. It will be put to rest by a large majority." And so it was. The debate, Cambreleng added, "will be of service to the Bank." Two weeks later, the Albany *Argus* published a Washington letter which condemned Barbour's unwise move, indicating that Cambreleng and the Regency were not out of step on this question. In 1829, Cambreleng performed a valuable service for the BUS when he traveled to western New York as Biddle's agent to recommend a site for a new branch. Buffalo got the nod, and Cambreleng got the thanks of a grateful Biddle for a job well done. Soon Biddle was hard pressed to find a kind word for his erstwhile employee. The prosecution of the Bank war found Cambreleng in the Democratic vanguard, fighting the good fight against aristocracy and Biddle bank privilege with an enthusiasm which may have permitted him to forget his previous labors in the enemy camp.

Regency discipline did not extend full force to New York City. This is clear from the legislature's votes on anti-BUS resolutions in 1831 and 1832. The resolutions of 1831 originated in Washington not Albany, claimed Biddle, but he did not identify Van Buren as the mastermind. In any case, it soon became evident that wherever in the Democracy the idea germinated, New York City members of the legislature were not prepared to rush into the anti-BUS crusade with alacrity, if at all. And Nicholas Devereux, Biddle's Utica branch cashier, reported that the majority of Democratic members from all parts of the state were leery of any anti-BUS move, not wishing to make the issue a sharp party test. On April 6, 1831 the resolutions came up in the assembly. Only one of the eleven New York City members voted against a motion to postpone indefinitely; eight men supported the motion, and two abstained. Three days later, the motion to postpone having failed on a tie vote, the resolutions passed, seventy-three to thirty-five. In the interim, party managers had whipped in stragglers and the faint-hearted, but of the New York City delegation of eleven, only three joined the upstate Democracy in declaring "that the present charter of the Bank of the United States ought not to be renewed." Two of the City men casting aye votes, Gideon Ostrander and Mordecai Myers, had fled the assembly floor on the sixth to avoid voting on postponement. In the senate, the New York City senators, Democrats Stephen Allen and Alpheus Sherman, voted against the resolutions. As Silas E. Burrows informed Biddle, the Regency "were disappointed as it respects our City. Most of our members remained true to the Bank."

An analysis of the city assemblymen's banking connections makes one pause before launching glib generalizations about New York City Democrats with interests in state banks, and their hatred of the BUS. Five of the eleven assemblymen were directors of New York City banks: Nathaniel Jarvis, Isaac L. Varian, and Myers, all of the Greenwich Bank; Ostrander of the Butchers and Drovers Bank; and Selden of the National Bank. All were Jacksonian Democrats, as were the other city assemblymen, and only Selden of the five bank directors later defected to the Whigs.

Next year, 1832, similar resolutions appeared, and this time the political stakes were higher. By then, Biddle had applied for recharter, and the Democracy prepared for full-scale war. Yet the best the Jacksonians could get at Albany from their New York City colleagues was a truce or divided vote in the assembly and a clear rebuff in the senate. City Democrat Charles L. Livingston, one of the men who had supported the BUS in 1831, became assembly speaker, much to the chagrin of the Regency. This time the senate acted first, producing the same two pro-BUS city votes as the year before, and the city assemblymen who voted split evenly, five to five. An earlier assembly motion to soften the resolutions resulted in only four anti-BUS votes from the city.

So the very men who were supposed to profit politically and economically by the destruction of the Philadelphia Bank, the New York City Democrats, many of them directors and investors in New York City banks, refused to accept Regency dictation and condemn the BUS. These were the men who stood to gain most from any pro-New York City money market conspiracy. Their votes on the resolutions of 1831 and 1832 show that however powerful the Regency machine may have been in the Hudson River and central counties of New York, the state leaders did not rule in New York City. The Tammany men were allies, not lackeys.

This New York City autonomy helped produce the misgivings frequently aired by Regency leaders contemplating the potential dangers of the bustling, unorthodox city—the same city which had nurtured the Regency's *bête noire*, DeWitt Clinton. At the constitutional convention of 1821, Van Buren, in opposing unlimited manhood suffrage and in cataloging the evils which might result from it, named a swollen and irresponsible New York City electorate as a major cause for concern. The new city voters would debase the electoral process, he warned. Next year, a New York City politician warned Van Buren that disgruntled city Republicans were likely to revolt at the polls because of the legislature's refusal to grant all applications for bank charters.

A decade later the distrust had not abated. State Adjutant General Dix reported gloomily to the legislature that New York City needed more police protection: "Wherever great wealth is accumulated are sure to be found those vices which seek an unlawful sustenance by preying upon it. . . . The dangers to be apprehended from riots . . . are much increased by the presence of such an abandoned class of transient persons." Many city Democrats were suspect. Campbell White had been a strong Clinton man, and when Duff Green journeyed north in 1831 seeking support for John C. Calhoun, he tried to charm the old Clinton men at Tammany. He failed, but that he should try caused the orthodox Regency men to whisper knowingly and apprehensively. The distrust of New York City emerged clearly at the Democratic state convention which chose delegates to the national convention in 1832. The national convention was extremely important to the Regency, since, following the Senate's rejection of Van Buren as minister to Great Britain, he was to be nominated for the vice-presidency and succeed the Old Hero. To ensure a solid and safe New York vote, the Regency insisted upon framing a statewide slate of delegates, not the county tickets which the independent-minded New York City politicians wanted. The city men fought hard but lost. Croswell then filled a column of the *Argus* with labored explanations. It was not true, he protested too much, "that the delegates from the city of New York, were arrayed in hostility against their friends from the country," although "they differed, it is true, in relation to . . . a form of proceeding." The result was a lethargic Democratic campaign in New York City which alarmed Jackson forces in Washington and worried the Regency because of the city's supposed greater susceptibility to BUS bribes.

New York City businessmen and bankers fared little better in Regency estimation. The city banks had almost derailed the Safety Fund System at its start by refusing for over a year to accept charter renewals within the System. Ironically, the BUS helped induce the city banks to join, reluctantly, but the Regency did not forget the banks' collective obstructionism. Later, during the removal-of-deposits crisis, Wright said he feared the "cursed Wall Street" operators more than any other group, and this feeling was shared by Dix, who opposed the request of a New York City clique for another two-million-dollar bank as an "overgrown monopoly." These fears were anything but groundless, for these same Tammany bank directors and merchants led the conservative revolt in New York City that saw many of them permanently desert the Democratic party in 1837.

The anti-New York City views held by the Regency conform to one of the standard patterns of state politics, the antagonism between metropolis and hinterland. The Wall Street conspiracy thesis would have one believe that in this instance the upstate interests put aside their long-standing jealousy and fear of the city—that is, that Albany and its environs worked consciously to ensure the financial domination of New York City. If true, that would have constituted statesmanship of a very high caliber indeed.

But the economic condition of Albany at the juncture leads to another conclusion. In the early 1830s Albany enjoyed its greatest period of growth and prosperity, and the state capital was never in a better position *vis-à-vis* New York City. Albany could never surpass New York City, of course, but between 1825 and 1830 its population grew considerably and at a faster rate than the city's. In 1825 New York City had ten times the population of Albany; by 1830, only eight times the number of persons. The fabled prosperity created by the Erie Canal seemed to work its quickest miracles at Albany. This was hardly the moment for capitulation to the metropolis.

Albany's banks shared to an inordinate degree the benefits of the capital's expansion. The Regency had prudently kept New York City banking capital as low as was politically and economically feasible. The Albany banks—all of them, not just the much-maligned Mechanics and Farmers—exercised almost despotic control over credit, westward from Albany. In urging the selection of a second pet bank for Albany in 1836, Democrat Greene C. Bronson informed Secretary of the Treasury Levi Woodbury that "Albany is only second in importance to New York [City], and, in consequence of its local position, Albany exercises almost as wide an influence over the banking operations of the State as does our commercial emporium." Croswell argued that "the banks in Albany are perhaps of more general application to the business of the state than those of any other place. Directly connected with the trade of the West, and with the banks and moneyed operations of all that portion of the state . . . . Indeed they can scarcely be regarded as *local* institutions, so diffused, in many respects, are their operations, connected with the exchange and business of the interior." It is difficult to see what the bankers of Albany, including Olcott and Corning, the Regency bankers, had to gain from Wall Street domination of their concerns.

Assuming that Van Buren and the Regency had little or no interest in fostering the rise of Wall Street, and that the political and economic power of New York City lay outside the range of Regency domination, the possibility remains that Van Buren and the Regency may yet have instigated the Bank war to serve their own immediate political and economic interests. The economic interest view is barely tenable. Having just painted a picture of Albanian (so they styled themselves) power at its peak, and with the banks of Albany wielding much of that power, it may be that dreams of glory kept the presidents and cashiers of Albany banks happily restless in their beds. But most Bank war observers who broached the subject of a newly-located national bank stipulated either New York City or Washington. Albany, the political capital, never imagined itself the financial capital of New York state, and the cashier of the Regency bank, Olcott of the Mechanics and Farmers Bank, knew even better than Thurlow Weed that Weed's editorials imputing to his bank a stranglehold on the entire state's finances were the customary anti-Masonic gloom-and-doom hyperboles.

Politically the Regency did not need the Bank war. Lee Benson's summary account of New York state politics in the 1830s labels the belated Regency attack upon the BUS a diversion intended to blunt the anti-Masonic assault upon its own state banking "monopoly" system. But Regency timing suggests an alternative explanation: that it was foot-dragging over a policy imposed by Washington. If the anti-Masonic critique proved so waspish, so infuriating, and so harmful to the Regency, why then the delay until the summer of 1832 to launch the clever diversion? Nothing had changed during the previous three years. The anti-Masonic attacks on the Safety Fund System "political engine" in general, and on the Mechanics and Farmers Bank in particular, continued at the same level of ferocity and speciousness. Nothing had changed except the declaration of Jackson's war against the BUS. Benson notes that the Regency held back until reception of the Bank veto, but he avoids the conclusion that the Regency shied away from the Bank war and avoided commitment until the last minute, until Jackson's ultimatum forced Democrats to show their colors by their Bank stand. Once in the bank war, the Regency sought political advantage where it could.

The anti-Masonic threat had subsided after the perilous election of 1828 when Van Buren won the governorship on a plurality vote. Two years later the bumbling Regency governor, Enos T. Throop, was able to carry the election with a higher percentage of the vote than Van Buren. In 1832 New York Democrats ran scared—and they took no chances by nominating Senator Marcy for governor—but a good part of the Regency's fear stemmed from the same Bank war they are accused of fomenting. Flagg knew this only too well, and he lamented the necessity for omitting an anti-BUS resolution at the Democratic state convention in March 1832. He feared that such a move, attempted outside of the legislature, "might aggravate some of our weak sisters who are more attached to the root of evil than to sound principles." Van Buren and his friends knew that many Democrats, in and out of the city, would oppose the destruction of the BUS, and that some of them might bolt. How many, they could not tell; nor could they yet know how valuable the anti-BUS crusade would prove to the Jacksonian Democracy.

Van Buren wanted to become President of the United States. Any assessment of his political course during the Jackson administrations which subordinates this cardinal consideration is bound to wither on careful scrutiny. Hammond, in commenting on Van Buren's presidential fixation, relates that two things stood in his path to the White House: Calhoun and the BUS. Calhoun's competition for Jackson's favor proved short-lived, and after the South Carolinian's apostasy, Van Buren could turn his attention to, and the administration's power against, the BUS.

But the question remains, why did Van Buren have to destroy the Bank? Was this a vital step in his rise to the presidency? In answer, Hammond submits the geo-economic solution: to ensure New York's triumph over Pennsylvania. But did the assault on the BUS correspond with Van Buren's political interests?

First, there is no evidence that the Bank represented a political threat, or even a serious political inconvenience, to the Democracy. When the specter of political recrimination arose concerning the personnel of branch boards, Biddle, to demonstrate his goodwill and political neutrality, responded by pointing out that many Democrats sat on BUS boards at New York City and elsewhere. He also appointed many additional Jacksonians to branch and mother bank directorships. One can make much of Biddle's dealings with complaisant editors and politicians in 1831 and 1832 when he had his back to the wall, but the fact remains that prior to the Jacksonian assault the BUS threatened no political party. Van Buren could have become President whether or not there was a monster in Chestnut Street.

Second, an attack on the BUS, planned in 1829 and 1830 by a Democrat aspiring to the presidency, was foolish. The position of Pennsylvania is central to this analysis, an analysis which Van Buren undoubtedly took into consideration during his tenure as Secretary of State. As Fritz Redlich, the dean of American banking historians, observes about Van Buren's autobiography, it "at every turn shows his incapacity to think along economic lines, as well as the overgrowth of politics in his reasoning." Political savants of the late 1820s accepted as almost axiomatic the premise that to win the presidency, Jackson would have to carry, among others, the state of Pennsylvania. It was no idle slogan which had referred earlier to Pennsylvania as the "Keystone of the Democratic Arch." And the Pennsylvania equation involved another factor: the secondary premise that one could not carry the state on an anti-BUS platform. Such was the belief, and the near unanimity of political opinion among the pro-BUS Pennsylvania Democratic establishment seemed to take the matter out of the realm of argument. Van Buren's plans depended on Jackson's reelection. Could it be that this supremely ambitious political hopeful would have pressed on his chief a course which in the consensus of that hour promised little but trouble? By November 1832 the Pennsylvania equation proved incorrect. The state could be carried against the Bank, as Jackson demonstrated, although many a Pennsylvania Democrat found it prudent to tread water for several months pending the outcome. A year before, such a victory on those terms seemed highly improbable—

and Van Buren was a man who had done well in the business of measuring political probabilities.

To repeat, Van Buren did not have to put down the BUS, and to fight it before 1832 was risky. This last assertion may seem questionable in view of retrospective wisdom, since it is known that Jackson crushed Biddle. But the Bank as a historical fossil is far different from the Bank as it then was—a powerful institution, fighting, however clumsily, for its life in the political arena. Van Buren's many critics, contemporary and historical, have absolved him of the sin of indiscretion, and provoking unnecessary quarrels is perhaps the worst type of political indiscretion.

With Van Buren out of the picture as the initiator, where do we stand? Is there a comprehensive substitute key to the Bank war, one that is revisionist as well? Unfortunately for that hope, any account which deemphasizes Jackson cannot stand up. Jackson still remains central to the Bank war, not only in the obvious constitutional sense (that is, that he had to put his signature to the veto), but in that most of the impetus came from the President himself, seconded by his two intimate advisors, Amos Kendall and Blair. Van Buren was close to Jackson, but the Red Fox had his presidential ambitions to cultivate, while the Kitchen Cabinet had no independent political capital worth mentioning. This comes through clearly in the respective newspapers of Kitchen Cabinet and Regency. The *Globe* and the *Argus* did not react in unison to the development of the Bank issue. The official anti-BUS word came from Washington and the *Argus* followed haltingly and often halfheartedly. Although emphasis on Jackson is nothing new (pro-Jacksonian historiography made a ritual out of chronicling his noble deeds), one should not return to the old Jackson-versus-Biddle morality play. More intensive work on Jacksonian politics is needed at all levels, work devoid of the clichés of previous historiographical battles.

To return the focus to Jackson, even assuming the appearance ultimately of a completely convincing analysis of Jackson's and the Kitchen Cabinet's motives and aims, is not to answer some of the most intriguing and important questions about banking and politics in the 1830s. There is much to learn about the many Bank wars of that decade. The use of the plural "wars" is advisable, since the maxim which holds that pre-Civil War politics was state politics applies to banking as well. In short, it is necessary to "Namierize" the Bank war, investigate the tangles of economic interests and banking struggles which took place in every state, and then extract from them their political significance. This is no small task, but it should prove a worthwhile one. Much has been done, but much more remains unexplored. Analysis of these Bank wars will tell a good deal that is new about politics in the states, and more importantly, it will allow meaningful generalization about the Bank war and its effects.

14 / The Working Men's Party Revisited

Edward Pessen

By the end of the 1830's, many wealthy Americans were frightened. It seemed to them that the Jacksonians had created an antibusiness feeling that threatened the basic rights of property. They called the feeling, and whatever else displeased them politically, Loco-Focoism. As difficult as it may be to believe today, such measures as Van Buren's subtreasury proposal, under which the federal government would discontinue using private banks as depositories for its money, were denounced as "radicalism" and a danger to everything that America had previously stood for or had come to stand for.

The aftermath of the Panic of 1837 increased conservative fears in a way that paralleled the Southerners' constant anxieties over possible slave revolts, fears that existed more in *their* minds than in those of their slaves. Northern businessmen reacted apprehensively to social protest movements. The city "mob" was revealed to be more interested in improved wages, than in waging revolution, but one would never have known it from the gloomy pronouncements of conservative spokesmen and businessmen.

The Working Men's Party, although never large or politically potent for very long, performed an important task. It articulated the feelings and some of the demands of the growing body of urban wage earners. Its relationship to the Jacksonian Democratic Party was a shifting one and one that indicated the political turns that transformed the Jackson Party of 1828 into the Democratic Party of 1840. The "Workies" kept their ideas in circulation independently, until the Democrats late in the 1830's were willing to adopt a more pronounced "antibusiness" line than they had originally used. This is not to label either Jackson or Van Buren as anticapitalist in any meaningful sense, but the Bank War and the subsequent alignment of most businessmen in the Whig camp injected a class element into the two-party system. In his essay, Edward Pessen reviews and analyzes the literature bearing on the Working Men's Party and then offers his evaluation of the party's historical significance.

Labor History, IV (Fall, 1963), 203–226. Reprinted by permission. Footnotes have been omitted.

For further reading: Walter Hugins, *Jacksonian Democracy and the Working Class: A Study of the New York Workingmen's Movement, 1829–1837*
(1960); Carl N. Degler, "The Loco-Focos: Urban 'Agrarians'," *Journal of
Economic History,* XVI (September 1956), 322–333; Richard Hofstadter,
"William Leggett, Spokesman of Jacksonian Democracy," *Political Science
Quarterly,* XLVII (December 1943), 581–594; Edward Pessen, *Most Uncommon Jacksonians: The Radical Leaders of the Early Labor Movement* (1967).

The unique feature of the American labor movement during the Jacksonian era was
the establishment of Working Men's parties. Beginning in Philadelphia in 1828,
a Working Men's movement spread throughout the country, reaching its climax
in the 1830s. For the only time in American history, workers formed separate
political organizations, largely independent of the major parties. Since one of the
classic features of the modern American labor movement is precisely the extent to
which it has eschewed politics, the appearance of this movement is of obvious
significance. This essay will examine aspects of the movement as well as some of the
issues still in controversy concerning it.

If no attempt will be made here to give a blow-by-blow account of the rise and
fall of the Working Men's parties, it is because it is by now a much-told tale. A substantial literature has appeared since George Henry Evans and his contemporaries in
ante-bellum America first chronicled the activities of the New York Working Men.
The Working Men's movements of particular cities have been studied recently by
Walter Hugins, William Sullivan, Louis Arky, Seymour Savetsky, Milton Nadworny
and myself, among others, to supplement the modern accounts of the broader movement by Joseph Dorfman, Arthur M. Schlesinger, Jr. and Alden Whitman. In
addition, of course, such modern authors of volumes on the history of labor as Joseph
Rayback, Foster Rhea Dulles, Herbert Harris and Philip Foner also have dealt with
the labor parties. To date, though, the most comprehensive and probably still the most
valuable study remains the pioneering effort of Helen Sumner in John R. Commons'
History in 1918. In many respects it remains the basic structure on which all later
works have built.

The modern discussion, focussing as it has on a few major cities, has perhaps
obscured what Miss Sumner's researches long ago uncovered: the ubiquitousness of
the Working Men's party. Operating under a variety of names—"Working Men's
Parties," "Working Men's Republican Associations," "People's Parties," "Working
Men's Societies," "Farmer's and Mechanic's Societies," "Mechanics and Other Working Men," and just plain "Working Men"—they appeared in most of the states of the
union. Pennsylvania was the home of the first known group, the Philadelphia party
of 1828, which developed out of an earlier organization, the Mechanics' Union of
Trade Associations. Other groups in Pennsylvania, some of them unknown to Miss
Sumner, were organized in Phillipsburg, Lancaster, Carlisle, Pike Township in
Clearfield County, Pottsville, Harrisburg, Erie, Allegheny and Mifflin Counties.

In New York State the leading, and certainly the most interesting, group was
organized by Thomas Skidmore and others in New York City. Brooklyn had its own
organization in which the later trade unionist John Commerford played a leading
role. Parties also appeared in Troy, Albany, Rochester, Buffalo, Genesee, Utica,

Syracuse (Salina), Schenectady, Geneva, Ithaca, Auburn, Batavia, Brockport, Hartford in Washington County, Canandaigua Village, Kingsbury, Lansingburgh, Glens' Falls, Palmyra, and Saratoga. A Working Men's convention in 1830 was attended by delegates from the counties of New York, Albany, Rensselaer, Cayuga, Oneida, Washington, Onondaga, Tioga, Tompkins, Montgomery, Kings, Cortland and Ontario, while it was reported that a number of other counties also had chosen delegates who for some unknown reason did not attend.

In New Jersey, groups formed not only in Newark and Trenton, as Miss Sumner noted, but in Hanover (Morris County), Orange County, Centerville, Caldwell, Paterson and Essex County as well. Organizations—albeit questionable ones which may have been "Working Men" in name only—were started in Washington, D.C. and Canton, Ohio. Working Men also formed in Zanesville and Columbiana County. In Delaware there were branches in Wilmington, New Castle County, Brandywine and Red Clay Creek.

New England had a lively movement whose Association of Farmers, Mechanics and Other Working Men has been heralded by some writers as the country's first true farmer-labor party, and by others as the first trace of industrial unionism. In addition to this group, whose members came from a number of states, Working Men organized in Boston, Dedham, Northampton, Dorchester, Hampshire and Franklin Counties in Massachusetts; New London and Lyme in Connecticut; Dover, New Hampshire, Portland and Brunswick in Maine; and Woodstock, Burlington, Middlebury, and Calais in Vermont.

Most of our information concerning these parties comes from the pages of the dozens of journals which sprang up in this period in support of the Working Men. According to the *Delaware Free Press,* one of these journals, at least twenty newspapers in a number of states had appeared by August, 1830, which might be classified as pro-labor. Miss Sumner found evidence of "some fifty newspapers in at least fifteen states" for the period 1829-32. Naturally, these papers varied in the degree of support or attention they gave to the Working Men's cause but a substantial number of them can properly be described as organs of the political movement, so completely were they dedicated to the Working Men's issues both in their coverage and in their news slant.

In the case of several of the movement's leaders, their identification with labor consisted precisely in the fact that they edited these journals. George Henry Evans was such a figure. Another was William Heighton, an Englishman who came to this country as a youth, became a cordwainer, the founder of the Philadelphia Mechanics' Union of Trade Associations and, early in 1828, the chief editor of the *Mechanic's Free Press,* the official journal of the Philadelphia movement. This weekly has been described as the "first of the mechanics' newspapers in this country edited by journeymen and directed to them." In Philadelphia, Heighton's journal prodded workers "along the path of reform and into politics," thus helping to *initiate* the political movement. More typical was Evans' *Working Man's Advocate* in New York City, which appeared shortly *after* the Working Men organized there. In many cases the journal followed so soon after the party that the two were practically simultaneous, as in Newark, where a Newark *Village Chronicle and Farmers, Mechanics and Working Men's Advocate* came out immediately after the political movement started.

Louis Arky's description of the *Mechanic's Free Press* could apply to numerous other papers as well: "its pages presented a spectrum of reform, from Pestalozzian educational ideas and cooperative store suggestions to the views of free thinkers and reprints from works like [John] Gray's Lecture [*Lecture on Human Happiness,* London 1825, a socialistic tract]." In addition the journals carried accounts of the Working Men's activities in other cities as well as their own, announcements of future activities, romances, advertisements, literary excerpts and a potpourri of other material. From the point of view of the student of American labor, however, most rewarding were their editorials, the letters of contributors—often polemical and therefore piquant as well as infomative—and the listings of the demands and the programs of the Working Men. Students of the history of American journalism and those who are interested in our social history also will find a treasure of material in the *New England Artisan and Farmer's, Mechanic's and Laboring Man's Reposi- tory,* the New York *Daily Sentinel,* the Indianapolis *Union and Mechanics' and Working Men's Advocate,* and the other labor journals of the period.

If the worth of Miss Sumner's contribution endures, it is also true that the recent discussion, certainly that of the past two decades—based on new evidence and re- flecting new scholarly interests and frames of reference—has not only added to our knowledge but in many cases severely modified and brought into serious question her conclusions concerning some rather important matters. In this respect, the trend is perhaps similar to that in American historical writing in general: an iconoclastic revisionism which accepts no previous interpretations as sacred, inspired as it is by a relativism to which all old judgments are merely the ephemeral reflections of a forever bygone time. $_{aN}$

It would be understatement to describe the main questions raised by the recent literature as a challenge to the traditional thesis. For these questions concern nothing less that the fundamental nature of the Working Men's movement. They simply ask: Was the movement authentic? Was it composed of bona-fide wage earners battling in the interests of wage earners? Or was it spurious, consisting instead of wily politicians who wrapped themselves in the Working Men's mantle only to hide their real identity?

According to Miss Sumner, the issue that divided the true Working Men's parties from the fraudulent was the tariff. For although her study expressed few doubts about the authenticity of most of the organizations which carried the title, she did believe that in some cases "advocates of a protective tariff assumed without warrant the popular name—'mechanics and workingmen'." She also suspected that these "associ- ations of so-called workingmen which favored protection generally avoided commit- ting themselves to the usual demands of the Working Men's party." But if the organi- zation were for free trade and in addition raised the "usual demands," her study accepts it at face value.

In challenging the authenticity of these parties, critics have focussed on a number of issues. One point of contention has been the party's origins, since the way in which the organization was started, the nature of the men involved, and the issues propelling them into action obviously tell us whether the organization was of and for working- men or whether it was something else again—at least in its infancy.

The political movement in Philadelphia grew out of a decision by the city's Mechanics' Union of Trade Associations to enter into politics in order to promote "the interests and enlightenment of the working classes." This organization, the "first union of all the orgainzed workmen of any city," had been organized largely through the energetic activity of William Heighton. It included the individual unions—or societies, as they were then called—of journeymen bricklayers, painters, glaziers, typographers and other groups, as well as the journeymen house carpenters whose strike for the ten-hour day in the summer of 1827 spurred the formation of the broader union. There can be little doubt as to the authenticity of the Mechanics' Union, whose appeal to its constituent societies rested primarily on its down-to-earth promise of financial support to journeymen on strike against their masters. A few months after it was organized, the bylaws of the Union were amended to provide that three months prior to general elections the membership should "nominate as candidates for public office such individuals as shall pledge themselves . . . to support and advance . . . the interests and enlightenment of the working classes." The new bylaws took immediate effect. Several months later the *Mechanic's Free Press* reported that "at a very large and respectable meeting of Journeymen House Carpenters held on Tuesday evening, July 1st [1828] . . . the Mechanics' Union of Trade Associations is entering into measures for procuring a nomination of candidates for legislative and other public offices, who will support the interest of the working classes." Thus, in the promise made by some journeymen workers to support at the polls individuals sympathetic to the working class, was born the Working Men's party of Philadelphia. The most skeptical observer can hardly deny the true workingmen's character of the party, at least at the time of its birth.

In New York City a Working Men's party appeared for the first time in 1829, when in the elections for the State Assembly held early in November eleven candidates nominated by the new party made a remarkable showing. The decision to run Working Men's candidates on a separate ticket was made at a general meeting of mechanics on October 19, 1829. In addition to approving a number of other resolutions presented by the executive body—called the Committee of Fifty—the meeting resolved "that past experience teaches that we have nothing to hope from the aristocratic orders of society; and that our only course to pursue is, to send men of our own description, if we can, to the Legislature at Albany; . . . [and] we will make the attempt at the ensuing election; and that as a proper step thereto we will invite all those of our fellow citizens who live on their own labor and none other, to meet us . . ."

This Committee of Fifty had been elected at the second of two meetings of journeymen mechanics held earlier that year (in the last week of April). They were to give leadership in the struggle to protect the ten-hour day against an alleged employers' plot to lengthen it. The first meeting of the mechanics, which was in fact to lead directly to the nomination of candidates, and which can therefore properly be described as constituting the first meeting of the New York Working Men's party, had been called in order to combat "all attempts to compel them to work more than ten hours a day." It would appear, then, that in its origins the political movement of the New York Working Men was clearly a response of bona-fide workers to an attack on their working conditions.

Seymour Savetsky, however, after a close study of this movement which appeared to establish an intimate relationship with the Republican (or Jackson) party, concluded that "the explanation for the origin of the . . . party is to be found in the bitter internal dissensions and schisms that were wrecking the Republican party of New York. In the fractionalization of the Republican party . . . resides the explanation for the appearance of the New York Working Men's Party." While there is evidence that the emergence of the New York movement owed something to the disenchantment of some Republican (or Democratic) voters with the Tammany machine, it seems to me impossible to disagree with Walter Hugins that the party's "initial impetus was economic, a protest against unemployment and a defense of the ten-hour day." Even Jabez Hammond's contemporary account, while stressing the complexity and heterogeneity of the State movement, saw the beginnings of the New York City party as essentially due to the concern of mechanics in the building trade with onerous economic conditions. Of three leaders of the New York Working Men— Robert Dale Owen, George Henry Evans and Thomas Skidmore—it is true that only the last might be classified a worker. These men were to steer the movement in directions determined largely by doctrinaire philosophies. But this fact is no way contradicts another: that the New York Working Men's party originated in a movement of journeymen mechanics to defend their positions against an anticipated attack by masters and employers.

For Boston, as for Newark and other towns in New Jersey, the evidence is not clear. The program adopted by the Boston Working Men's party, as well as the methods advocated to attain it and the candidates nominated to represent the organization politically, all raise doubts as to the nature of the movement. But according to the correspondents who reported on its first meetings in the summer of 1830, these early meetings were attended by large numbers of men who "from appearance, were warm from their workshops and from other places of daily toil, but who bore on their countenances convictions of their wrongs, and a determination to use every proper means to have them redressed."

There is considerably fuller information on the origins of the much more significant New England Association of Farmers, Mechanics and Other Working Men. Described by Miss Sumner as a "new type of labour organization, in part economic and in part political," this association was formed when delegates from the New England states, convening in Providence in December 1831, agreed to hold the first convention in Boston the following spring. The advertisement for the first convention emphasized that "the object of that convention is to mature measures to concentrate the efforts of the laboring classes, to regulate the hours of labor by one uniform standard." In short, this was a call for the ten-hour day. It is no coincidence that the date set by the first convention for the establishment of the ten-hour system —March 20, 1832—happened to be precisely the date that Boston's shipyard workers also began their strike for the ten-hour day. Certainly the workers went on strike not because the Association's Constitution directed them to do so. Rather, the Association incorporated the idea of a ten-hour system, a strike to achieve it, a war chest to finance it, and expulsion of all those who would work more than ten hours per day after March 20, because of the great influence that Boston's shipyard workers and their allies had in its councils. It was the defeat of the ten-hour strike that led the delegates to the second convention held at Boston in September to modify the clause calling for the expulsion from the Association of those who worked more than the ten-hour day. It appears incontestable that New England's most important Working Men's party was organized by workingmen to achieve—in contrast to its New York City counterpart, which sought to maintain—the ten-hour day.

The sharpest questions as to the authenticity of the Working Men's parties have been provoked by the accumulating evidence on the social and economic back-grounds of their members and leaders. The organ of the Philadelphia Working Men liked to think that in contrast to the two major parties of the time—the "Federalists," made up of lawyers and aristocrats, and the Jackson party, composed of bank speculators and office hunters—"on the Working Men's ticket . . . the candidates from first to last have been taken from the ranks of the people." But William Sullivan has shown that during its four years of existence the Philadelphia party nominated and supported very few workers as candidates for office. According to his tabulation, of the party's one-hundred candidates only ten were workingmen. Twenty-three were professional men, fifty-three were merchants and manufacturers, eleven were "gentlemen" and three had no occupations recorded. Among these were some of the wealthiest men in the city, including Charles Alexander, pub-lisher of the conservative *Daily Chronicle*. These facts lead Sullivan to doubt that the Philadelphia organization was a true workingmen's party. Louis Arky, on the other hand, found a high percentage of its early leaders—better than seventy-five per cent, in fact—workers or artisans.

The leading student of the New Jersey movement, Milton Nadworny, found little solid information about the occupations or incomes of the leaders and candidates there, although for Newark he ventures the understatement that "undoubtedly, not all of the men in the group were pure, unadulterated workingmen." Despite his find-ings that small businessmen and merchants often played leading parts in the move-ment, Nadworny nonetheless accepts it as essentially authentic.

The New York City Working Men split into at least three factions shortly after their striking political success in the fall of 1829, and there is no doubt that the largest faction had little in common with true workmen. But prior to the infiltration of the party by opportunistic elements, culminating in their ascendancy by the time of the 1830 elections, the evidence indicates that bona-fide workers were active in its ranks. Of the eleven candidates put up for the State Assembly in 1829, ten were workers; the other, a physician, got significantly fewer votes than all the rest of his colleagues in the election. In its early stages, according to George Henry Evans, the party sought not only to confine leadership to workingmen but to see that the leaders were journeymen rather than masters. That it was not successful, however, is shown by the fact that the following year even Evans' faction was supporting manufacturers as candidates for political office.

For that matter, Evans' definition of working man was a rather broad one. Accord-ing to him, only one member of the seventy-man General Executive Committee of the New York party of 1830—a broker—was not a working man. Evidently, he con-sidered the five grocers, the two merchant tailors, the oil merchant, the teacher and the farmer to be workers. The complete occupational breakdown for this committee unfortunately does not distinguish between masters and journeymen, but it does range over a broad category of occupations including carpenters, smiths, masons, painters, pianoforte makers, sash makers and porter housekeepers. Savetsky, who is not inclined to take this organization's claims at face value, nonetheless concedes that on this committee "a majority . . . belong to the laboring element in the community." His close study of the property owned by this group established that just under fifty per cent were propertyless, another ten per cent had only personal property, while only three individuals owned property assessed at more than $10,000. For the years after 1831 it has been rather conclusively shown, both by the contemporary, Jabez Hammond, and by Walter Hugins, writing in 1960, that the New York Working Men included a wide variety of social and economic types.

The Boston Working Men's party did not last long, though while it lasted it showed no animus towards men of wealth. Years ago I did a study of the social position of the candidates it supported in the municipal election of 1830 and in the state congressional contest of 1831. Their mayoralty candidate, Theodore Lyman, Jr., was a wealthy ship owner, while four of their seven aldermanic candidates were among the wealthiest men in Boston. Thirty-five of their sixty choices for the State Assembly belonged to that elite group whose property was valued in excess of $2,600. Since less than two thousand persons in a population of seventy-eight thousand had this amount of property, it would appear that forty of the party's sixty-eight nominees belonged to the wealthiest segment of the community. I must admit, however, that I am now not so sure of what I wrote then, that these figures "do not imply anything fraudulent," and that they reflect "middle-class aspirations and a certain naiveté" more than they raise doubts "as to the true workingmen's character" of the Boston Working Men's party. Doubts as to the actual nature of the party are indeed raised by such figures.

Doubts have also been raised by the programs of the Working Men's parties. Joseph Dorfman has not been alone in noting that some of the measures they advocated bore no relation to the economic needs of workingmen. But it is true, of course, that workingmen had needs that ranged beyond the economic. That Working Men's parties raised aloft a standard which included a wide variety of political, social, intellectual, occasionally even religious, as well as economic issues, does not necessarily testify to anything but their breadth of interests and hopes.

The programs of the parties were amazingly similar. For, as Miss Sumner observed, "substantially the same measures were advocated by the workingmen in most of the western and southern cities, as well as in New Jersey, Delaware and New England, as were advocated by their comrades in Philadelphia and New York." The program of the Philadelphia Working Men was to become the nucleus of all other programs. It included, above all, a call for a free, tax-supported school system to replace the stigmatized "pauper schools" which, according to Sullivan, provided a "highly partial and totally inadequate system of education for their children." The final copies of the *Mechanic's Free Press* contained on the masthead the following additional reforms: abolition of imprisonment for debt; abolition of all licensed monopolies; an entire revision or abolition of the prevailing militia system; a less expensive legal system; equal taxation on property; no legislation on religion; a district system of election. In addition, the Philadelphians intermittently protested against the unsanitary and overcrowded housing conditions of workingmen; the high cost of living; the long hours, low wages and poor conditions of labor, as well as the low esteem in which manual work was held; the hostility of the major parties towards labor; the mistreatment of labor unions; the lottery system—"the fruitful parent of misery and want to numberless heart-broken wives and helpless children, who have beheld the means of their subsistence lavished in the purchase of lottery tickets"; the "pernicious operating of paper money"; and such down-to-earth grievances as insufficient "hydrant water for the accommodation of the poor" and "the failure of the city to clean the streets in the remote sections of the city where the workingmen reside." And earlier they had pressed successfully for the passage of a mechanics' lien law to assure workingmen first claim on their employers' payrolls. Nor does this exhaust a list which from time to time carried criticisms of banks and banking, charitable institutions, the sale of liquor, conspiracy laws—and, when invoked against unions, the use of prison labor, and the complexity of the laws and of the legal system.

The Working Men of New York and of other cities did not of course slavishly follow the Philadelphia program, even though they put forward grievances and demands which concentrated on the same essentials. In New York City, for example, Thomas Skidmore early won the Working Men over to the approval of an "agrarian" program calling for "equal property to all adults," a plank in the platform which was supported until the expulsion of Skidmore from the party at the end of 1829. Later, Robert Dale Owen, George Henry Evans and their supporters, championed a unique educational system known as "State Guardianship," under which working class children not only were to receive an improved education under a tax-supported program but were to board out in the new public schools as well. At one time or another, the party also stressed anti-clericalism, compensation for jurors and witnesses, direct election of the mayor, smaller electoral districts, the payment of certain political officials (for the classic reason, later emphasized by the English Chartists, that otherwise only wealthy property holders could afford to hold office), the reduction of the salaries of others, civil service reform, abolition of capital punishment, pensions for Revolutionary War veterans, a single municipal legislative chamber, and free trade. As to the half-dozen or so issues which were most emphasized, the mastheads of the labor journals which proclaimed them could have been interchanged without notable difference. On many occasions the New York *Working Man's Advocate* and the Philadelphia *Mechanic's Free Press* carried precisely the same slogans.

As has been indicated, some programs were related to local problems and issues. The New England Association reflected its rural composition by calling for a reform in land tenure laws, and its sympathy with factory operatives by insistence on factory legislation. The Working Men of Boston advocated a reduction of the fees charged by professionals as well as a reduction in what were considered to be the exorbitant expenditures of the State government. And in Cincinnati the Working Men added "improvements in the arts and sciences" to the classic appeal for equal universal education and for the abolition of licensed monopolies, capital punishment, unequal taxation on property, the prevalent militia system, and imprisonment for debt.

There is no question but that this was a broad program, substantial portions of which were supported by men and groups having nothing to do with labor. Imprisonment for debt, for example, was opposed by many people outside of the Working Men's movement—on broad humanitarian grounds in some cases, and on grounds of economic inefficiency in others. Its victims were not always the "laboring poor." The same is true for other of the reforms, including education. Yet it would be economic determinism of a very rigid sort, indeed, to insist that authentic labor organizations confine their programs to economic issues advantageous only to workers.

Much of the Working Men's program *was* in fact concerned with the economic interests of labor. Naturally, workers sought larger wages and better working conditions. But they also sought improved status in society, and some of them organized in order to support the perfectionist demands put forward by their idealistic leaders as the means of achieving this status. The program of the Working Men's parties reveals them to have been champions of social justice and a more perfect democracy, as well as critics of every kind of social abuse.

Still other questions as to the authenticity of the Working Men have been raised over the alleged closeness of their relationship with the Jacksonian party. While Arthur M. Schlesinger, Jr. sees a coalition between the two movements, critics of his thesis have interpreted the same evidence as indicating the essential fraudulence of the Working Men's parties, seeing them as being no more than front organizations for the Democrats. It is perhaps a source of comfort to these critics that their charges are similar to those made 130 years ago by some National Republican leaders and publishers.

With regard to this issue, as with others, the evidence is either inconclusive or too complex to permit black and white generalizations. Assuredly, from time to time on certain issues the two movements behaved as one. The organ of the Newark Working Men, the Newark *Village Chronicle and Farmers, Mechanics, and Workingmen's Advocate,* admitted in April of 1830 to its sympathy with the Jacksonians. And there seemed to be more than coincidence in the decision by the two parties in New Jersey that year to hold their nominating conventions for the State legislature in the same small town on the same date. Nor is it surprising that after the fall elections the Whig press denounced what it felt to be the collusion between the two parties. Five years later, the Newark Democrats still evidently depended to a large extent on the political support of the Working Men, while in 1836 the two groups jointly supported a number of legislative candidates. The leading student of the New Jersey Working Men concludes that they consistently supported the Democrats and their candidates.

In New York City the striking political success achieved by the Working Men in 1829 seems to have been the result largely of a shift in the voting habits of people who ordinarily voted for the "Republican" or Jackson party. The New York party broke into several splinter groups shortly after the 1829 election. The so-called *Sentinel* or *Advocate* wing, named after the journals published by the younger Owen and Evans, supported much of the Democratic program, especially its anti-monopoly features. In fact, according to Savetsky, this faction was simply absorbed or assimilated into the New York Jacksonian organization after its defeat in the elections of 1830.

In New England the decision in 1833 of the New England Association to support as their gubernatorial candidate Samuel Clesson Allen, the erstwhile champion of Andrew Jackson and opponent of the Bank of the United States, led more than one Whig journal to denounce the unholy alliance of Working Men and Jackson men. This same fact serves as the basis for Schlesinger's conclusion that at this time the Massachusetts Working Men increasingly threw themselves behind Jackson's monetary program. Yet this same New England Association Convention urged the formation of a pro-labor national political organization. When the Association again nominated Allen for Governor at its last convention in September 1834, at Northampton, it simultaneously urged rejection of the candidates of the major parties for State office. A close study of its programs, conventions, resolutions and actions indicates that from its birth in Providence in December 1831, until its demise not three years later, this organization was little concerned with, let alone sympathetic to, the Democratic Party. As for the Boston Working Men's Party, not only did it show no support whatever for the Jacksonian party, but its slate of candidates for the Board of Aldermen and the State House of Representatives included a good number of National Republicans. Although its mayoralty candidate, Theodore Lyman, Jr., had worked for Jackson's victory in 1828, he had broken with Old Hickory's party well before the 1830 municipal elections. The non-support of the Democrats by the poorer wards in the 1831 elections provoked David Henshaw, Jackson's appointee to the strategic collectorship of the port of Boston, to charge that Boston Workingmen were the enemies of the Democratic Party. (The evidence indicates that workmen were no great friends to the Working Men, either.)

In New York City not only Skidmore, but Evans and Owen and their supporters as well, regularly voiced their opposition to both major parties. Despite their occasional agreement with the Democrats on a particular issue, their press warned that Jackson had no interest in important reform. If the mid-century commentator, Jabez Hammond can be believed, the men who "flocked to the standard of the Workingmen" in New York State were "opposed to the Albany Regency and the Jackson party."

The Philadelphia Working Men had no objections to supporting candidates of whatever social background or political persuasion. Yet their journal saw no contradiction in denying any connection with either of the major parties; in fact, it stressed the danger represented by the Democrats, "for as most of us are deserters from their ranks they view us with the same sensation as the mighty lord would the revolt of his vassals: there cannot be so much danger from the Federalists as, generally speaking, we were never inclined to trust them." In the elections of 1829, the one year in which the Philadelphia Working Men achieved an outstanding success, they combined with the anti-Jacksonians in support of eight local candidates, while endorsing only one Jackson supporter. Sullivan has concluded that "an analysis of the [Philadelphia] Working Men's Party reveals that both in its composition and its predilections, it was amazingly regular in its support of the anti-Jackson forces."

Even for New Jersey the situation was more complex than the allegations of some National Republicans would make it appear. The original platform of the New Jersey Working Men refused to align the group in support of Jackson. As the Working Men of Morris showed in 1834, they had no compunctions about nominating a Whig to office. His success goaded the Democrats into charging that the Whigs used the Working Men as tools! The following year an election rally of Newark's Working Men's party expressly stated that it preferred neither of the major parties. And although in 1836 there was a degree of cooperation between the two groups, there was evidently a falling out (before the end of the year) that may have been due to the Working Men's resentment at being used by the Jackson party.

Two points should be stressed. The program of the Working Men's Parties called for reforms that in most cases went unmentioned by the Democrats, whether on a local, state or national level. This would indicate that the movement's organizers were motivated precisely by the failure of the Democrats—not to mention the National Republicans—to work towards goals these organizers deemed of the highest importance. In addition, despite the attempt by some historians to treat the political issues and the major parties of the era in striking ideological terms, as though they represented diametrically opposed social and class viewpoints, the facts are otherwise. As Charles Sellers, Glynden Van Deusen, Bray Hammond, Richard Hofstadter and others have shown, the major parties had similar views on many important issues, differing more in tactics than in fundamental objectives, with neither party dedicated to a drastic alteration of the fabric of society. Of course there were Democrats and Democrats. But Jackson himself, and the leaders of the Democratic party in most of the states, were practical men. All of which is to say that it is to misinterpret the nature of the Democratic state machines or the national Democratic party of Andrew Jackson's day to believe that so loose, opportunistic, all-inclusive and eclectic a coalition would devote itself to the kinds of reform urged by the Working Men.

What conclusions can be drawn about the relationship between the Working Men, led by radicals who often sharply criticized the Democratic party, and Jacksonian democracy? To the extent that it, too, opposed aristocratic privilege and monopoly, the Working Men's movement may perhaps be interpreted as part of a broadly defined "Jacksonian Revolution." But neither organized nor unorganized workingmen became a fixed part of a Democratic political coalition. And if the Jacksonian movement was in fact a movement primarily devoted to achieving a freer competitive capitalism, the Working Men clearly had demands which went far beyond that objective. Yet in the large view which seeks to impose a pattern on the era, reforms of varied character, championed by diverse groups—each seeking the achievement of its own objectives—somehow merge together in a broad, all-embracing reform movement. It is only in this general sense that the Working Men of the Jacksonian era can be said to have been a part of the large, sweeping movement towards whose political expression—the Democratic party—they often displayed indifference if not actual hostility.

If it does nothing else, the discussion of the various controversies concerning the authenticity of the Working Men's parties should clearly establish one thing: it is impossible to generalize about the movement as a whole, as though all of its constituent parts were alike in all important particulars. There were Working Men and Working Men. The origin of some was obscure; of others, dubious. Some arose out of economic struggles, others out of concern for status. Some came to be dominated by opportunists, others by zealots. Thus, the only safe generalization perhaps would be that no two parties experienced precisely similar careers.

Yet it is also clear that despite inevitable differences in their circumstances and behavior these organizations, arising more or less simultaneously and calling for like reforms, had much in common. Common to the Working Men's parties in the major cities, in my opinion, was their authenticity—at least for part of their history. By authenticity I mean that they were formed by workers or men devoted to the interests of workers, sought to attract workers to membership in or at least to support of the new organizations, worked for programs designed to promote the cause and welfare of workers, and entered politics because of the failure of the major parties to concern themselves with important reforms and in the hope that these parties could be goaded or influenced into showing such concern. The authenticity of a party that conforms to this standard is not lessened by the fact that in supporting candidates to office, it asked only that they support the program, or important elements of it, while it evinced no interest in the size of their bank accounts or their social status. Nor is there anything suspect in the fact that parts of the program might also be supported by non-workers.

The origins of the Working Men in Philadelphia, New York City, Newark, and the cities of New England, stressing as they did either the working class backgrounds or the aims of their founders, strengthen the belief that the parties were not misnomers. It is true that the parties contained many men who by present definitions would not qualify as workers. But the definition of that earlier day was much more flexible. The prevailing concept was that all who performed "honest toil" were working men. Even to such a radical as George Henry Evans in 1830, only lawyers, bankers, and brokers could be designated as persons not engaged in the kind of useful occupation qualifying them for membership either in the Working Men's party or the working class. (It is interesting testimony to the growing conservatism of the New York City Working Men that a resolution incorporating Evans' sentiments was defeated as too restrictive. In the fall of 1829, on the other hand, there was strong support for the principle of confining leadership in the party to journeymen and, in Evans' words, denying a vote to any "boss who employed a large number of hands.") Additional light on this issue is thrown by the similar discussion that arose among the Philadelphia Working Men. According to the *Mechanic's Free Press,* early in the party's history (in the summer of 1828) it was decided that while employers might be present at meetings, they could not hold office. Yet one year later its Ricardian Socialist editor, William Heighton, could write: "If an employer superintends his own business (still more if he works with his own hands) he is a working man. . . . If this view of things be correct, shall we look with a jealous eye on those employers who prefer being considered working men? Who are willing to join us in obtaining our objects?" Not only for political candidates but also for mere membership in the party, the important issue evidently had become simply whether the man would join in "obtaining our objects."

It is also true that at a certain point in its career the New York party, for example, seemed to be in the hands of men who had little sympathy with its expressed program. But contemporary participants and later scholars alike are unanimous in agreeing that these elements infiltrated the party only after the dramatic success it achieved in the 1829 elections and succeeded in taking it over only by the use of money, inner party intrigue, extra-legal tactics, and newspaper excoriation, all the while continuing to pay lip service to reform. The New York Working Men underwent a *transition* that powerfully testifies to the fact that in its heyday it was not only an authentic but also an impressive organization, even frightening to some politicians. Perhaps nothing more dramatically suggests that the New York and other Working Men's parties were bona fide than the opposition, to put it mildly, they inspired in Democratic and National Republican politicians alike, and above all in most of the press. The Boston *Courier* was not alone in arguing that "the very pretension to the necessity of such a party is a libel on the community." The underlying thought of its editors, the Buckinghams, was that rich and poor, publishers and typesetters, skilled and unskilled—all are workingmen and therefore there was no need for a separate Working Men's party.

In the nation's cities, however, not only did a Working Men's party appear; it would be more accurate to say that it burst forth on the political community like a meteor, either electing its candidates, or obtaining the balance of power on its second attempt, as in the City of Brotherly Love or, in other cities, immediately after putting forward its original slate. Less than two weeks before the election, in New York City, for example, a ticket nominated for the State Assembly elected one and came near to electing several other of its candidates, amassing better than 6,000 out of 21,000 votes cast. And yet in this as in other cases the political success was decidedly ephemeral. Decline set in almost immediately, culminating a brief few years later in the party's demise and disappearance.

What accounted for the almost immediate downfall of the Working Men's party? From that time to this, attempted explanations have not been lacking. Some Philadelphia leaders bitterly blamed the workers themselves, both for their blindness to their own true interests and for their lack of courage. Other sympathizers attributed the failure to the party's mistaken policy of supporting wealthy candidates, themselves personally sympathetic to monopolies. Thomas Skidmore, himself cashiered out of the New York party for his radical views and his uncompromising fight for them, charged that the party's doom was sealed by its permitting rich men to take over, men who had no business in the party in the first place. Evans, his one-time opponent, later came to agree with him. Hammond also noted that the New York State party had within its ranks men who made their living at jobs they professed to criticize, not excluding banking. By his view, "this party, if it deserves the name of a political party, was too disjointed and composed of materials too heterogeneous to continue long in existence." New York friends of the Boston Working Men, on the other hand, explained the pathetic political showing of the New England party by its preoccupation with issues, such as religious infidelity, that were not properly the concern of a workingmen's political organization.

In her summary of the causes of the failure of the Working Men's parties, Miss Sumner listed, in addition to some of the factors mentioned by contemporaries of the movement, the onset of a general prosperity which turned the attention of workers from "politics to trade unionism"; dissension—"legitimate" when resulting from heterogeneity, "illegitimate" when started and nurtured by "professional politicians of the old parties, who worm themselves in the new party"; the inexperience of leadership with regard to the practical problems in managing a political party; the hostile activities of the parties' open enemies; and, "last but not least, the taking up of some of its most popular demands by one of the old parties." Most recent literature on the subject tends to confirm many of her judgments. For New York, both Hugins, and Savetsky before him, stress the way in which Tammany and the Democrats absorbed the program, above all its anti-monopoly features; Savetsky also calls attention to the lack of dynamic and energetic leadership such as might have been provided by a person like Frances Wright—erroneously designated by contemporary opponents of the party as its high priestess, with an eye toward tarring it with the same infidelity brush that was applied to her. Arky emphasizes the Philadelphia party's inept machinery: "for political purposes the movement was clumsily organized." Sullivan, on the other hand, stresses the lack of class consciousness of its members, threats made by employers against those who supported it, and, above all, the very nature of the party and its candidates. It is Arthur Schlesinger, Jr.'s provocative conclusion that the Working Men disappeared because "their own parties [were] engaged in kindhearted activity on the periphery of the problem"—on such issues as education, imprisonment for debt, or clericalism, whereas the Democrats stressed the core issues that really counted. Thus, "during the Bank War, laboring men began slowly to turn to Jackson as their leader, and his party as their party." Not the least questionable feature of his interpretation is its assumption that the Working Men's parties and "laboring men" were one and the same thing. If it appears to be true, rather, that most laboring men did not vote for Jackson, it is equally true that a few exceptional cases notwithstanding, at no time did they vote even as a significant minority for the parties organized in their name.

Their own political ineptitude and inexperience, internal bickering, heterogeneous membership, lack of funds, and the infiltration of their ranks by men interested only in using them, all played an important part in bringing about the downfall of the Working Men; so did the opposition of the press, and the shrewdness and adaptability of the Democrats. Several related points also might be mentioned. Better than the major parties then or now, the Working Men's party represented the Burkean definition of a political party as a group of men united in behalf of certain political, social, and economic principles. Its membership may have been broad but the party's program was not all things to all men; it was certainly not a grab bag aimed primarily at winning office for those who professed to support it. In the American society of Tocqueville's day a distinctly class-oriented program could not expect success at the polls.

On the other hand, for a party that presumes to speak out in behalf of labor to open its lists to individuals who embody the opposite of everything it stands for is perhaps fatally to blur its image—at least in the minds of workingmen—while failing to shake the loyalties of other citizens for the traditional parties who were so much better at practical politics. Speak out the Working Men did, in a message that was idealistic and radical; and as the message became clearer, an American public seeking the main chance and increasingly optimistic about its possibilities, lost interest in the nay-saying of the radical dissenters who formulated the Working Men's program. It may well be, then, that a reform party was doomed to failure in the American society-in-flux (bemoaned by a James Fenimore Cooper), whose characteristic members quivered in anticipation of the material fortunes to be made. Such optimism, when shared by workers, is the stuff that kills off ideological politics.

Notwithstanding their failings and their ephemeral vogue, a final assessment of the Working Men's parties cannot fail to note their significance. Immediately after the results of the striking Working Men's showing in New York became known, the Democrats promised to pass the lien law for which the new party had been agitating. Nor was it a matter of a lien law alone. Even in the short run, the Democrats in New York and elsewhere hastily showed greater concern than ever before for the various reform provisions of the Working Men's program. Thus one of the factors that helped bring about their disappearance as a separate political entity was also an indication of their strength. If it is the function of radical parties in America to act as gadflies, to goad and influence rather than win elections, then the Working Men succeeded admirably.

Of course the degree of success they enjoyed is hard to measure. The Working Men were not alone in championing public education, abolition of imprisonment for debt, banking reform, reform of the militia system, factory laws, general incorporation laws, recognition of labor's right to organize unions, shorter hours of work for labor—to name some of the leading issues. It is impossible to fix with precision their contribution in comparison with that of other individuals and groups who supported one or another of these measures. But there would seem to be no question that the role of the Working Men's parties was an important one, in some cases even greater than is usually believed. In the struggle for the creation of a public school system free from the stigma of charity or pauperism, for example, it has long been the fashion (certainly since Frank Carlton pointed it out) to accord considerable credit to the Working Men. Yet, as Sidney Jackson has shown, not only did the Working Men agitate for the establishment of such a system; they also advocated sophisticated qualitative measures that seem remarkably prescient. Among the changes they sought were an improved curriculum, less concerned with pure memory and "superannuated histories," less emphasis on strict discipline, better physical conditions for children, better trained and better paid teachers, and better equipped schools, free of clerical influences. In sum, Helen Sumner's generous estimate does not seem overdrawn: "The Working Men's party, in short, was a distinct factor in pushing forward measures which even conservative people now recognize to have been in the line of progress toward real democracy."

It has been suggested that one of the factors working against the long-run popularity of the Working Men's party was a radicalism uncongenial to opportunistic Americans. But on the other hand the party's relative popularity, brief though it was, suggests that some contemporaries were receptive to the voice of protest. The fact that a Thomas Skidmore, who favored a redistribution of property, could win acceptance as a leader of the New York party; that in removing the slogan, "all adults (are entitled to) equal property," from the third issue of the *Working Man's Advocate*, George Henry Evans went to great lengths to explain that he continued to believe essentially in the same goals; that the program of the "conservative" Cook-Guyon faction, which came to dominate the party, continued to pay lip service to radical reform—all of this indicates not only that an important minority in the Jacksonian era were disenchanted with their society and its institutions, but that it was considered politic by some astute men to cater or defer to this mood. A final significance, then, of the Working Men's party lay in the testimony its career afforded that the United States of the Jackson era was not altogether devoid of that sense of alienation that in England and on the Continent provided fertile ground for the spread of Owenite, Chartist, Fourierist and other socialist doctrines.

15 / Political Aspects of the Van Buren Era

William G. Carleton

Extending the analysis beyond the critique of the Workie leaders, William G. Carleton deals with the general political and social climate of the unhappy years of the Van Buren administration in terms of social conflict. He shows the extent of the rift then developing between the classes and its political effects upon the development and polarization of major political parties.

The principal paradox of the Van Buren era lay in the fact that it produced a President who failed to gain reelection in 1840, presumably on the grounds that he behaved like an aristocrat and a dandy, and at the moment his Democratic Party was undergoing a short-lived "radical-democracy" phase. Van Buren, as Jackson's political heir, gained more than the Presidency. He also inherited the high level of political acrimony that characterized the Jackson years. Van Buren, the slick accomodator, did not have Jackson's talent for battling with his political opponents. The depression that followed the Panic of 1837 doomed Van Buren to 4 frustrating years in the White House.

The significance of these years in American political history has been slighted. During this time a major reshuffling occurred that altered the political structure although it did not permanently revolutionize it. Businessmen aligned themselves with the Whigs, giving the parties after 1837 a greater class orientation than before. The Calhoun states'-rights men (a minority among Southerners) returned to the Democrats. To a greater degree than in most administrations, the parties of the Van Buren era represented substantial political alternatives. A political earthquake had briefly opened the landscape, allowing a glimpse of the underlying realities.

For further reading: Reginald C. McGrane, *The Panic of 1837: Some Financial Problems of the Jacksonian Era* (1924); Douglas T. Miller, *Jacksonian Aristocracy: Class and Democracy in New York, 1830–1860* (1967).

South Atlantic Quarterly, L (April 1951), 167–185. Reprinted by permission.

At the turn of the century Richard T. Ely wrote that the historian would find the Democratic party of Van Buren's time to be more proletarian than any other major party in American history. During the first decade of this century Frederick J. Turner pointed out that the historian of the Van Buren administration would discover the origins of some of the social ideals and aims that later came to dominate American politics. Turner advised historians to seek in Evans and Jacques and Byrdsall and Leggett the sources of the progressive politics of the twentieth century.

In our own day Arthur M. Schlesinger, Jr., in his *Orestes A. Brownson: A Pilgrim's Progress* and in his better-known *The Age of Jackson* has drawn attention to the importance of the Van Buren period, emphasizing some of the origins which Turner foretold. Perhaps Schlesinger has discovered more of the present in the Van Buren past than the actual historical record warrants and has read into that period more proletarian consciousness and more New Dealism than are justified. In his treatment of the Van Buren period Schlesinger rendered a service by emphasizing the significance of the East in the politics of the Jackson-Van Buren period. But he probably went too far; Turner would not have agreed with Schlesinger's minimizing of the West. The labor elements of the East were important, but so also were the Western agrarians, ably led by such men as Thomas H. Benton, Thomas L. Hamar, and Benjamin Tappan.

Undoubtedly, the party politics of the Van Buren administration reached a pitch of intensity rarely equaled in American history. A number of causes contributed to this: the fact that by Van Buren's time party tensions carried over from Jackson had become cumulative; the effect of the prolonged economic depression in fraying political tempers and exacerbating party passions; the fact that while in Jackson's time the administration engaged in a fight on the Bank of the United States, in Van Buren's time the administration engaged in a fight on nearly all the banks of the country.

In any case, the significance of the epochal year 1837 in the history of American political parties has been neglected. It witnessed the last of the important secessions from the Democratic party into the Whig party and the beginning of those reverse currents which were to carry important elements back into the Democratic party. The Whig party had been building rapidly since the defeat of Clay in 1832. By 1837 that party was composed of three main elements: the old National Republicans, the Anti-Masons, and the bolting Democrats. The ranks of the piebald Whigs had steadily grown as group after group of seceding Democrats went over to the new opposition. Even before 1832 the Calhoun Democrats, following the Jackson-Calhoun break, had left the Democratic party. During 1832 and thereafter the secessions had increased. The veto of the recharter of the Bank of the United States had alienated many conservative Democrats. The nationalist and consolidationist tone of the Nullification proclamation had caused many sincere states-rights men and strict constructionists to leave the party. But the greatest exodus came during the last years of the Jackson regime as the result of the controversy over the removal of the deposits and the celebrated expunging resolution. At the very time these secessions were taking place among conservatives because of the alleged radicalism of the Jackson administration, in New York the more advanced Democrats, known as Locofocos, had cut themselves off from the party on the grounds that it was not radical enough.

In 1837, the first year of the Van Buren administration, occurred the last of the formidable secessions due to the revolt of the state banks from the Independent Treasury and the Specie Circular principle. Such state banking interests as were still in the Democratic party (most of them had been Whig from the beginning) now left it and gravitated into the Whig party. On the national stage this revolt was led politically by William C. Rives, Nathaniel P. Tallmadge, William L. May, Josiah Caldwell, John Ruggles, and F. O. B. Smith. These Conservatives were the last important additions to the Whig party. With their accessions, the Whig party contained its constituent elements; it was fully "made."

The same months which saw the Conservative revolt saw also the return to the Democratic party of important elements to the right and to the left, elements which were to have tremendous influence inside the Democratic party. On the left, the Locofocos returned, attracted by the Independent Treasury and the Specie Circular principle. During the Van Buren administration they and their policies were to exert a great influence within the Democratic party; the Whigs indeed proclaimed that the Democratic party had been swallowed by the Locofocos. On the right (though not so rightist in 1837 as they later were to become), Calhoun and many of his followers went back into the fold. These Southern Democrats returned on the same issue that brought back the Locofocos. This movement back to the Democratic party was felt not only in South Carolina; in Virginia it was represented by the return of R. M. T. Hunter and his followers, in Georgia by the return of such men as Mark A. Cooper, Walter T. Colquitt, and Edward J. Black. Thirty years later Alexander H. Stephens was to state that his own failure to return at this time had been an error. The return of the Calhoun Democrats was to have a more profound effect than the return of the Locofocos. It checked the growth of the Whig party in the South, forced the Whigs of that section into a more disciplined organization, compelled the Southern Whigs into greater acceptance of Northern policies and leadership, made the Democratic party the dominant party in the South, and enabled the Democracy of that region, because of its growing numerical strength, to exert an increasing influence in the affairs of the Democratic party nationally. There is irony in the fact that Calhoun and other planters returned to the Democratic party on the same measures which brought back the Locofocos, for the return of the Calhoun men ultimately transformed the radical, agrarian, small-farmer party of Jackson, Van Buren, and Benton into the conservative and planter party of Pierce, Buchanan, and Davis.

Rarely in American history have the economic and social differences between the major parties been so clear-cut as in the Van Buren period. The only comparable periods in this respect are the Federalist period and that since the advent of the New Deal. In the period immediately preceding the second Adams, political differences were blurred and amorphous. Much of the political division seemed personal and sectional. In the period following Van Buren there was an increasingly growing emphasis on the slavery question, which brought to politics moral and irrational considerations in an unusual degree and finally divided the country on sectional lines. Following the Civil War, the carry-over of sectionalism and war issues lingered. Indeed, the Republicanism of the corn and wheat states and the one-party system of the South were due in part to the unnatural continuation of the war issues, some of them emotional.

On the other hand, the Van Buren period witnessed well-defined party differences based on economic and social realities. Class and group politics cut across sectional lines in a way reminiscent of the Hamilton-Jefferson rivalry. This situation was developing in Jackson's time; it was an accomplished reality in Van Buren's day. Foreign commentators, domestic politicians, and local newspaper editors of the period were conscious of these sharp party differences and of their economic and social basis. In a generation not yet familiar with the term economic determinism, the substantive ideas of that hypothesis were boldly proclaimed. Foreign travelers in America commented on the sharp cleavage of the parties. Michel Chevalier noted that the Whigs were largely composed of the upper classes and the Democrats of farmers and mechanics. James S. Buckingham observed that the Whig party was made up of the rich capitalists, merchants, wealthy tradesmen, the clergy for the most part, lawyers, and the medical profession, in short, of all those who desired to rank with "the aristocratical and genteel portion of society." British visitors were struck with the ideological similarity of the American Whig and the British Tory parties. Thomas Hamilton, spending some time in Boston during the Jackson administration, found Boston Whigs as intransigently conservative as British Tories. Buckingham discovered a like feeling on the part of the Whigs of New York City and reported that these American Whigs would like to see the radicalism of British Whiggery checked and the Duke of Wellington and a Tory ministry restored to power.

Commentators from abroad were not a little puzzled by the extreme fears entertained by American Whigs of their Democratic opponents. Charles Lyell, who traveled in the United States in the 1840's, reported the resentment of the merchant class at the political ascendancy of the small farmers. Frederick Von Raumer was told by Whigs that the Locofocos might finally subject all laws to public license and abolish the right of property. Buckingham found that the Whigs spoke of their Democratic opponents as "atheists, infidels, agrarians, incendiaries, men who were without religion and without honesty." According to Buckingham, the Whigs thought that the Jacksonian Democrats "desired to pull down all that was venerable in the institutions of the country, to seize the property of the rich and divide it among the poor, to demolish the churches, to destroy the courts of justice, to let loose all the criminals from the jails, to abolish all government and to produce only a chaos of anarchy and confusion." Foreigners were also impressed by the length to which the Whigs apparently would like to go in order to check their opponents. Harriet Martineau was told that the "grand question of the time was whether the people should be encouraged to govern themselves or whether the wise should save them from themselves." Buckingham found that the Whigs with whom he talked in New York City frankly wished to establish a relatively high property qualification for voting. Also, he found that the Whigs opposed any discussion of the slavery question for fear that such discussion might affect adversely their own wealth.

Domestic politicians and journalists boldly described the conflict of economic interests—of class and group interests—as the basis of the American party struggle. On the floor of the House of Representatives, Francis W. Pickens, of South Carolina, flatly rejected the interdependence of classes, claimed such interdependence to be merely theoretical, and declared the fundamental fact of politics to be group and class conflict. John C. Calhoun, subscribing to the same doctrine, declared that Daniel Webster spoke not merely for a single section but for a single class within that section. Orestes A. Brownson's *Boston Quarterly Review* became the spokesman of the Locofocos and of the radical intellectuals; in every issue Brownson or his contributors enunciated the doctrine of group conflict. History was viewed as a class struggle. The conflict in the Middle Ages had been between barons and kings; in the sixteenth, seventeenth, and eighteenth centuries, between landed capital and commercial capital. In the nineteenth century it would increasingly become a conflict between "the operative and his employer, between wealth and labor." The middle class had been a valuable historical agency in humbling the classes above it, but was an inveterate foe of the classes below it. The Chartist movement foreshadowed the capitalist-labor conflict in Britain; the growing socialist movement against Louis Philippe's government foreshadowed it in France. In America "the proletaries" were better off than in Europe, but the conflict could not long be postponed even in America. Growing industrialization had cheapened the cost of production and raised the standard of living, but the accumulators and capitalists were pocketing most of the gains, and the gap between capital and labor was getting wider and wider. Universal suffrage and political democracy were but forerunners of social democracy. Brownson suggested as a specific reform for his own day the abolition of the inheritance of property.

Charles J. Ingersoll of Pennsylvania declared the specific class conflict of the time to be a clash of the rural communities with the cities. In one of the most realistic speeches ever made in Congress, Representative Pickens declared it to be a conflict of laboring men and planters with capitalists. He pointed out that the Southern planters owned their laborers and therefore were interested in the "bona-fide profits of daily labor," since the planters received the economic rewards of their laborers. The interests of Southern agrarians and Northern laborers were thus related, and planters and wage earners were natural allies in politics. Pickens's speech became all the more pointed when, upon its conclusion, Ely Moore, a Locofoco representative from New York City, arose from his place, ostentatiously went over to Pickens's seat, and warmly clasped the South Carolinian by the hand. Brownson's *Boston Quarterly Review* viewed the party struggle in the United States as largely between landed capital on the one hand and commercial and manufacturing capital on the other; he predicted that the laborers would thus gain more from a triumph of the landed interest than from that of the commercial and manufacturing interest, though in the end labor would come into conflict with all capital. Thomas L. Hamar, next to C. C. Cambreleng the most important Democratic leader in the House of Representatives, thought the merchant class to be the central opposition to the Democratic party; on one occasion he attacked bitterly the members of that class, reviving the charges of treasonable conduct on their part during the War of 1812 and assigning to them an ignoble role thoughout human history. Charles J. Ingersoll agreed with Hamar's estimate of the merchant class.

The Whigs responded to the Democrats in three ways. They admitted the conservative nature of their party and appealed frankly to the conservative classes; they claimed that the Democrats represented revolutionary radicalism; finally, they emphasized the fluidity and interdependence of classes. They defended the merchant class and frequently described the merchants as the pillars of society. In the Senate Nathaniel P. Tallmadge paid a glowing tribute to the merchants. A meeting of Whig businessmen of New York City, presided over by Philip Hone, declared that the Whigs would not interfere with the rights of property anywhere. Caleb Cushing proclaimed the Whig party to be that of law, order, and property on both sides of the Mason-Dixon line. Later, enemies of the Whigs put it another way, calling the

Whig party an alliance of "the lords of the lash" and "the lords of the loom." "Law, law, law is the call of the Whigs," asserted a correspondent of the *National Intelligencer,* chief Whig organ in the country.

The Whig press and politicians attempted to tar the whole Democratic party with the taint of Locofocoism. The chief scare-word of the Federalists had been "Jacobin"; the bogey word employed by the Whigs came to be "Locofoco." The Locofocos were denounced as French revolutionaries, Robespierrians, Jacobins, social incendiaries, "Fanny Wright men," "Slam Bang Fellows," "low lived levellers," and "the odds and ends of this big earth." The New York correspondent of the *National Intelligencer* wrote, ". . . a terrible war has commenced in all this great country between European Radicalism of the worst kind and American Conservatism." Ogden Hoffman, of New York, termed the Locofocos the followers of Jack Cade, who swore that "his horse would graze in Cheapside." Caleb Cushing saw a Jacobinical radicalism of temper running through society, as different from true democracy as darkness from light. The obvious tendency was general confusion. What were the objects of men who would put an end to legal indebtedness, abolish institutions of religion, have no protection of life or property by law, and whose warfare against the banks was but an item in their general warfare against all good orders?

The declaration of Whig principles written by Webster and adopted by the Whigs of Massachusetts for the campaign of 1840 denounced the "new democracy" as characterized by "revolutionary rapidity"—a democracy which would establish the boldest agrarian notions, assail the rights of property, deny the sacred right of inheritance. In the course of a speech in the Senate, Webster declaimed against the leftists of the day and predicted that their activities would lead to "disturbance and disorder, the diffusion of corrupt principles, and the destruction of the moral sentiments and moral habits of society." But Calvin Colton, the leading Whig pamphleteer of the period, best expressed the fears of the conservatives. His literary productions were redolent of the Federalist pamphlets of 1796, 1798, and 1800, when "the rich, the wise, and the good" were alarmed by Jacobinism. In the trend of the times Colton saw a fundamental struggle between a constitutional republic and a radical democracy. If the Jacksonians were not checked, the forces of radicalism would overthrow the republic. The strife in Europe was between despotism and an absolute monarchy on the one hand and a constitutional monarchy on the other. In America a constitutional republic, "as originally set up," was struggling against a radical democracy. Colton saw in the offing revolution, the "most protracted and devastating war" which the world had ever witnessed, the destruction of Christianity and morality, and the establishment of a complete despotism.

In their more suave moments the Whigs emphasized the fluidity and interdependence of classes. Senator Tallmadge declared the interest of all classes in America to be reciprocal. "Neither the farmer, manufacturer, the mechanic, nor the merchant can get on advantageously the one without the other." Whig merchants in a meeting in New York City formally resolved that "the interest of the capitalists, merchants, manufacturers, mechanics, and industrious classes are dependent upon each other, and any measures of the government which prostrate the active business men of the community will also deprive honest labor of its reward." William Cost Johnson, of Maryland, asserted on the floor of the House of Representatives that public functionaries "should be cautious in awakening prejudices against any class in the community when the interests of all are so naturally dependent upon each other, and are knit together like the woof of the spider's web, so that whatever touches or deranges a part must be felt at the most remote and attenuated extremities."

Cushing pointed out that the property in corporations and banks "is not, for the greater part, property of the rich. They are for the greater part the property of those not rich, and especially of the earnings of the industrious, the investments of females or other persons desiring safe investments of their small property and trust funds." William B. Calhoun, an able Whig member of Congress from Massachusetts, observed: "The men of business in the North, the men who manage and control all these institutions, are the great middle class of society—the men who by their own industry and intellect have made themselves what they are. The banking institutions are owned not by the great capitalists but by the active, thriving, energetic men of business. The proprietorship of these institutions is for the most part in the hands of men of moderate property, of females, of orphans, of charitable societies." Why envy and persecute the rich man? Johnson denied that the rich constituted a danger, since by "the laws of descent of the states it is impossible that any family or class of individuals ever can accumulate so much wealth as to be enabled to oppress any portion of the people." Besides, the "rich man of last year is the poor man of this; and the poor man this, is the rich man next year; so the changes go round the circle, from year to year, from generation to generation." Colton wrote that America was the poor man's heaven and the rich man's hell. The poor man could easily get enough to live on and easily acquire independence and wealth; the rich man found it hard to keep what he had got because his sons, who neither knew the pains it cost nor its value, were sure to dissipate it. By the revolutions of the wheel of fortune, those who were poor would be at the top, and the children of those who were rich would be at the bottom. Charles Naylor, a Whig Representative from Philadelphia, declared that in America any laboring man worth his salt could become a capitalist. Northern capitalists of that day were but the penniless apprentices of the preceding day. The Whigs pictured the system of bank credit as advantageous to the poor, without which a man of humble station would never rise in society. Speaker after speaker and editor after editor among the Whigs emphasized this aspect of the credit system.

There are three plausible generalizations with respect to the attitude of political parties in the United States toward centralization. It may be said that the party out of power tends to be against a stronger government, and the party in power tends to favor it. The classic illustration of this point of view is in Henry Adams' history of the Jefferson and Madison administrations. Adams in a spirit sometimes approaching malicious glee shows how the Jeffersonians, once in power, adopted more and more the centralizing tendencies of the Federalists. Parties out of office almost invariably accuse parties in office of being power-hungry. During the Jackson-Van Buren period this attitude became a Whig stereotype. John Quincy Adams thought that there was a good bit of cant about the Whig harping on government usurpation; he wrote in his diary that the enormity of power was one of the commonplaces of all oppositions. But this generalization should be adopted with caution. There are examples of administrations in office rejecting more power; the spectacular resistance of positive power measures in the Pierce and Buchanan administrations, in the second Cleveland administration, and in the Coolidge and Hoover administrations shows how dangerous it is to press this position too far.

It may be said, further, that in a given long-range period of our history one major party will rather consistently favor centralization, whether in or out of office, and the other lean to decentralization. There is much truth in this position provided it is regarded merely as a tendency and due regard is given to exceptions which frequently appear. Richard Hofstadter emphasizes the continuity between Jefferson and Jackson laissez-faire ideology and views Democratic action under Van Buren as being inspired by and contributing to the laissez-faire tradition. On the other hand, the younger Schlesinger describes the Van Buren administration as a "people's government" acting "on behalf of the people as freely as in the past the capitalists' government had acted on behalf of the capitalists."

Still another generalization suggests that political parties are for or against centralization in proportion as these policies affect the groups composing the parties, that at any given moment a political party may be both for and against centralization. The activities of political parties during the Van Buren administration are an example of this pragmatic attitude. In general, the Democrats opposed government aid to capitalists and businessmen. They rejected the old mercantilist view that government should positively stimulate business with bounties, subsidies, tariffs. Hence they opposed the United States Bank, special charters for corporations, subsidies to canals and railroads and internal improvements generally, and the protective tariff. In this attitude they were but responding to what their constituent elements—farmers, wage-earners, and "small fellows" generally—regarded as their best interests.

On the other hand, the Democrats of Van Buren's time did not hesitate to extend government powers to help their own groups and to regulate business. The Van Buren administration limited the work day of wage-earners on federal public works to ten hours a day without any corresponding reduction of wages. Within the states, the Democrats stood for the regulation of banks: compulsory publicity, periodic inspection, requirement of a broad specie basis for circulation and discount, denial to the banks of the power to issue bank notes of low denominations. On the federal side, the Independent Treasury and the requirement that federal dues be paid in specie were designed in part to force banks to keep adequate specie reserves. In his message to the special session of Congress in the fall of 1837, President Van Buren went so far as to recommend the application of a federal bankruptcy statute to state banks as a means of regulating excessive issues of paper money. And in 1837 John C. Calhoun, now returned to the Democratic party, spoke for considerable planter opinion when he came out boldly for a system of government credit. Calhoun insisted that the question before the country was not credit or no credit, as the Whigs contended, but the way credit could best perform the function of a safe and sound currency. The question was whether credit should be extended by private bankers for private profit or by the government. Calhoun ranged himself squarely on the side of a system of government credit. It was his impression that the sum necessary for the wants of the treasury should be raised by paper, which should at the same time have the requisite qualities of a paper currency.

The Whigs have long been regarded as the exponents of a strong government in general and of a powerful and paternal federal government in particular. The famous words of Clay, that we "are all—people, States, Union, banks—bound up and interwoven together, united in fortune and destiny, and all, all entitled to the protecting care of a paternal government," have often been quoted. It must not be supposed, however, that the Whigs always favored an extension of the powers of the state and federal governments. They did so only when such an extension accrued to the benefit of the capitalist and entrepreneur classes. They advocated government stimulation of business endeavor and consequently supported tariffs, bounties, internal improvements, and the distribution to the state governments of the proceeds of the sales of public lands, bank charters, and the receipt by the federal government of bank notes. On the other hand, they tended to oppose the extension of government activities which threatened to regulate business or which came into conflict with private capitalistic enterprise.

In state after state the Whigs opposed the regulation of banks. They resisted laws designed to deny the banks power to issue bank notes of low denominations. They rallied in opposition to the Van Buren proposal that a federal bankruptcy statute be applied to the state banks. Clay declared this to be an attempt to prostrate the whole of the state banks by one blow. Webster said that corporations and banks had never been within the purview of bankruptcy statutes. But even if bankruptcy should be so extended as to include moneyed corporations and banks, he could not see how an act which singled them out and embraced them alone could be defended.

The Whigs opposed Calhoun's contention that the credit system should be based upon government rather than private bank credit. They saw in this proposal the lurking ghost of John Law and the likely return of the Continental currency system. They went beyond mere opposition to federal issue of irredeemable paper money and opposed a redeemable government currency convertible into gold and silver. They contended that the national government had no constitutional power to issue paper money. Cushing, intimate with Webster, contended that the federal government had no power to create a paper currency or to emit bills of credit. Treasury notes were bills of credit and therefore beyond the authorized power of the federal government to issue. William Halstead, of New Jersey, one of the leading Whigs in the lower House, supported this proposition that the federal government had no power to issue paper money or emit bills of credit. Thus the great extension of the federal government's fiscal operations during the Civil War, particularly the issuance of greenbacks, was anticipated not by the "nationalistic" Whigs but by John C. Calhoun.

The attitude of the Whigs toward the Independent Treasury system reflected their fear of a "bank" that might come into conflict with private banking enterprises. Clay sounded the alarm that the Independent Treasury system would drive the notes of the state banks out of circulation and destroy the banks themselves. In almost every speech made between the fall of 1837 and the repeal of the Independent Treasury in 1841 Clay conjured up this frightful specter of a national government bank, leveling against this huge bank of his imagination all the arguments of the Jacksonians against the Bank of the United States. This federal bank would be a money monopoly, an intolerable monster; "here would be no imaginary, but an actual, visible, tangible, consolidation of the moneyed power." It would crush out the state banks, prostitute the voters, and buy up elections. "What opportunity does it not afford to reward a partisan or punish an opponent?" Clay felt a federally chartered national bank, controlled by private stockholders, managed by private directors, and operated for private profit to be a less dangerous agency than the government itself and more to be trusted with the regulation of the currency and domestic exchanges. So hostile was Clay to this "government bank" that he said he "would greatly prefer the employment of the agency of the State banks."

Whigs sometimes voiced the general philosophy that government should not regulate private business affairs or interfere with free capitalistic enterprise. In the fall of 1837 Cushing said in the House, "Once more I welcome the general idea, that Government should not be over-prone to interfere in the private pursuits of the citizen." William B. Calhoun, also of Massachusetts and one of the most respected Whigs leaders, saw all the troubles of the country as having their origin in "the unhallowed connection of politics and business." During the Presidential campaign of 1840, Colton emphasized the doctrine that government should not interfere with private business activities. In a famous electioneering tract distributed by the Whig managers during the pre-election campaign, he rejoiced that the doctrine of American democracy—"DON'T GOVERN US TOO MUCH"—could not easily be dislodged from the public mind. *"Let the people alone,"* urged Colton. "Obviously we are governed too much. The best Government is that which is neither seen, nor felt, by the innocent and good citizen. This is true American democracy."

This apparent inconsistency of political parties need not surprise us, since the principles of political parties are usually but rationalizations of the needs and interests of the groups which constitute them. Political principles are generally arguments to disguise the underlying motives behind them; to use James Harvey Robinson's phrase, they are *good* reasons but not the *real* reasons.

The important economic fact of the Jackson-Van Buren period was not the destruction of the Bank of the United States or even the establishment of the Independent Treasury, but the multiplication of business corporations and banks and the weakening in state after state of the system of special charters along with the passage of general laws regulating incorporation. The nation was undergoing a capitalist revolution; the way was being prepared for an industrial revolution. The credit system, brilliantly analyzed by Thorstein Veblen as the basis of modern business enterprise, was in process of development. Men were accordingly debating the fundamentals of banking, credit, and incorporation.

Richard Hofstadter and Bray Hammond tend to view this liberal capitalist revolution as the expression of Jackson-Van Buren Democracy and to regard the Democratic party of the period as spearheading this revolution. The destruction of the Bank of the United States and the consequent greater freedom resulting for small banks, the growth of general incorporation laws and free banking statutes, and the decision in the Charles River Bridge case are cited as evidence in support of this view. Undoubtedly there was a wing of the Democratic party—mostly in the East, led by such men as Henry Edwards, Preston King, Colonel Samuel Young, A. C. Flagg, William Leggett, and William Cullen Bryant, and given newspaper expression in the New York *Evening Post*—which had some idea of the nature of liberal capitalism and which favored its positive development. On the other hand, large segments of the party were critical of capitalism and sought to check its development. Most Democrats of this period were agrarians and shared the agrarian aversion to corporations, banks, and paper money. Andrew Jackson was among these. In his Farewell Address he attacked the "moneyed interest" and declared that the continuance of popular government itself depended upon the curtailing of corporations, banks, and bank notes. Jackson mainly had in mind banks of circulation, but the distinction between banks of circulation and banks of discount was not made clear and definite. This blurred conception was characteristic of the rank and file of Democratic politicians. A great majority of them favored an exclusive "federal coin currency"; if that caused many banks to close, "so much the better, if done gradually," according to a typical Democratic politician of the day, Charles J. Ingersoll. Some Democratic politicians, notably Benton, made a distinction between banks of circulation and banks of discount; President Van Buren usually made it plain that he was not attacking banking *per se* but only abuses. But a wide reading of the Congressional debates and the political press of the period shows that the run-of-the-mill politician made no such clear distinction. The Locofocos held to the agrarian view of money and banking, had an aversion to banks in general, and particularly opposed bank notes and paper money. A typical Locofoco manifesto declared that banks were "dangerous to the interests of the people, whether as one great institution or as a number of small ones." The Locofocos favored a metallic currency. Democrats of the wage-earner wards of Philadelphia and Baltimore took similar positions. It was possible for Van Buren to take a "Locofoco" position on the money question in federal politics because on this question agrarians and proletarians saw eye to eye. The Calhoun Democrats were outspoken in opposition to the developing capitalism. Calhoun himself preferred government paper money to bank notes.

To call the liberal capitalist revolution *Democratic* is to ignore the part played in that revolution by the Seward-Weed-Greeley-Hildreth-Stevens-Ritner wing of the Whig party. The forerunner of such measures, the New York Free Banking Act of 1838, was carried by the liberal Whigs, not the Democrats; most Democrats in the New York legislature opposed it. Hofstadter in his interpretation of the Jackson-Van Buren support of liberal capitalism seems to make Calvin Colton say in effect, "Praise be for Andrew Jackson!" But were the merchants, the bankers, the businessmen of that day in the wrong party? Perhaps these economic and social groups were themselves the best judges of their political and economic interests. According to the Hofstadter-Hammond school of thought the majority of businessmen and bankers should have been Democrats; in fact, they were not. Even Hammond admits that the honeymoon between capitalist enterprise and the Democratic party was brief and that in 1840 business enterprise "eloped with the Whigs." In fact, most business enterprise, including banking, had supported the Whigs since the inception of that party. David Henshaw is usually mentioned as a representative of the banking class inside the Democratic party, but there were relatively few David Henshaws. In 1837, on the Independent Treasury issue—not in 1840—the banking interests that had continued in the Democratic party moved over to the Whigs.

Arthur M. Schlesinger, Jr., and William Trimble view the Democratic party of Van Buren's time as the party of a growingly class-conscious proletariat and as imbued with a spirit of government regulation for social ends. It is true that Democrats favored very definite regulation of banks and the ten-hour day on federal works, but the regulations advocated by the Democratic party were, in the light of the total economic picture, rather few; and many of these regulations failed of adoption, or were never codified when adopted. The Independent Treasury, the most centralizing measure of the Van Buren administration, later was used by the industrialists in the Civil War and post-Civil War periods as an agency to effectuate their own purposes.

The truth seems to be that both the Hofstadter-Hammond school and the Schlesinger-Trimble school are reading back into the Jackson-Van Buren administration too much of the politics of later periods. The Hofstadter-Hammond school is reading back too much capitalist influence in politics, too much Republicanism of the 1850's and the 1860's; the Schlesinger-Trimble school, too much of the Progressive-New Deal approach, too much proletarianism. Both are minimizing the dominant political groups of the time—the agrarian groups of the South, of the West, even of the East.

It is easy to be misled about the significance of the role played by the Democratic party of the Jackson-Van Buren period. We usually think of a politically dominant party as affecting decisively historical trends; as a matter of fact, the politically dominant party of the Jackson-Van Buren period failed to achieve its major economic objective. The majority of Democrats—the Western agrarians, the Southern planters, and the Eastern Locofocos—wanted to check the rising capitalism. In this they failed, and capitalist enterprise grew apace. In fact, American agrarianism never developed either in theory or practice a positive program to check capitalism. Agrarianism was largely negative; it would keep life as it was; it would oppose corporations, banks, bank notes, the credit system. Even the Independent Treasury system was conceived not so much as a means of regulating banks as of divorcing banks and government. Those who made the distinction between banks of circulation and of deposit and discount were traversing a blind alley; the differences between note and deposit liabilities, as Gallatin pointed out, are of form; one is as capable of abuse as the other. Those like Calhoun, who were willing to have the government provide a paper currency, were not willing to have the government assume the deposit and discount function, and it was precisely in this area that the credit system was to do most in bringing a capitalist and business revolution. A system of government credit designed for planters and farmers—a kind of green socialism—would have been fantastic in the 1830's and the 1840's.

What were the underlying conditions at work in the Jackson-Van Buren era which will explain the multiplication of business corporations and banks and the enormous expansion of the credit system? These were: the phenomenal development of capitalism and industrialism in Europe; the expansion of the United States and the growth of the American population; the rapid increase in capital savings and their more widespread distribution. Here were the fundamental causes of the economic revolution taking place; the proliferation of general incorporation laws and free banking statutes was the result of these basic causes. It is a mistake to emphasize political action as a major cause, as Hofstadter and Hammond and Joseph Dorfman seem to do. It is also a mistake to think that capitalism and industrialism had progressed far enough to breed the proletarianism sometimes suggested by the younger Schlesinger and by Trimble.

Failing to check capitalism, some of the Democrats in the older and more commercial states acquiesced and in effect joined the progressive Whigs in helping to liberalize it. Confronted with choice between a monopolistic capitalism and a free capitalism, Democrats, even the majority noncapitalist Democrats, preferred a liberal and competitive capitalism. In truth, the positive achievements of the Jackson-Van Buren Democrats are to be found not in the economic but in the political field—in the extension of political democracy, in the organization and practices of political parties, in political campaign techniques, in the development of an American political folklore. Even here the Democrats were checked; they failed in their major attempts to democratize the federal judiciary.

As the developing capitalism in the 1840's and 1850's spread across the North, enveloping even the West, only the South held out against it. By the late 1850's those in the North who remained genuinely agrarian in their outlook and who still resisted banking and industrial capitalism appeared to be more and more pro-Southern, for they found their strongest allies in the South. This carry-over of Jacksonian anticapitalist bias to a later period explains why most wage-earners in the Eastern cities remained Democratic through the 1850's and why Jacksonian labor leaders such as George H. Evans, John Commerford, Mike Walsh, Fitzwilliam Byrdsall, John H. Hunt, and John Windt resisted Republicanism, remained Democrats, and even supported Calhoun and his doctrines to the bitter end. Even historians, who mostly write history as though it could not have come out any other way than it did, are often surprised at this persistence of anti-capitalist attitudes.

Similarly, most groups in the Whig party represented frustrations. The National Republican wing of the Whig party, the neo-Federalists, was routed all along the line as political aristocracy gave way to political democracy and as economic monopoly gave way to economic freedom. The Southern Whigs, men of large agricultural property in alliance with men of industrial property in the North, were unwittingly hastening the industrial revolution which they disliked and were thus contributing to their own ultimate ruin, as Alexander Stephens suggested thirty years later.

Only one group of the Jackson-Van Buren period was to come out triumphant, a group which in the period itself was a distinct minority: the Seward-Weed-Greeley-Stevens Whigs. This group, in the origin largely Anti-Masonic, had to a marked degree welcomed the political democracy and the political methods of the Jacksonians and had always been hostile to Clay, the Bank, and the National Republican economic philosophy of monopoly capitalism. This group welcomed and encouraged the coming of liberal capitalism, and underlying economic forces were working in its behalf. In the 1850's this group was to be joined by the liberal capitalist wing of the Democratic party—Preston King, William Cullen Bryant, and the group for which the New York *Evening Post* spoke. The slavery question has been too much emphasized as a force bringing these groups together; liberal capitalism has been stressed too little as a cohesive force. As members of the Republican party in the 1860's they were to raise to flood tide the revolution of liberal capitalism with the opening of the West, the building of the transcontinental railroads, the passage of the Homestead Act, and the bringing of the national banks to Main Street. This revolution, of course, contained seeds out of which were to grow again a new centralization and a new monopoly capitalism, but that is another story.

16 / The Jacksonian Persuasion

Marvin Meyers

What was the essence of the Jacksonian "message"? Answers to this question have been almost as numerous as the corps of investigators. In attacking the problem, Marvin Meyers concentrates on one of the most readily available (and thus perhaps neglected) sources for Jacksonian history: the public papers and addresses of the "Old Hero" himself. After all, people were listening to and reading these pronouncements, more so than we do today, giving them an importance far beyond their immediate use as oratory or apologetics. Meyers isolates several recurrent themes and argues that the theme of restoration assumed the greatest importance. Not that the others—the egalitarianism of virtue, or specific responses to financial problems, for example—were unimportant. But all tended to be blended into the need for the restoration of old republicanism as a value system. The Jacksonians knew that the clock could not be turned back, but in facing an uncertain future they wished to rely as much as possible on the moral philosophy of the Republican Founding Fathers. In addition to their desire to learn from history, the Jacksonians wanted to *use* it.

For further reading: Marvin Meyers, *The Jacksonian Persuasion Politics and Belief* (1957); Richard Hofstadter, "Andrew Jackson . . ." Chap. III of *The American Political Tradition* (1948).

An artful editor of the works of eminent Jacksonians might arrange one volume to portray the revolt of the urban masses against a business aristocracy; a second in which simple farming folk rise against the chicanery of capitalist slickers; a third volume tense with the struggle of the fresh forest democracy for liberation from an

American Quarterly, V (Spring 1953), 3–15. Copyright, by the Trustees of the University of Pennsylvania. Reprinted by permission.

effete East; and still another book of men on the make invading the entrenched positions of chartered monopoly. With no undue demand upon editorial resourcefulness, the Jacksonian series might turn next to the party machine, managing a newly made mass electorate through the exploitation of some of the preceding themes. The terminal volume might well rest in the shadow of Jefferson: the patriotic friends of wise and frugal government, equal rights and equal laws, strict construction and dispersed power, resisting the eternally scheming tory, monocrat, and rag-baron.

This partial list of possible uses of Jacksonian thought does not quite suggest that Jacksonian Democracy may mean all things to all men. Some omissions have been made with a point: for example, it is not suggested that any plausible editorial selection could identify Jacksonian Democracy with the rise of abolitionism; or (in an exclusive sense) with the temperance movement, school reform, religious enthusiasm or theological liberalism; or (in any sense) with Utopian community building. Yet the variety of meanings which can command some documentary support is too wide for easy assimilation in a coherent interpretation of Jacksonian Democracy. Here there is, I think, a fair field for the critical examination of the major contending theses and, of greater importance, for a fresh reading of the most obvious Jacksonian sources.

The present approach takes its departure from the debunking theses of recent writers like Dorfman and Abernethy, who in their separate ways have corrected a number of major and minor errors by an exemplary regard for original sources viewed carefully in historical context. Yet their very suspicions of such things as campaign appeals and public messages lead them to discount as meaningless a large part of the sustenance of the Jacksonian public, in order to pursue the "real thing"—i.e., the objective import of legal and institutional changes. If, for example, in Dorfman's terms, the major economic consequences of Jacksonian reform politics in New York were to establish free banking and incorporation laws and constitutional limits upon credit undertakings of the state—then what is the meaning of the highly-charged polemical jargon, the vague class appeals, the invocation of grand principles? Why, in short, did the language go so far beyond the practical object?

Simply to say "propaganda" does not tell why a particular lingo makes good propaganda and another kind does not. Nor is there obvious reason for regarding the traffic in "propaganda" as less significant intrinsically than the traffic in harder goods. And so these notes return to a staple of pre- or non-revisionist historians, the popular political discourse, in an attempt to identify the social values expressed or implied by opinion leaders of the Jacksonian persuasion.

The difficulties in such an enterprise are no doubt abundant and serious: the subject matter is in its nature elusive; the temptation is powerful indeed—as the debunking writers have been quick to note—to select passages from selected spokesmen, with considerable neglect of textual and situational context, in order to find some grand motif establishing the spirit of Jacksonian Democracy; and always one faces the relatively easy out of fabricating some systematic theory of Jacksonian Democrats from fragmentary words and acts, with results which tend to be laborious, intellectually arid, and unrevealing of the qualities of the Jacksonian movement.

There is nevertheless a commanding case for examining the sort of values offered to and preferred by the Jacksonian public; the popular political statement would seem a prime example of such communication; and the first spokesman must be Andrew Jackson. His presidential papers taken in all their dimensions, theory, policy, and rhetoric, and searched for certain constant, elementary moral postures, provide a revealing and somewhat unexpected commentary upon the character of Jacksonian Democracy.

THE "OLD HERO" AND THE RESTORATION

Andrew Jackson, most students agree, rose to national leadership on the strength of reputed personal qualities: the blunt, tough, courageous "Old Hero" of New Orleans—honest and plain "Old Hickory." "Old" refers to age, of course, but perhaps more to "old-style." Again, not so much to old-style ideas as to the old *ways* of our fathers. He could be—and was in a boy's capacity—a fit companion for the Revolutionary heroes. Jackson never figured as the speculative statesman. In his own estimate and the public's, he was executor of a republican tradition which required not elaboration or revision but right action, taken from a firm moral stance.

It is no novelty to say that the world revealed in Andrew Jackson's public statements appears, like the public image of the man, strikingly personal and dramatic, built upon the great struggle of people *vs.* aristocracy for mastery of the republic. In relation to such issues as the Bank War, the view offers a sharp pattern: on one side, the great body of citizens, demanding only an equal chance; on the other, their tempters and adversaries, the small greedy aristocracy, full of tricks and frauds, absorbing power and privilege. Yet the grand conflict, as it emerges from Jackson's public statements, has its ambiguities—*viz.*, the variant interpretations of Jacksonian Democracy. Within the gross polemical image of social drama much remains for further explication and explanation.

* On the side of virtue, in Jackson's world, one finds the plain republican—direct decendant of Jefferson's yeoman hero—along with Poor Richard and such other, lesser friends. The presence of the sturdy, independent citizen-toiler has been no secret to historians—yet some interesting possibilities have been missed. In creating the character and rôle of the plain republican Jackson has provided, I think, an important clue for the interpretation of Jacksonian values.

* "Keep clear of Banks and indebtedness," Jackson wrote to his adopted son after settling the boy's debts, "and you live a freeman, and die in independence and leave your family so . . . and remember, my son, . . . that we should always live within our means, and not on those of others." Read this little paternal homily against the familiar public statements. Can it be that Jacksonian Democracy appeals not to some workingman's yearning for a brave new world; not to the possibilities of a fresh creation at the Western limits of civilization; not to the ambitions of a rising laissez-faire capitalism—not to any of these so much as to a *restoration* of old virtues and a (perhaps imaginary) old republican way of life?

It will be my contention that the Jacksonian appeal evokes the image of a calm and stable order of republican simplicity, content with the modest rewards of useful toil; and menacing the rustic peace, an alien spirit of risk and novelty, greed and extravagance, rapid motion and complex dealings. In short, we may discover in the political discourse of Jacksonian Democracy a powerful strain of restorationism, a stiffening of republican backs *against* the busy tinkerings, the restless projects of innovation and reform—against qualities so often set down as defining characteristics of Jacksonian America.

Of course this is not to say that the Jacksonians—master politicos and responsible rulers—designed to whisk away the given world, nor that their public actions yielded such a result. In practice they met issues as they came out of the play of current politics, adapting skillfully to the requirements of local conditions, special interests, and party rule. If the plain-republican theme is a substantial component of the Jacksonian persuasion, it need not dictate the precise policy line or control the objective consequences of party action in order to qualify as significant. The degree of coincidence or divergence is another (most important) question which cannot be approached until one knows what appeared in that dimension of political life which consists in the effective communication of value-charged language.

THE REAL PEOPLE

Jackson's contemporary rivals damned him for appealing to class against class; some modern writers praise him for it. Beyond question, his public statements address a society divided into classes invidiously distinguished and profoundly antagonistic. But to understand the meaning of such cleavage and clash, one must see them within a controlling context. There is for Jackson a whole body, the sovereign people, beset with aristocratic sores.

The relentless and apparently irresistible use of "the people" in Jacksonian rhetoric is reflected in the diary of a wealthy New York City Whig, Philip Hone, who daily grinds the phrase through his teeth; or, with accumulated effect, in the growling humor of a Whig delegate to the New York Constitutional Convention of 1846—"The love of the people, the dear people was all that the gentlemen said influenced them. How very considerate. The love of the people—the dear people—was generally on men's tongues when they wanted to gain some particular end of their own. . . ."

In the opposition view Jackson—and Jacksonians generally—were the worst sort of demagogues who could appropriate with galling effectiveness both the dignity of the sovereign people and the passion of embattled classes. That is just the point for Jackson: nasty imputations about demagoguery aside, there are the whole people and the alien aristocracy, and the political advantages which result from the use of this distinction further confirm its validity. Jackson's notion of the-class-of-the-people is grounded first in the political order, more precisely in the republican order. From this fixed base, and with this fixed idea of the double character of the people, Jackson's representation of the group composition of society may be analyzed first in the standard terms of Jacksonian scholarship, and then, by what seems to me a necessary extension, in the context of the restoration theme.

In the most inclusive and high-toned usage, the people would comprise "all classes of the community" and "all portions of the Union." From their midst arises a general "will of the American people" which is something considerably more than a fluctuating majority vote (though the vote for Jackson is acknowledged as a fair index). There are interests of a class and sectional character, legitimate and often illegitimate; but also a pervasive common interest (which corresponds neatly with the main items of the Democratic platform). The general will is originally pure—("Never for a moment believe that the great body of the citizens of any State or States can deliberately intend to do wrong . . ."); liable to temporary error through weakness—(corruptionists will sometimes succeed in "sinister appeals to selfish feelings" and to "personal ambition"); and in the end, straight and true—("but in a community so enlightened and patriotic as the people of the United States argument will soon make them sensible of their errors").

A brief, sharp exemplification of this view occurs in Jackson's argument for direct election of the president. The extent of American territory—Madison's chief reliance for controlling the threat of majority faction—suggests to Jackson the dangerous prospect of sectional parties, which in turn will present sectional candidates and, in the zeal for party and selfish objects, "generate influences unmindful of the general good." Evil comes from the official apparatus, the mechanical contrivances of the complex electoral system. However, "the great body of the people" armed with a direct presidential vote which can express the general "will" must always defeat "antirepublican" [sic.] tendencies and secure the common good.

These "antirepublican" forces are identified as the "intriguers and politicians" and their tools, who thrive on political consolidation, chartered privilege, and speculative gain. Jackson sums up in relation to the bank war:

> The bank is, in fact, but one of the fruits of a system at war with the genius of all our institutions—a system founded upon a political creed the fundamental principle of which is a distrust of the popular will as a safe regulator of political power, and whose ultimate object and inevitable result, should it prevail, is the consolidation of all power in our system in one central government. Lavish public disbursements and corporations with exclusive privileges would be its substitutes for the original and as yet sound checks and balances of the Constitution—the means by whose silent and secret operation a control would be exercised by the few over the political conduct of the many by first acquiring that control over the labor and earnings of the great body of the people. Wherever this spirit has effected an alliance with political power, tyranny and despotism have been the fruit.

In these rough outlines there is enough to reconstruct what there is of a Jacksonian theory concerning the people and the classes. I doubt that the job is worth doing in any elaborate way. The Jacksonian persuasion is both more and much less than a theoretic structure; and Jackson's "people" are not reducible to a lump-quantity in a formal democratic scheme. What is missing is a sense of the nurture, character, and worth of the people as they are represented in Jackson's public papers. In Jackson's revealing phrase, there are still *"the real people"* to be considered.

When Jackson speaks of the people—the real people—he regularly specifies: planters and farmers, mechanics and laborers, "the bone and sinew of the country." Thus a composite class of industrious folk is marked off within society. It appears to be a narrower group than "the sovereign people" of democratic doctrine—though it would surely encompass the mass of enumerated inhabitants of the Jacksonian era. Historians who identify the favored Jacksonian class simply as the common man tell too little. Others, who make the separation upon wage-earner lines, or by rich/poor, town/country, East/West, or North/South, accept what seem to me variable secondary traits. Jackson's real people are essentially those four specified occupational groups, whose "success depends upon their own industry and economy," who know "that they must not expect to become suddenly rich by the fruits of their toil." The lines are fixed by the moral aspects of occupation.

Morals, habits, character are key terms in Jackson's discussion of the people—and almost every other subject. Major policies, for instance, are warranted by their capacity to "preserve the morals of the people," or "to revive and perpetuate those habits of economy and simplicity which are so congenial to the character of republicans." And so with the differentiation of classes according to worth: the American "laboring classes" are "so proudly distinguished" from their foreign counterparts by their "independent spirit, their love of liberty, their intelligence, and their high tone of moral character." At a still higher level within the bloc of favored classes, those who work the land—"the first and most important occupation of man"—contribute to society "that enduring wealth which is composed of flocks and herds and cultivated farms" and themselves constitute "a hardy race of free citizens."

The positive definition of the real people significantly excludes pursuits which are primarily promotional, financial, or commercial. This does not mean that Jackson raises a class war against mere occupational categories. (He was himself lawyer, office-holder, land-speculator, and merchant at various times.) The point seems to be that virtue naturally attaches to, and in fact takes much of its definition from, callings which involve some immediate engagement in the production of goods. Vice enters most readily through the excluded pursuits, though it may infect all classes and "withdraw their attention from the sober pursuits of honest industry." As indicated before, vice is to be understood largely in terms of certain occupational ways, the morals, habits, and character imputed to the trades which seek wealth without labor, employing the stratagems of speculative maneuver, privilege-grabbing, and monetary manipulation.

Like the Jeffersonians, Jackson regularly identifies the class enemy as the money power, the moneyed aristocracy, etc. There is in this undoubtedly some direct appeal against the rich. The mere words call up the income line as an immediate source of invidious distinction. Yet I would maintain that this is a secondary usage. First, Jackson's bone-and-sinew occupational classes clearly allow for a considerable income range—it would be fair to say that upper-upper and lower-lower could enter only exceptionally, while there would be a heavy concentration at the middling-independent point. Income as such does not become a ground for class preference in the usual terms of differential economic or power interest. Instead, Jackson links income with good and evil ways. The real people cannot expect sudden riches from their honest, useful work. And surplus wealth would in any case prove a temptation to the anti-republican habits of idleness and extravagance, as well as an engine of corruption. Briefly, a stable income of middling proportions is generally associated with the occupations, and with the habits, morals, and character of the real people.

More important, however, is the meaning given to phrases like "money power"— and note that Jackson typically uses this expression and not "the rich." The term occurs invariably in discussions of corporations and, particularly, of banking corporations; it signifies the *paper* money power, the *corporate* money power—i.e., concentrations of wealth arising suddenly from financial manipulation and special privilege, ill-gotten gains. If the suggestion persists in Jackson's public statements that such is the common road to wealth—and certainly the only quick way—then it is still the mode and tempo of acquisition and not the fact of possession which is made to damn the rich before Jackson's public.

Further, the money power—as I have defined it—is damned precisely as a *power,* a use of ill-gotten gains to corrupt and dominate the plain republican order. Any concentration of wealth may be a potential source of evil; but the real danger arises when the concentration falls into hands which require grants of special privilege for economic success. So a wealthy planter (and Jackson was this, too) should need no editorial or legislative hired hands; a wealthy banker cannot do without them.

Thus, Jackson's representation of the real people in the plain republican order supplies at least tentative ground for an interpretation of Jacksonian Democracy as, in vital respects, an appeal to an idealized ancestral way. Beneath the gross polemical image of people *vs.* aristocracy, though not at all in conflict with it, one finds the steady note of praise for simplicity and stability, self-reliance and independence, economy and useful toil, honesty and plain dealing. These ways are in themselves good, and take on the highest value when they breed a hardy race of free citizens, the plain republicans of America.

HARD COIN AND THE WEB OF CREDIT

As a national political phenomenon, Jacksonian Democracy drew heavily upon the Bank War for its strength and its distinctive character. The basic position Andrew Jackson established for the Democratic party in relation to money and banking continued to operate as a source of political strength through the eighteen-forties. So powerful, in fact, was the Jacksonian appeal that large sections of the rival Whig party finally capitulated on this issue explicitly for the purpose of saving the party's life. First, shrewd Whig party managers like Weed of New York, and later the generality of Whig spokesmen were forced to plead in effect: a correct (Old Whig) position on banking is incompatible with political survival in America.

The standard outlines of Jackson's case against banking and currency abuses have already been sketched above. Within the matrix of his Bank War, the crucial class split is discovered and the general principles of Jacksonian Democracy take shape. However, the Bank War—viewed as a struggle for possession of men's minds and loyalties—does not simply offer a self-evident display of its own meaning. Out of the polemical language there emerges a basic moral posture much like the one which fixes Jackson's representation of the republican order.

Jackson's appeal for economic reform projects, at bottom, a dismantling operation: to pull down the menacing constructions of federal and corporate power, and restore the wholesome rule of "public opinion and the interests of trade." This has the sound of laissez faire; it is laissez faire with a difference suggested by the previous discussion of the real people and their natural, legitimate economic interests. Poor Richard and economic man may be given a common enemy with the plain republican; surmounting serious difficulties, the forest democrat, poor man, and workingman might be recruited for the same cause. Indeed the sweeping effect of Jackson's negative case may be explained in part by his touching off a common hatred of an all-purpose villain. Yet, if the dismantling operation gives promise of catching several particular enemies in the broad aristocracy trap, does it not promise still more winningly a *dismantling,* and a restoration of pure and simple ways?

Tocqueville, though he reaches an opposite conclusion, suggests very effectively this unmaking spirit:

> The bank is a great establishment, which has an independent existence; and the people, accustomed to make and unmake whatsoever they please, are startled to meet with this obstacle to their authority. In the midst of the perpetual fluctuation of society, the community is irritated by so permanent an institution and is led to attack it, in order to see whether it can be shaken, like everything else.

But what is it about the great establishment which provokes hostility and a passion for dismantling? How can the permanence of the Bank, set over against the perpetual fluctuation of society, explain the ceaseless Jacksonian complaint against the tendency of the Bank to introduce perpetual fluctuation in the economic affairs of society? There is, I think, another and better explanation of the symbolic import of the Bank War.

The Bank of the United States, veritable incarnation of evil in Jackson's argument, assumes the shape of "the monster," which is to say, the unnatural creature of greed for wealth and power. Its managers, supporters, and beneficiaries form the first rank of the aristocracy, i.e., the artificial product of legislative prestidigitation. The monster thrives in a medium of paper money, the mere specter of palpable value. The bank system suspends the real world of solid goods, honestly exchanged, upon a mysterious, swaying web of speculative credit. The natural distributive mechanism, which proportions rewards to "industry, economy, and virtue," is fixed to pay off the insider and the gambler.

To knock down this institution, then, and with it a false, rotten, insubstantial world, becomes the compelling object of Jackson's case. He removed the public deposits, so he said, "to preserve the morals of the people, the freedom of the press, and the purity of the elective franchise." Final victory over the Bank and its paper spawn "will form an era in the history of our country which will be dwelt upon with delight by every true friend of its liberty and independence," not least because the dismantling operation will "do more to revive and perpetuate those habits of economy and simplicity which are so congenial to the character of republicans than all the legislation which has yet been attempted."

The Jacksonian appeal for a dismantling operation and the restoration of old republican ways flows easily into the course of the hard coin argument. Hard coin, I have already suggested, stands for palpable value as against the spectral issue of the printing press. In plainer terms, Jackson argues before the Congress: "The great desideratum in modern times is an efficient check upon the power of banks, preventing that excessive issue of paper whence arise those fluctuations in the standard of value which render uncertain the rewards of labor." Addressing a later Congress, Jackson pursues the point: Bank paper lacks the stability provided by hard coin; thus circulation varies with the tide of bank issue; thus the value of property and the whole price level are at the mercy of these banking institutions; thus the laboring classes especially, and the real people generally, are victimized, while the few conniving speculators add to their riches.

A related appeal to the attractions of stability, of sure rewards and steady values and hard coins, can be found in Jackson's warnings against the accumulation and distribution of the revenue surplus: an overflowing federal treasury, spilling into the states, would produce ruinous expansions and contractions of credit, arbitrary fluctuations in the price of property, "rash speculation, idleness, extravagance, and a deterioration of morals." But above all it is the banks and their paper system which "engender a spirit of speculation injurious to the habits and character of the people," which inspire "this eager desire to amass wealth without labor," which turn even good men from "the sober pursuits of honest industry." To restore hard coin is to restore the ways of the plain republican order. Dismantling of the unnatural and unjust bank and paper system is the necessary first step.

THE SUM OF GOOD GOVERNMENT

The one essential credential of public or private worth—whether of individual, or class, or trade—is conveyed by Jackson through the term "republican"; that which is anti-republican is the heart of evil. With all valuations referred to the republican standard, and that standard apparently a category of politics, one might expect some final revelation of the Jacksonian persuasion in Jackson's representation of the good state. The truth is, on my reading, somewhat different: Jackson rather defines republican by ways of living and working, than refers those ways to republicanism in the strict political sense. The good republic he projects—and remembers from the Revolutionary days of '76 and 1800—is on the political side the ornament, the glory, and the final security of the worthy community, not its creator.

Jackson's sketch of a political system congenial to old republican ways uses nothing beyond the memorable summation in Jefferson's First Inaugural Address: "a wise and frugal government, which shall restrain men from injuring one another, shall leave them otherwise free to regulate their own pursuits of industry and improvement, and shall not take from the mouth of labor the bread it has earned. This is the sum of good government, and this is necessary to close the circle of our felicities." The literal Jacksonian translation prescribes: the Constitution strictly construed; strict observance of the "fundamental and sacred" rules of simplicity and economy; separation of the political power from the conduct of economic affairs.

His political appeal both parallels and supports the general themes discussed in previous sections. This is no government of projects and ambitions. It does its simple, largely negative business in a simple, self-denying way. Firm and strong, it trims drastically the apparatus of power. The hardy race of independent republicans, engaged in plain and useful toil, require no more than a stable government of equal laws to secure them in their equal rights. In Jacksonian discourse, government becomes a fighting issue only when it grows too fat and meddlesome. Again, the republic is defined and judged positively by its republicans and only negatively by its government.

The Bank War once more provides the crucial case. Jackson mobilized the powers of government for what was essentially a dismantling operation. His cure avoids with terror any transference of the powers of the Bank to another agency: to give to the president the currency controls and the power over individuals now held by the Bank "would be as objectionable and as dangerous as to leave it as it is." Control of banks and currency—apart from the strictly constitutional functions of coinage and regulation of value—should be "entirely separated from the political power of the country." Any device is wicked and dangerous which would "concentrate the whole moneyed power of the Republic in any form whatsoever." We must, above all, ignore petty, expediential considerations, and "look to the honor and preservation of the republican system."

PARADOX

And so the circuit of Jackson's public appeal may be closed. Plain, honest men; simple, stable economy; wise and frugal government. It reads less as the herald of modern times and a grand project of reform than as a reaction against the spirit and body of the changing world. Jacksonian Democracy, viewed through Jackson's public statements, wants to undo far more than it wishes to do; and not for the purpose of a fresh creation, but for the restoration of an old republican idyl. The tremendous popularity of Andrew Jackson and his undoubted public influence suggest that this theme can be ignored only at great peril in any general interpretation of Jacksonian Democracy. We must prepare for a paradox: the movement which in many ways cleared the path for the triumph of laissez-faire capitalism and its culture in America, and the public which in its daily life acted out that victory, held nevertheless in their conscience an image of a chaste republican order, resisting the seductions of risk and novelty, greed and extravagance, rapid motion and complex dealings.

17 / Spoilsmen and Interests
in the Thought and Career of John C. Calhoun

William W. Freehling

The traditional interpretation of Southern politics before the Civil War creates visions of a united section marching directly toward secession while chanting the ideological catchphrases of its political philosophers. There were such philosophers, some of them self-appointed sectional gurus, but in the decades before secession a real struggle occurred in the South over principles and tactics. This essay, and the one following, chip away effectively at the monolithic picture of the South.

William W. Freehling examines important parts of Calhoun's political philosophy to discover that the Great Nullifier was not beyond making sidesteps over logical inconsistencies, nor, since he was a politician all his adult life, was he beyond calculating the political dividends to be gained from the application of his ideas. This does not detract from nor is it meant to diminish the importance of the man and his intellectual effort to bolster what he considered vital Southern interests, but the essay rightfully places the Calhoun philosophy in the political context that created it.

Calhoun's mind combined Southern sectional interest and his own peculiar political vision. The South Carolinian became increasingly fearful of democratization and the inevitable "evils" it created: political parties seeking to resolve the interests of conflicting groups and professional politicians to run them. The politics of the Jacksonian era and its democratic credos did not impress Calhoun. Indeed since they had deflated his presidential ambitions, they left him apprehensive over his section's future.

For further reading: Charles M. Wiltse, *John C. Calhoun* (1944–1951); Charles S. Sydnor, *The Development of Southern Sectionalism, 1819–1848* (1948); Gerald M. Capers, *John C. Calhoun, Opportunist* (1960).

Journal of American History, LII (June 1965), 25–42. Reprinted by permission. Footnotes have been omitted except where they are necessary for an understanding of the text.

Over a century after his death John C. Calhoun is still considered one of America's outstanding political theorists. In a culture which has usually exalted the doctrine of majority rule, he stands out as an entrenched defender of minority rights. The South Carolinian's political theory has been equally renowned for its emphasis on economic interests, and even detractors heap praise on his insight into the economic roots of political events. Political scientists term him a founding father of pressure group theory, while historians point to him with pride as an American counterpart of the great European theorists of economic determinism. Recently, two leading historians have suggested that Calhoun anticipated Marx in his contention that the struggle between classes determines political controversy. In a more traditional interpretation the Carolinian's overriding theme remains the conflict between the great geographical subdivisions in a nation. But whether viewed as a theorist of class or of sectional interests, Calhoun is usually considered a leading American exponent of a consistently economic theory of politics.

No one would deny that the clash of pressure groups alarmed Calhoun. But he was far from a thoroughgoing economic determinist. The crucial reason why his political philosophy is hopelessly inconsistent is that he had only a sporadic commitment to an economic interest theory of history.

First of all, Calhoun had a morbid appreciation of the political power of antislavery ideology. For the last two decades of his life the abolitionist campaign was Calhoun's master concern, and he feared the antislavery "fanatics" not because they appealed to northern pocketbooks but because they engaged the nation's conscience. Calhoun often reiterated his conviction that "a large portion of the northern states believed slavery to be a sin," and he always dreaded the moment when the Yankees would feel "an obligation of conscience to abolish it." The notion that ideas can be the decisive force in politics makes Calhoun a rather milktoast Marxist, and marks his first important step away from a thoroughly economic conception of history.

The dangers wrought by corrupt spoilsmen, Calhoun's second deviation from an economic interest theory of politics, is even more significant in his political thought. To a Marxist, or to any consistent believer in economic determinism, the politician's quest for the spoils of office is of minor importance. Politicians are the tools of the interests they represent, and the commands of the interests—not the intrigues of the spoilsmen—form the driving force of the historical process. But Calhoun always believed that demagogic spoilsmen could delude the rabble, control popular elections, ignore the desires of the great communal interests, and turn the political scene into a mere scramble for patronage. As a disdainful patrician in the age when the two-party system first became an American fixture, he feared that democracy could not survive the race for the spoils. This alarm about emergent spoilsmen is the neglected theme in the thought and career of the Carolinian.

Calhoun's concern with corrupt politicians is particularly evident in "A Disquisition on Government," the most systematic statement of his political philosophy. The Disquisition has long been regarded as Calhoun's definitive formulation of, and solution to, the problem of warring economic interests. However, to read the Disquisition in this way is to miss half of Calhoun's intention. The Disquisition presents a picture of democracy gone to seed. Corruption in government has been a prime cause of its swift decline; spoilsmen feuding over patronage will soon bring on anarchy and revolution; the unscrupulous political boss will emerge the despotic victor. Calhoun's concern with the war of selfish economic interests is no more acute than his very different concern with the clash of scheming political spoilsmen. These twin obsessions, inseparable yet irreconcilable, produce a political theory which can best be termed a mass of contradictions.

For the purpose of analysis the two theories which are intertwined in the Disquisition have been termed the "theory of interests" and the "theory of spoilsmen." The theory of interests designates Calhoun's contention that the leading interest groups —the different classes, separate sections, various economic groups—dominate political events. The theory of spoilsmen deals with his contention that corrupt demagogues control the democratic process.

The theory of interests is the well-known portion of the Disquisition, and hence a brief summary will suffice. Calhoun began with the assumption that man "is so constituted, that his direct or individual affections are stronger than his sympathetic or social feelings." It follows that a group of men with similar concerns is more self-interested than disinterested. Therefore, in a democracy, if one interest group contains a numerical majority, it will "pervert its powers to oppress, and plunder the other." If no pressure group can muster a majority, "a combination will be formed between those whose interests are most alike." In both cases minority riches will soon be transferred into majority pockets by legislative edict, a form of legal plunder which rivals the exactions of the most despotic prince. Neither a separation of powers nor a written constitution can relieve the plight of the hapless minority. The numerical majority will elect the president and the congress; the majority president will appoint majority judges; and the appointed judges will interpret the constitution, stripping away minority rights by judicial decree.

A government of the concurrent majority, on the other hand, will end the danger of majority tyranny by giving each pressure group a veto on all legislation. Since each interest will have to concur for any law to pass, successful selfishness will become impossible, and the various social interests will be forced to send disinterested compromisers to the legislative chambers. There remains the possibility that the constant use of the veto power will lead to governmental paralysis and to social anarchy. Calhoun confessed that an impotent government would be an intolerable evil. But he presented two crucial reasons why the concurrent majority will produce creative compromise rather than a permanent stalemate. First, since anarchy is "the greatest of all evils," the various interests will have every selfish reason to cooperate whenever pending legislation becomes an "urgent necessity." Secondly, this desire to seek compromise will inspire the leading pressure groups to elevate to power the very statesmen who are most able to find grounds for conciliation.

Under the numerical majority, argued Calhoun, each interest elects unscrupulous and designing politicians, since such men are best equipped to devise means of plundering other interests. These sordid schemers are incapable of seeking the common good through disinterested compromise. But in governments of the concurrent majority, interests will realize that they must cooperate instead of compete, and hence the politician's craft will give way to the statesman's art. Calhoun held that "each portion, in order to advance its own peculiar interests, would have to conciliate all others, by showing a disposition to advance theirs; and, for this purpose, each would select those to represent it, whose wisdom, patriotism, and weight of character, would command the confidence of the others."

This combination of interests determined to compromise and statesmen dedicated to conciliation will insure the success of the concurrent majority. Thus the pack of selfish interests will be forced to maintain a disinterested government and to elevate its handful of selfless men to power. Calhoun waxed lyrical at the beneficent prospect: "instead of faction, strife, and struggle for party ascendency, there would be patriotism, nationality, harmony, and a struggle only for supremacy in promoting the common good of the whole."

Before turning to the theory of spoilsmen, it would be well to underscore the assumptions upon which the theory of interests is based. The problem posed by warring interests and the solution achieved by the concurrent majority both assume that the legislators perfectly represent the desires of their constituents. Discord in Congress merely reflects conflict between economic interests. When the pressure groups are neutralized, the legislative feuds will cease. The new objectives of the economic interests even produce the growing quality of political leadership. As the pressure groups' thirst for plunder gives way to the necessity for compromise, statesmen inevitably replace politicos at the head of the state. The major economic interests are the guiding, primal force in the political drama. The men who sit in the halls of Congress are mere servants who speak, maneuver, and vote as their constituents direct.

The theory of spoilsmen, like the theory of interests, is based on the primordial selfishness of human nature. However, the focus shifts from the economic interests to their politicians, and the servants become masters. Spoilsmen, breaking free from the control of the interests which selected them, emerge as the primary historical force. This time, the pot of gold which turns men into plunderers is the spoils of office rather than the riches of minorities. Since nations—like individuals and economic interests—are primarily selfish, governments must maintain "vast establishments" to deter aggressive enemies. The politicians who are elected to the higher offices in the government control the hiring, paying, and firing of the thousands of employees which such huge military preparations require. Since politicians—like almost everyone else—are self-interested, they will employ every effective method to gain a monopoly of the spoils.

The spoilsmen have the supreme weapon of demagoguery at their disposal. Calhoun assumed that the average voter is a greedy and gullible creature who will respond to inflammatory appeals to his passions. Demagogues bent on securing patronage need only make full use of "cunning, falsehood, deception, slander, fraud, and gross appeals to the appetites of the lowest and most worthless portions of the community." Soon the nation will be "thoroughly debased and corrupted." Demagogic spoilsmen will completely control their depraved constituents.

Meanwhile the party structure will be refined and extended. Patronage will be used to control wayward legislators, and the party boss will demand absolute obedience from his immediate subordinates. As Calhoun's dirge unfolds, politicians forget their constituents and engage in the most violent struggle for patronage. Those "seeking office and patronage would become too numerous to be rewarded by the offices and patronage at the disposal of the government"; the disappointed would shift their allegiance causing the control of the government to "vibrate" between the factions until "confusion, corruption, disorder, and anarchy" become so destructive that all social interests seek peace from their politicians by turning to a military despot. Thus in the imminent destruction of democracy spoilsmen rather than interests will tear down the last walls of the republic.

Nothing better shows the extent of Calhoun's fear of spoilsmen than the historical examples he developed in the Disquisition. Calhoun believed that the Romans and the English had experimented with the concurrent majority, and he employed their histories to demonstrate his principles. The resulting narratives bear little resemblance to historical truth, but they supply an excellent illustration of Calhoun's own logic and fears. With both Rome and England, Calhoun viewed his historical material through the perspective of his social theory. And in each narrative the war of spoilsmen poses the greatest threat to the concurrent majority.

In ancient Rome, argued Calhoun, two distinct classes of interests existed, the patricians and the plebeians. A violent conflict between the two classes was at last resolved by giving the Tribune, controlled by the plebeians, the power to veto all laws that the Senate, controlled by the patricians, passed. But the concurrent majority soon broke down. The enormous wealth gained in conquest caused

> the formation of parties, (irrespective of the old division of patricians and plebeians,) having no other object than to obtain the control of the government for the purpose of plunder. . . . Under their baneful influence, the possession of the government became the object of the most violent conflicts; not between patricians and plebeians,—but between profligate and corrupt factions. They continued with increasing violence, until, finally, Rome sank, as must every community under similar circumstances, beneath the strong grasp, the despotic rule of the chieftain of the successful party;—the sad, but only alternative which remained to prevent universal violence, confusion and anarchy.

Thus the concurrent majority, introduced to end a bloody conflict of class interests, was itself overturned by the equally violent strife of political spoilsmen. However, the concurrent majority wins its vindication in Calhoun's panegyric on the political genius of the English. For in Calhoun's England the concurrent majority successfully ends the supremacy of spoilsmen.

The miraculous success is gained by totally ignoring the conflict of pressure groups. Calhoun's visionary England is undisturbed by controversies between classes or occupations or sections. The sole problem revolves around the spoils of office. The prime contestants include the citizens who pay the taxes, the monarch who dispenses the patronage, and the lords who receive the offices. Each of the disputants controls a segment of the government, and each segment has a veto on all legislation. The House of Commons represents "the great tax-paying interest by which the government is supported." The King is "the conduit through which, all the honors and emoluments of the government flow." The conflict between Commons and King would necessarily "end in violence and an appeal to force" were it not for the stabilizing influence of the House of Lords. Whereas the King dispenses the patronage, the Lords receive the spoils. Since the members of the House of Lords are "the principal recipients of the honors, emoluments, and other advantages derived from the government," their most profound desire is to preserve the system. Thus the Lords interpose to maintain the equilibrium between Commons and King.

The genius of the system, continued Calhoun, is most evident when the British kingdom expands. Rome collapsed because the bounty gained in conquest inspired a resurgence of spoilsmen. But in England an increase in patronage only adds stability to the system: "the greater the patronage of the government, the greater will be the share" which the House of Lords receives; "the more eligible its condition, the greater its opposition to any radical change" in governmental form. No matter how lush the spoils become, the Lords, Commons, and King will go on checking each other, thus preventing a war over patronage and demonstrating the supreme virtue of the concurrent majority.

In both the Roman and English narratives, then, corruption in government emerges as Calhoun's prime concern. In Rome, the concurrent majority checked the clash of interests and then succumbed to a conflict of spoilsmen. In England, communal pressure groups are nowhere to be found, and the system is devised to avert a war over patronage. These historical fantasies reveal once again how profoundly Calhoun was disturbed by the intrigues of the spoilsmen.[1]

Calhoun never really explained how the success of the concurrent majority in England points the way toward a cure for the disease of spoilsmen in a democracy. As Calhoun described it, the alleged absence of spoilsmen in England depends as much on the principle of monarchy as on the doctrine of the concurrent majority. Spoilsmen do not develop in England, he wrote, partly because the dispenser of patronage is an hereditary king rather than an elected politician, which prevents "in consequence of its unity and hereditary character, the violent and factious struggles to obtain the control of the government,—and, with it, the vast patronage which distracted, corrupted, and finally subverted the Roman Republic." Calhoun was hardly proposing that a democratic nation save itself by adopting a king. The question remains, how could the concurrent majority cure the disease of spoilsmen in a democracy?

First of all, Calhoun believed that governmental revenues would inevitably shrink when each minority interest could veto any tax bill. Reduced taxes would result in diminished patronage, thereby removing the cause of the clash between spoilsmen. On the other hand, under a government of the numerical majority, the minority interests would continually be forced to pay higher taxes, thereby increasing patronage and stimulating spoilsmen.

But, as Calhoun indirectly admitted, minority veto would never reduce patronage enough to discourage the spoilsmen for long. Calhoun is remembered today more for his later years as a determined sectionalist than for his early career as an ardent nationalist. Yet the fundamental premise of the early Calhoun, the assumption that strong national military preparations alone insure lasting peace, is what destroys his later political theory. Calhoun could legitimately expect that minority veto would remove one of the two causes of huge bureaucracy, a majority's systematic perversion of the power of taxation to exploit the minority. However, the South Carolinian hoped and believed that no interest would veto the necessary

[1] Calhoun's discussion of the problems of minority interests also superbly illustartes the central importance of his theory of spoilsmen. Calhoun sometimes assumed that the principle of periodic elections would be of no help to minority interests, for the numerical majority would simply re-elect the same representatives at subsequent elections. But in the Disquisition Calhoun admitted that minority interests could become part of a new majority coalition when the polls reopened. The problem is that the war between spoilsmen will lead to a revolution which will close the polls forever. "It is true," Calhoun conceded, "that . . . the minor and subject party, for the time, have the right to oppose and resist the major and dominant party, for the time, through the ballot box, and may turn them out, and take their place. . . . But such a state of things must necessarily be temporary. The conflict between the two parties must be transferred, sooner or later, from an appeal to the ballot-box to an appeal to force."

expenses for national defense—the second reason for vast government—and he maintained that legitimate appropriations for military survival would alone produce a government large enough to stimulate violent conflicts between spoilsmen.

Thus Calhoun's first solution to the problem of spoilsmen fails because, even under the concurrent majority, patronage will be extensive enough to attract demagogues. But Calhoun did not rely solely on reducing the spoils to put down the politicians. He also believed that the very nature of government under the concurrent majority would elevate to power men of enlarged and enlightened views. Since pressure groups would have to cooperate instead of conflict, they would elect disinterested statesmen rather than scheming politicians. The concurrent majority would effectively force interests to destroy the spoilsmen.

The difficulty with this solution to the problem of spoilsmen is that it rests on the premises of the theory of interests; it assumes that pressure groups control their politicians. But the theory of spoilsmen assumes that demagogues can delude the rabble and break free from all control. If the concurrent majority would force interests to elect statesmen, the spoils of office would continue to call forth the demagoguery of the spoilsmen. Since the "vast" military establishments would still offer rich patronage harvests, corrupt politicians would have not reason to cease their electioneering. And since the masses would remain as gullible as ever, statesmen would still have little chance of defeating demagogues in a popular election.[2] Thus the need for disinterested compromisers, like the reduction in the size of government, may slow down but cannot stop the rise of spoilsmen. In both cases the "vast" military establishment remains to invite the resurgence of demagogues. Under the concurrent majority in the future, no less than under the numerical majority in the past, the supremacy of spoilsmen will continue to threaten the republic.

The concurrent majority's failure to end the disease of spoilsmen is serious enough in itself. The race for patronage alone leads to revolution and dictatorship. However, the continued supremacy of political spoilsmen also has a disastrous effect on an ultimate reconciliation of economic interests. Critics of the Disquisition have always maintained that minority veto would destroy a democratic system by completely paralyzing the governmental process. As has been seen, Calhoun conceded the overriding importance of this consideration, but he countered with the assertion that the concurrent majority would inevitably produce compromise because enlightened statesmen would be elevated to power. With "representatives so well qualified to accomplish the object for which they were selected," argued Calhoun,

[2] At one point in the Disquisition Calhoun claimed that demagogues would pose no threat to a government of the concurrent majority. His reasons, however, are unconvincing. Under the numerical majority, he argued, "the wealthy and ambitious" would inevitably "excite and direct" the "more ignorant and dependent portions of the community." Thus suffrage would have to be severely restricted. But under the concurrent majority, continued Calhoun, suffrage could be well nigh universal. "Mere numbers" would no longer control the govenment, and hence demagogues "would have neither hope nor inducement" to delude the masses "in order to obtain the control." Ibid., 45–46. Of course Calhoun is right that the concurrent majority would prevent the masses from passing laws detrimental to a propertied minority. But this would not affect the motivation of the spoilsmen. The spoils of office would still give demagogues every "inducement" to debase the mob in order "to obtain the control." And as Calhoun readily conceded, whenever "party triumph and ascendency" is placed "above the safety and prosperity of the community," the combined force of "falsehood, injustice, fraud, artifice, slander, and breach of faith" will "overpower all regard for truth, justice, sincerity, and moral obligations of every description."

the prevailing desire would be, to promote the common interests of the whole; and, hence, the competition would be, not which should yield the least to promote the common good, but which should yield the most . . . herein is to be found the feature, which distinguishes governments of the concurrent majority so strikingly from those of the numerical. In the latter, each faction, in the struggle to obtain the control of the government, elevates to power the designing, the artful, and unscrupulous, who, in their devotion to party,—instead of aiming at the good of the whole,—aim exclusively at securing the ascendency of party.

It is hardly necessary to trace the ultimate defect in Calhoun's theory. The concurrent majority, to be successful in conciliating interests, must result in compromise; statesmen are likely—but by Calhoun's own admission, spoilsmen unlikely—to seek the general interest; the concurrent majority fails to stop the war of spoilsmen; hence politicos, not the wise and virtuous, will be elected; thus governmental deadlock and social anarchy are likely to ensue; therefore the concurrent majority cannot successfully end the clash of interests.

The failure of the concurrent majority is the result of the fundamental contradiction in Calhoun's political philosophy. The concurrent majority, expressly designed to end political strife by preventing clashes between different portions of the community, assumes that the interests control their politicians. The theory of spoilsmen rests on the premise that demagogues control their constituents. The concurrent majority, in curing the disease of the interests, will not affect the intrigues of the demagogues. Even a completely disinterested government will supply enough patronage to whet the appetites of the spoilsmen. Thus corrupt demagogues will still use the rabble to obtain high office to enrich themselves. And the continued success of unscrupulous politicians will undermine the chance of a disinterested compromise between communal interests. In the end, Calhoun's attempt to unite in one theory two irreconcilable conceptions of political causation topples the entire logical structure.

The central importance of the theory of spoilsmen in the Disquisition leads to the obvious question, why was Calhoun so distressed about political corruption? The answer comes from two directions. First of all, as a political philosopher well versed in the ideology of the Founding Fathers, Calhoun inherited that strain of late eighteenth-century thought which considered democratic politics the pursuit of gentlemen and disdained legislative cabals and mass parties. Secondly, as the political leader of the South Carolina planters during the Age of Jackson, Calhoun had special reasons to deplore the emerging spoils system. A brief consideration of Calhoun's intellectual heritage and his political career will help to explain the emphasis on corrupt politicians in his formal political theory.

To the men who led the American Revolution and founded the federal republic, the possibility of party conflict always seemed one of the great dangers which beset a democracy. The Founding Fathers were upper class republicans, and they sought "to refine and enlarge the public view" by insuring that a propertied elite would rule. If political parties developed, corrupt demagogues might "first obtain the suffrages, and then betray the interests, of the people." As John Taylor of Caroline put it, "all parties, however loyal to principles at first, degenerate into aristocracies of interests at last; and unless a nation is capable of discerning the point where integrity ends and fraud begins, popular parties are among the surest modes of introducing an aristocracy."

The Founding Fathers' distrust of political parties received its classic expression in George Washington's famous "Farewell Address" of 1796. Washington could not take leave of his countrymen without warning them "in the most solemn manner against the baneful effects of the spirit of party generally." Party agitation, he declared, "is seen in its greatest rankness" in republican governments "and is truly their worst enemy." The spirit of party "serves always to distract the public councils and enfeeble the public administration. It agitates the community with ill-founded alarms; kindles the animosity of one part against another; foments occasionally riot and insurrection." Only "a uniform vigilance," said Washington, can "prevent its bursting into a flame."

During the early years of the republic the Founding Fathers' political practices often belied their antiparty principles. The election of 1800, in particular, was a bitterly fought contest between two aggressive political parties. However, the Jeffersonian and Federalist parties remained only half developed; they had all but dissolved by 1820. More important, the new nation's early presidents were usually enlightened aristocrats, philosopher statesmen who spent less time than their mid nineteenth-century successors perfecting partisan political organizations.

During the Age of Jackson more systematic national political parties emerged, requiring a different style of political leader and making the struggle for the spoils of federal office of high importance. A plentiful supply of patronage could knit together the diverse factions which made up a national party. Moreover, leading this hybrid of local factions required flexibility, tact, and political maneuver. By 1850 the Founding Fathers' vision of a republic without political parties had been rendered hopelessly obsolete, and the age of the philosopher statesman had given way to the age of the political manager.

Calhoun's career spanned the years of transition. Educated at Yale College and the Litchfield Law School at the beginning of the nineteenth century, the South Carolinian studied under Timothy Dwight, James Gould, and Tapping Reeve, three high priests of the Federalist faith. Calhoun remained a Jeffersonian in spite of his mentors. But Jefferson himself prayed that popular majorities would select "natural aristocrats" to govern and the young Calhoun probably raised few objections to the elitist side of the dogmas handed down at Litchfield and Yale. Calhoun emerged from his encounder with the Federalists steeped in the eighteenth-century conviction that democracies could best survive if enlightened aristocrats continued to rule.

Throughout his ensuing national career Calhoun fought to preserve the Founding Fathers' principles against the onslaught of the emerging political managers. In his brilliant early years as Secretary of War under James Monroe, Calhoun opposed the presidential aspirations of William H. Crawford partly because the Geogian hoped "to attain favor, not by placing himself on principles and policy . . . but by political dexterity and management." Calhoun's crusade against John Quincy Adams' administration was also partly motivated by growing concern with base political methods. Adams had risen to power, according to Calhoun, by a "corrupt bargain" with Henry Clay in which Adams bought the presidency by paying Clay with the appointment as Secretary of State. In late 1829, when the political craftiness of Martin Van Buren had begun to drive Calhoun to the rear of the Jackson movement, the South Carolinian wrote John McLean that "I deeply apprehend, that the choice of the chief magistrate will finally be placed at the disposition of the executive power itself, through a corrupt system to be founded on the abuse of the power and patronage of the government."

Thwarted by Van Buren and isolated from Jackson in 1831, Calhoun became a leader of the South Carolina nullifiers. One of the many reasons for his action was the belief that South Carolina's veto of the tariff would lower governmental revenues and thereby reduce executive patronage. By 1835 the South Carolinian was obsessed with the notion that Jackson's use of the patronage to promote the ascendancy of his own handpicked candidate was turning democracy into dictatorship. Arguing in his "Report on the Extent of the Executive Patronage" that the executive corps was becoming "so strong as to be capable of sustaining itself by the influence alone, unconnected with any system or measure of policy," Calhoun urged Congress to enact controls on "King Andrew's" manipulation of the spoils. Thereafter, in every major policy decision, from distributing the surplus revenue to enacting the Independent Treasury, from lowering the tariff to entering the Mexican War, the "Cast Iron Man" from South Carolina carefully weighed the effect on executive patronage. For a time, in the late 1830s and early 1840s, Calhoun believed that patronage could be successfully dried up. But by 1848 an embittered Calhoun had almost admitted defeat. He did not see "how any man who has the ability and the disposition to correct abuses and reform the government can in the present state of politics be elected. The governing, I might with truth say, the exclusive object of both parties, in electing the President, is to obtain the spoils. They are both equally ready to sacrifice any other considerations to it."

In denouncing Crawford's use of the congressional caucus, in castigating the "corrupt bargain" between Clay and Adams, in thundering against Jackson's distribution of the spoils, Calhoun was not merely echoing the antiparty rhetoric of the Founding Fathers. He was also voicing the typical disdain of a South Carolina patrician for the new political methods in the Age of Jackson. Throughout the first half of the nineteenth century the South Carolina planters remained solidly committed to a quasi-aristocratic version of democracy, and no other group in American society clung more tenaciously to the eighteenth-century ideal of a nation ruled by gentlemen. In his campaign against the spoilsmen, as in so much else, Calhoun can only be understood against the background of the state whose cause he made so peculiarly his own.

The South Carolina patrician was a democrat with the brakes on; he had faith only in the right kind of democracy. If the natural aristocracy was allowed a free hand to govern, the Carolina planter could afford to be a democrat. He conceded that the people should choose which aristocrats would rule. As James Hamilton, Jr., put it, "The people expect that their leaders in whose . . . public spirit they have confidence will think for them—and that they will be prepared to *act* as their leaders *think.*"

The South Carolina Constitution of 1790 as amended in the early nineteenth century institutionalized this qualified faith in democracy. Any adult white male who had resided in South Carolina for two years could vote for state legislators. However, the legislators elected almost all other state officials from the governor to the tax collectors, as well as United States senators and presidential electors. A high property qualification for the legislature kept lower class opportunists outside the statehouse. Finally, the apportionment of legislative seats gave the small minority of lowcountry aristocrats control of the senate and a disproportionate influence in the house. Political power in South Carolina was uniquely concentrated in a legislature of large property holders which set state policy and selected the men to administer it.

The characteristics of South Carolina politics cemented the control of upper class planters. Elections to the state legislature—the one control the masses could exert over the government—were often uncontested and rarely allowed the "plebeians" a clear choice between two parties or policies. Even in the state legislature, the Carolina gentry eschewed organized parties. Leaders of a well-disciplined legislative party might organize a statewide popular ticket and encourage the "mob" to overreach themselves by debating issues. Unscrupulous demagogues would subsequently seize control from disinterested patricians by bribing and deluding the rabble. Political parties would overturn the rule of the rich, well born, and able, and would thus upset the precariously balanced, qualified democracy which alone won the approbation of the South Carolina patricians.

Although sensitive souls throughout the country were disgusted with the emerging spoils system in the Age of Jackson, the South Carolina aristocrats shrieked the longest and the loudest. The rise of the political manager upset their delicately balanced, limited democracy and produced some of the evils they most feared—a passion for federal patronage, the rule of party hacks, the rise of inferior demagogues. South Carolina's participation in the political parties was occasional and superficial. The Calhounites, quickly disillusioned by their bitter experience with the early Jackson movement, usually remained aloof from national coalitions. And when Calhoun sporadically and suspiciously rejoined the Democratic party, he always insisted that taxes should be lowered so that the party would be based on principles rather than spoils.

However, Calhoun's attempt to reform the Democratic party was not solely the disinterested campaign of a South Carolina patrician to reestablish the ideals of the Founding Fathers. His rhetoric on executive patronage also probably reflects the bitter disappointment of a brilliant and supremely ambitious young man who climbed with incredible speed to the higher ranks of federal power and then never achieved his ultimate goal. Political maneuvering had destroyed his presidential prospects in 1832 and threatened to produce a life of personal frustration. Calhoun may well have realized that his marked superiority at political reasoning was somewhat offset by his notorious failings as a practical politician. In this sense, he may have hoped that reduced executive patronage would produce a nation where the Calhouns rather than the Van Burens, the philosopher statesmen rather than the party managers, would once again have a chance to be President of the United States.[2]

But Calhoun's obsession with political corruption was more than a response to unfulfilled ambition, more than a patrician's distrust of the new political managers. It was also one expression of that violent South Carolina radicalism in the crisis of the 1830s which produced both the nullification crusade against the tariff and the

---

[2] This is not to say that Calhoun always shunned the methods he deplored. The South Carolinian enthusiastically directed his own presidential campaign in the early 1820's, and—as Charles G. Sellers has pointed out to the author—the Calhounites tried to use Van Burenite methods to defeat Van Buren himself in the contest for the Democratic nomination in 1844. But even at such times, Calhoun was somewhat uneasy about using partisan political techniques. Calhoun's disdain for the new style of democratic politics may have been an important reason for his ineptness as a practical politician.

gag rule fight against the abolitionists. The South Carolinians, morbidly aware of their own weaknesses—depressed economically, frightened by recurrent slave conspiracies, able to defend slavery only with the doctrine that bondage was a "necessary evil" (and secretly believing that necessary or not the evil was grave)—found themselves faced for the first time with a mounting abolitionist attack and a high protective tariff, both of which seemed to threaten slavery and the future of southern white civilization. The planters devised (and tried to believe) a proslavery argument, developed a closed, rigid, restrictive society, and even endeavored (a bit lamely) to acquire some of that Yankee spirit of commercial enterprise which they held in such contempt. But for their ultimate salvation they turned to national politics. Convinced that their only hope lay in the most rigid adherence to principle, the South Carolina aristocrats were made desperate by the apathy of natural allies throughout the nation. Many southerners seemed content to compromise with the abolitionists. Most Democrats, both North and South, refused to engage in an uncompromising fight against Clay's American System. There could be only one explanation. Politicians were compromising with abolitionists and monopolists to keep their party together and to increase their chances of grabbing a share of the spoils of office. If the American System could be destroyed and patronage reduced, the South might be brought to defend itself in time and the Democrats brought to stand steadfast on the only principles which could save the union. And surely Calhoun's belief that politicians often ignore their constituents in their race for the spoils originated in part with what he considered the shame of the spoilsmen in the 1830s.

Thus, in his practical career as in his political theory, Calhoun's concern with spoilsmen was as important as his fear of interests. By exorcising the new political brokers Calhoun could hope to bring the republic back to the enlightened rule of disinterested patricians, fulfill his presidential ambitions, and develop national political movements based on principles rather than spoils. When statesmen replaced spoilsmen, the clash between fundamental interests over the American System and over abolition could also be resolved.

Yet Calhoun's practical program was vitiated by the same logical contradiction between the theory of interests and the theory of spoilsmen which destroyed his political philosophy. The South Carolinian was again unable to decide whether pressure groups or politicians caused historical events. On the one hand, Calhoun held that the Democratic party would be run by spoilsmen rather than statesmen until the American System ceased to supply patronage. On the other hand, he maintained that the American System would only be destroyed when statesmen replaced spoilsmen at the head of the Democratic party. If interests could be neutralized, spoilsmen would disappear. Yet spoilsmen must disappear before interests could be neutralized. The reformer hardly knew where to begin. As Calhoun saw the dilemma in a more practical situation, Jackson's Democratic politicos—although elected by interest groups opposed to Clay's brainchild—compromised with an American System which fed them patronage, thereby frustrating their constituents.

Nullification was, among other things, a desperate way out of the vicious circle. South Carolina, by nullifying high duties, could at once neutralize interests and reduce patronage. For a time in the late 1830s Calhoun was almost sanguine. But even nullification was no real escape, for by Calhoun's own admission the unnullified military establishments remained to invite the resurgence of spoilsmen. More im-

portant, in the 1840s, with nullification discredited, the South Carolinian was again
trapped in his own logical nightmare. Thus when Democrats like Thomas Ritchie and
Van Buren compromised a bit with the American System and with the abolitionists,
Calhoun's profound bitterness was the logical culmination of the inconsistencies in
his own political program.

The Disquisition, written in the late 1840s, reflects Calhoun's despair as his career
drew to a close. The increasingly angry controversy between northern and southern
interests seemed disastrous enough in itself. But in addition the vast federal patronage
seemed certain to perpetuate the regime of the spoilsmen. With unscrupulous
politicians in power the North and South would never find grounds for reconciliation.
Thus the Disquisition represents one of Calhoun's last desperate attempts to restrain
the interests and spoilsmen which together seemed destined to break up the republic.

In one sense, the Disquisition is a justly celebrated contribution to the American
democratic tradition. Calhoun was a political realist who ranks with James Madison
and John Adams in his mordant analysis of the defects of a democracy. As Calhoun
endlessly reiterated, entrenched majorities can ignore constitutional restraints and pay
little heed to minority rights. The South Carolinian was also clearly right that the
clash of interests and the intrigues of spoilsmen often threaten the efficiency of a
democratic government.

The problem with the Disquisition lies not in its diagnosis but rather in its
exaggeration of the weaknesses in a republic. Calhoun's critics have often argued
that the theory of interests overstates both the helplessness of democratic minorities
and the selfishness of economic interests. It must now be added that the theory of
spoilsmen magnifies the threat posed by scheming politicians. Ambitious demagogues
may sometimes exert more political influence than the economic determinists like to
think. But Calhoun surely overestimated the spoilsmen's capacity to delude the
masses and overthrow the system. Indeed Calhoun's rhetoric on the evils of patronage
often sounds suspiciously like that of a late nineteenth-century mugwump, fighting
his curious crusade to save democracy by enacting civil service reform. The combination of this exaggerated fear of spoilsmen and Calhoun's exaggerated fear of interests
simply posed problems too grave for the concurrent majority, or any constitutional
reform, to solve. The resulting inconsistencies in the Disquisition must create renewed doubts as to whether Calhoun deserves his reputation as America's most
rigorous political logician. It would be closer to the truth to call the author of the
Disquisition one of the more confused political philosophers in the American tradition.

The contradictions in Calhoun's Disquisition provide a particularly revealing illustration of that ambivalence toward democratic principles which so often marked
the political thought of the more aristocratic southern slaveholders. As historians
have often reminded us in the past two decades, the clash between American
politicians has characteristically taken place within a consensus of belief in democratic government. Calhoun paid his personal testimonial to this pervasive Amercian
consensus by straining to remain both a statesman and a theorizer of the democratic
persuasion. But the deeper significance of Calhoun's tragic career is that despite his
fascination with abstract political argument he could not put together a consistent
democratic theory. The key to Calhoun's thought is not just his concern with class
or any other kind of economic interests, not just his concern with moral fanatics, not

just his concern with demagogic spoilsmen. Rather, the secret of his political philosophy—the reason why it is inevitably inconsistent—is that Calhoun distrusted democracy for so many exaggerated and contradictory reasons. An eighteenth-century elitist increasingly disillusioned with the emerging political order in the Age of Jackson, Calhoun by the end of his career no longer quite believed in American democracy.

18 / Who Were the Southern Whigs?

Charles Sellers

During much of the Jacksonian period the Whig Party of the South was a nationally oriented group, aligned with the capitalistic-commercial interests of the entire country. Charles Sellers develops this theme clearly in the following article. By the late 1830's, the nation enjoyed the short-lived luxury of sustaining two major parties that were strong in every section.

The Southern Whig of 1840, the year of the first Whig presidential victory, had more in common with his partisan counterpart in the North than he had with the "dangerous Loco Focos," or Democrats, of his own Southern state. Such issues as banking, internal improvements, and the tariff created national economic interests that by that time were clearly discernible in terms of party alignment. Sellers also shows that although Calhoun and his followers prepared the way for the rationalization of secession in the years ahead, most of the South rejected extremist formulas during the Jacksonian period.

But almost as soon as this national, two-party system had been established, it began to break down in the sectional conflicts of the late 1840's and the 1850's. The end of the system signaled the end of the Jacksonian coalition and ultimately the end of an era.

For further reading: Arthur C. Cole, *The Whig Party in the South* (1913); Joel Silbey, *The Shrine of Party* (1967); Frederick Jackson Turner, *The United States, 1830–1850* (1935).

Students of the Old South have spent much of their time in recent years dispelling myths about that fabled land of moonlight and magnolias. Our understanding of the

American Historical Review, LIX (January 1954), 335–346. Reprinted by permission. Footnotes have been omitted except where they are necessary for an understanding of the text.

social, intellectual, and economic life of the ante-bellum South has been considerably revised and immeasurably widened by the work of a large number of able scholars.

Political history, however, has been unfashionable and one of the results has been the survival of a series of myths about the political life of the South in the 1830s and 1840's. The key myth may be called the myth of a monolithic South: a section unified as early as the 1820's in its devotion to state rights doctrines and its hostility to the nationalistic, antislavery capitalistic North. The result of approaching ante-bellum history by way of Fort Sumter and Appomattox, this point of view found its classic statements in the apologias of Jefferson Davis and Alexander H. Stephens, but it was made respectable in the first generation of professional scholarship by such historians as Herman Von Holst and John W. Burgess. "It colored such early mono-graphs as U. B. Phillips' "Georgia and State Rights" and H. M. Wagstaff's *States Rights and Political Parties in North Carolina, 1776–1861*, and is to be seen in most of the more recent works on the pre-Civil War South.[1] It has also given rise to the corollary myths that Calhoun was the representative spokesman and political leader of the South after about 1830, and that the Whig party in the South mainly reflected the state rights proclivities of the great planters.

These myths have been strengthened by Frederick Jackson Turner's sectional analysis of our early national history. Turner's approach has been extremely fruitful, but its sweeping application has tended to exaggerate differing sectional tendencies into absolute differences. The application of geographic sectionalism to individual states, moreover, has fostered the further myth that political strife within the Old South was confined largely to struggles over intrastate sectional issues between up-country and low country, hill country and "black belt."

All of these myths have some basis in fact. They are, however, the product of a misplaced emphasis which has permeated nearly all the studies of pre-Civil War southern politics. Sectionalism and state rights have been made the central themes of southern political history for almost the entire ante-bellum period. Southern opposition to nationalistic legislation by Congress has been overemphasized. And the social, economic, and ideological lines of political cleavage within the slave states have been obscured. The early history of the Whig party below Mason and Dixon's line shows the character of these distortions.

It is too often forgotten that in the ante-bellum period the South had a vigorous two-party system, an asset it has never since enjoyed. Until at least the later 1840's, the voting southerner was much more interested in the success of his own party and its policies than in banding together with southerners of the opposite party to

---

[1] Charles S. Sydnor, in what is, in many respects, the finest work on the ante-bellum South, presents a persuasive restatement of the traditional sectional-state rights interpretation. His chapter headings on politics from the Panic of 1819 to nullification describe a developing sectionalism: "From Economic Nationalism to Political Sectionalism," "End of the Virginia Dynasty," "The Lower South Adopts State Rights," and "Bold Acts and Bolder Thoughts." The 1830's and 1840's, however, present a paradox. Professor Sydnor finds a growing "Regionalism in Mind and Spirit," but a "decline of sectionalism in politics." This he explains as a result of the fact that "major Southern hopes and fears found no champion in either party," so that "party conflict south of the Potomac . . . had the hallow sound of a stage duel with tin swords," "The agrarian South felt little interest," writes Professor Sydnor, in that conflict between the "wealthier and more conservative segments of society" and the liberal, democratic elements "which formed a major issue between the Democratic and Whig parties" in the nation as a whole. *The Development of Southern Sectionalism, 1819–1848* (Baton Rouge, 1948), especially p. 316.

defend the Constitution and southern rights against invasion by the North. The parties were evenly matched, and elections were bitterly contested. It was rare for any southern state to be regarded as absolutely safe for either party. Of the 425,629 votes cast in the slave states at the election of 1836, the Whigs had a majority of only 243 popular votes. In this and the three succeeding presidential elections, a total of 2,745,171 votes were cast, but the over-all margin, again in favor of the Whigs, was only 66,295 or 2.4 per cent of the total votes. In these four elections the Whigs carried a total of twenty-seven southern states and the Democrats twenty-six.

An equally close rivalry is evident in congressional representation. In the five congressional elections between 1832 and 1842, southern Democrats won an aggregate total of 234 seats, while their opponents captured 263. Whigs predominated among southern representatives in three of these five Congresses, and Democrats in two. In three of them the margin between the southern wings of the parties was five or less. We have then a picture of keen political competition, with a vigorous Whig party maintaining a slight ascendancy.

What did this Whig party stand for? The pioneer account of the southern Whigs was the essay by U. B. Phillips which, significantly, appeared in the *Festschrift* to Frederick Jackson Turner. This study shows Phillips' characteristic tendency to generalize about the entire South on the basis of conditions in his native Georgia. "The great central body of southern Whigs," he declares, "were the cotton producers, who were first state-rights men pure and simple and joined the Whigs from a sense of outrage at Jackson's threat of coercing South Carolina."

Two years after Phillips' essay appeared, Arthur C. Cole published his exhaustive monograph on *The Whig Party in the South*. Less than a third of the Cole volume is concerned with the period before 1844, when Whiggery was of greatest importance in the South, and he generally follows the Phillips interpretation of its origins. His account of the birth of the party devotes three pages to early National Republicanism in the South, twenty to the anti-Jackson sentiment aroused during the nullification crisis, and only four and a half to the fight over the national bank and financial policy. "Various interests," he says, "linked in political alliance with the few southerners whose interests and inclinations led to the support of latitudinarian principles, a still larger faction made up of those who supported constitutional doctrines on the opposite extreme and whose logical interests seemed to point against such an affiliation."

An analysis, however, of the record of the Twenty-second Congress (1831–1833) leads to somewhat different conclusions. It was this Congress which dealt with the tariff, nullification, and national bank questions, and it was during this Congress that the groundwork for the Whig party was laid. Of the ninety southerners in the House of Representatives, sixty-nine had been elected as supporters of Andrew Jackson, while twenty-one, nearly a fourth, were National Republicans. Of the sixty-nine Democrats, twenty-five were subsequently active in the Whig party. Eighteen of the latter were state rights Whigs, while seven were not identified with the state rights wing of the opposition. These twenty-five men then, together with the twenty-one National Republicans, may be regarded as representative of the groups which formed the Whig party in the South.

These incipient Whigs voted twenty-four to twenty-one in favor of the tariff of 1832, a measure denounced by state rights men and nullified by South Carolina.

They also voted twenty-four to nineteen for the Force Bill, which was designed to throttle the nullifiers. This backing of administration measures was hardly a portent of an opposition state rights party. The real harbinger of Whiggery was the vote on the national bank bill, which this group supported twenty-seven to seventeen.

The Whig party actually took shape during the Twenty-third Congress (1833–1835), in which it gained the allegiance of fifty-two of the ninety-nine southern members of the House. They voted twenty-nine to sixteen in favor of rechartering the national bank and unanimously in favor of restoring the government deposits to Biddle's institution. By a closer vote of twenty-two to twenty they supported repairing and extending the Cumberland Road. In the Twenty-fourth Congress (1835–1837) the forty-eight Whig Representatives from the South divided thirty-eight to three in favor of Clay's bill to distribute the proceeds from sales of public lands to the states. Other votes showing similar tendencies might be cited, but enough has been said to suggest that, even in the beginning, a majority of southern anti-Jackson men were far from being state rights doctrinaires.

In the light of this record it is not so surprising that only a handful of southern Whigs followed Calhoun when he marched his supporters back into the Democratic household during Van Buren's administration.[2] The record also prepares one for the increasing manifestations of nationalism among southern Whigs which Phillips and Cole found so difficult to explain. The southern wing of the party backed Clay almost unanimously for the Presidential nomination in 1840. Tyler's nomination for Vice President was more a sop to the disappointed Clay men, of whom Tyler was one, than a concession to the state rights proclivities of southern Whiggery, the reason usually given for his choice.

The nature of southern Whiggery had its real test when Tyler challenged Clay for leadership of the party. Of the fifty-five southern Whigs in the lower house of the Twenty-seventh Congress (1841–1843), only three stuck by the Virginia President and his state rights principles, whereas Mangum of North Carolina presided over the caucus which read Tyler out of the party, and southern Whig editors joined in castigating him unmercifully. Southern Whigs supported Clay's legislative program —repeal of the Subtreasury, a national bank, distribution, and tariff—by large majorities. Even the Georgians, Berrien, Toombs, and Stephens, defended the protective features of the tariff of 1842.

Having said so much to the point that the Whig party in the South did not begin as and did not become a state rights party, it is necessary to add that neither was it consciously nationalistic. State rights versus nationalism simply was not the main issue in Southern politics in this period. It is readily apparent from the newspapers and correspondence of the time that, except for Calhoun and his single-minded little band, politicians in the South were fighting over the same questions that were agitating the North—mainly questions of banking and financial policy.

It is hard to exaggerate the importance of the banking question. State and federal governments, by their policy in this sphere, could cause inflation or deflation, make capital easy or difficult to obtain, and facilitate or hinder the marketing of staple

---

[2] Senator William C. Preston and Representative Waddy Thompson of South Carolina refused to leave the Whig party with Calhoun, and three other Representatives from the state took the Conservative, or anti-Subtreasury, position. Outside his own state Calhoun carried with him only seven members of Congress.

crops and commercial activity generally. And by chartering or refusing to charter banks, they could afford or deny to the capitalists of the day the most profitable field of activity the economy offered.

The banking issue is the key to an understanding of southern as well as northern Whiggery. Merchants and bankers were most directly concerned in financial policy, but their community of interest generally included the other business and professional men of the towns, especially the lawyers, who got most of their fees from merchants, and the newspaper editors, who were dependent on the merchants for advertising revenues. The crucial point for southern politics, however, is that the large staple producers were also closely identified economically with the urban commercial groups. These were the principal elements which went into the Whig party.

The Whigs generally defended the national bank until its doom was sealed, then advocated a liberal chartering of commercial banks by the states, and finally, after the Panic of 1837, demanded a new national bank. The Democrats fought Biddle's institution and either favored state-operated banks to provide small loans for farmers, as distinguished from commercial banks, or tried to regulate banking strictly or abolish it altogether.

Much of the misunderstanding about the Whig party in the South may be traced to the technique of plotting election returns on maps. Such maps tell us much, but they may also mislead. They show, for example, that the "black belts" of the lower South were the great centers of Whig strength. This has led scholars to reason (1) that the Whig party was a planters' party *par excellence,* (2) that planters were necessarily rigid state rights men, and (3) that the Whig party was, therefore, a state rights party. Q. E. D.!

What the maps do not illustrate, however, is the dynamics of the political situation —the elements of leadership, impetus, financing, and propaganda, which are the real sinews of a political organization. In the case of the Whig party, these elements were furnished mainly by the commercial groups of the cities and towns, with their allied lawyers and editors. Lawyers were the practicing politicians for both parties, but the greater influence of lawyers among the Whigs is an indication of the commercial affiliations of the party. Seventy-four per cent of the southern Whigs who sat in Congress from 1833 to 1843 are identified as practicing attorneys, as compared with fifty-five per cent of the Democrats. In the lower house of the Tennessee legislature of 1839, farmers predominated, but a fourth of the Whigs were lawyers, as compared with only a tenth of the Democratic membership.

The size and importance of the urban middle class in the Old South has yet to be fully appreciated. As early as 1831, Nashville, for example, contained twenty-two wholesale houses and seventy-seven retail stores, not to mention numerous other businesses, such as the sixty taverns and tippling houses. Even the little county seat town of Gallatin, Tennessee, boasted in 1840 ten mercantile firms, a grocer, a merchant tailor, three hotels, five lawyers, five doctors, a paper and grist mill, and eighteen artisans' establishments of one kind or another.

Businessmen dominated the towns socially, economically, and politically, and the towns dominated the countryside. This was particularly true of the "black belts" of the lower South, since the great cotton capitalists of this region were especially dependent on commercial and credit facilities for financing and carrying on their extensive planting operations. In recognition of the urban influence on politics, congressional districts were commonly known by the names of the principal towns in each—as, for example, the Huntsville, Florence, Tuscaloosa, Montgomery, and Mobile districts in Alabama.

Other evidence points in the same direction. A large majority of the stockholders in Virginia banks in 1837 lived in the areas of heaviest Whig voting. The principal commercial towns of the state—Richmond, Petersburg, and Norfolk—gave unbroken Whig majorities throughout the period 1834–1840. In North Carolina twenty of the twenty-one directors of the two principal banks in 1840 were Whigs. The first Whig governor of North Carolina was a railroad president; the second was a lawyer, cotton manufacturer, and railroad president; and the third was one of the wealthiest lawyers in the state.

Similar party leadership obtained elsewhere. In Virginia, younger men of the type of John Minor Botts of Richmond and Alexander H. H. Stuart of Staunton actually directed the party of which Tyler and Tazewell were nominal leaders. Senators George A. Waggaman and Judah P. Benjamin were typical of the New Orleans lawyers who guided Louisiana Whiggery. Poindexter and Prentiss in Mississippi were intimately associated both personally and financially with the bankers and business-men of Natchez. The Tennessee Whigs were led by John Bell, Nashville lawyer and iron manufacturer, who had married into the state's leading mercantile and banking house; Ephraim H. Foster, bank director and Nashville's most prominent commercial lawyer; and Hugh Lawson White, Knoxville lawyer, judge, and bank president.

This commercial bias of the Whig party did much to pave the way for the industrial development of the South after the Civil War. It was no accident that former Whigs provided a large part of the leadership for the business-minded Conservative-Democratic parties which "redeemed" the South from Republican rule and then proceeded to make the conquered section over in the image of the victorious North, often in the interest of northern capital.

Commercial considerations and the banking question did not, of course, determine political alignments in the Old South by themselves. Pro-tariff sentiment made for Whiggery among the sugar planters of Louisiana, the hemp growers of Kentucky, and the salt and iron manufacturers of western Virginia and Maryland. The more liberal policy of the Whigs toward internal improvements by both the state and federal governments won them support in landlocked interior sections and along the routes of projected transportation projects. And the fact that the Democrats gener-ally championed a broadened suffrage, apportionment of congressional and legislative seats on the basis of white population, and other measures for extending political democracy, inclined propertied and conservative men to rally to the Whig party as a bulwark against mobocracy.

These factors, however, merely reinforced the commercial nature of southern Whiggery. The business orientation of the Whigs and the relative unimportance of their state rights wing become quite apparent if the party is described as it actually developed in the various states, rather than on the basis of general assumptions about southern politics.

A state by state analysis would indicate that, in the four border slave states and Louisiana, Whiggery was simply National Republicanism continued under a new name. The National Republicans were also strong in Virginia, but here they were joined in opposition to the Democrats by a body of state rights men alienated from Jackson by his attitude toward nullification. The National Republican and commercial wing of the party, however, was the dominant one, especially after the business-minded Conservative Democrats joined the Whigs on the Subtreasury question. In North Carolina and Tennessee, the Whig party was formed by the secession of pro-Bank men from the Democratic party, aided in Tennessee by the local popularity of Hugh Lawson White as a Presidential candidate in 1835–1836.[3]

The state rights element was more conspicuous in the four remaining states of the lower South. But it was by no means the majority wing of the Whig party in all of them. Both Alabama and Mississippi had an original nucleus of pro-Clay, anti-Jackson men, and in both states the nullification episode caused a substantial defection from the Jackson ranks. In Mississippi, however, a greater defection followed the removal of government deposits from the national bank. The state rights men were clearly a minority of the opposition party, which elected an outspoken foe of nullification to the governorship in 1835 and sent the ardent Clay partisan, Seargent S. Prentiss, to Congress two years later.

The state rights defection seems to have been more important in Alabama, where it was led by the able Dixon H. Lewis. The Lewis faction, however, maintained only a tenuous connection with the regular Whigs, and in 1837 Lewis and his supporters followed Calhoun back into the Democratic party. The significant fact is that in neither Alabama nor Mississippi were the Whigs greatly weakened by the departure of Calhoun's admirers.

Only in South Carolina and Georgia did avowed state rights men make up the bulk of the anti-Jackson party. When the real nature of the new party alignments became apparent, the politicians of Calhoun's state gave proof of their sincerity (and of the Presidential aspirations of their chief) by moving back to the Democratic ranks at the first decent opportunity.

The principal Whig leader in Georgia was John M. Berrien, a Savannah lawyer and attorney for the United States Bank who had been forced out of Jackson's cabinet by the Peggy Eaton affair. At the time of the election of 1832, Jackson's Indian policy was so popular in Georgia that Berrien did not dare oppose the President openly. Indeed, he went about stirring up anti-tariff and state rights sentiment, while

---

[3] The difficulty historians have had understanding why the North Carolina planters perversely remained in the Democratic party arises from the initial error of regarding the Whig party as primarily a planter group. The basic explanation is that the Old Republican planters of North Carolina, unlike the agricultural capitalists of the lower South, were antagonistic toward the commercial-financial group, rather than identified with it. With a smaller investment in land and slaves than his Mississippi counterpart, with little chance to make large profits by further investments, and relying less on a single cash crop, the average North Carolina planter was much less dependent on the town merchant and banker. For some years before the Jackson era, the planters had been resisting demands for banks and internal improvements, while simultaneously trying to stem the tide of democratic discontent with planter rule. It was the union of these two anti-planter forces, commercial and democratic, which produced the Whig party in 1833–1835. Businessmen controlled the new party, but they retained popular support by championing constitutional reform and by progressive legislation in the fields of internal improvements and public education. There is no adequate account of the North Carolina Whigs in print. The situation in Virginia was somewhat similar, in that a majority of the planters, Phillips and Cole to the contrary notwithstanding, remained Democrats. In the period 1833–1843, the twelve congressional districts of plantation Virginia, lying east of the Blue Ridge and south of the Rappahannock, were represented thirty-eight times by Democrats and twenty-two times by Whigs or Conservatives, with nine of the Whig elections being won in the commercial Norfolk, Richmond, and Fredericksburg districts. The Democratic party of Virginia differed from that of North Carolina, however, in having a much larger popular element.

secretly trying to prevent anti-Bank resolutions by the legislature. Immediately after Jackson's re-election, however, Berrien and his allies managed to reorganize the old Troup political faction as an openly anti-Jackson state rights party. In view of Berrien's pro-Bank attitude and his subsequent staunch support of Clay's policies, it seems probable that he was merely capitalizing on state rights sentiment to defeat Democratic measures which he opposed on other grounds. At any rate, the Georgia Whigs were soon arrayed against the Jackson financial program, and they held their lines nearly intact in the face of the desertion of state rights Whigs to the Democrats on the Subtreasury issue. By 1840 Berrien had brought his Georgia followers into close harmony with the national party.

This summary sketch of southern Whiggery raises, of course, more questions than it could possibly answer definitively. It has attempted to suggest, however, that preoccupation with the origins and development of southern sectionalism has led to distortions of southern political history in the 1830's and 1840's. Specifically, it is suggested:

That only John C. Calhoun and a small group of allied southern leaders regarded state rights as the most important issue in politics in this period.

That the southern people divided politically in these years over much the same questions as northern voters, particularly questions of banking and financial policy.

That the Whig party in the South was built around a nucleus of National Republicans and state rights men, but received its greatest accession of strength from business-minded Democrats who deserted Jackson on the Bank issue.

That the Whig party in the South was controlled by urban commercial and banking interests, supported by a majority of the planters, who were economically dependent on banking and commercial facilities. And finally,

That this alliance of the propertied, far from being inherently particularistic, rapidly shook off its state rights adherents and by 1841 was almost solidly in support of the nationalistic policies of Henry Clay.

There is a great need for intensive restudy of southern politics in the 1830's and 1840's, and particularly for critical correlation of local and national developments. The story as it comes from the contemporary sources is full of the resounding clash of solid interests and opposing ideologies, hardly having "the hollow sound of a stage duel with tin swords" which one historian seems to detect. And recent events should make the student wary of state rights banners, especially when raised by conservative men against national administrations not conspicuously devoted to the interests of the propertied.

Part IV

SOCIAL
TENSIONS

19 / Introduction to Charles G. Finney, *Lectures on Revivals of Religion*

William G. McLoughlin

"There is no country in the world where the Christian religion retains a greater influence over the souls of men than in America," wrote Alexis de Tocqueville, the great French observer of Jacksonian America. Yet by the 1830's no church any longer enjoyed state support, a privilege widespread in colonial America and throughout Europe in the nineteenth century. The vitality of American Christianity lay in voluntarism and denominationalism. Denied the backing of government, no religious group had a monopoly, and the numerous sects that competed could neither survive nor prosper except through the exertions of their members. The churches, however, could not count on people flocking to worship in a society that offered extensive opportunities for worldly success. Lured by the opportunities to make money and improve their social position, Americans paid less attention to the condition of their souls than did earlier generations—closer in time to European experiences—for whom faith was a consolation for the disappointments of life.

Developed in the eighteenth century, the religious revival became American Protestantism's most effective weapon in the battle against religious indifference and infidelity. The greatest of the revivalists was Charles G. Finney, who systematized and perfected the technique in Jacksonian America. The revivalists preached before throngs at camp meetings and in cities and reawakened the guilt of sin, the fear of damnation, and the desire for salvation. The preacher filled the hearts of sinners with the terrors of Hell, but he also offered them hope.

One consequence of the work of Finney and the other revivalists was a

Excerpted by permission of the publishers from William G. McLoughlin (editor), *Introduction to Charles Grandison Finney, Lectures on Revivals of Religion* (Cambridge, Mass.: The Belknap Press of Harvard University Press, 1960). Copyright 1960 by the President and Fellows of Harvard College.

proliferation of reform movements through which the regenerate expressed their piety in concern for the slave, the drunkard, the blind, the deaf, and especially, the unchurched. Through revivalism, American Christianity strengthened its position by recruiting new members and playing an important role as the nation's moral instructor. In doing so, the churches modified their theology and techniques to suit American conditions. The following essay on Charles G. Finney by William G. McLoughlin analyzes how the churches adapted and were shaped by the forces that democratized Jacksonian America.

For further reading: William G. McLoughlin, *Modern Revivalism: Charles G. Finney to Billy Graham* (1959); Timothy L. Smith, *Revivalism and Social Reform in Mid-Nineteenth Century America* (1957); Alice Felt Tyler, *Freedom's Ferment: Phases of American Social History to 1860* (1944); Whitney R. Cross, *The Burned-over District: The Social and Intellectual History of Enthusiastic Religion in Western New York, 1800–1850* (1950); Sidney E. Mead, "Denominationalism: The Shape of Protestantism in America," *Church History*, XXIII (1954), 291-320.

This book, first published in 1835, has an important place not only in American religious history but in American social and intellectual history as well. Its importance to religious history has two dimensions. In the realm of theology it clearly marks the end of two centuries of Calvinism and the acceptance of pietistic evangelicalism as the predominant faith of the nation. In the realm of applied religion, as a textbook on how to promote revivals of religion, this book is the perennial classic to which all succeeding generations of revivalists have turned for authority and inspiration.

The volume's importance to American social and intellectual history lies in the fact that it constitutes a vigorous and dramatic expression of the religious side of the Era of the Common Man. In its underlying assumptions about nature, man, and society, it was in its way as ebullient an embodiment of the spirit of Jacksonian democracy as the speeches of Andrew Jackson, the editorials of John L. O'Sullivan and William Leggett, or the essays of Ralph Waldo Emerson. For in these lectures Finney gave characteristic expression to the views of those sincere believers in Christianity who took a middle ground between the ambitions of clerical Whigs, who hoped to erect a national church as a bulwark against atheistic mobocracy, and the efforts of those anticlerical Democrats who were trying to reduce Christianity to little more than an exalted system of ethics. Finney spoke particularly for those far-flung sons of New England who eventually abandoned both the Whigs and the Democrats to vote for the Republican Party of Abraham Lincoln. Opposing both the ecclesiastical pretensions of the conservatives and the freethinking propensities of the radicals, Finney stood for the evangelical outlook that became the prevailing one among middle-class churchgoers in mid-nineteenth century America. He believed, as the lectures in this book clearly testify, that a Christian nation must be based upon the devout personal faith in the revealed truth of God of each individual citizen. In this respect it might justly be claimed that he was more truly a spokesman of his age than any of the religious liberals or churchly Whigs who have commonly been granted that role.

Charles Grandison Finney, the son of a Revolutionary veteran and an heir of the Pilgrim tradition of seventeenth-century Massachusetts, was born in Warren, Connecticut, in 1792. He moved west with his family two years later, grew up in the "burnt-over district" of western New York, and in 1821, as the result of an intense religious experience, he gave up a promising career as a lawyer in order to become an itinerant evangelist. He was a tall, slim, handsome man with piercing blue eyes, sandy hair, and a burning conviction that he was "led by God" in his effort to convert and reform the nation. Because he was ordained as a Presbyterian minister and because orthodox Presbyterianism at this time was Calvinistic, many who have not read his works erroneously assume that Finney was a preacher of hellfire and damnation who excoriated the moral depravity of man and exalted the wrath of God. Because he ardently espoused such moral reforms as temperance, abolition, and Sabbatarianism, and because of his close association with such wealthy Whig merchants as Lewis and Arthur Tappan, David and William E. Dodge, and Anson G. Phelps, it has been commonly assumed that Finney was totally out of sympathy with the Jacksonian temper of his times. His famous revival meetings, conducted in towns and cities across the country in the second quarter of the nineteenth century, are mistaken for manifestations of a resurgent ecclesiasticism, a "Protestant Counter-Reformation" designed to put down the deistic radicalism of Tom Paine and Thomas Jefferson and to reassert Christian orthodoxy and clerical domination in the new nation. And despite the fact that in 1851 Finney became the President of Oberlin College, it is sometimes assumed that his evangelical theology brands him as anti-intellectual, antiscientific, and antiliberal.

Even a cursory reading of the *Lectures on Revivals* will soon dispel these misconceptions. Unlike the majority of his clerical colleagues, Finney was a child of his age, not an enemy of it. He had little use for Calvinism, and the basic philosophical and social principles underlying his thought were essentially the same as those associated with Jacksonian democracy. Like the Jacksonians, Finney had an ardent faith in progress, in the benevolence of God, and in the dignity and worth of the common man. Like the Jacksonians, he believed that the restrictive clerical and aristocratic traditions of the seventeenth and eighteenth centuries were out of date and that they must give way to a new and more liberal outlook if the nation was to continue to grow in peace, liberty, and prosperity under God. Finney was no backward-looking fundamentalist exhorter, longing for the good old days of Puritanism and inculcating a fear of hell to keep the wickedness of the common man in check. He was in fact just the opposite of a theocrat—he was a pietist. And that is why he spent his life at odds with the Calvinists of his day. He disliked man-made creeds; he saw no need for institutionalized denominational systems; he believed in the priesthood of all believers. His mission, as he saw it, was to create a universal Church based upon the fundamentals of the gospel. He sought to cut away the bonds of customs and liberate men from their blind obedience to the past. He wanted to help men free themselves from sin and learn to grow in wisdom and love as free Christian men and women. And he believed that the millennial age was about to dawn in the United States of America.

It is true that Finney never took the stump for Andrew Jackson. His antislavery convictions were sufficient to prevent this. Moreover, like Emerson, he preferred to vote against the party that shared his broad principles because he was convinced the other side had the more honest men. His pietistic evangelicalism made him see politics through moralistic eyes, and he cast his vote in terms of particular moral issues rather than in terms of party politics.

The clue to Finney's Jacksonian temper lies not in his attitude toward politics but in his attitude toward Calvinism. The first thing that strikes the reader of the *Lectures on Revivals* is the virulence of Finney's hostility toward traditional Calvinism and all it stood for. He denounced its doctrinal dogmas (which, as embodied in the Westminister Confession of Faith, he referred to elsewhere as "this wonderful theological fiction"); he rejected its concept of nature and the structure of the universe (especially its exaltation of the sovereign and miraculous power of God in regard to conversions and the promotion of revivals); he scorned its pessimistic attitude toward human nature and progress (particularly in regard to the freedom of the will); and he thoroughly deplored its hierarchical and legalistic polity (as embodied in the ecclesiastical system of the Presbyterian Church). Or to put it more succinctly, John Calvin's philosophy was theocentric and organic; Charles Finney's was anthropocentric and individualistic. It is little wonder that Finney was considered a renegade, a radical, and a "revolutionary" by so many of his strait-laced church brethren throughout his career. As one prominent Calvinist editor wrote in 1838 of Finney's revivals, "Who is not aware that the Church has been almost revolutionized within four or five years by means of such excitements?"

But this volume is more than a destructive attack upon "the traditions of the elders," as Finney scornfully referred to the old Calvinistic doctrines. It is a positive, ringing statement of the new religious, social, and intellectual philosophy that came to dominate popular American thought until well into the twentieth century—a philosophy that, however inconsistently, blended reason and faith, science and revelation, self-reliance and divine guidance, pragmatism and intuition, head and heart, moral self-denial and spiritual freedom, social reform and rugged individualism, humanitarianism and piety in a form perfectly adapted to the needs of the expanding and prospering American society. Within the broader frame of western civilization, Finney's faith, like that of the Jacksonians, was part and parcel of Thomas Reid's "Scottish Common Sense School" of philosophy, Jeremy Bentham's "philosophical radicalism," John Stuart Mill's "utilitarianism," Adam Smith's "laissez faire," plus that spongy modification of Jonathan Edwards' Calvinism in terms of John Wesley's Arminianism that is commonly called "evangelicalism." The one element that produced the tensile strength of this miscellaneous compound, and the strongest note in Finney's preaching, was the pietistic sectarianism he got from his separatist Pilgrim forebears.

Finney struck the keynote of the intellectual revolution for which this volume speaks in the very first lecture, when he stated it as axiomatic that a revival of religion "is not a miracle or dependent on a miracle. It is a purely philosophical result of the right use of the constituted means." This was obviously a direct contradiction of the theocentric cosmology of John Calvin and especially of the doctrines of God's arbitrary grace and inscrutable sovereignty that John Cotton and Jonathan Edwards had so vigorously upheld in America. Jonathan Edwards had described the famous revival in Northampton, Massachusetts, in 1734, as "a marvelous work of God," a "shower of divine blessing," which, like a shower of rain in a parched land, came miraculously through the divine hand of Providence. Finney, writing one hundred years later, insisted that the revivals with which he was so prominently connected in the years 1825–1835 were simply the result of cause and effect in which the revival preacher was the principal agent: "The connection between the right use of means for a revival and a revival is as philosophically sure as between the right use of means to raise grain and a crop of wheat." And as Finney went on to claim, the physical, psychological, and physiological laws of nature were now so well known (as perhaps they were not in Edwards' day) that it was clearly God's intention that men should make use of them to evangelize the world. Therefore, for the better advancement of God's kingdom, Finney designed the *Lectures on Revivals* to be a handbook, a how-to-do-it book, for ministers interested (as all ministers should be) in promoting revivals and winning souls. . . .

The truth of the matter is that the breakdown of Calvinism was one of the two or three great intellectual revolutions in American history, and a chronicle of its decline would constitute a history of almost a century of American civilization. Dr. Holmes's career indicated the revolution in science and medicine that accompanied the more naturalistic outlook of the post-Calvinistic era. In American literature a large segment of the romantic movement sprang from the nineteenth century's faith in man and nature and gave rise to a literary outburst later critics have called "the flowering of New England" and "the American renaissance." In philosophy the Transcendentalists produced their unique and talented contribution by inverting every tenet of Calvinism and making a virtue out of each inversion. The repudiation of the doctrines of original sin and an arbitrary God of wrath had its eccentric side in the perfectionist, the communitarian, and the physiological fads of the pre-Civil War era. And it had its ugly side in the spread-eagle oratory about "manifest destiny" and the "Order of the Star-Spangled Banner." Like all great intellectual revolutions the overthrow of Calvinism broke through the crust of custom and unleashed an uncontrollable flood of human energy in all areas of life. It is perhaps not too much to say that it provided the driving power which thrust the United States into the forefront of western civilization.

Finney's contribution to this revolution was made in the field of theology and ecclesiasticism. But he was not primarily a theologian or an ecclesiastic. He was primarily an evangelist, and as such he can best be understood in terms of the shifts in American religious life embodied in the first and second Great Awakenings.

To put the matter briefly, the first Great Awakening of 1725–1750, in which Edwards, Whitefield, Frelinghuysen, and the Tennents played major roles, had resulted in a restatement of seventeenth-century Calvinism in terms that made the individual more responsible than formerly for working out his salvation, without quite asserting that he could effectively attain it by any act of his own. As the theologians of the time put it, man had the natural ability to act rightly but he was morally unable to do so unless God, through the Holy Spirit, transformed or infused his soul with supernatural grace. The followers of Edwards in the Congregational and Presbyterian churches maintained the legalistic rigidity of his theology after 1750 without maintaining his homiletic fervor. The theology of the neo-Edwardeans, like Samuel Hopkins, Jonathan Edwards, Jr., Joseph Bellamy, Nathaniel Emmons, and Asa Burton, hardened into a series of arid formulae that produced endless quibbling among the clergy and increasing tedium, frustration, and skepticism among the churchgoers. The deistic ideology that underlay the Revolutionary zeal for human or natural rights aroused more fervor after 1765 than anything the churches were espousing. The demand for separation of church and state that began in Virginia in 1776 and ended in Massachusetts in 1833 was made easier by the desiccated state of theology in this period.

But the deistic anticlericalism of Ethan Allen, Thomas Paine, and Thomas Cooper went too far for the average American, who continued to respect the Word of God even when he found the words of His ministers incomprehensible. Toward the end of the eighteenth century, as the new nation stabilized its domestic and international position, a new interest in religion was stimulated by a group of itinerant evangelists—Presbyterians, Methodists, and Baptists—who rode through the newly settled frontier regions across the Appalachians preaching a new theology and holding four-day camp meetings under the trees to promote it. The Presbyterian Church in the Southwest was galvanized by great excitement and by grave schisms in 1804–1810 as a result of the new doctrines of Barton W. Stone, Finis Ewing, and Thomas Campbell. New Englanders also had a return to religious interest in the opening decades of the nineteenth century under the spirited but restrained preaching of Timothy Dwight, Lyman Beecher, and Asahel Nettleton, whose subtle modifications in New England Calvinism avoided the quarrels that rent the Presbyterian Church. And then in 1821 Finney began his astounding career as a revivalist in the middle colonies, starting in western New York and gradually moving eastward to the big cities of Philadelphia, New York, and Boston. He brought the Presbyterian and Congregational churches to their great schism of 1837 and completed the downfall of Calvinism.

The significant fact about this second Great Awakening (which can roughly be dated as 1795–1835) was that from the outset it minimized or denied entirely the arbitrary grace of God, which elected some to heaven but most to hell. The preachers of this awakening proceeded on the assumption that every individual had the free will and the moral ability to work out his own salvation. The five points of Calvinism, with their stress upon predestination and total depravity, were kept in the background even by revivalists who claimed to believe in the Westminster Confession. Instead, these revivalists concentrated upon putting new life into the dry bones of the churches by calling upon sinners to repent and submit to God without offering any clear doctrinal interpretations of what these terms meant. The average American, who had never been very fond of the mechanistic God of the deists, was ready to return to church when he found that an arbitrary God of wrath was being replaced by a comprehensible God of love and when he was told that religion was a reasonable service in which God merely asked the acceptance of a freely proffered salvation for all. It was an especial relief to be told that the Word of God plus the experience of receiving His Spirit was more important than adherence to any denominational creed or doctrinal confession. Between 1800 and 1835 church membership in America increased more than fivefold, considerably outdistancing the threefold increase in population.

To the more rigid Calvinist ministers who adhered closely to the standards of Edwards and the Westminster Confession the new revival was a mixed blessing. They were delighted at the multitude of new church members and the manifest evidence of divine blessings, but they soon began to question whether the bars of doctrine were not being lowered too far by some revivalists in their over-zealous efforts to fill the fold. By 1830 it was evident to the defenders of the Edwardean view of Calvinism that a stand would have to be taken against innovations all along the line if the faith of the founding fathers was to be maintained. The quarrel naturally centered in the Presbyterian Church, which since 1801 had been affiliated with the Congregationalists. These two denominations combined represented the most learned, numerous, and influential religious bodies in the nation. Their Plan of Union was consummated when the second Great Awakening was just getting under way. Its purpose was to prevent denominational quarreling among Calvinists over new converts in the West. Since Congregationalists and Presbyterians both claimed allegiance to the Westminster Confession and to the theology of Edwards there was thought to be no reason for competition between them. And since the Presbyterian form of church government was considered better suited to bringing order and stability to the frontier areas, most of the families that moved west from New England gave up their Congregationalism to form Presbyterian churches, especially in western New York, Ohio, Michigan, and Indiana. Nevertheless, these new Plan of Union (or "Presbygational") churches in the West more often chose pastors who had been trained at Yale, Andover, Williams, Middlebury, Hamilton, or in the home of some honored Congregational divine in New England than ministers trained at Princeton, Glasgow, Edinburgh, or under the guidance of the Scotch-Irish presbyteries of the Middle and Southern states.

As a result the doctrines taught in the Plan of Union territory were flavored with certain New England modifications of Calvinism that qualified the doctrines taught in strict Presbyterian churches. The neo-Edwardean theologians of New England honored Jonathan Edwards, as they did John Calvin, but they considered it possible to reinterpret his teachings in the light of further study and spiritual insight. And by 1830 many of the leading ministers of New England, particularly Lyman Beecher and Nathaniel W. Taylor, had so far departed from the old interpretations of Calvinism that they were openly being accused of heresy by their more rigid colleagues. However, Beecher and Taylor were not only adroit theological disputants, they were also ardent and successful revival preachers. By disclaiming any heretical tendencies in their views and by pointing to their revival converts as signs of divine approval of their ministries they made it very difficult for heresy-hunting Congregationalists and Presbyterians to bring them to account. And this was where Finney entered the drama.

Finney was a Plan of Union minister from Western New York. Ordained by a liberal "Presbyterian" presbytery and not having been trained in any theological school, he was unable and unwilling to split theological hairs in expressing his own divergence from what he called "hyper-Calvinism," whether it was of the Congregational or Presbyterian variety. Although he had been trained for the ministry by a graduate of Princeton Seminary, Finney had disavowed his belief in a strict interpretation of the Westminster Confession shortly after his ordination in 1824. His immediate and astounding success as a revivalist, preaching what came to be called "New School" theology (or the "New Divinity" or "New Haven theology") convinced him and many others in western New York that the Lord approved of his modifications of hyper-Calvinism or "Old School" Calvinism. . . .

While few of the New School Calvinists had departed quite so far from orthodoxy as Finney did in his *Lectures on Revivals* and his *Sermons on Various Subjects,* it was nevertheless apparent that in this review the Rev. Mr. Dod was throwing down the gauntlet to the whole group of theologians who were trying to pour the new wine of pietistic evangelicalism into the old bottles of Calvinism. "We tender him our thanks," said Dod of Finney, "for the substantial service he has done the church by exposing the naked deformities of the New Divinity." And he took every occasion to connect Finney with Beecher and Taylor during the course of his review.

Dod spelled out his complaints against Finney's theology (and the New Divinity in general) under three headings: the nature of God's government; the nature of sin and depravity; and the nature of regeneration and conversion. In each case he concluded that Finney was guilty of the heresy of Pelagianism. Pelagianism, the fifth-century heresy in opposition to which Augustine had formulated the predestinarian theory that constituted the basis of Calvinism, became the predominant heresy of the nineteenth century and is still deeply imbedded in Protestantism. Dod may have been unfair in laying the blame for its resurgence thus heavily upon Finney, nevertheless the fact that, as a responsible spokesman for the orthodox viewpoint, he did so, is another reason why Finney must rank as an important figure in American intellectual history. The charge is worth examining in some detail.

Finney's great error in relation to "the government of God," said Dod, was that he adopted the view (earlier put forward and then qualified by Nathaniel W. Taylor) "that God could not prevent the introduction of sin" in the world. This view was, as Dod saw it, advanced by Finney for the primary purpose of exalting the self-reliance of man at the expense of the sovereignty and omnipotence of God. Finney naturally claimed that his view was commensurate with God's sovereignty and that, more clearly that Calvinism, it placed upon men the responsibility for sinning against the moral law of God's government. This point of divine sovereignty arose in the very first lecture on revivals, where Finney defended the view that revivals are not miracles but are subject to the operations of cause and effect in which man has as important a part to play as God. The Calvinistic doctrine of God's sovereignty, Finney said, had been misunderstood. Many "supposed it to be such an arbitrary disposal of events, and particularly of the gift of his Spirit, as precluded rational employment of means for promoting a revival of religion." Finney denied that this view was justified either by Scripture or by experience. "Everything goes to show that God has connected means with the end through all the departments of his government—in nature and in grace." Of course, Finney went on, this does not justify the deistic concept of God as the great clockmaker of the universe. "He has not built the creation like a vast machine that will go on alone without his further care. He has not retired from the universe, to let it work for itself. This is mere atheism. . . . And yet every event in nature has been brought about by means. He neither administers providence nor grace with that sort of sovereignty that dispenses with the use of means." In short, the deists were wrong but so also were those Calvinists who talked about the arbitrary grace of God, which, like the wind, bloweth where it listeth and no man knows how or why.

The question of divine sovereignty came up again in even more significant form when Finney discussed the regeneration and conversion of individuals. Here, as Dod pointed out, Finney went so far in his theory of means and ends that he actually gave to the sinner the power to thwart the will of God by hardening his heart against the converting power of the Holy Spirit: "When the Son of God approaches you, gathering motives from heaven, earth, and hell and pours them in a focal blaze upon your mind, how is it that you are strong enough to resist? You . . . can exert such a giant strength, I had almost said the strength of Omnipotence, in resisting the infinite weight of motive that rolls upon you from every quarter of the universe to obey God." Could anything be more diametrically opposed to the Calvinist doctrine of irresistible grace?

Dod was particularly wroth with Finney's statement on the very first page of the *Lectures on Revivals* that (and the italics are Dod's) "God has found it *necessary to take advantage* of the excitability there is in mankind to produce powerful excitements among them before he *can* lead them to obey." If this were true, Dod noted, then "God, thwarted in his wishes and plans by the obstinacy of the human will, is literally grieved by the perverse conduct of men; and sinners may properly be exhorted, as they have been, to forsake their sins from a compassion for their suffering Maker!" This was to become a very common argument in evangelical preaching later in the century, but to Dod, as to any seventeenth- or eighteenth-century Calvinist, the idea was little short of blasphemy: "We know of nothing which ought more deeply to pain and shock the pious mind" than this, he said; "If the perverseness of man has been able in one instance to prevent God from accomplishing what he preferred, then may it in any instance obstruct the working of his preferences. Where then is the infinite and immutable blessedness of the Deity? . . . We can see, indeed, but little to decide our choice between such a God as this and no God."

What, in the broad range of intellectual history, is most significant about Finney's assault upon the Calvinist doctrine of God's unlimited and arbitrary sovereignty is that it so clearly made man and not God the measure of all things. Finney, like the deists of the Enlightenment, preferred to think of God simply as the Creator and Governor of the universe, the God of nature, who works according to the fixed laws of physics and of psychology that he has made known to man. In presenting God to the sinner, as Dod rightly pointed out, Finney "takes his stand amid the wonders of Creation" and, having pointed out the benevolence of God, the reasonableness of his commands, the utility of his moral law, and the wisdom of cause and effect, he then chastises the selfish, unreasonable, hardhearted sinner with having "set his unsanctified feet upon the principles of eternal righteousness, lifted up his hands against the throne of the Almighty, set at naught the authority of God and the rights of man!" When Presbyterian revivalists began to chastise sinners for setting God at naught and interfering with the rights of man, Calvinism was clearly dead. Finney was in effect saying that while God "proposes" the general terms of earthly and eternal life, it is man who "disposes." God offers the possibility for a happy universe, but man rejects it. Thus man is the captain of his fate, not God. And by this means Christianity was made to conform to the nineteenth century's optimistic belief in human progress, humanly controlled, toward an eventual utopian society, a New Eden, in which all men could voluntarily and joyfully live and work in harmony with all God's moral and spiritual laws, provided they would only "accept" or "get right with" God.

This self-reliant, optimistic outlook, which pervades all Finney's work, naturally collided with another basic tenet of Calvinism, and that was the doctrine of original sin, or the innate depravity of man. On this point Finney and Dod clashed swords over the interpretation of the prevailing theory of pure and applied psychology. Twentieth-century readers of Dod's review will at this point be apt to cry "a plague on both your houses," for the terminology of the old "faculty psychology" in which they argued is now as antiquated as it was inadequate. Even a novice in Freudian theory can punch holes in it. But it is not necessary to plunge into the ancient quagmire of nineteenth-century "mental science" in order to understand the importance of the intellectual issues at stake. Finney and Dod were here arguing the age-old question of the freedom of the will and with it the problem of whether human nature is basically and irremediably bad or whether it is basically good or reasonable and capable of improvement. Finney took the eighteenth-century view, the view of the Enlightenment (which he glossed over with a Christian veneer) that human nature is (with God's help) perfectible. Dod took the older view that even with God's help men are incurably sinful and while they remain on earth will always be so.

Theologically they were arguing over whether God was or was not the author of sin; psychologically they were trying to define the basis of human volition or motivation. Finney argued, with some justice, that as Calvinism was generally preached and understood, its doctrine of innate or natural depravity made God the author of sin because it defined man as a creature incapable of acting rightly. Hyper-Calvinists, said Finney, "have spoken of depravity, and of the pollutions of our nature, as if there were some moral depravity cleaving to, or incorporated with, the very substance of our being." To which Dod answered that Finney was confusing the sinner's moral inability (which Calvinists did believe in) with the theory of physical inability (which they did not believe in). According to Jonathan Edwards, men were physically capable of obeying God's laws but they were, because of Adam's sin, born with an innate or constitutional preference or disposition for evil (that is, for satisfying selfish or animal desires) that made them morally incapable of obeying God's laws or accepting His grace. Finney insisted that this theory of an innate constitutional preference or disposition toward evil in effect denied men freedom of will and thereby failed to make men morally responsible for their actions. He claimed that the Calvinists preached a theory of physical inability, whether they called it that or not, because they implied that the nature of man was so deformed at birth that only the supernatural action of the Holy Spirit could convert the mind (or the heart or the soul) into a state where it could (the Calvinist's said "would") act rightly. . . .

The clearest statement Finney ever made of his theory of regeneration appeared in the sermon, "Sinners Bound to Change Their Own Hearts," which was the first in his *Sermons on Various Subjects*. Finney repeated verbatim the central portion of this sermon in Lecture XII of his *Lectures on Revivals*; this is the famous metaphor in which he compared the conversion of a sinner to the way in which a man, walking in a reverie near Niagara Falls, was saved from falling over a cliff by a passer-by who shouted "Stop!" just in the nick of time. In explaining the metaphor Finney pointed out that there were four agencies at work saving the life of this foolish daydreamer: from the brink of destruction. Obviously the daydreamer is the sinner, the passer-by acting upon the dulled mind of the daydreamer to awaken him to his danger, and there was the action of the daydreamer himself in stopping short and turning back from the brink of destruction. Obviously the daydreamer is the sinner, the passer-by the revivalist, the word is the Scripture, and the force behind the word is the Holy Spirit.

In his review of Finney's books Dod rightly pointed out that Finney's theory of regeneration and conversion explicitly reduced the roles of God and the Holy Spirit to positions of equality with those of the revivalist and the sinner, while implicitly it almost pushed them out of the picture entirely. Finney's description of the agency of the Holy Spirit in regeneration, said Dod, was so limited that "it is strictly parenthetical" if not in fact "superfluous." Instead of supernaturally transforming the heart by "imparting a new relish for spiritual objects" or "implanting a new principle" into it, as the Calvinists taught, "the Spirit" in Finney's theory, said Dod, "merely presents the truth and the moral suasion of the truth regenerates the sinner, or rather, induces him to regenerate himself." This is the heart of Pelagianism, said Dod, and "we do utterly deny that man is able, in the sense which Mr. Finney contends for, to obey the divine commands" until such time as his heart is "renewed" by God. "Nor are we able to see," he went on, still speaking for all the Old School Calvinists, how a sinner can be turned from selfishness to benevolence, from sin to virtue, from enmity toward God to love of God "unless his mind be illuminated, his heart renewed, by the influence of the Holy Spirit." If "Mr. Finney asserts the perfect, unqualified ability of man to regenerate himself," Dod concluded, then he has forgotten the Bible. For Christ said, "No man can come to me except the Father which hath sent me, draw him," and Paul taught, "The natural man receiveth not the things of the spirit of God; neither can he know them, for they are spiritually discerned."

Finney's attempts to utilize such texts as "make to yourself a new heart" and "my son, give me thy heart" were distortions of the Bible, according to Dod. In order to make these texts support his view Finney was required to rely not upon the words themselves but upon an appeal to "our natural sense of justice" or to "the common sense of mankind" (an appeal, Dod might have added, often used by Paine and the deists when they sought to discredit the Bible). Finney maintained that the text "make you a new heart and a new spirit, for why will ye die," and others like it, were direct commands from God to all sinners ordering them to effect their own salvation. If God, said Finney, commands his creatures to do something, it is only common sense to believe that he gives them the ability to obey. "Obligation and ability are commensurate" was Finney's famous phrase for it. And he insisted that if the Calvinists taught that men could not change their own hearts then they were either denying the word of God or else were making "God an infinite tyrant."

Although Dod maintained that "the Bible does not inform us that there is any tyranny in God's commanding men to do what they cannot do" and although he claimed that "the common sense of mankind" substantiated the Calvinist view of inability (as for example in such cases as that of "a man under the influence of any dominant passion," such as drink or gluttony, who knows he ought to reform but cannot), nevertheless Finney's argument was clearly more in harmony with the spirit of the age than Dod's. Americans who had wrested their political freedom from the British Empire and their economic self-sufficiency from the seas and the forests of the New World were ready to believe with Finney that God had endowed them with the intelligence, the conscience, and the will power to wrest their spiritual freedom from the grip of Satan. And as good democrats who had, under Jacksonian leadership, won control of American politics from the Federalist aristocrats by laws granting universal manhood suffrage, "the common sense people" (as Finney called them) were persuaded rather than shocked, as Dod was, by Finney's declaration that "the object of the ministry is to get all the people to feel that the devil has no right to rule this world but that they ought all to give themselves to God and vote in the Lord Jesus Christ as the governor of the universe."

In emphasizing this rationalistic and Pelagian aspect of Finney's doctrines, however, it is necessary to remember, as Dod did not do, that there was also a strong pietistic strain in Finney's theology. This is amply demonstrated in the *Lectures on Revivals* by his three lectures on prayer and his lecture on the need for being "filled with the Spirit." For all his lawyer-like logic, for all his comparisons of the Holy Ghost to an advocate arguing before a jury, and his carefully reasoned arguments taken step by step, there was a strong element of mysticism about Finney. (In this regard he again resembles Jonathan Edwards, whom he quotes.)

Time and again in his lectures he speaks of prayer as a means of obtaining close communion with God. He even speaks of prophecies and coincidences bordering on miracles that were brought about by "the prayer of faith." Finney's revivals, like those of the second Great Awakening in general, were evidence of a resurgent pietism in American Protestantism, a pietism that had been dormant but not dead since the first Great Awakening. The hysterical outbursts in the frontier camp meetings demonstrated just how emotionally and spiritually starved by the arid legalism and formalism of Old School Calvinism the average, unsophisticated churchgoers were. Among the more devout, continual fasting and agonizing all-night prayer meetings became common. The ultimate limit of pietism came with the various perfectionist movements after 1830 and the adventist movement led by William Miller. To most Old School Calvinists, and even to such dignified New School ministers as Beecher and Taylor, pietism was far too powerful an explosive to be trusted. To their minds Finney was guilty of encouraging the worst excesses of the camp meeting exhorters when he spoke approvingly (as he does in Lecture IV of this volume) of a person who prayed so fervently that his nose bled. Finney himself, in the early days of his ministry prayed and fasted so rigorously, "without ceasing," that he frequently had visions in which "a light perfectly ineffable, shone in my soul" and "almost prostrated me to the ground." And throughout his career Finney continually spoke of his being "led by the Spirit" or "instructed by God." He implored his readers in the *Lectures on Revivals* to learn to watch for "leadings of the Spirit," and when these came to follow them without hesitation. If you wish to be filled with the Spirit, he said, "you must yield to his softest and gentlest motions and watch to learn what he would have you do, and yield yourself up to his guidance." This deep emotional reliance upon the leading of God's Spirit distinguishes the radical pietistic evangelical from the conservative ecclesiastical evangelical and indicates why both Beecher and Dod considered Finney a revolutionary. It also indicates a common bond between Finney's anti-ecclesiasticism and the Jacksonian's anticlericalism. Egalitarian reliance upon the innate common sense of the common man is, after all, only a secular form of the doctrine of the priesthood of all believers. . . .

One final remark is worth making about the Rev. Albert Dod's definitive critique of Finney's *Lectures on Revivals* from the Old School point of view. There can be no doubt that Dod, like Beecher and Nettleton in 1827, saw Finney as a "revolutionary" in more ways than in terms of theology and new measures. Fanaticism to all of these men was demagoguery, and demagoguery had social and political overtones that, as conservatives, these men feared and disliked. Dod noted that Finney's revivalism had already spread desolation through western New York, the "burnt-over region." In his review he expressed the fear that "if it should affect still larger masses . . . it will spread desolation and ruin" throughout the nation for ages to come. The association of gentlemen at Princeton were not great admirers of the self-reliant common men who heard Finney so gladly. They suspected that the lower classes throughout the United States were somehow getting out of hand under Jacksonian leadership. "The great improvements in the mechanic arts and the wide diffusion of knowledge have given a strong impulse to the popular mind," said Dod, "and everywhere the social mass is seen to be in such a state of agitation that the slightest breath may make it heave and foam. This being the case, should religion fall in with the excitement and institute measures for fostering it up to a certain point that she may gain a favorable moment for presenting her claims? We had thought that one great object of religion was to allay this undue excitement of the human mind; to check its feverish outgoings towards earthly objects and to teach it without hurry or distraction, in self-collectedness, to put forth its energies in a proper direction and to their best advantage."

These sentences provide a kind of key to the growing gap between the outlook of the Old School Calvinists and the New School Calvinists. It would be too much to say that the Old School looked upon religion as the opiate of the masses or even as a utilitarian method by which the better classes might keep "the social masses" in check. But it would not be wholly inaccurate to see the Old School as defenders of the status quo, aristocratic in temper, and generally unsympathetic to the democratic egalitarianism and optimistic self-reliance that characterized the spirit of the second quarter of the nineteenth century. The Old School clung to the ideal of an organic Christian society guided by the spiritual leadership of the clergy; the New School stood for the individualistic view of society in which each citizen made his own peace with God and went his own way in life. And to this extent Finney's "revolutionary" theology and revival measures, formed on the frontier and based upon the common-sense reasoning of the common man, deserve to be considered as part and parcel of the Jacksonian revolution in American social and intellectual history. This estimate of his work receives strong substantiation from the social philosophy revealed in the *Lectures on Revivals* as well as in all his other writings.

If the essence of Finney's Jacksonian temper lies in his attitude toward progress, this in turn is closely connected with his doctrines of millennialism, disinterested benevolence, and perfectionism. Progress Finney defined as the working out of God's will, and since God was by definition benevolent, His ultimate aim was to produce the great possible happiness in the universe. Because Finney no longer accepted the Calvinist view of God's inscrutable sovereignty and of man's ineradicable depravity and because he did not believe that the Bible justified the view that only a few predestined elect were eligible for salvation, he saw no reason why the whole world might not someday be made up of converted Christians living in brotherly love. Nor did he doubt that as the world became increasingly Christian through the conversion of more and more individuals it would become increasingly happy and prosperous. Men, especially regenerated men, would grow in wisdom, learn all the laws of science, and someday create a perfect utopia which would start the millennium of God's kingdom on earth. When he accepted the post as professor of theology at Oberlin early in 1835 (while still in the midst of writing his lectures on revivalism), he expressly did so in order to help educate "a new race of revival ministers," who would constitute the advance guard of the world-wide evangelistic movement.

Finney was sufficiently patriotic to believe that the United States was to be the first nation in which the whole population would be completely converted. Unlike those theocratically inclined Calvinists (Old School and New School) who saw an inevitable conflict between democracy and religion, Finney believed that democracy was the form of government most approved by God. There is an illuminating chapter on "Human Government" in his *Systematic Theology* (a book based upon his lectures at Oberlin and first published in 1846). In this chapter he stated explicitly that a republic is a "less pure form of self-government" than a democracy, and "a democracy is in many respects the most desirable form of government." In 1776 God, who controls the outcome of all revolutions (as John Locke said), permitted Americans to establish a republican form of government instead of continuing as subjects of a monarchy, because "God always allows his children as much liberty as they are prepared to enjoy" and "the intelligence and virtue of our Puritan forefathers rendered a monarchy an unnecessary burden." Consequently, if Americans continued to grow still more intelligent and virtuous, it was probable that God, in his benevolence, would someday grant them a democratic form of complete self-government that would be tantamount to a withering away of the state. Finney of course recognized the possibility of a nation's backsliding in virtue and hence slipping into a monarchy or a despotism, but he did not think this would happen in the United States where revivals were flourishing, education was expanding, and social reform was overcoming one evil after another. . . .

In the light of Finney's theology and social philosophy it is of some interest to compare briefly his views with those of a typical Jacksonian spokesman like John L. O'Sullivan in order to see how much they had in common. O'Sullivan, who was the part-owner and editor of the *United States Magazine and Democratic Review,* is generally acknowledged to have been a particularly articulate and representative spokesman of the Jacksonian spirit. In the first number of his newspaper, in October 1837, he issued a statement of his political and social philosophy that is often quoted as a manifesto of the age. Among the beliefs that O'Sullivan here espoused were "the principle of democratic republicanism," "an abiding confidence in the virtue, intelligence, and full capacity for self-government of the great mass of our people," and a deep-seated dislike for those "aristocratic interests" or "better classes" who claim a "more enlightened wisdom" than the average man and therefore a greater right to govern. Finney would have agreed with all of these beliefs. O'Sullivan then went on to advocate "the general diffusion of knowledge" among all classes, to acknowledge "the moral elements implanted by its Creator in human society," and to profess "a true and living faith in the existence and attributes of that Creator." Finney used more theological and Scriptural terminology, but he would have endorsed all of this. In his argument for the view that that government is best which governs least, O'Sullivan, like Finney, saw "the democratic principle walking hand in hand with the sister spirit of Christianity" down through time until "our theory and practice of government shall be sifted and analyzed down to the lowest point of simplicity consistent with the preservation of some degree of national organization." O'Sullivan attacked men, like Beecher and Dod, who "cast the weight of their social influence against the cause of democracy under the false prejudice of an affinity between it and infidelity." The cause of Democracy "is the cause of Christianity" he asserted. And just as Finney attacked the dead hand of Calvinism for trying to preserve the outmoded "traditions of the elders," so O'Sullivan argued that progress depended upon avoiding "that specious sophistry by which old evils always struggle to perpetuate themselves by appealing to our veneration for the wisdom of our fathers." Like Finney, O'Sullivan praised the great step forward made by those who led the American Revolution and declared that Americans were "a chosen people" with a "glorious destiny," which would be guided by the unseen hand of Providence. The whole of this manifesto breathes the optimistic faith in God, in man, in America, and in the future that underlies Finney's fervent pietism. Both men saw God as a benevolent Creator who has endowed humankind with moral principles and who requires of all men the abandonment of selfish desires and a devotion to the reformation of the world. There is even in O'Sullivan something of Finney's distrust of the wealth and social pretensions of the *nouveaux riches* of the wicked cities. O'Sullivan deprecates the rising "cities, where wealth accumulates, where luxury gradually unfolds its corrupting tendencies, where aristocratic habits and social classifications form and strengthen themselves, where the congregation of men stimulates and exaggerates all ideas."

There is no denying, of course, that there was a strong tinge of rationalism, free thought, and anticlericalism in the Jacksonian spirit, which runs directly counter to Finney's evangelical temper. And, too, the Jacksonian politicians were opposed to such moral reforms as temperance, Sabbath legislation, and abolition, just as Finney was uninterested in the political and economic reforms of the party platform. Finney probably shared the view of his close friend Lewis Tappan regarding Andrew Jackson. Tappan stated that the General was "a very unfit man to be at the head of the government." But there were many reasons why a pietist might dislike Jackson without disliking the principles of Jacksonian democracy. And it can be said that Finney and Jackson, each in his own way, were striving for much the same kind of free, individualistic, and egalitarian society.

20 / Some Themes of Counter-Subversion: An Analysis of Anti-Masonic, Anti-Catholic, and Anti-Mormon Literature

David Brion Davis

America has always been a nation of men on the move and a nation of immigrants. But during the second quarter of the nineteenth century—the years historians call approvingly or mockingly the Age of Jackson—internal mobility within the United States and foreign immigration to it accelerated at rates that kept pace with the transportation and economic revolutions. First, after the War of 1812, came large-scale movements from the farm areas of the eastern seaboard extending from northern New England to Georgia, to new lands in western New York and across the Appalachian chain. Although immigration had subsided early in the period between 1825 and 1850, by the 1840's it picked up again, and by the end of the decade it became an avalanche, with Irish Catholics comprising the bulk of the newcomers.

Both forces worked to weaken the social structures of traditional America, and both let loose or stimulated negative reactions among those frightened by social change and apprehensive over the existence of alleged perils to American institutions. David Brion Davis in the following article examines three organizational forms of this negative reaction and attempts to show what was common to all three, anti-Masonry, nativism, and anti-Mormonism. A conspiratorial element characterized the movements' philosophies, revealing a relationship between radical political groups and a conspiracy or devil theory that has persisted in America to this day.

For further reading: Whitney R. Cross, *The Burned-Over District: The Social and Intellectual History of Enthusiastic Religion in Western New*

Mississippi Valley Historical Review, XLVII (September 1960), 205–224. Reprinted by permission.

York, 1800–1850 (1950); Ray Allen Billington, *The Protestant Crusade, 1800–1860* (1938); Darrell W. Overdyke, *The Know-Nothing Party in the South* (1950); Fawn M. Brodie, *No Man Knows My History: The Life of Joseph Smith the Mormon Prophet* (1945).

During the second quarter of the nineteenth century, when danger of foreign invasion appeared increasingly remote, Americans were told by various respected leaders that Freemasons had infiltrated the government and had seized control of the courts, that Mormons were undermining political and economic freedom in the West, and that Roman Catholic priests, receiving instructions from Rome, had made frightening progress in a plot to subject the nation to popish despotism. This fear of internal subversion was channeled into a number of powerful counter movements which attracted wide public support. The literature produced by these movements evoked images of a great American enemy that closely resembled traditional European sterotypes of conspiracy and subversion. In Europe, however, the idea of subversion implied a threat to the established order—to the king, the church, or the ruling aristocracy—rather than to ideals or a way of life. If free Americans borrowed their images of subversion from frightened kings and uneasy aristocrats, these images had to be shaped and blended to fit American conditions. The movements would have to come from the people, and the themes of counter-subversion would be likely to reflect their fears, prejudices, hopes, and perhaps even unconscious desires.

There are obvious dangers in treating such reactions against imagined subversion as part of a single tendency or spirit of an age. Anti-Catholicism was nourished by ethnic conflict and uneasiness over immigration in the expanding cities of the Northeast; anti-Mormonism arose largely from a contest for economic and political power between western settlers and a group that voluntarily withdrew from society and claimed the undivided allegiance of its members. Anti-Masonry, on the other hand, was directed against a group thoroughly integrated in American society and did not reflect a clear division of economic, religious, or political interests. Moreover, anti-Masonry gained power in the late 1820's and soon spent its energies as it became absorbed in national politics; anti-Catholicism reached its maximum force in national politics a full generation later; anti-Mormonism, though increasing in intensity in the 1850's, became an important national issue only after the Civil War. These movements seem even more widely separated when we note that Freemasonry was traditionally associated with anti-Catholicism and that Mormonism itself absorbed considerable anti-Masonic and anti-Catholic sentiment.

Despite such obvious differences, there were certain similarities in these campaigns against subversion. All three gained widespread support in the northeastern states within the space of a generation; anti-Masonry and anti-Catholicism resulted in the sudden emergence of separate political parties; and in 1856 the new Republican party explicitly condemned the Mormons' most controversial institution. The movements of counter-subversion differed markedly in historical origin, but as the image of an un-American conspiracy took form in the nativist press, in sensational exposés, in the countless fantasies of treason and mysterious criminality, the lines separating Mason, Catholic, and Mormon became almost indistinguishable.

The similar pattern of Masonic, Catholic, and Mormon subversion was frequently noticed by alarmist writers. The *Anti-Masonic Review* informed its readers in 1829 that whether one looked at Jesuitism or Freemasonry, "the organization, the power, and the secret operation, are the same; except that Freemasonry is much the more secret and complicated of the two." William Hogan, an ex-priest and vitriolic anti-Catholic, compared the menace of Catholicism with that of Mormonism. And many later anti-Mormon writers agreed with Josiah Strong that Brigham Young "out-popes the Roman" and described the Mormon hierarchy as being similar to the Catholic. It was probably not accidental   that Samuel F. B. Morse analyzed the Catholic conspiracy in essentially the same terms his father had used in exposing the Society of the Illuminati, supposedly a radical branch of Freemasonry, or that writers of sensational fiction in the 1840's and 1850's depicted an atheistic and unprincipled Catholic Church obviously modeled on Charles Brockden Brown's earlier fictional version of the Illuminati.

If Masons, Catholics, and Mormons bore little resemblance to one another in actuality, as imagined enemies they merged into a nearly common sterotype. Behind specious professions of philanthropy or religious sentiment, nativists discerned a group of unscrupulous leaders plotting to subvert the American social order. Though rank-and-file members were not individually evil, they were blinded and corrupted by a persuasive ideology that justified treason and gross immorality in the interest of the subversive group. Trapped in the meshes of a machine-like organization, deluded by a false sense of loyalty and moral obligation, these dupes followed orders like professional soldiers and labored unknowingly to abolish free society, to enslave their fellow men, and to overthrow divine principles of law and justice. Should an occasional member free himself from bondage to superstition and fraudulent authority, he could still be disciplined by the threat of death or dreadful tortures. There were no limits to the ambitious designs of leaders equipped with such organizations. According to nativist prophets, they chose to subvert American society because control of America meant control of the world's destiny.

Some of these beliefs were common in earlier and later European interpretations of conspiracy. American images of Masonic, Catholic, and Mormon subversion were no doubt a compound of traditional myths concerning Jacobite agents, scheming Jesuits, and fanatical heretics, and of dark legends involving the Holy Vehm and Rosicrucians. What distinguished the stereotypes of Mason, Catholic, and Mormon was the way in which they were seen to embody those traits that were precise antitheses of American ideals. The subversive group was essentially an inverted image of Jacksonian democracy and the cult of the common man; as such it not only challenged the dominant values but stimulated those suppressed needs and yearnings that are unfulfilled in a mobile, rootless, and individualistic society. It was therefore both frightening and fascinating.

It is well known that expansion and material progress in the Jacksonian era evoked a fervid optimism and that nationalists became intoxicated with visions of America's millennial glory. The simultaneous growth of prosperity and social democracy seemed to prove that Providence would bless a nation that allowed her citizens maximum liberty. When each individual was left free to pursue happiness in his own way, unhampered by the tyranny of custom or special privilege, justice and well-being would inevitably emerge. But if a doctrine of laissez-faire individualism seemed to promise material expansion and prosperity, it also raised disturbing problems. As one early anti-Mormon writer expressed it: What was to prevent liberty and popular sovereignty from sweeping away "the old landmarks of Christendom, and the glorious old common law of our fathers"? How was the individual to preserve a sense of continuity with the past, or identify himself with a given cause or tradition? What, indeed, was to insure a common loyalty and a fundamental unity among the people?

Such questions acquired a special urgency as economic growth intensified mobility, destroyed old ways of life, and transformed traditional symbols of status and prestige. Though most Americans took pride in their material progress, they also expressed a yearning for reassurance and security, for unity in some cause transcending individual self-interest. This need for meaningful group activity was filled in part by religious revivals, reform movements, and a proliferation of fraternal orders and associations. In politics Americans tended to assume the posture of what Marvin Meyers has termed "venturesome conservatives," mitigating their acquisitive impulses by an appeal for unity against extraneous forces that allegedly threatened a noble heritage of republican ideals. Without abandoning a belief in progress through laissez-faire individualism, the Jacksonians achieved a sense of unity and righteousness by styling themselves as restorers of tradition. Perhaps no theme is so evident in the Jacksonian era as the strained attempt to provide America with a glorious heritage and a noble destiny. With only a loose and often ephemeral attachment to places and institutions, many Americans felt a compelling need to articulate their loyalties, to prove their faith, and to demonstrate their allegiance to certain ideals and institutions. By so doing they acquired a sense of self-identity and personal direction in an otherwise rootless and shifting environment.

But was abstract nationalism sufficient to reassure a nation strained by sectional conflict, divided by an increasing number of sects and associations, and perplexed by the unexpected consequences of rapid growth? One might desire to protect the Republic against her enemies, to preserve the glorious traditions of the Founders, and to help insure continued expansion and prosperity, but first it was necessary to discover an enemy by distinguishing subversion from simple diversity. If Freemasons seemed to predominate in the economic and political life of a given area, was one's joining them shrewd business judgment or a betrayal of republican tradition? Should Maryland citizens heed the warnings of anti-Masonic itinerants, or conclude that anti-Masonry was itself a conspiracy hatched by scheming Yankees? Were Roman Catholics plotting to destroy public schools and a free press, the twin guardians of American democracy, or were they exercising democratic rights of self-expression and self-protection? Did equality of opportunity and equality before the law mean that Americans should accept the land claims of Mormons or tolerate as jurors men who "swear that they have wrought miracles and supernatural cures"? Or should one agree with the Reverend Finis Ewing that "the 'Mormons' are the common enemies of mankind and ought to be destroyed"?

Few men questioned traditional beliefs in freedom of conscience and the right of association. Yet what was to prevent "all the errors and worn out theories of the Old World, of schisms in the early Church, the monkish age and the rationalistic period," from flourishing in such salubrious air? Nativists often praised the work of benevolent societies, but they were disturbed by the thought that monstrous conspiracies might also "show kindness and patriotism, when it is necessary for their better concealment; and oftentimes do much good for the sole purpose of getting a better opportunity to do evil." When confronted by so many sects and associations, how was the patriot to distinguish the loyal from the disloyal? It was clear that mere disagreement over theology or economic policy was invalid as a test, since honest men disputed over the significance of baptism or the wisdom of protective tariffs. But neither could one rely on expressions of allegiance to common democratic principles, since subversives would cunningly profess to believe in freedom and toleration of dissent as long as they remained a powerless minority.

As nativists studied this troubling question, they discovered that most groups and denominations claimed only a partial loyalty from their members, freely subordinating themselves to the higher and more abstract demands of the Constitution, Christianity, and American public opinion. Moreover, they openly exposed their objects and activities to public scrutiny and exercised little discrimination in enlisting members. Some groups, however, dominated a larger portion of their members' lives, demanded unlimited allegiance as a condition of membership, and excluded certain activities from the gaze of a curious public.

Of all governments, said Richard Rush, ours was the one with most to fear from secret societies, since popular sovereignty by its very nature required perfect freedom of public inquiry and judgment. In a virtuous republic why should anyone fear publicity or desire to conceal activities, unless those activities were somehow contrary to the public interest? When no one could be quite sure what the public interest was, and when no one could take for granted a secure and well-defined place in the social order, it was most difficult to acknowledge legitimate spheres of privacy. Most Americans of the Jacksonian era appeared willing to tolerate diversity and even eccentricity, but when they saw themselves excluded and even barred from witnessing certain proceedings, they imagined a "mystic power" conspiring to enslave them.

Readers might be amused by the first exposures of Masonic ritual, since they learned that pompous and dignified citizens, who had once impressed non-Masons with allusions to high degrees and elaborate ceremonies, had in actuality been forced to stand blindfolded and clad in ridiculous garb, with a long rope noosed around their necks. But genuine anti-Masons were not content with simple ridicule. Since intelligent and distinguished men had been members of the fraternity, "it must have in its interior something more than the usual revelations of its mysteries declare." Surely leading citizens would not meet at night and undergo degrading and humiliating initiations just for the sake of novelty. The alleged murder of William Morgan raised an astonishing public furor because it supposedly revealed the inner secret of Freemasonry. Perverted by a false ideology, Masons had renounced all obligations to the general public, to the laws of the land, and even to the command of God. Hence they threatened not a particular party's program or a denomination's creed, but stood opposed to all justice, democracy, and religion.

The distinguishing mark of Masonic, Catholic, and Mormon conspiracies was a secrecy that cloaked the members' unconditional loyalty to an autonomous body. Since the organizations had corrupted the private moral judgment of their members, Americans could not rely on the ordinary forces of progress to spread truth and enlightenment among their ranks. Yet the affairs of such organizations were not outside the jurisdiction of democratic government, for no body politic could be asked to tolerate a power that was designed to destroy it. Once the true nature of subversive groups was thoroughly understood, the alternatives were as clear as life and death. How could democracy and Catholicism coexist when, as Edward Beecher warned, "The systems are diametrically opposed: one must and will exterminate the other"? Because Freemasons had so deeply penetrated state and national governments, only drastic remedies could restore the nation to its democratic purity. And later, Americans faced an "irrepressible conflict" with Mormonism, for it was said that either free institutions or Mormon despotism must ultimately annihilate the other.

We may well ask why nativists magnified the division between unpopular minorities and the American public, so that Masons, Catholics, and Mormons seemed so menacing that they could not be accorded the usual rights and privileges of a free society. Obviously the literature of counter-subversion reflected concrete rivalries and conflicts of interest between competing groups, but it is important to note that the subversive bore no racial or ethnic stigma and was not even accused of inherent depravity. Since group membership was a matter of intellectual and emotional loyalty, no *physical* barrier prevented a Mason, Catholic, or Mormon from apostatizing and joining the dominant in-group, providing always that he escaped assassination from his previous masters. This suggests that counter-subversion was more than a rationale for group rivalry and was related to the general problem of ideological unity and diversity in a free society. When a "system of delusion" insulated members of a group from the unifying and disciplining force of public opinion, there was no authority to command an allegiance to common principles. This was why oaths of loyalty assumed great importance for nativists. Though the ex-Catholic William Hogan stated repeatedly that Jesuit spies respected no oaths except those to the Church, he inconsistently told Masons and Odd Fellows that they could prevent infiltration by requiring new members to swear they were not Catholics. It was precisely the absence of distinguishing outward traits that made the enemy so dangerous, and true loyalty so difficult to prove.

When the images of different enemies conform to a similar pattern, it is highly probable that this pattern reflects important tensions within a given culture. The themes of nativist literature suggest that its authors simplified problems of personal insecurity and adjustment to bewildering social change by trying to unite Americans of diverse political, religious, and economic interests against a common enemy. Just as revivalists sought to stimulate Christian fellowship by awakening men to the horrors of sin, so nativists used apocalyptic images to ignite human passions, destroy selfish indifference, and join patriots in a cohesive brotherhood. Such themes were only faintly secularized. When God saw his "lov'd Columbia" imperiled by the hideous monster of Freemasonry, He realized that only a martyr's blood could rouse the hearts of the people and save them from bondage to the Prince of Darkness. By having God will Morgan's death, this anti-Mason showed he was more concerned with national virtue and unity than with Freemasonry, which was only a providential instrument for testing republican strength.

Similarly, for the anti-Catholic "this brilliant new world" was once "young and beautiful; it abounded in all the luxuries of nature; it promised all that was desirable to man." But the Roman Church, seeing "these irresistible temptations, thirsting with avarice and yearning for the reestablishment of her falling greatness, soon commenced pouring in among its unsuspecting people hoardes of Jesuits and other friars." If Americans were to continue their narrow pursuit of self-interest, oblivious to the "Popish colleges, and nunneries, and monastic institutions," indifferent to manifold signs of corruption and decay, how could the nation expect "that the moral breezes of heaven should breathe upon her, and restore to her again that strong and healthy constitution, which her ancestors have left to her sons"? The theme of an Adamic fall from paradise was horrifying, but it was used to inspire determined action and thus unity. If Methodists were "criminally indifferent" to the Mormon question, and if "avaricious merchants, soulless corporations, and a subsidized press" ignored Mormon iniquities, there was all the more reason that the *will of the people* must prevail."

Without explicitly rejecting the philosophy of laissez-faire individualism, with its toleration of dissent and innovation, nativist literature conveyed a sense of common dedication to a noble cause and sacred tradition. Though the nation had begun with the blessings of God and with the noblest institutions known to man, the people had somehow become selfish and complacent, divided by petty disputes, and insensitive to signs of danger. In his sermons attacking such self-interest, such indifference to public concerns, and such a lack of devotion to common ideals and sentiments, the nativist revealed the true source of his anguish. Indeed, he seemed at times to recognize an almost beneficent side to subversive organizations, since they joined the nation in a glorious crusade and thus kept it from moral and social distintegration.

The exposure of subversion was a means of promoting unity, but it also served to clarify national values and provide the individual ego with a sense of high moral sanction and imputed righteousness. Nativists identified themselves repeatedly with a strangely incoherent tradition in which images of Pilgrims, Minute Men, Founding Fathers, and true Christians appeared in a confusing montage. Opposed to this heritage of stability and perfect integrity, to this society founded on the highest principles of divine and natural law, were organizations formed by the grossest frauds and impostures, and based on the wickedest impulses of human nature. Bitterly refuting Masonic claims to ancient tradition and Christian sanction, anti-Masons charged that the Order was of recent origin, that it was shaped by Jews, Jesuits, and French atheists as an engine for spreading infidelity, and that it was employed by kings and aristocrats to undermine republican institutions. If the illustrious Franklin and Washington had been duped by Masonry, this only proved how treacherous was its appeal and how subtly persuasive were its pretensions. Though the Catholic Church had an undeniable claim to tradition, nativists argued that it had originated in stupendous frauds and forgeries "in comparison with which the forgeries of Mormonism are completely thrown into the shade." Yet anti-Mormons saw an even more sinister conspiracy based on the "shrewd cunning" of Joseph Smith, who convinced gullible souls that he conversed with angels and received direct revelations from the Lord.

By emphasizing the fraudulent character of their opponents' claims, nativists sought to establish the legitmacy and just authority of American institutions. Masonic rituals, Roman Catholic sacraments, and Mormon revelations were preposterous hoaxes used to delude naïve or superstitious minds; but public schools, a free press, and jury trials were eternally valid prerequisites for a free and virtuous society.

Moreover, the finest values of an enlightened nation stood out in bold relief when contrasted with the corrupting tendencies of subversive groups. Perversion of the sexual instinct seemed inevitably to accompany religious error. Deprived of the tender affections of normal married love, shut off from the elevating sentiments of fatherhood, Catholic priests looked on women only as insensitive objects for the gratification of their frustrated desires. In similar fashion polygamy struck at the heart of a morality based on the inspiring influence of woman's affections: "It renders man coarse, tyrannical, brutal, and heartless. It deals death to all sentiments of true manhood. It enslaves and ruins woman. It crucifies every God-given feeling of her nature." Some anti-Mormons concluded that plural marriage could only have been established among foreigners who had never learned to respect women. But the more common explanation was that the false ideology of Mormonism had deadened the moral sense and liberated man's wild sexual impulse from the normal restraints of civilization. Such degradation of women and corruption of man served to highlight the importance of democratic marriage, a respect for women, and careful cultivation of the finer sensibilities.

But if nativist literature was a medium for articulating common values and exhorting individuals to transcend self-interest and join in a dedicated union against evil, it also performed a more subtle function. Why, we may ask, did nativist literature dwell so persistently on themes of brutal sadism and sexual immorality? Why did its authors describe sin in such minute details, endowing even the worst offenses of their enemies with a certain fascinating appeal?

Freemasons, it was said, could commit any crime and indulge any passion when "upon the square," and Catholics and Mormons were even less inhibited by internal moral restraints. Nativists expressed horror over this freedom from conscience and conventional morality, but they could not conceal a throbbing note of envy. What was it like to be a member of a cohesive brotherhood that casually abrogated the laws of God and man, enforcing unity and obedience with dark and mysterious powers? As nativists speculated on this question, they projected their own fears and desires into a fantasy of licentious orgies and fearful punishments.

Such a projection of forbidden desires can be seen in the exaggeration of the sterotyped enemy's powers, which made him appear at times as a virtual superman. Catholic and Mormon leaders, never hindered by conscience or respect for traditional morality, were curiously superior to ordinary Americans in cunning, in exercising power over others, and especially in captivating gullible women. It was an ancient theme of anti-Catholic literature that friars and priests were somehow more potent and sexually attractive than married laymen, and were thus astonishingly successful at seducing supposedly virtuous wives. Americans were cautioned repeatedly that no priest recognized Protestant marriages as valid, and might consider any wife legitimate prey. Furthermore, priests had access to the pornographic teachings of Dens and Liguori, sinister names that aroused the curiosity of anti-Catholics, and hence learned subtle techniques of seduction perfected over the centuries. Speaking with the authority of an ex-priest, William Hogan described the shocking result: "I have seen husbands unsuspiciously and hospitably entertaining the very priest who seduced their wives in the confessional, and was the parent of some of the children who sat at the same table with them, each of the wives unconscious of the other's guilt, and the husbands of both, not even suspecting them." Such blatant immorality was horrifying, but everyone was apparently happy in this domestic scene, and we may suspect that the image was not entirely repugnant to husbands who, despite their respect for the Lord's Commandments, occasionally coveted their neighbors' wives.

The literature of counter-subversion could also embody the somewhat different projective fantasies of women. Ann Eliza Young dramatized her seduction by the Prophet Brigham, whose almost superhuman powers enchanted her and paralyzed her will. Though she submitted finally only because her parents were in danger of being ruined by the Church, she clearly indicated that it was an exciting privilege to be pursued by a Great Man. When Anti-Mormons claimed that Joseph Smith and other prominent Saints knew the mysteries of Animal Magnetism, or were endowed with the highest degree of "amativeness" in their phrenological makeup, this did not detract from their covert appeal. In a ridiculous fantasy written by Maria Ward, such alluring qualities were extended even to Mormon women. Many bold-hearted girls could doubtless identify themselves with Anna Bradish, a fearless Amazon of a creature, who rode like a man, killed without compunction, and had no pity for weak women who failed to look out for themselves. Tall, elegant, and "intellectual," Anna was attractive enough to arouse the insatiable desires of Brigham Young, though she ultimately rejected him and renounced Mormonism.

While nativists affirmed their faith in Protestant monogamy, they obviously took pleasure in imagining the variety of sexual experience supposedly available to their enemies. By picturing themselves exposed to similar temptations, they assumed they could know how priests and Mormons actually sinned. Imagine, said innumerable anti-Catholic writers, a beautiful young woman kneeling before an ardent young priest in a deserted room. As she confesses, he leans over, looking into her eyes, until their heads are nearly touching. Day after day she reveals to him her innermost secrets, secrets she would not think of unveiling to her parents, her dearest friends, or even her suitor. By skillful questioning the priest fills her mind with immodest and even sensual ideas, "until this wretch has worked up her passions to a tension almost snapping, and then becomes his easy prey." How could any man resist such provocative temptations, and how could any girl's virtue withstand such a test?

We should recall that this literature was written in a period of increasing anxiety and uncertainty over sexual values and the proper role of woman. As ministers and journalists pointed with alarm at the spread of prostitution, the incidence of divorce, and the lax and hypocritical morality of the growing cities, a discussion of licentious subversives offered a convenient means for the projection of guilt as well as desire. The sins of individuals, or of the nation as a whole, could be pushed off upon the shoulders of the enemy and there punished in righteous anger.

Specific instances of such projection are not difficult to find. John C. Bennett, whom the Mormons expelled from the Church as a result of his flagrant sexual immorality, invented the fantasy of "The Mormon Seraglio" which persisted in later anti-Mormon writings. According to Bennett, the Mormons maintained secret orders of beautiful prostitutes who were mostly reserved for various officials of the Church. He claimed, moreover, that any wife refusing to accept polygamy might be forced to join the lowest order and thus become available to any Mormon who desired her.

Another example of projection can be seen in the letters of a young lieutenant who stopped in Utah in 1854 on his way to California. Convinced that Mormon women could be easily seduced, the lieutenant wrote frankly of his amorous adventures with a married woman. "Everybody has got one," he wrote with obvious pride, "except the Colonel and Major. The Doctor has got three—mother and two daughters. The mother cooks for him and the daughters sleep with him." But though he described Utah as "a great country," the lieutenant waxed indignant over polygamy, which he condemned as self-righteously as any anti-Mormon minister: "To see one man openly parading half a dozen or more women to church . . . is the devil according to my ideas of morality virtue and decency."

If the consciences of many Americans were troubled by the growth of red light districts in major cities, they could divert their attention to the "legalized brothels" called nunneries, for which no one was responsible but lecherous Catholic priests. If others were disturbed by the moral implications of divorce, they could point in horror at the Mormon elder who took his quota of wives all at once. The literature of counter-subversion could thus serve the double purpose of vicariously fulfilling repressed desires, and of releasing the tension and guilt arising from rapid social change and conflicting values.

Though the enemy's sexual freedom might at first seem enticing, it was always made repugnant in the end by associations with perversion or brutal cruelty. Both Catholics and Mormons were accused of practicing nearly every form of incest. The persistent emphasis on this theme might indicate deep-rooted feelings of fear and guilt, but it also helped demonstrate, on a more objective level, the loathsome consequences of unrestrained lust. Sheer brutality and a delight in human suffering were supposed to be the even more horrible results of sexual depravity. Masons disemboweled or slit the throats of their victims; Catholics cut unborn infants from their mothers' wombs and threw them to the dogs before their parents' eyes; Mormons raped and lashed recalcitrant women, or seared their mouths with red-hot irons. This obsession with details of sadism, which reached pathological proportions in much of the literature, showed a furious determination to purge the enemy of every admirable quality. The imagined enemy might serve at first as an outlet for forbidden desires, but nativist authors escaped from guilt by finally making him an agent of unmitigated aggression. In such a role the subversive seemed to deserve both righteous anger and the most terrible punishments.

The nativist escape from guilt was more clearly revealed in the themes of confession and conversion. For most American Protestants the crucial step in anyone's life was a profession of true faith resulting from a genuine religious experience. Only when a man became conscious of his inner guilt, when he struggled against the temptations of Satan, could he prepare his soul for the infusion of the regenerative spirit. Those most deeply involved in sin often made the most dramatic conversions. It is not surprising that conversion to nativism followed the same pattern, since nativists sought unity and moral certainty in the regenerative spirit of nationalism. Men who had been associated in some way with un-American conspiracies were not only capable of spectacular confessions of guilt, but were best equipped to expose the insidious work of supposedly harmless organizations. Even those who lacked such an exciting history of corruption usually made some confession of guilt, though it might involve only a previous indifference to subversive groups. Like ardent Christians, nativists searched in their own experiences for the meanings of sin, delusion, awakening to truth, and liberation from spiritual bondage. These personal confessions proved that one had recognized and conquered evil, and also served as ritual cleansings preparatory to full acceptance in a group of dedicated patriots.

Anti-Masons were perhaps the ones most given to confessions of guilt and most alert to subtle distinctions of loyalty and disloyalty. Many leaders of this movement, expressing guilt over their own "shameful experience and knowledge" of Masonry, felt a compelling obligation to exhort their former associates to "come out, and be separate from masonic abominations." Even when an anti-Mason could say with John Quincy Adams that "I am not, never was, and never shall be a Freemason," he would often admit that he had once admired the Order, or had even considered applying for admission.

Since a willingness to sacrifice oneself was an unmistakable sign of loyalty and virtue, ex-Masons gloried in exaggerating the dangers they faced and the harm that their revelations supposedly inflicted on the enemy. In contrast to hardened Freemasons, who refused to answer questions in court concerning their fraternal associations, the seceders claimed to reveal the inmost secrets of the Order, and by so doing to risk property, reputation, and life. Once the ex-Mason had dared to speak the truth, his character would surely be maligned, his motives impugned, and his life threatened. But, he declared, even if he shared the fate of the illustrious Morgan, he would die knowing that he had done his duty

Such self-dramatization reached extravagant heights in the ranting confessions of many apostate Catholics and Mormons. Maria Monk and her various imitators told of shocking encounters with sin in its most sensational forms, of bondage to vice and superstition, and of melodramatic escapes from popish despotism. A host of "ex-Mormon wives" described their gradual recognition of Mormon frauds and iniquities, the anguish and misery of plural marriage, and their breath-taking flights over deserts or mountains The female apostate was especially vulnerable to vengeful retaliation, since she could easily be kidnapped by crafty priests and nuns, or dreadfully punished by Brigham Young's Destroying Angels. At the very least, her reputation could be smirched by foul lies and insinuations. But her willingness to risk honor and life for the sake of her country and for the dignity of all womankind was eloquent proof of her redemption. What man could be assured of so noble a role?

The apostate's pose sometimes assumed paranoid dimensions. William Hogan warned that only the former priest could properly gauge the Catholic threat to American liberties and saw himself as providentially appointed to save his Protestant countrymen. "For twenty years," he wrote, "I have warned them of approaching danger, but their politicians were deaf, and their Protestant theologians remained religiously coiled up in fancied security, overrating their own powers and undervaluing that of Papists." Pursued by vengeful Jesuits, denounced and calumniated for alleged crimes, Hogan pictured himself single-handedly defending American freedom: "No one, before me, dared to encounter their scurrilous abuse. I resolved to silence them; and I have done so. The very mention of my name is a terror to them now." After surviving the worst of Catholic persecution, Hogan claimed to have at last aroused his countrymen and to have reduced the hierarchy to abject terror.

As the nativist searched for participation in a noble cause, for unity in a group sanctioned by tradition and authority, he professed a belief in democracy and equal rights. Yet in his very zeal for freedom he curiously assumed many of the characteristics of the imagined enemy. By condemning the subversive's fanatical allegiance to an ideology, he affirmed a similarly uncritical acceptance of a different ideology; by attacking the subversive's intolerance of dissent, he worked to eliminate dissent and diversity of opinion; by censuring the subversive for alleged licentiousness, he engaged in sensual fantasies; by criticizing the subversive's loyalty to an organization, he sought to prove his unconditional loyalty to the established order. The nativist moved even farther in the direction of his enemies when he formed tightly-knit societies and parties which were often secret and which subordinated the individual to the single purpose of the group. Though the nativists generally agreed that the worst evil of subversives was their subordination of means to ends, they themselves recommended the most radical means to purge the nation of troublesome groups and to enforce unquestioned loyalty to the state.

In his image of an evil group conspiring against the nation's welfare, and in his vision of a glorious millennium that was to dawn after the enemy's defeat, the nativist found satisfaction for many desires. His own interests became legitimate and dignified by fusion with the national interest, and various opponents became loosely associated with the un-American conspiracy. Thus Freemasonry in New York State was linked in the nativist mind with economic and political interests that were thought to discriminate against certain groups and regions; southerners imagined a union of abolitionists and Catholics to promote unrest and rebellion among slaves; gentile businessmen in Utah merged anti-Mormonism with plans for exploiting mines and lands.

Then too the nativist could style himself as a restorer of the past, as a defender of a stable order against disturbing changes, and at the same time proclaim his faith in future progress. By focusing his attention on the imaginary threat of a secret conspiracy, he found an outlet for many irrational impulses, yet professed his loyalty to the ideals of equal rights and government by law. He paid lip service to the doctrine of laissez-faire individualism, but preached selfless dedication to a transcendent cause. The imposing threat of subversion justified a group loyalty and subordination of the individual that would otherwise have been unacceptable. In a rootless environment shaken by bewildering social change the nativist found unity and meaning by conspiring against imaginary conspiracies.